NAPOLEON AND GROUCHY

The Last Great Waterloo Mystery Unravelled

NAPOLEON AND GROUCHY

The Last Great Waterloo Mystery Unravelled

Paul L Dawson

Frontline Books

NAPOLEON AND GROUCHY
The Last Great Waterloo Mystery Unravelled

This edition published in 2017 by Frontline Books,
an imprint of Pen & Sword Books Ltd,
47 Church Street, Barnsley, S. Yorkshire, S70 2AS

ISBN: 978-1-52670-067-4

CIP data records for this title are available from the British Library

For more information on our books, please visit
www.frontline-books.com
email info@frontline-books.com
or write to us at the above address.

Printed and bound in the UK by TJ International Ltd.
Typeset in 10.5/12.5 point Palatino

Contents

Acknowledgments

In the preparation of this book I would like to thank all those who have offered advice and support, all those who have helped me with my research. I am indebted to Mr John Franklin for his guidance, advice and provision of some research materials. Furthermore, I must also thank M. Yves Martin, Mr Ian J. Smith, John Lubomski and Sally Fairweather for their generous assistance with, and photographing of, archival material at the Archives Nationales and Service Historique de la Défence Armée du Térre, in Paris.

I must single out Ian Smith for his friendship, dedicated support to the project and excellent company during our numerous research trips to Paris. His advice and guidance during our many thousands of hours of conversation over numerous bottles of red wine was, and is, of immense help in understanding the wealth of data that we have gathered, to synthesise it into a cohesive narrative. Without this most generous support by Ian the book would have taken far longer to complete.

Erwin Muilwijk deserves a special word of praise, without his assistance in the provision of Dutch - Belgian source material this book could never have come to fruition. Lieutenant-Colonel Timmermans must be thanked for illustrations. I heartily encourage visitors to his excellent website http://Napoléon-monuments.eu/. Sally Fairweather must be thanked for proof reading this text.

Notes on the Sources

This study is based on two forms of evidence: personal testimony written after the events took place and empirical hard data in the form of orders and letters written on 17 and 18 June, as well as regimental muster lists. The material used has undergone a variety of processes before it was read by the author. Not all the archival paperwork prepared in 1815 has survived to the current day. Not all written memoirs of participants have survived. Those cited here are just those the author could identify—many more may exist in private collections, museums and libraries, and they may well tell a different narrative from that presented here. The narrative has been constructed from the sources available to the author.

In creating our narrative, we have endeavoured to let the primary sources speak for themselves without having to fit what they say into a superficial construct created by other authors. We must be aware, however, of the limitations and failings of these memoirs as a source of empirical data. The memoir, as Paul Fussell has established, occupies a place between fiction and autobiography.[1]

Since Fussell's work, recent research and developments in the fields of clinical and behavioural psychology, memory and the response to stress has called into question the value of memoirs and so-called eyewitness reports written by participants. Neuroscientist John Coates conducted research into memory; his study undertaken between 2004 and 2012 found that what is recalled from memory is what the mind believes happened rather than what actually happened. This effect is often referred to as 'false memory'.[2] A memoir, letter or other material used to help create a narrative of events is of limited value in terms of historical interpretation without context. This is defined as hermeneutics. Hermeneutics addresses the relationship between the interpreter and the interpreted; viz: What does it mean? What were the author's intentions? Is the source authentic?

Therefore, the historian's primary aim is decoding the language of the source used, to understand the ideological intentions of the author, and to locate it within the general cultural context to which the source material belongs.[3] The letters cited in this narrative were written down by combatants (or by family members) long after the events had taken place, and are not necessarily an accurate reflection of events that happened. Each of the writers of the letters included in this work had a personal and unique view of Waterloo—what they experienced will be different from participant to participant. The letters left by the participants recorded what was important to them. However, the closeness of the written narrative to the events that took place will affect what is recorded.[4] This is the reason why the police take statements immediately from as many eyewitnesses as possible without allowing the eyewitnesses to hear what others are saying. They then tease out the facts from this jumble of data.

Consulting the various archive boxes at the Service Historique de la Défence Armée du Térre at Vincennes in Paris quickly reveals that a lot of accepted fact on the battle cannot be verified. Marshal Grouchy, whose later life was obsessed with presenting his side of Waterloo, printed a vast amount of information in the 1840s, particularly orders, reports from field officers, marching orders, comments, etc. in order to verify his version of events. We do not know if the material produced by Grouchy is a word-for-word transcript, or if it has been edited, or if he published all the material he had. Grouchy, in order to corroborate his version of events, published the order book of Marshal Soult, the major-general of the Armée du Nord. The book exists in three forms: a) a hand written copy made by Grouchy housed in Archives Nationales de France; b) the published manuscript; and c) the du Casse copy made in 1865. The original is missing, so we cannot be sure that Grouchy's handwritten version is an exact copy. In order to strengthen his argument, he obtained and copied, but never published, Vandamme's correspondence register from 1815; the original document being lost. Grouchy also published his own, now lost, register of correspondence from 1815. Vandamme's correspondence and Grouchy's data tallies with the order book of Soult—a coincidence brought about by Grouchy, or are all three books in accord because they contain the same material generated on those fateful days in 1815? I believe all three books are word-for-word copies of the lost originals. Soult and Vandamme were still alive when Grouchy made his copies, and both men would have made comment. Vandamme did make comment on the 1815 campaign, not against Grouchy, but in support of him. Clearly if Vandamme felt he had lied, he would have made it obvious.

Into this mix comes the work of Albert du Casse. Pierre-Emmanuel-Albert, Baron du Casse (also Ducasse, 16 November 1813-14 March 1893), was a French soldier and military historian born at Bourges on 16 November 1813. He is best known for being the first editor of the correspondence of Napoléon I. He often published as Albert du Casse.

In 1849 he became aide-de-camp to Prince Jérôme Bonaparte, ex-King of Westphalia, then governor of the Invalides, on whose commission he wrote *Mémoires pour servir a l'histoire de la campagne de 1812 en Russie* (1852). Subsequently, he published *Mémoires du roi Joseph* (1853-1855), and, as a sequel, *Histoire des négotiations diplomatiques relatives aux traits de Morfontaine, de Lunéville et d'Amiens*, together with the unpublished correspondence of the Emperor Napoléon I with Cardinal Fesch (1855-1856). From papers in the possession of the imperial family he compiled *Mémoires du prince Eugene* (1858-1860) and *Réfutation des Mémoires du duc de Raguse* (1857), part of which was inserted by authority at the end of volume six of the *Mémoires*.

He was attached to Jérôme's son, Prince Napoléon, during the Crimean War, and wrote *Précis historique des operations militaires en Orient, de mars 1854 a octobre 1855* (1857), which was completed many years later (1892) by a volume entitled *La Crimée et Sebastopol de 1853 a 1856, docusnentl intiines et indits*, followed by the complete list of the French officers killed or wounded in that war. He was also employed by Prince Napoléon on the *Correspondence of Napoléon I*, and afterwards published certain letters, purposely omitted there, in the *Revue historique*. These documents, subsequently collected in *Les Rois fréres de Napoléon* (1883), as well as the *Journal de la reine Catherine de Westphalie* (1893), were edited with little care and are not entirely trustworthy, but their publication threw much light on Napoléon I and his entourage. His *Souvenirs d'un officier du le Zouaves, and Les Dessous du coup d'état* (1891), contain many piquant anecdotes, but at times degenerate into mere tittle-tattle. du Casse was the author of some slight novels, and from the practice of this form of literature he acquired that levity which appears even in his most serious historical publications. In our context, in 1870 he published *Le général Vandamme et sa correspondance*. It is in the production of this book that he collected a considerable amount of material on the 1815 campaign. His papers can be found at Vincennes in Paris. His material is clearly based on both order books of Soult and Grouchy, as well as material from other sources.

Into this mix of material need to be placed the original documents written by Grouchy between 15 and 29 June. These again can be found at Vincennes. This set of documents allows us to cross-check the material Grouchy published later with du Casse's work. In some cases, the original documents are not published by Grouchy, so when he published in 1847 we know some material was omitted. But in most cases this authentic material casts a new light on the campaign, as it has not been used in any reassessment of Grouchy, as all English language writers up to the present time (discounting the author) have used the published material rather than consult the archive sources.

A vast resource for understanding the Battle of Wavre and the Napoléonic era comes from personal service documents. Every officer and man who joined the army had their personal details recorded in a *controle* book. Every member of the Legion of Honour had a dossier of their military service, as well as baptismal certificates and other relevant material such as medical notes and date of death. These sources provided bias-free empirical data from which we can reconstruct the life story of the Battle of Waterloo from the French perspective. The *etat de service* also provided a wealth of detail on the battle. Many officers and men proudly write about their military achievements. A lot of officers and men left the army soon after Waterloo, and are thus writing about their experience of the battle while still fresh in their heads, and before their memories had become contaminated by what they had read about the battle. As legal documents, each had to be signed by the officer or regimental colonel and a review inspector, who would no doubt question the events the individual wrote about. Thus, these records have more value than memoirs and letters home, and have more validity as they are, in essence, sworn statements which would easily be questioned by comrades and senior officers. This untapped source of first-hand accounts for the battle, and campaign as a whole, has provided over 200 new accounts of the 1815 campaign.

The dossiers for legionnaires also hold medical records. These records report the injuries sustained during the empire period, or the injuries sustained at Waterloo, which cause the person to be invalided from the army. These data points help us to start to understand what happened to a regiment and the type of fighting it endured: a high proportion of men wounded with sabre cuts compared to gunshots suggest a cavalry attack; high, or exclusively, gunshot wounds indicate a fire fight between infantry.

Every man who served the in the French army had their details recorded in regimental muster lists, the *'Registre Controle Troupe'* and *'Registre Controle Officier'* held in the Service Historique de la Défence Armée du Térre. These volumes record information relating to every officer and man that was enlisted into a regiment. The information usually comprises age, height, place of birth, physical appearance, their service history in the army, dates of promotion and if the individual was wounded, captured or deserted. If men were killed, deserted or were made prisoner was important, so the regiment could stop the man's pay, and also request new recruits. Therefore, the data on the whole is largely bias-free. However, the fate of men in a battle was only recorded by the company adjutant into the register at muster parades after the battle, and the remaining men informing the adjutant of the fate of that person.

A lot of the personal testimony was written to prove a point, and thus a lot of material we are left with written after 1815 is written to serve an agenda, rather than source material which is bias-free. It is this later writing by eyewitnesses that has been used to damn Grouchy. We must judge Grouchy's actions based upon what he knew on 15 to 29 June, rather than what we know now in 2017, which is the approach taken in this book.

What I present in the narration is an interpretation of events based upon the experiences of those involved. It should be seen as *a* version of events and not *the* version of events. The evidence for the events of the attack of the Guard is, by its nature, part way between fiction and autobiography, and cannot be considered a true and accurate reflection of events. Indeed, eyewitness accounts are typically not written at the time of the events, but sometime after based on what the observer thought they observed, what they remembered and what they deemed important to write down. In relation to letters and memoirs, these cannot be seen as hard fact, but contain elements of fact as was noted in the introduction.

NOTES:
[1] Paul Fussell, *The Great War and Modern Memory*, Oxford University Press, Oxford, 1975, p. 311.
[2] John Coates, *The Hour Between Dog and Wolf*, Fourth Estate, London, 2012.
[3] Guverich, *The French Historical Revolution: The Annales School*, in Hodder et al, *Interpreting Archaeology*, Routledge, London, 1995, pp. 158-61. This short paper offers a good introduction to the notion and concept of the Annales School for those unfamiliar with the theory of history.
[4] Fussell, p. 311.

Chapter 1

The Road to Destiny

Emmanuel, Second Marquis de Grouchy, was touching fifty in 1815. He walked with a limp the result of a severe leg wound he had received at Craonne a year earlier, a wound which had taken a long time to heal. He had served in the French army for some thirty-six years, originally enlisting in the Corps Royal d'Artillerie in 1779. Despite his family background, Emmanuel—perhaps thanks to his intellectual mother, Gilberte Freteau de Peny, and his sister, the early feminist, Sophie de Condorcet—was an ardent supporter of the youthful French Republic, and fought in many of the major battles of the republic and Napoléon's empire. He was an able divisional and corps commander, but upon Napoléon's resumption of the French throne in spring 1815, he found himself promoted to the dignity of marshal of France. During this troubled and turbulent time, could he rise to the challenge set by Napoléon?

The story of Grouchy's controversial mission of 17 June 1815 has, ever since it happened, become dominated by hindsight and all kinds of personal and political interests from eyewitnesses who served under him in 1815. He had been accused of being one of the determining causes, if not the cause, of the defeat of the emperor at Waterloo. As a result of this, it is very hard to get down to the nub of the issues at hand due to complex self-interest of the men from 1815, and from later historians. What I aim to do with this book is to judge Grouchy and his mission, as far as possible, from what was known on those fateful June days and, where needed, to expose aspects of those events as either truth or lies. This is only possible with a thorough examination of all the original documents from 1815 that can be found by the author, a task not undertaken since at least 1840 by Grouchy himself.

In the words of Gregor Dallas, Napoléon's position in spring 1815 was built on 'wobbly foundations.' There was the very real prospect of civil war. Napoléon no longer possessed the means to re-impose a

1

dictatorship, and no single political faction was dominant; he presided over political and domestic chaos of his own making. In 1815, Napoléon did not represent national will, with the support from, it is estimated, 3 per cent of the nation. Revolt in the spring of 1815 was not just limited to France. In London, riots against the government and its punitive corn laws came to an end in mid-March. Nationalist riots broke out in the former French Confederation of the Rhine states against the Prussians. Europe, in spring 1815, was a tinderbox of discontent, into which came Napoléon.

Yet despite the worrying developments on the home front, Napoléon was determined to take the inevitable war to the Allies before they could attack France.

On the 3 June, Napoléon informed Marshals Soult and Davout that Marshal Grouchy had been named commander-in-chief of the cavalry of the Armée du Nord. Grouchy joined the Imperial Headquarters at Laon on 5 June, and began to work with Soult on establishing the movement orders for the forthcoming campaign.

The Imperial Guard left Paris on 8 June 1815. Napoléon left Paris on 12 June for Soissons to join headquarters. On the Belgian border were the two Allied armies; a force of 116,000 Prussians and Saxons, led by the Prussian Field Marshal Gebhard Leberecht von Blücher, was based at Namur, and a force of 93,000 British, Dutch, and German troops based at Brussels, commanded by the Duke of Wellington. Leading elements of the Allied armies were at Charleroi and Gilly on the evening of 14 June 1815.

NOTES:
[1] Gregor Dallas, *1815: The Roads to Waterloo*, Pimlico, London, 1996, p. 313.
[2] Dallas, p. 315.
[3] Dallas, p. 323.
[4] The *Morning Chronicle*, 18 March 1815.

Chapter 2

Invasion

In the early hours of 15 June, the French army began to cross the frontier; an army that was enthusiastic in its support of their 'Great Captain', who, like them, was confident of the expected outcome. The order of the day, issued on 14 June, proclaimed:[1]

> Soldiers, today is the anniversary of Marengo and Friedland, places where the destiny of Europe was decided on two occasions. Accordingly, like after Austerlitz and Wagram, we believed the arguments and the oaths of the princes that we left on their thrones! Today, however, in their coalition against us they take offence at the independence and at the most sacred rights of France. They started their aggressions on a precise manner: let us therefore march to meet them; them and us, are we not the same men?
>
> Soldiers, at Jena, against those same Prussians, who are today so arrogant, you were one against three, and at Montmirail, one against six.
>
> That those of you who were prisoners of the English tell you their stories of their pontoons and of the horrible evils that they suffered.
>
> The Saxons, the Belgians, the Hanoverians, the soldiers of the Rhine Confederation, groan at their obligations to help the cause of the princes who are enemies of the justice and the rights of all people. They know that this coalition is insatiable. After destroying twelve million Italians, one million Saxons, and six million Belgians, it will devour the smaller States of Germany.
>
> The fools! One moment of good fortune blinds them. The oppression and the humiliation of the French people are above their power! If they move into France, they will find their graves.

> Soldiers! We have to make forced marches, give battles, take risks; but, with steadiness, victory will be ours: the rights, the honour and the welfare of our country will be retaken.
>
> For each Frenchmen who has the courage, the moment has come to win or to die!

Napoléon's plans called for a concentric advance of three columns onto Charleroi. Reille's 2nd Corps and d'Erlon's 1st Corps formed the left wing of the army, and were to march from Solre-sur-Sambre, via Thuin, to Marchienne-au-Pont, a short distance outside of Charleroi. Pajol's cavalry in the centre, supported by Domon's cavalry, was to advance from Beaumont to Charleroi, with General Vandamme's 3rd Corps to follow under the protective cavalry screen. At the rear were Lobau's 6th Corps and the Imperial Guard. The right wing comprised General Gérard's 4th Corps, protected by one of Milhaud's cuirassier divisions.

Napoléon's plan was that if the army left its positions at 3.00, some 60,000 men would be at Charleroi by midday. However, things went very wrong before the campaign really began, as at 7.00 General-of-Division de Ghaisnes, Comte de Bourmont, who commanded the 14th Infantry Division, along with his staff, deserted their posts and headed off to join the Prussians. No doubt this caused widespread alarm among the division. General Hulot was named the new divisional commander by General Gérard. This was the first of many desertions that would happen over the next few days. Sergeant-Major Sylvain Larreguy, of the 93rd Regiment of Line Infantry, relates:[2]

> On 15 June … General de Bourmont deserted and went over to the enemy. He was able to shed light on our strengths and on the campaign plan. The indignation of the troops was high, and it will long echo in posterity.

Just as the shock of the desertion of de Bourmont was sinking into the officers of 4th Corps, the aide-de-camp carrying Napoléon's orders to General Vandamme had fallen from his horse and broken his leg, thus the orders were not delivered on time. Therefore, Vandamme had not broken camp until after 7.00, several hours later than had been accounted for in the meticulous timetable for the day.[3]

The avantgarde: Pajol
Marshal Grouchy was clearly aware of the importance of sticking to Napoléon's timetable as closely as possible. Early on the morning of 15 June he dictated his orders to General Pajol:[4]

Bossus-les-Ralcourt 15 June 1815

If you please, dear general, instruct your army corps to mount at two o'clock in the morning and to reunite with the cavalry division of General Domon, to whom I have passed orders to form the avantguarde for the army and head to Charleroi; the division of General Domon will be on the left, and the division of General Soult to be on the opposite flank.

Attached to this order is a copy of the movement orders. March with the three other cavalry corps which will be taking different routes, you are to act with General Vandamme.

You will receive immediate orders ether from Vandamme or the emperor, who is marching with the rearguard.

I desire you to go to Charleroi and to pass through Bossus, Henneux and Gares, or on the main road from Philippeville to Charleroi.

Be sure to keep in communication and report to me any news.

Receive my dear general, etc.

The marshal commanding the cavalry

Comte de Grouchy.

Pajol left his positions around 3.00, and his troops marched, it seems, in three columns, all of which were destined to converge on Charleroi. Domon's command was the western-most column, taking a direct route to Charleroi. Pajol, with Soult and Subervie taking the centre and eastern-most columns, took a less direct path. In essence, they would come against Charleroi in a pincer movement from the south and south-east. General Reille and 2nd Corps would, it was hoped, approach at the same time from the south-west.

The 1st Cavalry Corps—or at least elements of it—arrived at Ham-sur-Heure at approximately 6.00 on the morning of 15 June 1815. This small town was about one mile from Marbais. The town was essentially square in plan, with a central block of buildings, and an outer ring of buildings following the town's quadrangular plan. According to the Prussian officer, Wagner, Domon's cavalry brigade (4th, 9th and 12th Chasseurs à Cheval, belonging to 3rd Corps) made contact with the Prussian 11th Company of the 28th Infantry Regiment.[5] The Prussian infantry made a stiff resistance, but was forced to withdraw to Couillet.[6] General Domon comments that the attack was led by Squadron Commander Petit, of the 9th Chasseurs à Cheval, and made 300 prisoners.[7]

Combat at Couillet

At approximately 8.30, General Pajol arrived at the outskirts of Couillet, which was defended by the Prussians. Couillet lies on the northern edge of the immense woods of the Prince de Liège, de la Fereye and de Hublembue. The village itself was entered on its southern side by the metalled *Grand Chemin de Philippeville* (Philippeville road), which ran approximately due south, and the *Grand Chemin de Charleroi* (Charleroi road), which ran south-east. Both of these roads, we assume, would have been utilised by Pajol and Vandamme. Two roads entered the village from the west and converged at the centre of the village. All four roads funnelled into a single road that ran north-west to Marcinelles and was bounded by hedges on each side. At the north-eastern edge of the town was a shallow ford across the River Sambre. A second ford could be found at Ecluse, a short distance to the north-east of the village.

Here, at Couillet, about a mile below Charleroi, Pajol fell on a company of the 3rd Battalion of the 28th Prussian Infantry Regiment and forced it to surrender.[8] Colonel Biot himself mentions that he encircled the Prussians at a farm off the main road, set back among fields. He brought up a howitzer and in result to a short bombardment, the Prussians surrendered.[9] A French general of the Imperial Headquarters states these troops, around three hundred men, were former Grand Duchy of Berg soldiers, which a French general demanded to return to French service.[10] This appears to be the same incident in which General Letort was killed at Gilly (as we shall see below), so the writer appears to be mistaken, but these troops had formerly been in French service. Elsewhere, the 4th Company of the 2nd Westphalian Landwehr Regiment was captured by the French.[11]

Combat at Marcinelles
As Pajol was arriving at Couillet, Domon was arriving at Marcinelles. He was at Jamignon at 7.00, with the division of Pierre Soult marching via Bommeree. The attack here coincided with General Reille's attack at Marchienne-au-Pont. The cannonade was heard by Colonel Biot, the senior aide-de-camp to General Pajol. The small village of Marcinelles consisted of three conjoined hamlets, the primary focus a roughly rectangular hamlet, orientated north-west to south-east, centred upon a church and its cemetery. It was entered on the south-east by three roads, the Charleroi road and two lesser parallel roads. Running approximately east-west was a long row of houses. From the north-west point of the village ran the road to Charleroi. According to the Prussian writer Wagner, the road from Marcinelles to Charleroi was defended by a 500 metre-long palisaded dyke and a covered bridge connecting the village to Charleroi. Hedges lined with Prussian sharpshooters bordered the dyke and road.[12] The road entered Charleroi past a square redoubt on the town's south-eastern angle, and then turned north-west

as the road passed through the outer circuit of defences. Control of this road controlled access to the town of Charleroi and its vital bridge. The French 4th and 9th Chasseurs à Cheval made a sortie and encountered the 5th Battalion of the Prussian 23rd Infantry Regiment. The Prussians were surrounded and forced to surrender, the 4th Chasseurs à Cheval lost one officer killed and two wounded. The French cavalry then captured the village, but was repulsed by sharpshooters that lined the hedgerows and field boundaries, as well as the gardens and some of the village houses.[13] Without infantry support, there was little Domon could do to push the Prussians from the village. His dismounted chasseurs with their short carbines were no match for the Prussian sharpshooters.[14] General Ameil and the 5th Hussars were sent in the direction of Couillet to search for a ford to cross the river and come behind the enemy. Not being able to take the town, according to Pajol, Domon, along with Subervie, withdrew to the head of the wood of Hublembue.[15] Around 10:00 Napoléon was at Jamignon.[16]

Combat at Marchienne-au-Pont

General Reille's 2nd Corps marched out at dawn and occupied Thuin, Lobbes and Montignies-le-Tilleul. In doing so they pushed back Prussian outposts. At Lobbes, the 1st Chasseurs à Cheval debouched and pushed the Prussian pickets from the 2nd Battalion 1st Westphalian Landwehr Regiment and the 6th Uhlans back. Elements of Bachelu's division pushed the Prussians back through Lobbes, with the bulk of the division moving onwards to Maladrie and Thuin.[17]

General Reille was marching to Marchienne-au-Pont. The town was a mile or so due west of Charleroi and was protected by a valuable bridge over the Sambre, but he did not reach it until 10.00. Bachelu was ordered to storm the town, parts of which were dominated by a monastery to gain possession of the bridge. This operation would take time, and Bachelu was not across the Sambre until, it seems, 13.00. At Marchienne-au-Pont was the 2nd Battalion of the 6th Prussian Infantry Regiment. The bridge was barricaded and supported by two artillery pieces.[18] The Prussians note that the French attacked three times to capture the town and seize the bridge, but eventually fell back to Dampremy, to the north-east, and over the Sambre. General Reille in his report dated 15 June at 21.00 at Gosselies to Marshal Soult, notes that the cavalry of generals Piré and Hubert, with the 1st Chasseurs à Cheval, charged the Prussian infantry with vigour and took 200 prisoners.[19]

With Vandamme's troops delayed, and the Prussians putting up more resistance than Napoléon had anticipated at Marciennes and

Marchienne-au-Pont, Napoléon was forced to improvise to maintain the momentum of his advance. The Imperial Guard, marching in front of 3rd and 6th Corps, was ordered to take the lead over 3rd Corps and to move by forced marches.[20]

By this time, Napoléon was at Jamignon where an embarrassed Pajol informed him that he had failed to take Marcinelles and Couillet.[21] Pajol was ordered to renew the attack, supported by two batteries of horse artillery and the Young Guard. The Young Guard, or more likely only a single regiment of the Young Guard (perhaps the 3rd Voltigeurs who are recorded as having casualties at Charleroi)[22], led by General La Bédoyère,[23] supported by the sailors of the Guard, advanced and drove off the Prussian sharpshooters.[24] As more of the Imperial Guard arrived it was not long before all of Marcinelles and Couillet were held by the French, along with the defensive dyke which, importantly, lead to the intact bridge over the Sambre.[25] The 3rd Battalion of the 28th Prussian Infantry Regiment withdrew to Chatellet, where Gérard's 4th Corps found them, along with the 11th Company of the 1st Battalion of the 2nd Westphalian Landwehr Regiment.[26] Placed in the churchyard at Dampray was the 1st Battalion of the 2nd Westphalian Landwehr Regiment, supported by two guns. Both these bodies of Prussian troops had orders to retreat to Gilly.[27] Reille was at Jumet by 15.00 and he began his movement to Gosselies, advancing his cavalry to the left of the Monceaux Wood, through which his infantry marched.

The capture of Charleroi
With Marcinelles captured and the vital roadway into Charleroi taken, it was only a matter of time before the Prussian garrison was overwhelmed and the town and its bridge captured by the French. With more and more French troops flooding the area, Prussian Major von Rohr, commander of Charleroi, deployed his beleaguered force from the 6th Prussian Infantry Regiment: the 1st Company was placed on the road leading to Marchienne-au-Pont; the 2nd Company was on the road leading to Marcinelles; the 3rd and 4th Companies were placed in the central square of the town. A jäger detachment was on the road leading to Marchienne-au-Pont.[28] The sailors and engineers of the Imperial Guard stormed the barricade at the end of the dyke from Marcinelles to Charleroi.[29] Renee Bourgeois, surgeon-major of the 12th Cuirassiers, writes the following about the incident:[30]

> The light cavalry of the centre followed the movement of the 2nd Corps on the road to Charleroi, and sweeping away through several

successive charges all that opposed them, repulsed the enemy with force onto the Sambre, behind which he hastened to take positions to dispute the passage.

A serious fight ensued in front of Charleroi, and was maintained for some time with great vivacity. While many sharpshooters defended the approach of the bridge, the Prussians took care to make it impracticable, in order to evacuate the city, and their columns were formed on the river, they received the French by a brisk fire, which stopped the impetuosity of their march for a few moments, but they soon became renewed again with vigour and such fearlessness that the Prussians pressed so strongly, and shelled by our batteries, were compelled to abandon the bridge without being able to destroy all of it, they managed to cause some damage that was easily repairable. The sappers and the marines of the Guard thither and soon ironed out difficulties, and then the enemy hastily withdrew from the city, and reached the heights which border on the side of Brussels. Our cavalry pursued them very closely, and the army that made its way without experiencing other obstacles, immediately took possession of Charleroi.

Twenty-three year-old Captain Marie Denis Larabit, who had accompanied Napoléon to Elba, and who during the Hundred Days had served in the engineers of the Imperial Guard, wrote:[31]

He crossed the river at Marchienne and Charleroi. M. Larabit was sent with the engineers of the Imperial Guard to destroy any barriers that would prevent our easy passage through Charleroi. He had barely entered the city when he found himself in front of a Prussian post, which fired at him from almost point-blank range. Immediately the fighting started and the Prussians were chased from the city. The engineers took up positions at the other end of Charleroi. The emperor arrived: he ordered that we were to entrench and fortify the first houses. The army filed off and marched forward.

With the removal of the barricade around midday, Pajol's horsemen had clattered through the village pushing the Prussians back towards Gilly and Fleurus.[32]

Coming under increasing pressure, the Prussians began an orderly withdrawal, and by 11.00 the town was evacuated.[33] Major Pierre François Tissot, officer commanding the 92nd Regiment of Line Infantry, notes that Napoléon arrived at Charleroi at 11.00.[34] Four hours had been lost in Napoléon's methodical timetable.[35]

Jean Baptiste Berton, commanding the 14th and 17th Dragoons under the orders of General Chastel, formed part of Excelmans's reserve cavalry and writes:[36]

> The light cavalry division of General Domon strongly pursued the enemy to Charleroi; a square of Prussian infantry wanted to stop us short of that city, to give them time to cut the bridge over the Sambre they had not yet mined. Colonel Desmichels, head of the 4th Chasseurs à Cheval Regiment, supported by the 9th, attacked the square and made four to five hundred prisoners. The corps of light cavalry of General Pajol, composed of six regiments, followed this division to cross the bridge of Charleroi, and then it moved to the right after detaching General Clary, with the 1st Regiment of Hussars, to Gosselies, where he sabred a Prussian battalion and took its flag.

Captain Aubry, of the 12th Chasseurs à Cheval, recalls that:[37]

> We reached the environs of Charleroi, the 12th Chasseurs forming the extreme avantgarde. I, with my squadron, were the first to penetrate the town, we found a small number of the enemy. We had been accompanied by a company of *pontonniers* who quickly re-established the bridge over the Sambre. We then took prisoner a battalion of Prussian light infantry who formed part of the Prussian rearguard, and who had remained to destroy the bridge, the emperor was satisfied with our conduct.

Aubry is one of two sources to tell us that the *pontonniers* repaired or established a bridge at Charleroi. If a second bridge was established it would have eased the bottleneck in getting troops across the river. The bridge at Charleroi was narrow, restricting the movements of soldiers north and west. Here in Charleroi, field hospitals were established, which, following the action at Gilly housed forty wounded soldiers, most of who were from the cavalry of the Guard.[38] Here, too, a huge quantity of stores was captured and distributed:[39]

24,000 rations of bread, of which 4,000 were issued to troops in the town;

126 sacks of flour each weighing 190 *livres*, sufficient for 800 rations over four days;

1,200 rations of oats;

1,600 rations of hay;

2,000 rations of straw; and

200 head of cattle.

Charleroi was to be garrisoned by elements of 6th Corps, and become a field hospital.

Ney's dispositions

Upon arriving at Charleroi, Pajol was ordered by the emperor to detach the 1st Hussars towards Gosselies. He was then instructed to advance with the remainder of 1st Cavalry Corps towards Gilly.[40]

The vanguard was led by the French 1st Hussars, which encountered Prussian cavalry and infantry as it headed off.[41] At the start of the Hundred Days, the 'Hussard du Roi' the regiment's royalist incarnation, had been ordered to join the army of the Duke of Berry. At Chateauneuf, Captain Morel mutinied and headed to Paris with two companies in the name of the emperor. In consequence, General Clary[42] was appointed colonel in place of Oudinot, the son of Marshal Oudinot. An analysis of 200 men with the regiment on 1 June 1815 gives the average age as twenty-five years three months. The regiment was a mix of veterans taken into the regiment in 1814 to bulk out the conscripts from 1813 and 1814, as the best men from the hussars were passed to the 'Hussard du Roi'.[43] In October 1814, the bulk of the regiment's clothing was described as needing to be replaced. This seems to have occurred, as on 10 October 1814 the depot held 521 metres of *bleu celeste* wool cloth, which was almost entirely used up, assuming no more stocks were purchased over the following year, making new dolmans and pelisses.[44] A painting by Vernet of Colonel Clary commanding the regiment shows the regiment's elite company wearing colpacks—these items certainly did not exist either in use or in the magazine—and also scarlet side stripes to their blue breeches, and other troopers wearing the shako *Rouleau.*

The leading echelons of Reille's 2nd Corps, were also moving upon Gosselies, presumably to cut off the line of retreat of Ziethen's troops along the Brussels road, and to effect the separation of the Prussians from Wellington's army. d'Erlon's 1st Corps received orders to follow and support Reille's 2nd Corps.

About 16.00, Gosselies fell into French hands when the Prussian garrison retreated to Fleurus. Marshal Ney and General Lefèbvre-Desnoëttes pushed back a small Allied contingent out of Frasné and pursued it until just short of Quatre-Bras. Perponcher had taken up defensive positions. Not knowing the strength of the Allied forces here, Ney broke off the action and wrote the following dispatch to Marshal Soult:[45]

11

Gosselies, 15 June 1815. Eleven o'clock in the evening

To His Excellency the marshal major-general,

Monsieur marshal, I have the honour to inform you, Your Excellency, that in conforming to the orders of the emperor that I received, with the cavalry of General Piré and the infantry of General Bachelu, I was able to dislodge the enemy from Gosselies. The resistance of the enemy was quite obstinate, but after an exchange of between twenty-five to thirty cannon shots, they retired to Heppignies via Fleurus. I captured 500 to 600 Prussian soldiers from the corps of General Ziethen.

Here is the location of my troops:

General Lefèbvre-Desnoëttes with the lancers and chasseurs of the Guard at Frasné;

General Bachelu with the 5th Division at Mellet;

General Foy with the 9th Division at Gosselies;

The light cavalry of General Piré at Heppignies.

General d'Erlon is based with the majority of his corps around Jumet; unfortunately, I am not able to transmit to you, Your Excellency, in this letter any further details about these dispositions.

I send with this letter a report by General Lefèbvre-Desnoëttes. Ney.

Grouchy at Gilly

Elsewhere, with the French across the River Sambre in ever increasing numbers, Pirch withdrew his troops from the line of the river and concentrated his troops at Gilly. The defending forces under General Pirch comprised:[46]

1st and 2nd Battalions 28th Infantry Regiment (around 1,200 men);

1st and 2nd Battalions 2nd Westphalian Landwehr Infantry Regiment (around 1,200 men);

1st and 2nd Battalions 1st West Prussian Infantry Regiment (the 6th Infantry regiment) (around 1,200 men);

The 3rd Battalion was in reserve;

1st West Prussian Dragoons;

Four squadrons of the 1st Regiment of Westphalian Landwehr Cavalry; and

Foot Battery Number 3.

Pirch had around ten thousand men at his disposal. He initially deployed four battalions of infantry in the village, supported by an artillery battery on his right. The road to Fleurus was barricaded. Skirmishers were placed in hedgerows and ditches and the cavalry was drawn up in reserve. The 2nd Westphalian Landwehr Regiment was deployed on either side of the road, supporting the artillery. The regimental history of the 6th Prussian Infantry Regiment describes the positions occupied by the Prussians as follows:[47]

> The fusilier battalion was deployed in a small copse at the forward slope of the heights of Gilly. Four cannon were placed on a mount to the right, with two cannon between this point and the cobbled road to Fleurus, and the remaining two cannon on the road facing towards the exit of Gilly. The battalion's skirmishers were placed behind hedges between the cannon to protect them.
>
> The 28th Regiment stood astride the road leading to Lodelinsart, with the regiment's two musketeer battalions placed 200 paces behind the front, in the second line. Communications with the 1st Brigade, deployed at Gosselies, could not be maintained as the village of Ransart was too far away from the positions of both brigades for either of them to occupy it. The right flank of the brigade was all the more exposed when the village was occupied by French light infantry. The road to Fleurus was blocked with an abatis.

The 2nd Westphalian Landwehr Regiment was deployed on either side of the road, supporting the artillery.

Sub-Lieutenant Charles Etienne Philippe Gerbet[48] (37th Regiment of Line Infantry) notes that Vandamme arrived at Charleroi at 13.00, and as soon as he arrived he began crossing the river and debouched on to the plain overlooking the town.[49] Napoléon, however, incorrectly states that Vandamme arrived at Charleroi only some two hours later, around 15.00.[50] Marshal Grouchy himself notes Napoléon ordered Vandamme to speed up his rate of march, and confirms that the dragoons marched across low ground to enable them to attack the Prussian left without being observed.[51]

The village comprised a long row of houses and, with the hedges swarming with sharpshooters; it was clearly not terrain for cavalry. Napoléon sent Vandamme's infantry, Excelmans's cavalry and, it appears, the Imperial Guard to the front. The first tentative moves occurred around 15.30. Napoléon, who arrived around half an hour later (16.00),[52] directed the action from the windmill at Cobreil, on a small hill some 500 metres south of the church at Gilly. Close by the mill was a house owned by a man called Lambert, the owner of a local mine.[53]

Due to a village being entirely unsuitable for cavalry operations, General Ameil sent the 5th Hussars to reconnoitre, and, upon reaching the far end of the village, was met by a fusillade of Prussian musketry and artillery fire.[54] Grouchy, concluding that Pajol's cavalry alone could not carry the position, ordered up infantry support. The engineers and marines of the Guard were ordered to attack.[55]

At 15.30, Marshal Soult informed General Gérard of 4th Corps that the emperor had encountered enemy troops and his object was to attack the enemy at the head of the Lambusart Wood. As soon as Gérard had crossed the Sambre, he was to attack any enemy troops he encountered and was to send a report of his dispositions to Soult.[56] Captain Aubry, of the 12th Chasseurs à Cheval, notes that:[57]

> In the evening, the emperor arrived, and was supported by a picket of grenadiers à cheval and they crushed many Prussian battalions; it was a good start.

Captain Coignet, attached to the Imperial Headquarters, confirms the presence of the picket of the grenadiers à cheval:[58]

> In order to gain a footing in the plain of Fleurus, the emperor went on in advance, following the main road with his staff and a squadron of the horse grenadiers. He talked a while with his aide-de-camp. He looked over to his left, took his small glass, and examined attentively a perpendicular eminence far off from the road in an immense plain. He saw some dismounted cavalry.

Despite Napoléon having arrived at 16.00, no attack was made for a further two hours, until 18.00. Why was there yet further delay? Neither of Napoléon's wings were secure: on the right, Gérard and the 4th Corps were not yet across the Sambre (hence he was sent an order at 15.30 to urge him into action), while the left wing under d'Erlon was also slow. Reille was on the left with Ney, but until Napoléon knew that Gosselies was secure, he did not risk an attack in the centre not knowing where the Prussians were. If Napoléon attacked and pushed the Prussians back, and his flanks were open, Prussian troops could have separated him from Reille and 2nd Corps, perhaps leaving him isolated and cut off from the bulk of the French army, as Pierre de Witt makes clear:[59]

> Seen in the context of the strategy of the central position, the left wing was, on 15 June, eventually to be in a position between Gosselies and Marchienne-au-Pont, while securing the road to Mons. At the same time, the left flank of this position was to be reconnoitred towards Mons, Nivelles, etc.
>
> Within this position, it becomes clear that the 2nd Corps, based at Gosselies had a prominent orientation and vigilance to the east

towards the Prussian army, while the 1st Corps had one to the south-west, to a point where Wellington was expected to be concentrating.

In time, the accent shifted that day from an orientation from Charleroi as a starting point to both north (Brussels road) and west (Mons road) in general, to Gosselies in particular. In this process, the forces put against Wellington's army through Marchienne-au-Pont towards Mons were reduced in strength, while the measures securing the crossings of the Sambre further south were withdrawn.

In looking at the orientation towards Mons and the concern for main passages over the Sambre, Napoléon clearly felt uneasy about a possible irruption of Wellington's army over this river into the French rear on the operation line running back through Beaumont and Laon towards Paris.

Battalion Commander Guillaume Baudus (aide-de-camp to Marshal Soult) suggests that the battle did not start early, simply because Napoléon was exhausted and had fallen asleep:[60]

> After passing the Sambre at Charleroi, Napoléon, wanting to see his troops defile past, climbed the hill overlooking the right bank of the river, and as the road is very narrow in the place where he stopped, he placed himself in the entrance of a large courtyard, and sent for a chair on which he settled, and soon fell deeply asleep. We can get a fair idea, having not seen, the enthusiasm of the soldiers passed him, and I cannot render the indignantly of which I was transported to when I saw that the cheers, the cries of joy, a noble and energetic translation of the infamous exclamation of Roman gladiators, *Morituri te salutamus, Cesar*, had no more power to get him out of his sleep than they had.

Napoléon disingenuously notes that Vandamme and Grouchy 'wasted' two hours, had been misled by false reports exaggerating the Prussian strength (200,000 men), that it was only through his personal intervention that the true strength of the Prussians was realised, and so he immediately ordered an attack.[61] This contradicts both Grouchy and his aide-de-camps, Bella and Baudus. Neither Coignet nor Aubry mention Grouchy accompanying Napoléon. Napoléon notes that Vandamme arrived at Charleroi at 15:00.[62] Grouchy further notes that when Vandamme arrived, he immediately attacked without orders and was repulsed. In this attack, in the 1st Brigade of the 8th Infantry Division (part of 3rd Corps), the 15th Regiment of Light Infantry had one officer wounded and one died of wounds that day. These are the only known casualties for all of the infantry of 3rd Corps for that day, without further archive research being undertaken. The Prussians notes the start of the action as follows:[63]

> Right in front of our eyes the enemy cavalry corps of Pajol and Excelmans, with large numbers of infantry and artillery, crossed the Sambre for the attack. The artillery duel had already begun, as had a skirmish fight in which Major von Quadt had a horse shot from under him, when the order arrived to break off the battle and fall back on Fleurus. This order was made all the more difficult to carry out because the artillery limbered up and then withdrew immediately, leaving the first line of the infantry to withdraw across an open field in front of the French cavalry corps.

The action began with the French directing the battle from the windmill near the farm of Grand Dieu. We are told that Napoléon in person, along with Marshal Grouchy, reconnoitred the enemy positions and judged that two divisions from General Ziethen's command of around 15,000 to 18,000 men occupied the Lambusart Wood.[64] At this stage, it seems the French had moved up a horse artillery battery in support.[65] The battle commenced with a short barrage by sixteen guns from 3rd Corps, commanded by Colonel Dougerou.[66] Prussian General Pirch observed three dense infantry columns assaulting the heights. One went in the direction of the fusilier battalion of the 1st West Prussian Infantry Regiment which occupied the woods, the second attacked in the centre of the village of Gilly and the third in support. Initially the Prussian artillery fired back, but, outnumbered, their guns fell silent.[67] Napoléon proposed that Excelmans's dragoons were to attack the Prussians in the flank after crossing the River Sambre at the mill of Delhatte, to the south-east.[68] The terrain prevented the Prussians observing this movement, so the dragoons fell on the Prussian left flank unopposed.

General Berthezène recalls that Letort charged with no support from Excelmans:

> The impatience of the emperor, and perhaps also that of the troops of the service squadrons to attack Gilly, before they could be supported, either by infantry or by another corps of cavalry, passing in front of the hillock on which the enemy was, were ordered to take them in the rear. In this hasty attack, General Letort, adjutant of the emperor and who commanded the squadrons, was killed. He was an officer of great resolution. A few minutes later, the cavalry arrived, debouched and sabred the enemy, which was formed in hollow

square, and, without waiting for our infantry to attack, they broke and fled into the woods, where the next morning many were made prisoners.

A clear narrative of events here is lacking from the eyewitness material. The charge of the Imperial Guard cavalry is absent from the narratives of Pajol, Excelmans and Grouchy in any clear detail. Grouchy suggests that the charge was initiated to extricate Vandamme's infantry.[70] Gourgaud suggests that Napoléon became impatient with the lack of success and ordered what turned out to be a 'death or glory charge' for the Empress Dragoons.[71] Prussian writer Damitz tells us that the Guard dragoons charged after the dragoons of Burthe and Bonnemains had attacked and cut up the West Prussian dragoons.[72]

Perhaps we will never know the true turn of events. Gustave Pontécoulant, of the Imperial Guard horse artillery, tells us that after the dithering of Vandamme and Grouchy, Napoléon ordered the duty squadron to charge to break the then impasse between the French and Prussians. He writes:[73]

> The infantry of the 3rd Corps, formed in column, was to march directly on Gilly, while General Excelmans, with his cavalry, was to pass on the right that crosses the creek, to flank to the Prussians, and advance to the defile of the Lambusart Wood and they were obliged to traverse to retire on Fleurus. These provisions were a great success: General Ziethen, who soon realised he would be crushed, hastened to evacuate Gilly, and took a position back and forth between this village and that of Fleurus, his back against a wood.
>
> The emperor had given the movement orders to march forward and to dislodge him, but this order was feebly executed, General Vandamme and Grouchy, deceived by false reports, had imagined that the entire Prussian army, with more than 100,000 men, was waiting at the entrance of the woods, in order of battle on the plain of Fleurus; they had lost two hours of unnecessary trial and error, and advanced with extreme reluctance. Napoléon, who meanwhile had dismounted and was talking on the edge of the Lambusart Wood with some officers of his staff, impatient because of all these delays, and to see before him escape a Prussian corps when a little more daring and activity could have taken them, mounted his horse to go himself to reconnoitre the enemy, believing that the woods were only occupied by two divisions of Ziethen's corps that had moved from Charleroi, forming eighteen or twenty thousand men at most, he gave new orders to march forward to force the issue.

Pontécoulant then narrates that Napoléon ordered forward the four duty squadrons of the Imperial Guard, headed by General Letort.[74] Both French and Prussian sources say that Letort led forward the duty squadron, which comprised on that day of a squadron each from the grenadiers à cheval, Empress Dragoons, chasseurs à cheval and the lancers.

However, the immediate picket to Napoléon on 15 June was, according to Aubry and Coignet (both independent writers), composed of the grenadiers à cheval and not the Empress Dragoons. If Letort was ordered to lead forward the duty squadron in the manner described by Pontécoulant and other French writers, then the body of cavalry immediately to hand was the grenadiers à cheval. Analysis of the casualty returns for the grenadiers à cheval compared to the Empress Dragoons shows that the grenadiers à cheval lost men from all four squadrons.[75] In comparison, the Empress Dragoons suffered a single trooper killed compared to the five killed, eleven wounded and twenty horses lost for the grenadiers à cheval.[76]

As well as the Guard cavalry duty squadrons, here at Gilly was a large concentration of French cavalry under Excelmans: General Stoltz's[77] division, comprising General Burthe's[78] brigade (5th Dragoons and the 13th Dragoons, totalling perhaps 930 men) and General Vincent's[79] brigade (15th and 20th Dragoons, mustering some 1,431 men). We are told that three squadrons of the 20th Dragoons were in action by Napoléon's bulletin. It also seems that General Chastel's command was in action. The 1st Brigade, lead by General Bonnemains[80] (comprising of the 4th and 12th Dragoons), also took part in the attack.[81] Bonnemains does not mention the 15th or 20th Dragoons and says that his command alone supported the duty squadrons.[82] Given that it seems that the Empress Dragoons charged with three squadrons of the 20th Dragoons and a squadron of the 15th Dragoons, it is not impossible that the 4th and 12th Dragoons, supported the duty squadron, and that the grenadiers à cheval attacked without support. The 15th Dragoons were in action that day, as Captain Antoine Lucien Deligny, Sub-Lieutenant Jean Gabriel Borde and Sub-Lieutenant Jean Baptist Louis Mony were all wounded. As they were all from the same squadron, this confirms Berton's claim that only a single squadron was in action from 15 June.[83] The 20th Dragoons recorded no officers dead or wounded. For whatever reason, Excelmans, in his report of 16 June, only mentions the 15th and 20th Dragoons and denies he suffered any casualties, which we know to be a lie.[84]

General Berton was a fascinating individual, one who would ultimately pay the price for his ardent Bonapartism when he was executed by the state in 1822.[85] He commanded the 2nd Brigade, comprising the 14th and 17th Dragoons, and seems to have been involved at some point.[86] To this were added the 4th and 9th Chasseurs à Cheval from Pajol, as well as the grenadiers à cheval and Empress Dragoons of the Imperial Guard. Captain Jean Roche Coignet, serving on Napoléon's staff as baggage-master, witnessed, it seems, a charge conducted by cuirassiers:[87]

> It was, I believe, on the 14th that we met a large body of the Prussian advance-guard beyond Gilly. The cuirassiers went through the town at such speed that the horses' shoes flew over the houses. The emperor watched them go through before leaving. It was a steep ascent, but it was impossible to imagine the rapidity with which that body of cavalry could go over a mountain. Our intrepid cuirassiers fell upon the Prussians, and sabred them without taking any prisoners. They were driven back upon their front with considerable loss. The campaign had begun.

Were these Delort's men? Or has Coignet mistaken the body of cavalry, as he notes the attack at Gilly was on 14 and not 15 June? If Coignet is wrong about the date, is he also wrong about what he observed? Colonel Biot notes that once Gilly had been stormed the cavalry debouched along the *faubourg* in the direction of Lodelinsart.[88] In the pursuit, General Stroltz's dragoons ran into the Prussian dragoons of Moisky at Chatelineau, and pursued them through the Pironchamp Wood to the edge of the Lambusart Wood.[89] Grouchy had initiated a skilful cavalry pursuit that was stopped by Ziethen's reserves. Grouchy himself notes:[90]

> Village de Campimarie, the 15th, ten o'clock in the evening
> Sire,
> I have the honour to report to Your Majesty that the corps of General Excelmans aimed to overwhelm the position occupied by the enemy beyond the village of Gilly. He crossed the ravine which separated us and charged onto the plain above Chatelineau; he has not pushed up beyond Ronchamps, and having repulsed their cavalry, fell onto squares of infantry, they were crushed and he made over 400 prisoners.
> The enemy, trying to hold the wood, sought to seek protection from the fire of his infantry, several companies of dragoons were dismounted and opened fire on the Prussian infantry which gave time for the infantry of General Vandamme to arrive. The march on the road through the woods was again supported by dragoons who

continued to pursue the Prussians to the village of Lambusart, which General Chaste[91] is still hunting. It is impossible to show greater intrepidness than that by the corps of General Excelmans, including the brigade of General Vincent, composed of the 15th and 20th regiments of Dragoons. Squadron Leader Guibourg, of 15th Regiment, destroyed a square and made 300 prisoners. I recommend him to Your Majesty's kindnesses.

Summarily, Pajol, at the head of the 1st Corps, drove the enemy from the direct route of Gilly to Fleurus, he made several hundred prisoners and was no less distinguished than General Excelmans, and I cannot do enough to praise him to Your Majesty. He is constantly shouting *'Vive l'Empereur'* and with an enthusiasm difficult to describe. His men have everywhere addressed the enemy.

Please accept my sincerest regards sire,

Marshal Comte de Grouchy.

Grouchy here talks extensively about the operations of Excelmans, perhaps as he had not received that of Pajol. About the day's action, General Excelmans writes to Grouchy as follows:[92]

I have the honour to inform Your Excellency that in the battle which took place yesterday, under your eyes, the brigade of General Vincent had two officers wounded, and with twenty-seven dragoons killed. This brigade has done his duty perfectly. They were led by the brave General Vincent who has extensive experience, showed great firmness and has the rarest of composure, I beg Your Excellency to request him to the emperor to be promoted a grade more in the Legion of Honour.

Colonel Bricqueville[93] (20th) was of good conduct and also Squadron Commander Guibourg[94] (the 15th) who led the 1st Squadron, as this officer is very old, I ask for him the rank of major.

The following men designated are those who have distinguished themselves in the affair of yesterday.

20th Dragoons, MM. Captains Marguiennes and Ramorette. Lieutenant Jory, Adjutant-Sub-Officer Barie, Sub-Lieutenant Warin, Sergeant-Majors Marcey (injured) and Iley, and Grenadier Pisse, who made twenty-seven of the enemy prisoners.

In my staff, Colonel Ferroussat[95] behaved at his best: the officer is fit to command a regiment. Squadron Commander Sensier, my aide-de-camp, also behaved with great bravery. Captain Franchen, attached to my small staff, acted with great daring: I ask for him the rank of battalion commander.

I ask the Cross of the Legion of Honour to M. Dibon,[96] my aide-de-camp, to M. Gemarmon, First Lieutenant of chasseurs, who behaved well. The latter is quite dangerously wounded; he was attached to my staff.

I have the honour, etc.

However, General Pajol writes at 22.00 on 15 June to Marshal Grouchy that:[97]

I would have occupied the village if General Vandamme had sent me some infantry support, but it seems that this general has taken to endeavour to do everything that is against the principles of war, because he failed to occupy the Lambusart Wood at Gilly and Fleurus, which are the two main points in the position where we are.

My troops have been perfectly conducted today. I seized Charleroi, I was the first to pass the Sambre, and with no support, for four hours I resisted all the efforts of the enemy, which must earn those who have distinguished themselves the kindness of His Majesty. I have the honour of addressing you tomorrow their names. I am, etc.

Pajol's inference is that between 12.00 and around 16.00, he kept at bay Prussian skirmishers between Charleroi and Gilly. This long, drawn out skirmish to control the road may well explain the time it took for the French to get to Gilly. This delaying action on the part of the Prussians, however, enabled sufficient time for Vandamme to arrive. However, Vandamme seems to have been unaware of who his direct field commander was, or perhaps, was being bellicose and belligerent in not wanting to support Grouchy's attack. General Sénécal, aide-de-camp to Marshal Grouchy, writes:[98]

15 June, at the allotted time Marshal Grouchy crossed Charleroi, followed by a portion of the light cavalry of General Pajol. We were not to a quarter of a league from that town when we discovered the Prussian corps of General Ziethen in battle order on the other side of a deep valley, where a stream flows, and he crowned the heights that dominated it.

The marshal sent me to inform the emperor, and, after reviewing with him the position of the enemy, ordered them to be attacked as soon as the dragoons of General Excelmans, who were still behind, had arrived. The attack took place as soon as they had joined. The Prussians were driven back and were pursued through the woods until near Fleurus, where he could not have captured the place having no infantry support. The marshal sent to General Vandamme, who had arrived with his corps to Lizière Wood on the hills that dominated Fleurus, the orders to hasten into the city and to use the little daylight left to attack in concert with him the Prussians, and pursue them to Fleurus, and complete the rout.

General Vandamme refused and marshal sent one of his officers to the emperor, to prevent and complain about it.

The emperor, who had remained at Charleroi, replied that the strictest orders were given to the generals commanding the infantry corps, that they might not escape the execution of the orders of the marshal.

Clearly there was some ill-feeling between Vandamme and Grouchy. We are told by Baron Gourgaud that Grouchy asked in person for infantry support and was rebuffed by Vandamme. He then sent General Excelmans on the same mission, who told the general that it was important that he released some of his infantry support to Grouchy. Gourgaud says he sent only a single battalion.[99] How reliable this narration of events is we can only judge against the words of Grouchy; Pajol, Excelmans and Vandamme are silent about this episode.

Despite the infighting between Grouchy and Vandamme, the action at Gilly had been a success. The personality clashes between Grouchy and his subordinates were to have an impact on the days ahead. Napoléon claims that the army captured five Prussian artillery pieces:[100]

At three hours after midday, General Vandamme debouched with his corps on Gilly.

Marshal Grouchy arrived with General Excelmans's cavalry.

The enemy occupied the left of the position of Fleurus. At five hours after midday, the emperor ordered the attack. The position was turned and carried. The four duty squadrons of the Guard, commanded by General Letort, aide-de-camp of the emperor, forced three squares: the 26th, 27th and 28th Prussian regiments were put to rout. Our squadrons sabred 400 to 500 men and took 1,500 prisoners.

During this time, General Reille passed Sambre at Marchienne-au-Pont, to move on Gosselies with the divisions of Prince Jérôme and of General Bachelu, the enemy attacked, he took 250 prisoners and continued on the road to Brussels.

We thus became masters of all the position of Fleurus.

At eight o'clock in the evening, the emperor returned to his Charleroi headquarters.

This day cost the enemy five artillery pieces and 2,000 men, including 1,000 prisoners.

But, Napoléon, in a letter to his brother dated 15 June (timed at 21.00), notes:[101]

> The army has forced the Sambre close to Charleroi and pushed the advanced guard's halfway from Charleroi to Namur and from Charleroi to Brussels. We took 1,500 prisoners and captured six pieces of artillery. Four Prussian regiments were crushed. The emperor lost little, but he had a loss which is very sensitive for him: it is his aide-de-camp, General Letort, who was killed on the Fleurus plateau leading a charge of cavalry. The enthusiasm of the inhabitants of Charleroi and all the countries which we cross cannot be described.

Clearly, either the Prussians are mistaken that the Prussian artillery withdrew or Napoléon was exaggerating his success of the day. We note he is inconsistent with the number of artillery pieces captured. Therefore, we cannot take at face value these two statements made by Napoléon: they contradict each other and in places are incorrect. He also, it seems, played down the strength of the French force engaged against Pirch. He honours the 20th Dragoons and the duty squadron, but fails to mention the grenadiers à cheval, the Young Guard, the Old Guard and the 15th Regiment of Light Infantry. Thus, Napoléon's firsthand testimony of the day cannot be relied upon as an accurate statement of events.

Tactical summary

Napoléon's plan for the day had been to keep the two Allied armies from uniting—this he had achieved, but in doing so had divided his own forces. This turned out to be a major tactical mistake by the emperor in hindsight. Despite success, the emperor's carefully planned timetable was in shreds. When the French came against Charleroi on the morning of 15 June, no immediate assault began until 8.00, simply because Vandamme was not where he was supposed to have been.

Gilly was an important position for the Prussians. It had to be maintained to keep the line of retreat open to Sombreffe. Holding the positions also allowed the Allies to assess where exactly Napoléon was. Perhaps, if Grouchy had been supported at Fleurus on 15 June, the Prussians would not have been able to concentrate at Sombreffe, and would have split both the Prussian forces in two, but also separated the British and their allies from the Prussians.[102] Clausewitz notes:[103]

> Since the enemy had already begun attacking at four o'clock in the morning and had therefore spent the night and the whole previous day on the move and in combat, it was pretty clear that he would neither undertake anything further during the night, nor even resume his attack very early the next day. It could thus be foreseen that if a battle was going to take place at Sombreffe on the 16th, it could begin only in the afternoon, so the armies would have until midday to assemble. General Ziethen's losses on the 15th are given as 1,200 men, but they may have been as high as 2,000. With this sacrifice, the 1st Corps had delayed the enemy's army for thirty-six hours, which is no unfavourable result.

The regimental history of the 6th Prussian Infantry Regiment narrates that:[104]

> The brigade had moved through the Lambusart Wood and deployed in front of the village. Shortly beyond the edge of the wood was a path to the Sambre valley. Here, General von Pirch had placed Major von Rohr with the 1st Battalion to cover the flank of the retreat. The 2nd Battalion replaced the fusiliers, forming the rearguard of the brigade. The entire regiment was deployed directly behind the wood. The enemy, meeting such determined resistance, did not stop attempting to pursue, but had to wait for substantial reinforcements of infantry which gave the regiment time to fall back slowly to positions at Lambusart, threatened only by cavalry.

The 6th Prussian Infantry Regiment arrived at Ligny at 23.30 that night.[105] The large losses sustained by the Guard cavalry show that this engagement was more serious than has been implied by most writers on the campaign. Napoléon himself suggests that the battle was of little or no significance, and that the duty squadrons easily overran the Prussians. Clearly this does not seem to be the case. The Prussians held out for as long as they could against superior numbers. The attack at Gilly was one part of a string of attacks along a wide front to prevent the French from advancing into Brussels and, by holding the French troops up, bought the Allies time to start concentrating their troops for a larger engagement on the following day.

The long, drawn out rearguard from Gilly to Fleurus bought the Prussians time to concentrate at Sombreffe; their chosen location for an engagement with the French.

NOTES:
[1] SHDDT: C15 5 *Correspondence Armée du Nord 11 Juin au 21 Juin 1815*. Dossier 15 June.
[2] Silvain Larreguy de Civrieux, *Souvenirs d'un cadet, 1813-1823*, Hachette, Paris, 1912.
[3] E. F. Janin, *Campagne de Waterloo*, Chaumerot Jeune, Paris, 1820, pp. 6-7.
[4] SHDDT: C15 5. Dossier 15 June 1815. Grouchy to Pajol.
[5] August Wagner, *Plane der Schlachten und Treffen, welche von der Preussischen Armee in den Feldzügen der Jahre 1813, 14 und 15 geliefert worden*, Reimer, Berlin, 1825, p. 13. See also: Karl von Damitz, *Geschichte des Feldzuges von 1815 in den Niederlanden und Frankreich*, E. S. Mittler, Berlin, 1838, p. 69.
[6] Wilhelm Neff, *Geschichte des Infanterie-Regiments von Goeben (2. Rheinischen) Nr. 28*, Ernst Siegfried Mittler und Sohn, Berlin, 1890, p. 21.
[7] SHDDT: Xc 192 *4e Chasseurs à Cheval*. Dossier 1815. Domon to Minister of War, 6 July 1815.
[8] Maurice Fleury, *Souvenirs anecdotiques et militaires du colonel Biot*, Henri Vivien, Paris, 1901, p. 235. See also: William Siborne, *The Waterloo Campaign 1815*, A. Constable, 1900, p. 103.
[9] Fleury, p. 235.
[10] *Nouvel Revue Rétrospective*, January 1896, p. 362.
[11] Emile von Conrady, *Geschichte des Könglich preussischen sechsten Infaterie-regiments*, Glogau, 1857, p. 240.
[12] Wagner, p. 14.
[13] Fleury, Vol. 3, p. 191.
[14] Fleury, ibid.
[15] Fleury, Vol. 3, pp. 191-2.
[16] SHDDT: C15 *Registre d'ordre et de correspondance du major-general à partir du 13 Juin jusqu'au 26 Juin au Maréchal Grouchy*, p. 12.
[17] SHDDT: C15 22 *Registre correspondence 2e corps observation Armée du Nord*, p. 27. After-action report of 15 June 1815, timed at 21.00. Reille to Soult.
[18] Toussaint-Jean Trefcon, *Carnet de la campagne du colonel Trefcon, 1793-1815*, E. Dubois, Paris, 1914, p. 179.
[19] SHDDT: C15 5. Dossier 18 June 1815. Reille to Soult, 15 June 1815.
[20] Hippolyte de Mauduit, *Les derniers jours de la Grande Armée* (Vol. 2), Paris, 1848, p. 11. See also, Gaspard Gourgaud, *La campagne de 1815,* P. Mongie, Paris, 1818, p. 45.
[21] Fleury, Vol. 3, p. 192.
[22] Compiled from SHDDT: GR 20 YC 55. See also: SHDDT: GR 20 YC 56.
[23] *Revue de l'Empire*, 1842.
[24] Fleury, p. 236.
[25] Wagner, p. 14. See also: Damitz, Vol. 1, pp. 69-70, and Karl Rudolf von Ollech, *Geschichte des feldzuges von 1815 nach archivalischen quellen*, E. S. Mittler und Sohn, Berlin, 1876, p. 103.
[26] Wagner, p. 14.
[27] Siborne, *The Waterloo Campaign*, p. 103.
[28] Conrady, p. 240.
[29] *Carnet de la Sabretache*, 1899, p. 243.
[30] François-Thomas Delbare, *Relation circonstanciée de la dernière campagne de Buonaparte, terminée par le bataille de Mont-Saint-Jean, dite de Waterloo ou de la Belle-Alliance*, J. G. Dentu, Paris, 1816, p. 30.
[31] Germain Sarrut, *Biographie des Hommes du Jour, etc*, Paris.
[32] Wagner, pp. 14-15. See also: Damitz, Vol. 1, p. 83.
[33] Wagner, p. 14. See also: Damitz, Vol. 1, pp. 69-70, and Ollech, p. 103.
[34] Pierre François Tissot, *Histoire de Napoléon, rédigée d'après les papiers d'État, les documents officiels, les mémoires et les notes secrètes de ses contemporains, suivie d'un précis sur la famille*

Bonaparte (Vol. 2), Delange-Taffin, Paris, 1833, pp. 263-4.

[35] Fleury, p. 236. See also: Damitz, Vol. 1, p. 83.

[36] Jean Baptiste Berton, *Précis historique, militaire et critique des batailles de Fleurus et de Waterloo, dans la campagne de Flandres, en juin 1815*, J. S. Wallez, La Haye, 1818, p. 15.

[37] Thomas Joseph Aubry, *Mémoires d'un capitaine de chasseurs à cheval*, Jourdan, Paris, 2011, p. 150.

[38] SHDDT: C15 5. Dossier 15 June 1815. Daure to Soult.

[39] ibid.

[40] *Nouvel Revue Rétrospective*, January 1896, p. 362.

[41] Fleury, p. 237.

[42] AN: LH 542/61. François Joseph Marie, Comte Clary, was born at Marseille on 3 October 1786. He was admitted to the 9th Dragoons on 8 February 1803 as a volunteer and was quickly rewarded by being made sub-lieutenant of the 22nd Dragoons on 7 December 1803. He is listed as a lieutenant in the 10th Dragoons on 3 May 1805 and was made aide-de-camp to Joseph Bonaparte on 17 January 1806, before being named as colonel of the voltigeurs of the Royal Spanish Guard on 10 January 1810. He became the aide-de-camp to Marshal Berthier on 22 April 1813 and then colonel of the 1st Hussars on 27 June 1813, aged twenty-seven with ten years' service. He was promoted to marshal-du-camp on 23 August 1814 and was placed on the non-active list. He is listed again as colonel of the 4th Chasseurs à Cheval on 26 March 1815, and took command of the 1st Hussars again on the 30 March. Following Waterloo, he was placed on half-pay.

[43] SHDDT: Xc 238 *1e Hussard*. Dossier 1814.

[44] ibid.

[45] SHDDT: C15 5. Dossier 15 June 1815. Ney to Soult, timed at 23.00.

[46] Wagner, pp. 17-20.

[47] Conrady, pp. 241-2.

[48] AN: LH 1121/44. Charles Etienne Philippe Gerbet was born on 6 November 1791 and was admitted to the Ecole Militaire on 20 April 1809, before he graduated as sub-lieutenant in the 37th Regiment of Line Infantry on 9 November 1812. He was discharged on 1 September 1815.

[49] Philippe Gerbet, *Souvenirs d'un officier sur la campagne de Belgique en 1815*, Émile Javal, Arbois, 1866, pp. 8-9.

[50] Anon, *Memoires pour servir a l'Histoire de France*, Richard Phillips & Co, London, 1820, p. 74.

[51] Emmanuel Grouchy, *Relation de la campagne de 1815*, n.d, p. 11.

[52] Emmanuel Grouchy, George Grouchy, *Mémoires du maréchal de Grouchy* (Vol. 4), E. Dentu, 1873, p. 126.

[53] Damitz, Vol. 1. p. 92. See also: Wagner, Vol. 4, p. 20.

[54] Fleury, p. 237.

[55] Fleury, p. 237.

[56] SHDDT: C15 *Registre d'ordre et de correspondance du major-general a partir du 13 Juin jusqu'au 26 Juin au Marechal Grouchy*, p. 17.

[57] Aubry, p. 150.

[58] Jean-Roch Coignet, *The Narrative of Captain Coignet Soldier of the Empire, 1776-1850*, Chatto & Windus, London, 1897, pp. 278-9.

[59] Pierre de Wit, personal communication, 14 July 2012.

[60] Marie Élli Guillaume de Baudus, *Études sur Napoléon*, Debecourt, Paris, 1841.

[61] Anon, *Memoires pour servir a l'Histoire*, pp. 77-8.

[62] Anon, *Memoires pour servir a l'Histoire*, p. 74.

[63] Neff, p. 23.

[64] Charles Paris Nicholas Beauvais, *Victoires, conquêtes, désastres, revers et guerres civils des Français, de 1792 à 1815*, C. L. F. Panckoucke, Paris, 1821, Vol. 24, p. 178. See also: SHDDT: C15 5.

[65] Grouchy, *Relation de la campagne de 1815*, p. 12.

[66] Damitz, p. 90.

[67] Damitz, Vol. 1, p. 90.

[68] SHDDT: C15 5. Dossier 18 June 1815.*Rapport Colonel Blocqueville*. See also: '*Declaration du Colonel de Bloqueville*' in Emmanuel Grouchy, *Relation succincte de la campagne de 1815 en Belgique*, Delanchy, Paris, 1843.

[69] Pierre Berthezène, *Souvenirs militaires de la republique et de l'empire*, J. Dumaine, Paris, 1855, pp. 360-1.

[70] Grouchy, *Relation de la campagne de 1815*, p. 11.

[71] Gourgaud, p. 50.

[72] Damitz, Vol. 1, p. 91.

[73] Gustave de Pontécoulant, *Souvenirs militaires: Napoléon à Waterloo*, J. Dumaine, Paris, 1866, p. 26.

[7] Pontécoulant, *Souvenirs militaires*, p. 26.

[7] SHDDT: GR 20 YC 137.

[7] ibid.

[7] Jean Baptiste Alexandre Stroltz was born at Belfort on 6 August 1771 and was admitted into the army on 8 April 1793, before being promoted to sub-lieutenant of the 16th Chasseurs à Cheval on 22 September 1794. He is listed as aide-de-camp to General Kléber in 1795, and in this capacity he was promoted to lieutenant on 25 December 1796, to captain on 23 June 1798, to squadron commander on 10 February 1800 and then named as aide-de-camp to General Moreau. He became a colonel of the light horse regiment of the Kingdom of Naples on 25 July 1806 and was promoted to brigadier-general in the Kingdom of Naples on 30 October 1807. Stroltz commanded an infantry brigade under General Mathieu in the Sicily campaign. He was then appointed as aide-de-camp to Joseph Bonaparte, and then promoted to general-of-division on 1 July 1813. He died in Paris on 27 October 1841.

[78] André Burthe was born in Metz in France on 8 December 1772, allegedly into a family of Irish refugees who had followed King James II of England to France. He entered military service on 6 April 1791 at the age of nineteen as a simple cavalier in the 2nd Regiment of Dragoons, after which his career had a meteoric rise. He served in the Armée du Rhine 1794-1795 and entered the general staff as an adjutant-general to Solignac in the Armée d'Italie in February 1796. In 1797, he was promoted to capitaine-d'Etat-major to the army in Italy and in October the following year became first aide-de-camp to André Masséna in the Armée d'Helvétie. He took part in the campaign in the Helvetic Republic and was promoted to Chef d'Escadron in the field at the First Battle of Zurich in 1799. He was seriously wounded twice by musket balls at the Siege of Genoa (1800). Masséna, recognising the young man's merit, honoured him with a particular friendship and charged him, once he was recovered, with the formal presentation of the Italian enemy flags captured at the Battle of Marengo on 14 June 1800 to the new First Consul of France (Napoléon Bonaparte, following a coup the previous year). The general raised him to the rank of adjutant-general, a promotion confirmed on 14 July 1800 when the presentation took place at a public display on the Champ de Mars in Paris: an address was made by Lannes and Burthe also made a speech. On the Bourbon Restoration, Burthe retired from military service; on 6 January 1825, he was granted a pension of 4,000 *francs*. He died on 2 April 1830.

[79] AN: LH 2725/17. Henri Catherine Balthazard Vincent was born on 22 May 1775 and was made a Commander of the Legion of Honour on 11 August 1814.

[80] Pierre Bonnemains was born 13 September 1773 and was admitted to the National Guard aged eighteen. He passed to the 12th Dragoons on 20 May 1793 with the rank of sub-lieutenant, and then named as aide-de-camp to General Tilly in 1797. He was promoted to squadron-commander on 21 April 1800, and to major of 16th Chasseurs à Cheval on 28 October 1803, before becoming colonel of 5th Chasseurs à Cheval on 20 September 1806. He was promoted to general-de-brigade on 6 August 1811. He served in the 1823 campaign. He and Armand de Bricqueville were noted for being ardent Bonapartists in the revolution of 1830. He served in Algeria in 1839 to 1848 and died on 9 November 1850.

[81] ibid.

[82] SHDDT: C15 5.

[83] Berton, p. 13.

[84] SHDDT: C15 5. Dossier 16 June 1815. Report from General Excelmans to Grouchy 16 June 1815.

[85] Jean Baptiste Berton was born on 15 June 1769 at Euilly in the Ardennes. He was admitted to the military school at Brienne aged twenty-seven and then passed to the artillery school at Chalons in 1793. He was attached to the staff of Bernadotte, and served at Austerlitz and Jena, and was with Victor's staff at Friedland, before serving in Spain with Soult's staff from 1808 to 1814. He never took a field command until 1815, nor had any experience as a regimental colonel. On leave from July 1815, he agitated against the Bourbons and was executed for treason on 5 October 1822.

[86] Berton, p. 15.

[87] Coignet, p. 280.

[88] Fleury, p. 237.

[89] 'Breife eines Preussischen Offiziers uber den Feldzug' in Militar Wochenblatt, Berlin, 1822, p. 462.

[90] SHDDT: C15 5. Dossier 15 June 1815, Grouchy to Napoléon dated 15 June 1815.

[91] Louis Pierre Aimé Chastel was born on 29 April 1774. He first joined up in 1792, in the Légion des Allobroges, under the name of Jacques François Dugommier, and was then transferred to the Armée des Pyrénées and saw service in Italy. He took part in Bonaparte campaign in Egypt, where he discovered the Dendera Zodiac. He was made major-en-second (lieutenant-colonel) of the grenadiers à cheval of the Imperial Guard in 1803, and his actions at Austerlitz got him recognised by Napoléon. In 1812 he was summoned to join the French invasion of Russia, where he led the 3rd Light Cavalry Division in the 3rd Cavalry Corps. His bravery at Borodino gained him a mention in dispatches. He died on 26 September 1826 in Geneva.

[92] SHDDT: C15 5. Dossier 15 June. Report from General Excelmans to Grouchy 16 June 1815.

[93] AN: LH 1227/40. Armand de Bricqueville was born at Bretteville in 1785 and was listed as a sub-lieutenant of the 18th Dragoons in 1803, as a major of the 2nd Light Horse Lancers of the Imperial Guard in 1813, and named as a colonel of 20th Dragoons during the Hundred Days.

[94] AN: LH 1227/40. Marie Jacques Emmanuel Guibourg was born on 15 December 1775.

[95] AN: LH 963/46. Jean Louis Ferroussat was born in London on 3 July 1780 and was admitted to the 9th Dragoons on 2 January 1797, before being promoted to corporal on 14 November 1798, to sergeant on 3 June 1800, to sous-lieutenant on 19 September 1801, to lieutenant on 7 January 1804, and to captain on 27 February 1806. He was named as the ADC to General Monpetit on 27 June 1806, and promoted to squadron commander on 17 September 1811. He was listed as major of 10th Chasseurs à Cheval on 18 July 1813, as colonel on 3 April 1814 and as chief-of-staff to 2nd Cavalry Corps on 15 May 1815. He was then listed as colonel of the 2nd Lancers in place of Colonel Sourd on 3 July 1815, before being discharged on 22 September 1815.

[96] AN: LH 771/50. Jean Baptiste William Dibon was born on 8 April 1793 and admitted to the Military School at Saint-Germain on 11 November 1812, before being named as sub-lieutenant in the Chasseurs à Cheval of the Young Guard on 19 February 1814, and admitted to the 1st Cuirassiers on 10 July 1814. He was promoted to lieutenant on 23 March 1815 and became aide-de-camp to Excelmans on 27 June 1815, before being dismissed on 22 June 1819.

[97] SHDDT: C15 5. Dossier 15 June. Pajol to Grouchy 15 June 1815, timed at 22.00.

[98] Sénécal, General le Sénécal campagne de Waterloo, Philadelphia, 1818, pp. 2-6.

[99] Nouvel Revue Rétrospective, January 1896, p. 366.

[100] Napoleon I, Correspondance de Napoleon 1er, vol.28, H. Plon, J. Dumaine, Paris, 1858. Order No. 22056 Bulletin of the Army.

[101] Napoleon I. Order No. 22055 to Prince Joseph 15 June 1815, timed as 21.00.

[102] Grouchy, Relation succincte de la campagne de 1815, pp. 31-2. See also: Gourgaud, p. 68.

[103] Christopher Bassford, Daniel Moran, Gregory W. Pedlow, Clausewitz, Wellington and the Campaign of 1815, On Waterloo, available at https://www.clausewitz.com/readings/1815/TOC.htm [accessed 12 April 2012].

[104] Conrady, p. 242.

[105] ibid.

Chapter 3

Morning of 16 June 1815

Following the action at Gilly, Sombreffe had become the concentration point for Blücher's army. At first light, just a few minutes before 4.00, Napoléon was on horseback. He was seemingly in good spirits, intending to reach Brussels as soon as possible. By daybreak he had had no news of Wellington's movements, or of Blücher. At 8.00 he received Grouchy's dispatch, which read:[1]

16 June 1815 five o'clock in the morning

M. marshal

The four corps of cavalry are established in the following locations:

The 1st has the 1st Division at Lambusart and the 2nd on the road to from Gilly to Fleurus, where they have established their camp.

The 2nd Corps has the 1st Division at Lambusart and another in the rear of the valley of Touchamp.

The 4th Corps has established the 2nd Division at the villages of Saint-François and the environs of Lenden [sic]

The 3rd Corps is between Charleroi and the point where they charged the Prussian infantry squares. General Kellermann is between this point and Charleroi, where he has established himself on the flank closest to us.

I have not received the reports of losses that the 1st and 2nd Corps have sustained during the day, and I have asked for them to be sent to me. Attached to this are copies for the emperor.

The total number of prisoners taken by the cavalry during the day total between 800 and 900 men.

Be assured, marshal, of my fraternity and high consideration of you,

The marshal commanding the cavalry

Comte de Grouchy

P. S. The 1st Hussars have been detached from the 1st Corps on your orders and I desire that they are returned to the division as soon as it is possible to do so.

In response, about the broader picture, Soult wrote to Grouchy about Ney and the broader plan of operations:[2]

Soult to Grouchy timed at 8.00. Carried by Colonel M. Lion
Marshal,
The emperor orders that you are to march with 1st, 2nd and 4th Cavalry Corps, and to direct them onto Sombreffe, where you will take up position. I have passed similar orders to Lieutenant-General Comte Vandamme for the 3rd Corps and to Lieutenant-General Gérard for the 4th Corps. I have informed these two generals that they are to act under your orders, and that they are to immediately send you officers carrying news of their movements, and to carry your instructions. I have informed them that they will take His Majesty's direct orders and to keep me informed of their news and movements.

I have also advised General Gérard that in his movement towards Sombreffe he is to keep Sombreffe on his left; and you are to direct him so that he marches with his men concentrated and within close reach of the 3rd Corps, so as to be able to contribute to the attack on Sombreffe. In consequence you will give orders to Vandamme if the enemy puts up resistance during the attack on Sombreffe.

I have the honour to inform you that I ordered the Comte de Valmy, as soon as he received my order, to move to Gosselies with the 3rd Cavalry Corps, where he will be at Ney's disposal.

The 1st Regiment of Hussars will return to the 1st Cavalry Corps, where they shall be placed under the orders of the emperor.

I have the honour to inform you that Marshal Prince of the Moskowa has received orders to move with the 1st and 2nd Infantry Corps and the 3rd Cavalry Corps to the intersection of the roads, at Trois-Bras, on the Brussels road, and he will detach a strong corps to Marbais, which will be available to you to support your operations at Sombreffe. After you have taken Sombreffe, you will immediately send an advanced guard to Gembloux and send out reconnaissance patrols, particularly in the direction to Namur, and at the same time establish communications with Marshal Ney.

The Imperial Guard is to move to Fleurus.

In the order, Ney was to detach a corps to aid Grouchy as needed. No word at all of sending Kellermann to Marbais. Here, Napoléon was beginning to form his plan of operations. Grouchy was to attack with 3rd and 4th Corps, and a corps from Ney's command with Kellermann's cavalry corps were to stand *en potence* ready to intervene at what would become the Battle of Ligny in a flanking assault to take the Prussians in the rear. Napoléon was clearly developing his strategy. Ney was under no illusion that part of his command was to be sent to Grouchy, and by inference Napoléon. He must have realised that he would only have to hand Reille's 2nd Corps, Piré's cavalry and the Guard cavalry. Napoléon issued the following set of orders:[3]

> My cousin,
>
> I'm sending you La Bédoyère, my aide-de-camp, who will present you this letter. The major-general will have made known to you my intentions, but because he has some badly mounted officers at his disposition, my aide-de-camp could arrive earlier. My intention is that you will command the right wing, and be in command of the 3rd Corps of General Vandamme, the 4th of General Gérard, the cavalry corps of the Generals Pajol, Milhaud and Excelmans, together around fifty thousand men.
>
> The rallying point of the right wing will be at Sombreffe. In consequence, you have to ensure that the corps of generals Pajol, Milhaud, Excelmans and Vandamme will start out immediately to continue your movement to Sombreffe. The 4th Corps, which is at Châtelet, will receive directly the order to go to Sombreffe, without passing through Fleurus. This is important because I will establish my general headquarters in Fleurus and we have to avoid any traffic jams.
>
> Send immediately an officer to General Gérard in order to let him know your movement and that he will execute his accordingly.
>
> It is my wish that the generals take their orders directly from you. They will take mine only when I am there. I will be at Fleurus between 10 and 11 a.m. Afterwards, I will go to Sombreffe, leaving the infantry and the cavalry of the Guard at Fleurus, and I will take them only to Sombreffe in case of necessity. If the enemy is at Sombreffe I want to attack him. I want even to attack him in Gembloux and take this position, because it is my intention to depart this night, after taking the two positions, and operate with my left wing, commanded by Marshal Ney, against the English. Do not lose a moment, because I will be moving soon to continue the operations.
>
> I suppose that you are at Fleurus; you have to communicate on a permanent basis with General Gérard, so that he could help you in attacking Sombreffe when it is necessary. The division of Girard

will be in the vicinity of Fleurus. Do not use them unless there is an absolute necessity to do so, because they had to march all night. Also, let my Young Guard and the attached artillery stay in Fleurus. The Comte de Valmy, with his two divisions of cuirassiers, is marching on the road to Brussels; he will join Marshal Ney in order to contribute with the manoeuvring this evening on the left wing.

Like I said, I will be at Fleurus from 10 to 11 a.m. Send me your reports concerning all that you hear of; make sure that the road to Fleurus will be free from congestion. All the information I have says that the Prussians cannot oppose us with more than 40,000 men.

Napoléon.

Thus, Girard was passed to Grouchy's command from Ney, without a word about this getting to the latter. The order informs us that on the morning of 16 June, the emperor had already decided to send off Grouchy to chase the Prussians, and was to swing north, we assume, with the Guard to take 1st and 2nd Corps to Brussels, leaving 4th Corps as a reserve. If this order is genuine, then why did the emperor dither on the morning of 17 June in putting his plan into action? In his order to Ney, the emperor clearly outlined his plan of operations for the day:[4]

Charleroi 16 June

M. marshal, the emperor orders that you are to march with 1st and 2nd Army Corps as well as the 3rd Cavalry Corps, which is now at your disposal, and lead them to the intersection of so called Trois-Bras of the Brussels roads, where you will take up position. You will undertake reconnaissances along the Brussels and Nivelles roads, along which the enemy probably withdrew. His Majesty desires that despite any setbacks, you are to establish a division with cavalry at Genappe and he orders you to send another division to Marbais to cover the area between Sombreffe and Trois-Bras. You can place with this division the cavalry of the Imperial Guard commanded by General Lefèbvre-Desnoëttes, as well as the 1st Regiment of Hussars, which was seconded to you yesterday, to stand at Gosselies.

The corps that is to be placed at Marbais may also be used to support Marshal Grouchy in his movements on Sombreffe, and also support the position of Trois-Bras, as it may become necessary. You are to instruct the general who will be at Marbais to scout in all directions, particularly to Gembloux and Wavre.

If, however, the division of General Lefèbvre-Desnoëttes is not standing on the Brussels road, it is to be replaced at Marbais by the

3rd Cavalry Corps under the orders of Comte de Valmy, as well as the 1st Hussars.

I have the honour to notify you that the emperor will be moving onto Sombreffe, where Marshal Grouchy will debouch with the 3rd and 4th Infantry Corps and the 1st, 2nd and 4th Cavalry Corps. Marshal Grouchy will occupy Gembloux. Please send a report of your news and arrangements to the emperor, and execute the order and I sent you.

His Majesty charges me to remind you to tell all generals commanding army corps to concentrate their men and draw back in all isolated men, to maintain the most perfect order among the troops, as well as to concentrate your artillery and ambulances which may be in the rear.

These two orders clearly defined Grouchy and Ney's mission objectives. He was to occupy Quatre-Bras, as well as Genappe, and move a division towards Sombreffe to support Grouchy at Ligny. However, the general concept of the situation (that Ligny was the primary objective and Quatre-Bras the secondary objective) was not explained clearly enough to Ney for him to understand the plan of operations for the day. It is obvious, though, that from the tone of both orders that Ligny and the Prussians were the primary objective. The order also makes it very clear that an entire army corps was to be sent to Marbais to aid Grouchy. Ney had known since early morning that part of his command was to be sent to aid Napoléon. Yet he clearly forgot this, as we shall see later, with tragic consequences. Napoléon's plan was devastatingly simple: Grouchy with 3rd Corps was to head to Sombreffe and Gembloux and engage the Prussians. If needed, the Guard and 4th Corps could be ordered up. Depending on how the situation unfolded at Sombreffe, the entire corps placed at Marbais was ideally situated to sweep down behind the Prussians. This tactic is called 'manoeuvres sur les derrières'. For reasons best known only to Ney, he didn't realise that the action at Quatre-Bras was of secondary importance to the 'manoeuvres sur les derrières' that was outlined in this order. Ney had clear orders to concentrate his forces, yet he issued no order to do so until 11.00; a tragic mistake. He did not send any Corps to Marbais. When the 1st Corps, did start heading off to Marbais much later in the day, Ney called it back to him, clearly forgetting his earlier orders. He had spent the morning dithering and dallying, unlike Grouchy who set off in response to his orders to find and attack the Prussians. Napoléon issued to Vandamme the following order, which was carried by Guyardin:[5]

Charleroi 16 June 1815

M. Comte Vandamme

M. general, the emperor orders you to march with 3rd Corps and direct it to Sombreffe, where 4th Corps and the corps of reserve cavalry are also being directed. S. M. [His Majesty] orders that you are to take orders from Marshal Grouchy who is in command of this wing of the army.

A similar order was sent to Gérard, who was instructed to skirt around Fleurus on its left side.[6] A second order was sent to Grouchy, informing him that orders had been issued to Vandamme and Gérard, and that he was to take the 1st, 2nd and 4th Cavalry Corps to Sombreffe. He closed the order with these words:[7]

If the enemy are at Sombreffe, you will attack. I will attack at Gembloux; it is my intention that we take both positions.

Early on the morning of 16 June, General Vandamme issued orders to his divisional commanders:[8]

Monsieur the general

His Excellency the General-in-Chief Comte Vandamme has ordered that each division of infantry of the army corps is to furnish a detachment of fifteen men, commanded by a lieutenant that is to serve in the park and equipment train of the army corps.

Order each detachment to join the suite of the headquarters staff of His Excellency, and will take new dispositions from Colonel van Landten, who will take command.

Agree with me, my general, on the importance of these orders.

With respect

Adjutant-commandant, assistant chief-of-staff of the headquarters of the general-in-chief of 3rd Army Corps of the Armée du Nord

Trezel.

The order sent to General Berthezène, commanding the 11th Infantry Division, is the only copy of this order that has survived to the present day. It was carried by a corporal and four troopers from the 9th Regiment of Chasseurs à Cheval.

On the morning of 16 June, General Friant issued the following order to the four regiments of grenadiers à pied:[9]

The lieutenant-colonel-general of the army has seen with astonishment and discontent that many grenadiers are permitted to lead pack horses or drive saddle horses. He can solely assign this oversight of their duties from the negligence of the officers who do not require their men to their duties and tolerate too many women to follow the companies. He therefore directs the marshal-du-camp to remove from the column all those women who exceed the number fixed by the regulations that would not be allowed to follow the army. All those who after receiving the order to remove themselves from following regiments will be arrested and handed over to the police. Any grenadier who is found driving a horse or leading a pack horse will be taken to the lieutenant-colonel-general of the arm, who will take such steps as he deems appropriate.

The daily routine and fatigues will be carried out with more order. Men on fatigues will always have their arms with them, and there will always be an officer of the regiment at their head, the corporal-quartermasters commanding the companies. The lieutenant-colonel-general of the arm will be informed each day of the names of the men who have missed the roll calls.

MM. the marshals-du-camp will, during the day of the 15th, send to the chief-of-staff their situations following the model attached. It will show the number of men present in each corps from the moment of departure from Paris, with the exception of the detachment from the 1st Regiment which left for the service of the emperor, and who will re-join us. All the other men who have had their names removed from the roll and recorded as transferred elsewhere and as passed through the depot company. The list of names of the men and their location since departure from Paris are to be sent to M. Villeumeureux, the quartermaster in Paris, by MM.[10] the officers.

Regardless of the situation report of the 15th of this month, which are to be submitted every 14th and 29th day, a situation report will be sent daily as in the past, where we mention the loss and gain of each day and a narration of events within each twenty-four hour period.

General Friant.

Clearly the grenadiers à pied then camped at Charleroi were not up to Friant's expectations, with lax officers and sub-officers and, apparently, a whole gaggle of camp-followers behind. The Imperial Guard in 1815 was a shaky formation, with far lower standards of discipline, *esprit de corps* and quality of men than in previous years. This was not just a problem for the Guard, as General Radet makes clear:[11]

Armée du Nord, at the Imperial General Headquarters, in Charleroi, on 16 May 1815.

The Lieutenant-General Bon Radet, inspector-general, commander-in-chief of the Imperial Gendarmerie and His Majesty's provost marshal of the Armée du Nord

Report to His Excellency, the major-general.

Sir,

The marauding and the disorder are renewing themselves in the army, and the Guard gives the example. Yesterday I went through the column from the rear to the front to assure myself of the execution of the order of the 14th. I have removed more than a hundred baggage wagons which belonged to the general staff, the Guard and different army corps, and who had slipped themselves in the columns, and afterwards they were placed where they belong.

I have chased away and assembled a lot of stragglers who took drinks and food by force. I have stopped the looting of the grains and the fodder of many farms that the artillery and their crews were removing in disorder.

I have assembled several mounted artillery detachments, for instance a detachment of the Guard which was going back in order to forage without having an officer in charge or a written order or claim, not even some vouchers.

I was obliged to leave pickets in each village so that order could be maintained until after the passage of the column: this night they have re-joined the crews of the general headquarters which are stationed at Marcinville in the vicinity of Charleroi. They have reported to me that they have arrested several soldiers taken in the act and with stolen goods, but that all was retaken from them with force and with such fierceness, insults and bad treatment by the regiments on the march that it was not possible for the gendarmes to even know the number of those corps.

I arrived at Montigny at noon and I have released the elite gendarmes who were guarding the prisoners; I have placed the colonel with some forty men on police duty at Charleroi at the Grand Place, and I came to re-join Your Excellency at the upper town with the six men who were still with me.

Following his orders, I have returned downtown to restore the order that was said to be disturbed; the army paraded enthusiastically and did not commit the slightest disorder.

Only the artillery of the Guard looted a fodder granary in the upper town, and I have chased the looters and ordered that one should be arrested, which took place. A soldier of the train was taken, two gendarmes were bringing him to me passing the column, when the adjutant-major named Morel, of the foot chasseurs of the Guard, put him free of their hands saying that it was him who authorised the foraging; I sent a captain in order to verify this fact and he was insulted.

Until six o'clock in the evening the peace was maintained, but this night a store of brandy was looted by the Guard, in spite of the efforts of the gendarmes that I posted there; however, the inhabitants were neither looted nor ill-treated, although overloaded with billets.

Your Excellency will sense that with the handful of gendarmes at my disposal it was not possible to keep the army in order. I will receive the seventy-five men in excess of the army, but I have to beg you to observe that even if I have a thousand gendarmes it will not be possible to suppress the disorder if the gendarmerie is not respected, and also the general orders if the officers do not maintain the discipline and the obedience, at last if the regiments don't keep order themselves and execute the orders of the emperor.

I will try to make some examples, but a new general order is needed to prevent the army looting.

General Denzel has reported that the two columns of prisoners are gone. About fifty of them were wounded and unable to march, so they stay in Charleroi. I will send some gendarmes to the intendant general to fetch the unused carts behind the corps and will direct them with our own wounded towards Avesnes.

Signed: Radet.

At 11.00, Napoléon arrived on the field of battle and was greeted with loud shouts of *'Vive l'Empereur!'* de Mauduit, of the 1st Grenadiers, remembers the start to the day as follows:[12]

On the 16th, about eight o'clock in the morning, we received orders to take up arms and follow the emperor, who was preparing to move forward. At nine o'clock, we resumed our march to Fleurus, with the drums and band at our head. Our clothing was that of combat: the greatcoat, overall trousers and fur cap without ornament…it should have been full dress, as we were soon to play a role worthy of it…The sky was as clear as the sky of Marengo, which we would celebrate in some way…the sun and no clouds foretell a hot day, and indeed, it was in every respect!

> Above the village of Gilly, whose single-storey houses stood directly onto the road to Fleurus, we detached some men to go and bury the dead of the battlefield of the previous day. The dead were still waiting for their military burial.

de Mauduit had been part of a burial detachment and the dead numbered around three hundred men—a figure similar to the losses known for the regiment. He also mentions that he met similar parties from the Guard, suggesting that in the woods in front of Gilly, the Imperial Guard had been in action.[13]

Napoléon's plans

The Battle of Ligny was thrust upon Napoléon by Blücher. In response, the emperor began to make plans for the coming battle. He was also aware that Ney, to his left, had Allied troops before him, but in low numbers. Therefore, the emperor planned an encircling movement behind the Prussians.

The French army had finally concentrated on the battlefield by 14.00, at which time Napoléon sent the following order to Marshal Ney outlining his plan of operations:[14]

> In front of Fleurus 16 June about 14.00 hours
> Marshal,
> The emperor charges me to let you know that the enemy has united a corps of troops between Sombreffe and Brye, and that at 14.30 hrs, M. Marshal Grouchy will attack it with the 3rd and the 4th Corps; it is the intention of His Majesty that you will also attack what is in front of you, and that you, after having repulsed it vigorously, fall back on us in order to surround the corps I just mentioned to you. If this corps is pushed before, His Majesty will move in your direction in order to hasten your operations. Instruct at once the emperor of your arrangements and of what is happening on your front.
> Marshal of the empire, Major-General Duc de Dalmatie.

This order presumably arrived between 15.00 and 15.30, but we cannot be sure. The order outlined for Ney was for a *'manoeuvres sur les derrières'* by the left wing of the army against Blücher. However, the general concept of the situation wasn't explained to him. Rather than holding the Allies at bay, the order made Ney commit himself even more into the action at Quatre-Bras, as the order made it clear that the occupation of Quatre-Bras was to be completed before he was to move towards Ligny. Ney didn't realise that the action at Quatre-Bras was of secondary importance, and that the decisive battle was raging at Ligny, nor did Soult make this clear to Ney. At 15.30, Napoléon dispatched the following order to Ney:[15]

> S. M. gives me the responsibility to say to you that you must manoeuvre at once so as to envelop the right of the enemy and fall quickly on his rear; this army is lost if you act vigorously; do not hesitate a moment to make the movement which the emperor orders you and directs you on the heights of Brye and Saint-Amand to contribute to a perhaps decisive victory.

Napoléon, in sending the order, endeavoured to make it clear that Ney was to manoeuvre to join the fighting at Ligny, along with Lobau and 6th Corps. Rather than holding the Allies at bay, the 15.30 order made Ney commit himself even more into the action at Quatre-Bras.

Ney had not yet taken Quatre-Bras when the 15.30 arrived. In this, he had become somewhat mission-blind and was solely focused on the crossroads, and not the larger tactical picture. He only understood the situation around 19.00 with the arrival of Baudus from Soult, perhaps sooner with the verbal portion of the orders (which have been lost to history) transmitted by Laurent or de La Bédoyère. In defence of Ney, Soult's orders from Napoléon were vague. But, we only have the written portion of the orders as no doubt the orders carried a verbal portion which is lost to history. In the first orders issued on 16 June, Napoléon desired that Ney was to take a position at Quatre-Bras and at the same time make provisions to wheel around behind the Prussians in a *'manoeuvre sur les derrières'*. Ney's initial task was to take up a position at Quatre-Bras as a stage towards a march towards Brussels, while in the 15.30 order this occupation became a condition for the *manoeuvre sur les derrières* as Napoléon had planned it. In this way, Ney became very much focused upon the crossroads as his first priority, and in reading Ney's report of the evening of 16 June, it seems as if he almost disregarded the clear distinction of the primary and the secondary action that day. On 17 June, Napoléon had planned that having defeated the Prussians and not having dispatched Grouchy in pursuit, would have been able to concentrate his forces and crush Wellington at Quatre-Bras by wheeling the 1st, 3rd and 4th Corps from Ligny to Quatre-Bras. Ney disobeyed direct orders and prevented this from happening.

Napoléon had, it seems, underestimated the strength of the Prussian forces in front of him. He bargained that Ney had troops to spare to send to Ligny. History shows that he was misplaced in his assumption that Ney was carrying out his orders. For a fuller discussion see the author's book *'Ney at Quatre-Bras'*.

8th Division attacks

Commanding 3rd Corps was General Vandamme. Dominique René Vandamme was born in Cassel on 5 November 1770. He was the son of a Flemish surgeon from Poperinghe and enrolled at Marshal de Biron's military school in 1786. Vandamme was one of Napoléon's more capable generals and, like many of his contemporaries such as Masséna and Augereau, had a reputation for looting. He was also known for his violent temper, which he seemed to have little control over.

Battle commenced at 15.00, when General Vandamme sent forward General Lefol's division against Saint-Amand. Saint-Armand in 1815 was small village, comprising of a string of cottages along the three main streets, between which was a triangular area of open ground. The village was dominated by its church, which still stands today.

The division stormed through La Hameau and burst into La Haye Sainte, pushing back the Prussian garrison and threatening the Prussian right.[16] Charles Philippe Lefol, aide-de-camp to General Lefol, writes:[17]

> With all the deployments for the battle ended, our division had the honour of opening fire against Saint-Amand, which became the scene of heavy fighting.
>
> Everyone advised the emperor to direct his main attack there, avoiding some of the difficult terrain, and with Marshal Ney at Quatre-Bras committed against the vanguard of Wellington, he could bring or receive reinforcements, separate the Prussians from the English, and forcing them initially to retire on Namur; too carried away by the desire to exterminate the Prussian army, he decided he would deliver a general battle.
>
> …The order to attack Saint-Amand had finally been given. The general ordered that a large number of skirmishers were to be deployed and advanced to the head of his division, which he had formed into columns.
>
> The march against the enemy began with the sound of military music that continued to be heard until the noise of the cannon dominated and drowned out all other sounds. Several musicians of the 23rd Line were wounded.
>
> The first shots of the Prussian batteries fell into the masses of a company, killing eight men of the 64th Line, commanded by Captain Revest, since then he is now colonel of an infantry regiment. This event, far from checking the ardour of our soldiers, served only to excite them more, and thus they arrived at Saint-Amand and carried it with the bayonet.

From that moment on, the battle was of bloody character. Each party was supported by a formidable artillery, whose detonations imitated the noise of thunder, and these terrible attacks were an alternating movement of fluctuation between the two armies constantly returning to the charge, almost two hundred guns were pointed against the village by the two armies that fought for its possession: it was the key position for Blücher, commander of the Prussian army, and every effort of the battle was on Saint-Amand which was taken and retaken three times amid scenes of horrible carnage.

General Lefol was the first to enter Saint-Amand, he had his horse killed under him in an orchard and he would probably have been killed or taken prisoner when aide-de-camp Lefol (same name as the general), doing his duty, alighted from his horse amidst a scene of horrible carnage and was fortunate to get him out of this mess by giving him his horse. Both suffered from a volley of musketry, and would be killed or captured, when unexpectedly a company of the 64th arrived to the place where this event happened, and saved them, giving the general to mount his horse again and to re-join the company with his nephew.

The aide of Lefol had his epaulette carried away by a bullet and his horse was slightly injured. The whole division was able to witness his brilliant conduct in the perilous attacks at the cemetery of Saint-Amand.

The evening of this memorable day, the young Lefol, who had helped save the life of his commander, who already at that time had been decorated by the emperor himself (decree of 26 March 1815), was promoted on the battlefield to the rank of captain.

General Etienne Lefol commanded the 8th Infantry Division, which formed part of Vandamme's 3rd Corps. The 1st Brigade was commanded by Colonel Jean Honoure Vernier, of the 23rd Regiment of Line Infantry, and comprised the 23rd and 15th Regiment of Light Infantry. The 2nd Brigade was commanded by General Andre Philippe Corsin and comprised the 37th and 64th regiments of Line Infantry. At some stage in the attack, the 23rd Regiment of Line Infantry overran a Prussian artillery battery, as Battalion Commander Nicolas Darru writes:[18]

16 June 1815, at the Battle of Ligny, supported in my movements by two other soldiers, I captured a Prussian field gun and helped to chase away the gun crew from another piece of artillery.

Battalion Commander Darru seems to have been aided in his attack by veteran Sergeant-Major François Paillard. About his involvement in the Battle of Ligny he writes:[19]

> At the Battle of Fleurus on 16 June 1815, I captured a Prussian 12-pounder field gun.

Presumably this 12-pounder field gun was one of the cannon captured by Battalion Commander Darru. Twenty-three year old Louis Joseph Petit, of the 64th Regiment of Line Infantry, was another eyewitness of this struggle:[20]

> The first balls discharged by the Prussian batteries fell into the French masses and killed eight men of the 64th Line, commanded by Captain Revest. This event, far from checking the ardour of our soldiers, excited them and thus they came and carried Saint-Amand with the bayonet.

Fighting alongside was the 37th Regiment of Line Infantry, among whose ranks was Sub-Lieutenant Gerbet:[21]

> 16 June at ten o'clock in the morning, the right wing was destined to attack the Prussians, quit the positions in which they had passed the night and debouched onto the plane of Fleurus, the scene of the great victory by Jourdan.
>
> We perceived that the Prussians occupied the heights that faced us, along their front ran the road from Namur to Nivelles, and covered therefore the line of communication between the two enemy armies. In this position the Prussians were protected by the villages of Ligny, Saint-Amand and others, as well as many fields which were enclosed either by stone walls or hedges as well as the brook of Ligny. The left was supported on the village of Ligny, and the centre of Saint-Amand. The position occupied was very advantageous to the enemy army, who presented us with a battle.
>
> At two o'clock, the emperor, in proximity to our division, commanded by General Lefol, which was part of the 3rd Army Corps, was ordered to deploy into closed columns by division. The emperor ordered us to change our direction and march towards the village of Saint-Amand, the position was the key to the battle which we commenced.

The village was on a small hill. The gardens and orchards of the village, along with the ditches and hedges as well as the houses, which were solidly constructed of masonry, were occupied by the enemy. The terrain was not favourable in front of the village for our attack. General Lefol addressed our division, who reminded us of the importance of our attack and our duty. We replied enthusiastically with cries of 'long live the emperor!' A short time after, the brave General Lefol led us up to the enemy. We did not make smoke [i.e. did not open fire with muskets] at the start of the moment, and soon a rain of canister shot fell among our ranks, making frightful ravages.

The enemy's round-shot ploughed into our ranks, and carried away entire files. In a short moment, the enemy infantry opened fire from the gardens, hedges and buildings and began to decimate our closed column. We continued to march with steadfast courage with shouldered arms, without firing a shot as we marched to the village, despite cruel losses. We arrived at the fences and attacked the Prussians with the strokes of our bayonets.

We penetrated into the village, but balls rained down upon us from doors and windows; despite this we gained possession. However, we reached low ground where there flowed the brook of Ligny, which was bordered on both sides by tall trees, through which appeared on the other side of the brook, sheltered from our fire, a mass of Prussian infantry held in reserve.

The new battalions advanced to re-conquer the village and were supported by a hail of cannon balls and canister shots, and we had to retire back to the village. Without re-enforcements, we would not resist the attack, therefore we entrenched ourselves in the church and cemetery, which was a strong position for defence. The men attacked each other face-to-face with the bayonet. After a bloody melee, which covered the ground with dead bodies, we remained in possession of the village of Saint-Amand. However, these strong masses, held in reserve, advanced and began a new attack, and the number of new assailants forced us back to our entrenched position. The coming of night ended this obstinate struggle. It was ten o'clock in the evening. All the enemy positions, which he had taken, remained under our control. The battle was won, but it was costly for us as our ranks were greatly thinned. The enemy retired in good order, but left for us as trophies the debris of the battle and dismounted cannon.

A member of the 29th Prussian Infantry Regiment narrates the start of the attack:[22]

It was between two o'clock and half-past two o'clock when the French attacked the village. It was carried out with particular audacity by concealed groups of men, who came from all sides. It was a very picturesque view, the red, yellow, green plumes and epaulettes of the grenadiers, carabiniers and voltigeurs looking like poppies and cornflowers growing in the tall crops.

Writing about the defence of Saint-Amand was Major Eberhard von Hymmen, of the 29th Prussian Infantry Regiment. The Silesian Schutzen Battalion and the jägers from the Brandenburg Infantry Regiment were in reserve. The 2nd Battalion of the 29th Infantry Regiment was placed in the village itself, the and right wing of the village was defended by the 1st Battalion. Two companies were drawn up in the centre of the village, the cemetery being garrisoned by landwehr troops. About the French attack, he writes:[23]

> Towards two o'clock in the afternoon, the enemy started the attack by throwing a cloud of tirailleurs forward against my left flank, which were formed against my left flank and were countered by Captain von Rohr, the commander of the skirmish section of the 2nd Battalion, which were positioned close to my left wing. This flank was reinforced by First Lieutenant Geissler and a detachment of jägers from the various regiments. The French attacked and while the battle raged, three officers, first lieutenants von Geissler, Iltz and Messe, were severely wounded. However, the excellent defence undertaken by Major von Kleist at this point did not allow the enemy to penetrate the line and to enter the village.
>
> The enemy now moved forward a number of cannon which fired round-shot and shells at the village. For more than half an hour the contest remained in the balance; we defended ourselves and the terrain as resolutely as the circumstance would permit, and we had not given the enemy a single inch of ground, when he redoubled his artillery fire and launched an all-out attack with superior forces to storm the village. Major Chevallerie recalled his skirmishers and was personally engaged, replying with numerous salvos, but the strength of the enemy eventually forced him to order the battalions under his command to retire to the inner most part of the village, and in order to save themselves the troops fought the enemy with great determination, step-by-step, for possession of the village. During this terribly violent attack, the two companies from the 1st Battalion united close to the cemetery and covered the withdrawal of the 2nd Battalion with strong sustained fire, which caused the enemy to be

more cautious in his advance, although we had to abandon the right wing, which the enemy attacked in force along with the centre of the village.

I lost a horse, as did my adjutant, Lieutenant Feege, and likewise Lieutenant and Paymaster Brunhof, who was responsible for the distribution of the orders for the withdrawal, which they did with great vigour, and he took time to rally the troops as they withdrew. I joined the remainder of the regiment, which together with the Brandenburg Regiment advanced into the village at attack-pace with great determination, whereupon Major von Chevallerie was severely wounded and had his horse shot from beneath him. The second attack succeeded in regaining everything which had been lost and the enemy was forced to leave a great many times.

General Lefol wrote the following description of the day's events in his after-action report to Marshal Soult:[24]

Conforming to the orders of His Excellency, the General-in-Chief Comte Vandamme, at one hour past midday, the 37th Regiment of Infantry, commanded by General Corsin, attacked the village of Saint-Amand. The remainder of the division was readied to the support the attack.

The village was carried by the bayonet after a strong resistance, accompanied by the fire of the enemy's musketry and artillery. The division converged on the village just at the moment when the Prussians attacked. Despite their best efforts, they were not able to dislodge us.

There followed a general attack, led by the 1st Brigade, which debouched towards the centre of the enemy positions, while the 2nd Brigade was left in reserve, stationed in the village's cemetery.

All the soldiers did their best, and indeed the division captured from the enemy two 12-pounders and took them to our reserve artillery park.

I send to you the losses that were sustained by the different corps. I mention with honour to Your Excellency, the officers, sub-officers, and soldiers for their particularly-distinguished conduct.

Lieutenant-General Bon. Lefol.

In holding the cemetery and church, the 37th and 64th regiments of Line Infantry had been decimated. Colonel Marion presented the returns for the division to Marshal Soult on 17 June, showing the following losses:[25]

Regiment	Killed		Wounded		Missing		Total
	Officers	Men	Officers	Men	Officers	Men	
15th Light Infantry	2	39	19	390	2	72	524
23rd Line Infantry	1	10	9	166	0	65	251
37th Line Infantry	1	18	12	155	1	110	297
64th Line Infantry	0	17	12	151	0	391	571
Total	4	84	52	862	3	638	1,643
7th Company							
6th Foot Artillery	0	0	1	4	0	0	5
1st Company							
1st Squadron							
Artillery Train	0	0	0	2	0	3	5
Total	0	0	1	6	0	3	10

The 15th Regiment of Light Infantry had been shattered during the attack, losing twenty-three officers out of eighty-five present on 10 June. Of the 2,319 other ranks present, 524 were dead, wounded or missing—representing a loss of 22.6 per cent of effective strength. The 64th Regiment of Line Infantry was also badly affected in the attack. Of the 1,847 men under arms on 10 June, 571 were dead, wounded or missing, accounting for some 30.9 per cent of the regiment's strength being lost. In comparison, the 23rd Regiment of Line Infantry mustered 1,224 officers and men on 10 June, and lost some 251 men (20.5 per cent). Of interest, at the time of disbandment the regiment had 120 men in hospital, meaning forty-six men had clearly recovered. The muster list agrees that ten men were killed. The 37th Regiment of Line Infantry lost 297 officers and men from the sixty-two officers and 1,125 men originally present, equating to some 26.4 per cent of effective strength. The division as a whole had mustered 4,583 other ranks on 10 June, equating to a total loss of 34.8 per cent effective strength. In comparison, the Prussian losses were:[26]

Regiment	Killed		Wounded		Missing		Total
	Officers	Men	Officers	Men	Officers	Men	
2nd Silesian Jäger							
Battalion no. 6	5	8	6	77	0	6	102
24th Regiment of	Fourteen officers and 340 men						
Infantry	killed or wounded						354
12th Regiment of Infantry	No information available						
1st Westphalian							
Landwehr Regiment	No information available						

1st Regiment of Silesian Hussars	6	3	0	16	0	0	25
6th Uhlan Regiment	0	0	0	0	0	0	0
Total							481

Total brigade losses were 241 killed, 700 wounded and 1,439 missing (some 2,380 men) at Ligny, equating to 26 per cent of effective strength. The French 8th Division lost 1,636 men. Habert's 10th Division were also in action against the Prussian 1st Brigade once the 8th Division had been bloodied.

The attack of Girard

With Lefol's force checked, Vandamme committed General Girard's division from 2nd Corps, which moved towards the village of La Haye Sainte. The division stormed through La Hameau and burst into La Haye Sainte, pushing back the Prussian garrison and threatening the Prussian right.[27]

The division was formed of two brigades: the first, commanded by General-de-Brigade Louis de Villiers, comprised the 11th Regiment of Light Infantry and 82nd Regiment of Line Infantry; and the second, commanded by General Piat, comprised the 12th Regiment of Light Infantry and 4th Regiment of Line Infantry.[28] At the head of the 82nd Regiment of Line Infantry was forty-two year old Colonel Jean François de Sales Matis. About Ligny, he writes:[29]

> The French marched forward through fields of very tall rye, which prevented them from seeing anything that was before them. The senior officers who were mounted were detached behind the masses. I believed we had in front of us the Prussians. However, our general did not believe it, and instead believed they were the troops of General Vandamme that were retiring. A salvo of artillery fire soon changed his impression of things. It was in that moment that there was a great surprise and alarm among the ranks. After this, the order for the columns to march at double-time was given. As the columns progressed, they were fired upon by the Prussian artillery. The cannon balls wounded and mutilated many; entire ranks of men were swept down.
>
> General-de-Brigade Villiers commanded the division, and I commanded his brigade. He advanced the 2nd Brigade and marched to the Prussians, but hardly had we gone a mile when he was wounded by a bullet in the hand, and command of the division passed to me.

Surgeon-Major d'Heralde, of the 12th Regiment of Light Infantry, writes the following about the attack:[30]

The order to attack the village of Saint-Amand was received by General Girard on the afternoon of 16 June, and had been sent by the emperor. The place was occupied by the Prussians. General Girard was deeply concerned and believed that his division would be decimated.

The general called his orderly to help him remove his blue cloak and leave it with him. The general appeared at the head of his division in full uniform of a lieutenant-general. He ordered his artillery to move forward and deployed his masses by putting them into two lines. At the first movement of the attack our soldiers emitted very sharp cries of 'Vive l'Empereur'. But not by me, as I was apprehensive of the great dangers that they would run. I felt tears come to my eyes.

The enemy was before us.

A battalion of the 11th Regiment of Light Infantry, which was in that first line moved forward. But when it arrived at the entrance of the farm, a battery of six pieces opened fire with canister shot. This caused great disorder in the ranks and forced them to retreat with some disorder.

Lieutenant-General Girard came to take our 1st Battalion to the right. This occurred while we were engaged in a deadly exchange of fire with the Prussians. In less than five minutes, General Piat, our commander, our adjutant, and our Battalion Commander Crebiniers were either killed or wounded. The unfortunate General Girard, already hit by two severe contusions, received a third shot which was essentially mortal. It threw him to the ground paralysed: a single bullet had fractured his right arm, passing under the shoulder and had become embedded in his spine.

The fall of the general and others resulted in putting us into disorder. The young Colonel Sebastiani took command of the brigade, but it was attacked by superior numbers of Prussian forces, and was obliged to retreat for a time and was forced to abandon our injured, several of which were killed by the Prussians. I rushed to the general to give him some first aid, and assess the severity of his injury.

As we were quickly approached by the enemy, 'kill me' said the general, 'do not leave me alive'. Four carabiniers carried him off in a greatcoat...I ordered him to Charleroi and I remained there the whole day of the 17th to be able to get him the care of a surgeon guard who was there with General Letort, who had been mortally wounded on the night of the 15th at Gilly.

In response to Girard's advance, Blücher advanced the Prussian 2nd Brigade forward to push back the French and also to take the pressure off the attack at Saint-Amand. Pushed from La Haye Sainte by the impetuosity of the Prussians, Girard, with the 12th Regiment of Light Infantry and the 4th Regiment of Line Infantry carried out a stubborn resistance back to the farm of La Haye Sainte. The 11th Regiment of Light Infantry and the 82nd Regiment of Line Infantry, rallied and were ordered back on the offensive, pushing the Prussians back to the village until, in turn, a second Prussian assault wave pushed the beleaguered French back to the farm. In this attack, General Girard fell mortally wounded, and generals de Villiers and Piat were also wounded. Colonel Timburce Sebastiani, commanding officer of the 11th Regiment of Light Infantry, took commanded of the battered division. Moving up in support of Girard's division was the division of Habert. Combined, both divisions moved back to the attack, holding back the Prussians until the Young Guard of General Duhesme relieved them and finally broke Prussian resistance in this sector of the battlefield. In this struggle, the 7th Infantry Division lost 2,500 men and was sent to the rear.[31]

Colonel Auguste Louis Petiet, of the Imperial Headquarters staff, recounts the following scene:[32]

> The villages at the scene of action were taken and retaken several times after a dreadful carnage. Those of Saint-Amand and Ligny are mostly played over with invincible obstinacy.
>
> General Girard was mortally wounded, and his division was pushed back a moment in the greatest disorder. Napoléon sent La Bédoyère to rally and unite the brigades.
>
> General La Bédoyère said with fire in his voice: 'Soldiers, do not be ashamed to shrink from the same men that you have defeated so many times, who threw their weapons at your feet at Austerlitz, Jena, Friedland. March forward, you will see them flee again and again, recognise you as their conquerors'. The noble voice of this brave young man was heard; the infantry rallied, and managed to stay in the cemetery of Saint-Amand and stay there, despite repeated efforts to drive them out by the Prussians.

In the division, the following loses were incurred:

Regiment	Killed		Wounded		Missing		Total
	Officers	Men	Officers	Men	Officers	Men	
11th Light Infantry	No data available						
82nd Line Infantry[33]	No meaningful casualty data recorded						
12th Light Infantry[34]	27		327 men wounded or missing				354
4th Line Infantry[35]	1	12	24	182	0	4	223
Total							577

All we are seeing for the wounded are the men still in hospital in September 1815. The losses sustained on the day of battle are likely to be far higher than the recorded wounded. No doubt many men who were evacuated to the rear ambulances, or sent to hospital by September 1815, had recovered and joined the regiment again. We are not seeing the missing, as hundreds of men were written off in September 1815, and we have no idea when they had quit their regiments. The true losses, therefore, of wounded and missing men is not known. We are also totally missing any casualties for the 11th Regiment of Light Infantry and 82nd Regiment of Line Infantry. An accurate total of losses in the division are not known in consequence of this. Prussian losses were as follows:[36]

Regiment	Killed		Wounded		Missing		Total
	Officers	Men	Officers	Men	Officers	Men	
2nd Silesian Jäger Battalion no. 6	No information available						
2nd West Prussian Regiment no. 7	12	51	32	264	0	34	393
29th Regiment	8	50	27	265	6	120	476
3rd Westphalian Landwehr Regiment	No available information						
Total	20	101	59	529	6	154	869

Comparing the data (where it exists), Girard's 2nd Brigade suffered over 300 fewer killed and wounded than their Prussian adversaries. Without further information, we cannot make any more comment beyond that the fighting was bloody on both sides. Total losses of the Prussian 3rd Brigade were 195 killed, 716 wounded and 1,572 missing—a total of 2,483 men, or 34 per cent, of the brigade were lost in the fighting against the French.

10th Division attacks
Following the Prussian counter-attack, Habert's 10th Infantry Division was ordered to move up to Le Hameau. Colonel Louis Florimond Fantin

des Odoards, commanding the 22nd Regiment of Line Infantry, relates on 22 July 1815 that:[37]

> After passing Fleurus, which the enemy had not defended, we found them well positioned behind this town. Our corps was the first to attack. Our efforts were in the main theatre of operations in the environs of the village of Saint-Amand, where we fought hard until 8 p.m. Without going into strategic details that would lead me too far, I simply say that despite strong and honourable resistance, the Prussian army was beaten on all points and that night she was in full retreat, leaving forty pieces of artillery, the wounded, baggage and several flags. His loss is estimated at 25,000 men, ours at 8,000 or 9,000. Field Marshal Blücher, thrown from his horse in a moment of defeat of his cavalry, was nearly captured.
>
> The results would have been even greater if the action had started sooner. The darkness favoured retirement. I said just now that our left wing had taken no part in the Battle of Fleurus. It was directed to the English army, which advanced to meet the English. The affair that took place in part on this side, that same day 16 June, was bloody, but indecisive. The English, Hanoverians and Belgians have between 4,000 and 5,000 men and we are about the same. The Duke of Brunswick was killed there and the Prince of Orange wounded. Of both sides, the forces engaged were said to be of great valour.
>
> I had reason to be satisfied with my new regiment in this brilliant day. Having dislodged the Prussians from Saint-Amand, to which they directed constantly, new attacks, it formed in brigade with the 70th Line, and had to deploy beyond the village to the cover the place. The enemy cavalry charged, and from the start we are willing to receive them, each regiment is deployed in square in checkerboard formation. The 70th was to my left and the Prussians advanced first towards him with sufficient resolution. But I think they had not replied to their charge, and without them waiting for the shock, this unfortunate regiment, intimidated by the enemy, gave ground, and was soon attacked and sabred. If this panic had reached my 22nd, the brigade was lost, but it stood firm. Well-aimed musketry began, which strongly repelled the charge executed at the moment on them, and covered the plain with dead men and horses.
>
> The fugitives of the 70th Line were able to rally behind my square and soon they resumed their place to my left in the same order as before. Allured by the greater strength of the 70th, and by my vigorous musket fire, another Prussian cavalry corps tried new charges against us, but this time the 70th, led by their great Colonel

M. Maury, did their duty and the attackers were constantly pushed back.

Seeing their efforts were useless, the Prussians, aided by a rise in the ground, began to advance two guns, which fired against us until the general advance, which involved the Imperial Guard, which swept the battlefield and gave us the victory.

All of this did not happen without losing men. The 70th was roughly handed, and has seen its ranks greatly reduced; my 22nd had twenty-six dead, including one officer, and 194 wounded, including eight officers.

In order to try and understand the regiment in 1815, analysis of the regiment's muster list reveals some interesting nuggets of information. A sample of 220 men of the regiment shows that ages ranged from seventeen to forty-two years of age. The data shows three clear trends: the ages of seventeen to twenty-five (those admitted in 1814 under the royalists to re-generate the regimen); those aged twenty-five to thirty-four (those veterans admitted during the campaigns in Spain); and those aged thirty-eight to forty-three (being older veterans of the early wars of the empire). The average age, however, was twenty-three. Of the sample, over three-quarters had served since 1814. However, in 1815 the regiment's manpower was diluted by a large influx of raw conscripts who had never been in action, and also reduced the bonds of trust between all ranks in the regiment. The reservists came from a wide background of ages, so we cannot solely rely on the age of the men to give an idea of the manpower of the regiment's relative experience in this instance. Overall, the regiment had a high percentage of reservists and former National Guardsmen. The lack of cohesion and experience among the 22nd Regiment of Line Infantry was, we are sure, repeated throughout the army.[38]

We have no eyewitnesses from the 34th or 88th regiments of Line Infantry, so the story of the division at Ligny is rather limited.

Captain van Rueter, commanding a detachment of the Prussian 6th Artillery Regiment, describes the fighting at Saint-Amand as follows:[39]

I suppose it was between two and three o'clock in the afternoon when I received orders to take four guns of my battery forward and accompany the 4th Regiment in its advance to Saint-Amand, while the howitzers and two remaining guns took up position opposite Ligny, so as to be able to shell the open ground beyond the village, and the village itself too, in the event of our not being able to hold it. I halted my advance about six hundred paces from Saint-Amand,

and opened fire on the enemy's artillery in position on the high ground opposite, which at once began to reply with a well sustained fire of shells, and inflicted heavy losses on us.

Meanwhile, the 14th Regiment, without ever thinking of leaving an escort behind for us, pressed gallantly forward to Saint-Amand, and succeeded in gaining possession of that part of the village. I myself was under the impression that they had been able to occupy the whole of it. The battery had been thus engaged for some hours in its combat with hostile guns, and was awaiting the order to follow up the movement of the 14th Regiment, when suddenly I became aware of two strong lines of skirmishers which were apparently falling back on us from the village of Saint-Amand. Imagining that the skirmishers in front of us were our own countrymen, I hastened up the battery and warned my gun layers not to direct their fire upon them, but to continue to engage the guns opposite. In the meantime, the skirmishers in question had got within 300 paces of the battery.

I had just returned to the right flank of my command, when our surgeon, Zinkernagel, called my attention to the red tufts on the shakos of the skirmishers. I at once bellowed the order 'with grape on the skirmishers!' At the same moment, both their lines turned upon us, gave us a volley, and then flung themselves on the ground. By this volley, and the bursting of a shell or two, every horse, except one wheeler, belonging to the gun on my left flank, was either killed or wounded. I ordered the horses to be taken from one of the ammunition wagons, which had been emptied, and thus make my gun fit to be moved again, while I meantime kept up a slow fire of grape, that had the effect of keeping the skirmishers to my front glued to the ground.

But in another moment, all of a sudden, I saw my left flank taken in the rear, from the direction of the Ligny brook, by a French staff officer and about fifty horsemen. As they rushed upon us, the officer shouted to me in German 'surrender gunners, for you are all prisoners!' With these words he charged down with his men on the flank gun on my left, and dealt a vicious cut to the wheel driver, who dodged it, however, by flinging himself over on his dead horse. The blow was delivered with such force that the sabre cut deep into the saddle and stuck fast. Gunner Sieberg, however, availing himself of the chance momentary delay afforded, snatched up a handspike off one of the 12-pounders, and with the words 'I'll show him to how take prisoners!' dealt the officer with such a blow on his bearskin that he slumped forward with a broken skull from his grey charger, which galloped away into the line of skirmishers in our front.

Rueter notes he then ordered his battery to withdraw, abandoning one gun. Losses in 10th Division were as follows:

Regiment	Killed		Wounded		Missing		Total
	Officers	Men	Officers	Men	Officers	Men	
34th Line Infantry[40]	0	31	0	184	0	1	216
88th Line Infantry[41]	0	24	0	192	0	5	221
22nd Line Infantry[42]	1	25	8	186	0	0	220
70th Line Infantry[43]	0	14	0	68	0	3	85
2nd Foreign Regiment	0	0	0	0	0	0	0
Total	1	94	8	630	0	9	742
18th Company 2nd Foot Artillery[44]	0	2	0	2	0	0	4
4th Company 5th Squadron Artillery Train	0	0	0	0	0	0	0
Total	1	96	8	632	0	9	746

The division, on 10 June, mustered 5,856 officers and men. Of these, 5,613 were other ranks. Some 737 other ranks and nine officers are recorded as killed, wounded or missing at Ligny, where the data exists. This means that the division lost 12.7 per cent of effective strength.

11th Division attacks

With Girard's division moving up to La Haye Sainte, and Habert's command struggling in Saint-Amand, General Berthezène was ordered to move up to attack the village of Saint-Amand. General Pierre Berthezène, commander of 11th Division (part of Vandamme's 3rd Corps) notes that:[45]

> In bivouac 17 June 1815
>
> The 11th Division took up its allotted positions on 16 June at ten o'clock in the morning, to advance from Frasné. The enemy resisted valiantly, and I ordered my troops to deploy in column by division to the left of the town, and from this position we were able to observe the movements at Saint-Amand and Mellet.
>
> After an hour, we received orders to advance to Saint-Amand and the division was replaced by the 7th of the 2nd Corps. The general-in-chief ordered us to pursue their sharpshooters, who were placed in front of the village and to attack immediately the village.
>
> The first operation was, however, conducted without any difficulties and the village was attacked at half-past two in the

afternoon. The 12th led the charge and was supported by the 86th. The 56th outflanked the village to retard the advance of the enemy against this point. The 33rd was kept in reserve.

The attack on the village was quickly settled. A large calibre artillery piece harness with six good horses was captured. The capture of the piece was largely due to Sergeant Brossiere of the 12th Line and one of my ordinances took it to Fleurus.

The enemy then attacked and routed in the division of foreign troops in our corps, which retreated in great disorder behind the men of the 11th, in spite of this the colonel of the 86th [Pellecier] advanced with calmness and firmness and resumed the charge despite the difficulties of the terrain, and regained the ground we had just lost. At six o'clock the enemy made a great effort and attacked the left of the village, it was now that I lost the great part of the men under my orders. I intended to remain the master and led myself an attack on their position, and bit-by-bit their advantage was lost and we advanced for the second time onto the plain. A second very strong attack was made, and the division of Girard was obliged to deploy to support the troops of the 11th so that we did not abandon the village.

Towards eight o'clock, the division was replaced by four battalions of the Young Guard, which debouched en masse and carried the position from the windmill of Saint-Amand to the heights of Brye.

Many of the individual soldiers the division fought against had been decorated with the Iron Cross or the Bronze Medal for fighting in the campaigns of 1813 and 1814 against the armies of France, and we supposed that these were elite troops.

The lieutenant-general commanding

The 11th Division

Berthezène.

Captain Jean Marie Putigny, of 2nd Battalion 33rd Regiment of Line Infantry (part of 11th Division of 3rd Corps), narrates:[46]

We formed up in front of Fleurus. At ten o'clock in the morning the emperor, with other officers, galloped along the line of outposts and then stopped at the windmill, where, with his telescope, he regarded the scene. There were 45,000 entrenched behind the river.

The outposts and the bastions were taken. We pushed back Prussian bayonets on the other side; we were soon to join them at Saint-Amand. I emerged from a ravine at the head of my company; a discharge of artillery screamed its song of death and made me flatten myself against the ground. I wanted to stand up. My shoulder burned me in pain, I fell heavily to the ground, my arm was bleeding a little, but I refused any medical help.

Standing upright without support was not convenient. My right hand uselessly dropped my sword. Once I was back on my feet I picked it up and my lieutenant scolded me, telling me to get my wound dressed, but it would be crazy to miss a day like this.

Taking advantage of a lull in the fighting, I fixed my inert arm in a sling. The village was taken, lost, and then taken again. The regiment was seriously engaged, and my charitable lieutenant lay on the ground, disembowelled. But, then the enemy were pushed back in confusion and the next day on the field of victory the emperor passed the 33rd Line in review.

In order to try and understand the regiment in 1815, analysis of the regiment's muster list reveals some interesting nuggets of information. Looking at the details of a random sample of 220 men who served with the regiment in 1815 shows that the youngest members of the regiment were aged seventeen and the oldest thirty-eight; the average age was twenty-eight. All had been with the regiment since July 1814.[47] Overall, in 1815 the 33rd Regiment of Line Infantry needs to be considered among one of the more experienced regiments of the Armée du Nord. The regiment had been eviscerated in the Russian campaign.

Captain von Bismarck, of the 29th Prussian Infantry Regiment, narrates the new attack as follows:[48]

> Finally, the enemy moved a large mass of men towards the entrance of the village, which also reinforced their skirmishers at the same time, and thus forced us back. We tried several times to get back into the village. We were unable to make any headway, and had to fall back again; during the retreat I was almost captured, as I remained behind for a little too long. The village had many ditches and hedges; I had to pass over a small meadow, which was already occupied by about twenty or thirty French. I could do nothing else but ride full tilt at them.

During the attack the division lost heavily. On the morning of 17 June 1815, the following muster return was submitted to Marshal Soult:[49]

Regiment	Killed		Wounded		Missing		Total
	Officers	Men	Officers	Men	Officers	Men	
12th Line Infantry	0	28	6	194	0	0	228

56th Line Infantry	1	9	8	196	0	46	260
33rd Line Infantry	0	1	1	16	0	0	18
86th Line Infantry	0	0	3	69	0	0	72
Total	1	38	18	475	0	46	578

The division, on 10 June 1815, had mustered 165 officers and 4,371 men, representing a loss of 12.7 per cent of effective strength. However, the bulk of the fighting fell on the 1st Brigade. The 12th Regiment of Line Infantry lost 228 men out of 1,171 present under arms on 10 June, or 19.5 per cent of effective strength. The 56th Regiment of Line Infantry had mustered 1,276 men and lost 260 men (20.4 per cent) in the attack.

Ney's summons
By now it was a quarter-past three. The engagement was larger than anticipated for the emperor, but he had taken this possibility into consideration with the order he issued at daybreak to Ney and Grouchy. We should recall that Ney was to send an entire corps to Marbais, so as to be able to fall on the rear of the Prussians between Sombreffe at Gembloux. The only news he had had from Ney was a dispatch sent at 11.00, which told him that a cavalry division and an infantry corps was headed to Marbais. They had yet to arrive. In order to remind Ney of his duty in sending an entire corps to aid his offensive, he sent him the following order:[50]

> In front of Fleurus, June 16, between 15.15 and 15.30.
>
> Mister the marshal,
>
> I wrote to you, one hour ago, that the emperor would make an attack on the enemy at half-past two in the position which it took between the villages of Saint-Amand and Brye; at this moment, the engagement is very marked. S. M. gives me the responsibility to say to you that you must manoeuvre at once so as to envelop the right of the enemy and fall quickly on his rear; this army is lost if you act vigorously; the fate of France is in your hands. Thus, do not hesitate a moment to make the movement which the emperor orders you and directs you on the heights of Brye and Saint-Amand to contribute to a perhaps decisive victory. The enemy is taken in the act at the time when it seeks to unite with the English.
>
> The marshal of empire, major-general,
> Duc de Dalmatie.

Napoléon now made it clear that Ney was to manoeuvre to join the fighting at Ligny, along with Lobau and 6th Corps.

This order was to have fateful consequences. By now of course, Napoléon had assumed, with only a single dispatch from Ney timed at 11.00, that he had pushed back the Allied troops at the crossroads, thus d'Erlon had three infantry divisions free to be able to march to Ligny down the Nivelles to Namur road, emerge on the Prussian right, and comprehensively defeat the Prussians. Napoléon knew when he got Ney's 11.00 dispatch that one infantry division and one cavalry division were already on the march to Marbais. Yet, he felt he needed more troops to deliver the *coup de grace* to Blücher. However, Napoléon made several assumptions:

That d'Erlon was at Quatre-Bras; and

The enemy presence at Quatre-Bras was still minimal and had been overcome.

In both cases he was wrong—down to the lack of clear communication from Ney about what forces he faced. Ney had calculated the Allied troops at Quatre-Bras as 3,000, which it seemed did not factor in the reinforcements arriving on the field, which Adjutant-Commandant Jeanin, from 6th Corps, knew about all too well, and stated that 20,000 troops were at Quatre-Bras. Napoléon could only make plans with the information he had: Ney had more than enough troops to push back 3,000 Allies and had troops to spare to swing to right to take part in the Battle of Ligny. Yet, this was based on the assumption that Ney's dispatch was accurate.

Soult sent three couriers with this order to Ney. Yet, why had Ney not sent troops to Marbais as ordered? The non-appearance of troops on his left flank as ordered, and no news from Ney, the emperor probably had one of his characteristic temper tantrums and no doubt blamed Soult for sending unclear orders, and Soult's couriers for being useless good-for-nothings. So exacerbated by Ney's failure to obey orders, and no doubt wanting to stop the emperor screaming and shouting at him, in desperation Soult sent his own aide-de-camp to Ney to make it clear about what he was to do. The plan of action for the day was utterly compromised by Ney and the total failure by the officer corps of 1st Corps, as we shall see.

---

[1] SHDDT: C15 5. Dossier 16 June 1815. Grouchy to Soult, timed at 5.00.

[2] AN: AFIV 1939 *Registre d'Ordres du Major General 13 Juin au 26 Juin 1815*, pp. 35-7.

[3] SHDDT: C15 5. Dossier 16 June, Napoléon to Grouchy. Copy of the now lost original order made by Comte du Casse.

[4] AN: AFIV 1939, pp. 37-40. See also: Grouchy, *Relation succincte de la campagne de 1815*, pp. 13-14. Grouchy states this is a verbal order, but it is written into Soult's order book, so clearly Grouchy is mistaken on this point, unless Soult recorded verbal orders.

5   AN: AFIV 1939, p. 15.

6   ibid.

7   Grouchy, *Relation succincte de la campagne de 1815*, pp. 15-16. This order is not in Soult's order book, so we cannot be certain of its authenticity.

8   SHDDT: C15 5. Dossier 16 June 1815 *Order du Jour*.

9   SHDDT: C15 5. Dossier 16 June 1815 Friant to Petit, Christiani, Poret de Morvan, Harlet.

10 MM is plural for Monsieur and in essence is short hand for all officers.

11 SHDDT: C15 5. Dossier 16 June. Radet to Soult.

12 de Mauduit, Vol. 2, p. 39.

13 de Mauduit, Vol. 2, p. 39.

14 Michel Louis Felix Ney, *Documents inédits sur la campagne de 1815*, Anselin, Paris, 1840.

15 Ney, *Documents inédits sur la campagne de 1815*.

16 Paul Avers, *Historique du 82e Régiment d'Infanterie de Ligne et du 7e Régiment d'Infanterie Légère, 1684-1876*, Lahure, Paris, 1876, pp. 161-2.

17 Lefol, *Souvenirs sur le prytanée de Saint-Cyr sur la campagne de 1814, le retour de l'empereur Napoléon de l'île d'Elbe, et la campagne de 1815, pendant les Cent-jours*, Montalant-Bougleux, Versailles, 1854, pp. 59-60.

18 AN: LH 664/2.

19 AN: LH 2035/60.

20 See http://www.ligny1815.org/histoire/petit.htm.

21 Gerbet, pp. 10-12.

22 Hans Wellmann, *Geschichte des Infanterie-Regiments von Horn (3-tes Rheinisches) N. 29*, Lintzcher Verlag, Trier, 1894, p. 85.

23 John Franklin, personal communication, 21 July 2012.

24 SHDDT: C15 5. File 17, June 1815, Lefol to Soult.

25 SHDDT: C15 5. File 17, June 1815, *3e Corps Armée du Nord 8e Division Etat des pertes eprouver la journee du 16e Juin 1815*.

26 See http://www.waterloo-campaign.nl/bestanden/files/notes/june16/note.3.pdf.

27 Avers, pp. 161-2.

28 Avers, pp. 161-2.

29 *Revue des Deux Mondes*, Volume 36, 1861.

30 John Franklin, personal communication, 3 July 2014.

31 Avers, pp. 161-2.

32 Auguste-Louis Pétiet, *Souvenirs militaires de l'histoire contemporaine*, Dumaine, Paris, 1844, pp. 221-2.

33 SHDDT: GR 21 YC 640 *71e régiment d'infanterie de ligne (ex 82e régiment d'infanterie de ligne), formation au 11 Août 1814 (matricules 1 à 1,790)*. See also: SHDDT: GR 21 YC 641 *71e régiment d'infanterie de ligne (ex 82e régiment d'infanterie de ligne), 11-26 Août 1814 (matricules 1,791 à 3,281)*.

34 SHDDT: GR 22 YC 104 *12e régiment d'infanterie légère Août 1814-Avril 1815 (matricules 1 à 1,800)*. See also: SHDDT: GR 22 YC 105 *12e régiment d'infanterie légère Avril 1815-Mai 1815 (matricules 1,801 à 2,112)*.

35 SHDDT: GR 21 YC 40 *4e régiment d'infanterie de ligne dit régiment de Monsieur, 18 Août 1814-13 Avril 1815 (matricules 1 à 1,800)*. See also: SHDDT: GR 21 YC 41 *4e régiment d'infanterie de ligne dit régiment de Monsieur, 14 Avril 1815-16 Mai 1815 (matricules 1,801 à 2,103)*.

36 See http://www.waterloo-campaign.nl/bestanden/files/notes/june16/note.3.pdf.

37 Louis Florimond Fantin des Odoards, *Journal du général Fantin des Odoards*, E. Plon, Nourrit et Cie, Paris, 1895, pp. 403-10.

38 SHDDT: GR 21 YC 208 *registre matricule du 22e régiment d'infanterie de ligne 29 Janvier 1804 à 3 Juillet 1815*.

39 John Franklin, personal communication, 6 July 2014.

40 SHDDT: GR 21 YC 309 *33e régiment d'infanterie de ligne (ex 34e régiment d'infanterie de ligne), 19 Juillet 1814-4 Novembre 1814 (matricules 1 à 1,800)*. See also: SHDDT: GR 21 YC 310 *33e*

régiment d'infanterie de ligne (ex 34e régiment d'infanterie de ligne), 19 Juillet 1814-21 Juillet 1815 (matricules 1,801 à 2,572).

[41] SHDDT: GR 21 YC 681 *75e régiment d'infanterie de ligne (ex 88e régiment d'infanterie de ligne), 7 Juillet 1814-18 Juillet 1815 (matricules 1 à 1,681).*

[42] Fantin des Odoards, pp. 403-10.

[43] SHDDT: GR 21 YC 590 *65e régiment d'infanterie de ligne (ex 70e régiment d'infanterie de ligne), 16 Septembre 1814-15 Mai 1815 (matricules 1 à 1,800).*

[44] SHDDT: GR 25 YC 21 *2e Artillerie à Pied 1814-1815.*

[45] SHDDT: C15 5. Dossier 16 June 1815. Rapport 16 June 1815, dated 17 June 1815.

[46] Hubert Miot-Putigny, *Putigny, grognard d'empire*, Gallimard, Paris, 1950, pp. 241-2.

[47] SHDDT: GR 21 YC 302 *registre matricule du 32e régiment d'infanterie de ligne réorganisation de 1814 29 Mai 1815 à 25 Juin 1815.*

[48] Wellmann, p. 88.

[49] SHDDT: C15 5. File 17 June 1815, *3e Corps Armee du Nord 11e Division Etat des pertes eprouver la journee du 16e Juin 1815.*

[50] AN: AFIV 1939, pp. 42-3.

Chapter 4

Attack of the 4th Corps

Commanding 4th Corps was Maurice-Etienne Gérard. He was born on 4 April 1773 at Danvilliers in the Meuse. His military career began when he enlisted in a battalion of volunteers from his department in 1792. As Vandamme's men attacked Saint-Amand, General Gérard advanced with the 4th Corps onto the village of Ligny to the east. In 1815, Ligny consisted of two main streets that ran parallel to each other, either side of the Ligny brook; the rue d'En-Haut to the south, the rue d'En-Bas to the north. Between the two streets were a cluster of cottages and houses, the church and cemetery. The Prussians, having been expelled from the farm of La Tour and the rue d'En-Haut, barricaded themselves into the cottages and cemetery.

The strongly-built Chateau de Looz stood to the west of the village. Nearby was Prussian General Ziethen's 1st Army Corps, and General Roeder's powerful reserve cavalry stood in the hollow ground between Brye and Ligny

As the attacking French columns closed on the village, a murderous fire broke out, about which Henri Houssaye recounts the words of General Rome, written in 1823:[1]

> The soldiers advanced valiantly under a crossfire. Some dashed into the houses; others climbed the embankment around the cemetery. Thereupon a great body of the enemy, which had rallied under shelter of the church, charged the French, who were thrown into great disorder owing to these repeated assaults. The little square, too narrow for such a number of combatants, became the scene of a terrific contest, a hand-to-hand struggle with no quarter given or sought; a frightful carnage! They shot at one another point-blank, they charged with their bayonets, with the butt ends of their muskets, and even fought with their fists. The Prussians at last gave way. They abandoned the houses, the church and the cemetery, and retired in

61

disorder across the two bridges of the Ligny, and were pursued at the point of the bayonet. More than one was thrown into the muddy bed of the brook beneath. Still, on the left bank, the enemy, reinforced by the two last battalions of Henckel's division, re-formed and made a determined stand. The Prussians fired from the hedges and from the line of willows that bordered the brook, while others fired over the heads of their comrades from the houses of the Rue d'En-Bas, and from loopholes opened in the walls of the large farm on the left bank. In spite of this terrible fusillade, the soldiers of the 30th and the 96th crossed the bridges and forced back the tirailleurs in to the houses. However Prussian reinforcements forced their assailants on to the right bank; they even attempted to cross to the other side by the two bridges. It was now the turn of the French to defend the brook. From either bank, the soldiers shot at each other at a distance of only four yards, through dense clouds of smoke. A threatening storm hung heavy in the air, and its sultry heat increased that of the continuous firing and of the flames kindled by the falling shells. Ligny became a fiery furnace. Amid the roar of the battle rose the piercing cries of the wounded that were being burnt alive beneath the flaming ruins.

Rumigny[2], aide-de-camp to General Gérard, notes the following about the events at Ligny:[3]

General Gérard set off on the right of the village of Ligny, the Prussians gathered their forces, and he observed the Namur road while waiting for the infantry to arrive. Soon after, he moved forward with his staff, but he became spotted by a squadron of Prussian lancers and a few sharpshooters. The chasseurs à cheval who escorted the general opened fire, and during an exchange of musketry with the sharpshooters, the general who was always at our head, showed no concern of being without a strong escort.

Colonel de Carignan, with the 6th Hussars stood with him. Suddenly, a Prussian lancer officer with his squadron launched themselves into a gallop and charged us.

The general and his small escort made a brave stand until the approach of the enemy squadron, which overthrew eight or ten of our chasseurs à cheval.

The general and his chief-of-staff, wanting to escape, found themselves in a sunken road, and their horses fell. They were caught by a Prussian lancer, who galloped after them into the sunken road. Finding himself in front of the general, he gave five to six lance thrusts to Saint-Rémy. When we arrived, the Prussian prudently withdrew, leaving his two opponents on the ground. General Saint-Rémy[4] escaped with relatively light injuries, and General Gérard from mild bruising to his leg. I went to call the cavalry. They arrived at the trot, and in turn crushed the Prussian squadron, who fell back on Ligny.

About this charge at Ligny, General Domon himself adds his thoughts to the action that saved the general and his chief-of-staff:[5]

> In a charge at Fleurus, these men saved the life of Lieutenant-General Comte Gérard and the chief-of-staff of 4th Corps; Chasseurs Schneiblein and Ferrad.

Rumigny further notes:[6]

> We attacked the left of the village of Ligny, while a brigade, commanded by General Rome, former colonel of the 7th Light, approached the centre of the village of Ligny which the Prussians occupied very strongly. As the attack was vigorous, they sent up more and more troops. Soon the artillery fire became so violent that the batteries thundered over the houses of the village.

Captain François, of the 30th Regiment of Line Infantry, narrates:[7]

> Around three o'clock, General Pecheux gave orders to General Rome, commanding the 1st Brigade of his division, consisting of 30th and 96th Line, to form in column of attack, to march on the village of Ligny and to attack. We, the 30th, formed leading the brigade; despite the bullets, we marched under shouldered arms on this village. We arrived some 200 paces from some hedges, behind which were thousands of Prussian skirmishers, the regiment was formed in line of battle and marched on.
>
> We beat the charge and the soldiers broke through the hedges. The left half of the 1st Battalion, myself included, descended into a sunken road, which was blocked by abatis, vehicles, harrows, ploughs which we only got through with great difficulty, during which time we were under constant fire from the Prussians hidden behind the hedges.
>
> Finally, we crossed these barriers and entered the village of Ligny.
>
> We arrived at the church, [where] a brook separated us from the enemy. They fired at us from inside houses, behind walls, on roofs.

We experienced a significant loss from their musketry as well as their artillery, which rained balls and shrapnel down on us.

In an instant, Major Hervieux, commanding the regiment, Battalion Commander Richard Lafolie was killed and Battalion Commander Blain was slightly wounded when he had his horse killed under him. Furthermore, five captains were killed, and three injured, as well as two adjutant-majors, nine lieutenants and second lieutenants killed, seven were wounded and nearly 700 men killed or wounded. I only suffered slight bruises to the thigh of my right leg. Not for a long time had I fought with such bravery and dedication. The disorder into which we are put by the enemy made me curse my existence. I wanted to be killed. I was so angry to see a battle as badly ordered. No one commanded. We could see neither our general nor staff officers, nor aides. The regiment two-thirds destroyed without receiving reinforcement or orders. Thus, we were forced to retreat in disorder and had to abandon our wounded comrades and to try and rally near our batteries, which were roaring against the enemy.

Captain Christophe and I rallied the remnants of the regiment and I can say to my glory that the soldiers were happy to see me still among them and asked that I should renew the fight. Despite the proven failure, the battalion made about 500 prisoners. The moment we were busy with gathering the regiment, General Rome arrived and gave orders to return to the village of Ligny. The soldiers were in no way put off by their failure, nor alarmed from the loss of two-thirds of their comrades and shouted 'long live the emperor!' and marched in front. Captain Christophe made the charge be beaten, the battalion returned to the village, but was repulsed. We rallied and attacked the village three times, always experiencing the same setbacks. So, Captain Christophe and I were commissioned by General Rome to gather the men behind the batteries of the division, which continued to fire. About 200 men had gathered there. General Rome, seeing their fearlessness, ordered me to take one hundred (all wanted to follow me) and make another effort. These hundred soldiers, happy to see me at their head, shouted: 'long live the emperor and Captain Francis'. I was proud of this confidence they had in me, and General Rome said flattering things about it.

We arrived at the hollow road which led to the village. The enemy's fire had greatly diminished. I ordered silence. Just as we were about to enter the village, we met a company of Prussians commanded by an officer; we were both surprised at finding ourselves so close to each other. I hit General Rome's horse on the nose with my sword, for he was right in front of my men, and the general squeezed as close to the bank as he could. I stooped down, and gave the command, 'ready, present, fire!' The Prussians did the same, and though I was in front I was not hit. But, there were dead and wounded on both sides. I was hit by a bullet, but it was stopped by my cloak which was in a tight roll over one shoulder and across my body. I found the bullet afterwards in my cloak. All it had done was to give me a bruise on the left breast; but that made me spit blood for several days. I ordered my men to charge with the bayonet; the enemy defended himself, and for some minutes the carnage was terrible. In parrying the thrusts that were made at me, my sword broke. I was knocked down by the crowd, and trampled underfoot by my own men and the enemy.

At that moment, General Rome ordered the 96th Regiment to advance. The enemy fled. I was picked up, along with several of my wounded soldiers who had not abandoned me.

I was badly bruised in many places by being trampled underfoot, but I re-joined the regiment, which was posted behind our batteries. I had seven men killed and eleven wounded, but most of them only slightly. I had only been stunned, and was able to get back to the regiment, upon which the enemy was still firing.

A little later, the village was taken, the centre of the enemy's army was in result thrown into disorder, and the Duke of Brunswick killed.

During the night, I learned that we had gained the battle, taken forty guns and eight flags, and done prodigies of valour. So, in spite of the want of unison and order, the troops had done their duty, and, for my part, I had done mine…In our first attack on Ligny, the regiment took about 500 prisoners in the yards and houses round the church. Some of the cowards, of whom there are plenty in every regiment, offered to guard these prisoners, really to get out of danger themselves.

In order to try and understand the regiment in 1815, analysis of the regiment's muster list reveals some interesting information. Analysis of the 220 men who served with the regiment in 1815 shows that the youngest members of the regiment were aged seventeen and the oldest thirty-eight; the average age was twenty-eight years seven months. In the amalgam of 1814, the regiment was consolidated with the 1st Battalion of the 156th Regiment of Line Infantry and the 2nd Battalion of the 13th Regiment of Tirailleurs of the Imperial Guard.

All had been with the regiment since July 1814, at least half of the sample being with the regiment since 1813. This is not surprising, as the regiment was wholly rebuilt following the Russian campaign. The conscripts drawn into the regiment seem to have come from a wide range of ages, so therefore the number of veterans in the sample is low overall.[8] In 1815, the 30th Regiment of Line Infantry needs to be considered as among one of the veteran regiments of the army. About the dress of the officers of the regiment, Battalion Commander Coudreux writes on 1 June 1815:[9]

> Finally, my friend, by dint of patience I managed to get a battalion of the line. The Minister of War has just forwarded me the order to go to Sézanne (twenty-two miles from Paris) to take command of a battalion of the 30th Line. The 30th is a beautiful and magnificent regiment. A change in my arms will complete my ruin. My clothes, with minor repairs, I can use, but we must change epaulets, hat, sword and boots. Now I have white trousers. I will be forced to buy two horses. I am, my dear friend, in the greatest embarrassment, if you do not once again be kind enough to come to my rescue. This is certainly the last time I importune you, but do not abandon me in this last effort that I have to do. Send me by return of post 700 or 800 *francs* from some of your friends in Paris. I have almost as many before me, and, with that amount, I can cope with everything.

The regiment was well dressed and had good morale as it entered the campaign. About the operations of the 30th Regiment of Line Infantry, Marie Theodore Gueulluy, Comte de Rumigny, writes:[10]

> Around two o'clock, General Gérard ordered me to go and tell General Rome that he was not to become involved if the resistance was too strong. I found the 30th Line in the sunken lanes, which were filled with a sticky mud. The unfortunate soldiers were shot by the Prussians who occupied the gardens and hedges. The 30th suffered horribly and General Rome was soon severely wounded. I ordered the men of the 30th, which would have succumbed to the last, to attack the enemy, and I told the officers to remain behind the brook that is in the middle of the village. I went to report to General Lavigne who was in the middle of it all. Marshal Blücher was about to make a sustained attack with about twenty thousand men. The 30th and the brigade of General Rome could not support such an effort; the village remained temporarily the conquest of the Prussians. Their sharpshooters appeared in the hedges outside, from where the fire of their infantry was very strong.
>
> Right now, General Gérard calls me, he ordered me to take two

battalions and drive the Prussians from the village. I took a battalion of the 72nd [possibly the 76th Regiment of Line Infantry] and I placed myself at the head of the column. We passed the hedges without firing a single shot; the grenadiers came up with the cemetery without having fired a shot. There, a Prussian battalion, arrested by a defile, would be practically wiped with our bayonets. Then, placing the 2nd Battalion to keep what we had taken the village, I headed to the right column and, after walking along a wall and passing an inn, I directed the 72nd [76th] to where the hedges of Ligny ended. This movement took us beyond the left of the Prussians.

I went to report to General Gérard, asking for reinforcements to fall on the left wing of the enemy. Right now, the emperor was on horseback in an orchard; general said, 'go report to the emperor'.

I approached His Majesty and told him that I was behind the enemy's left, and that if I had some cavalry, I could make a large number of prisoners. The emperor then gave orders to send me his escort; unfortunately they could not do so because of the column head of the grenadiers of the Imperial Guard, which was then engaged on the hedge-lined road, blocking the road leading to the point occupied by enemy troops.

After experiencing myself a thousand difficulties I arrived at the 72nd [76th], with the fear that another company would have the honour to bring disorder in the left wing of the Prussians. I ordered the two battalions to march forward.

Prussian chasseurs were spotted lurking in the final hedges, and when I had instructed the battalion commander 'commander! Come to me' my horse collapsed from a musket ball to the head. I continued on foot at the head of the troops…we seized the enemy's weak point and we could sense victory was in our grasp, when coming out of the hedges, to our great joy, the Prussians were occupied with a roaring fire against the village, but had their backs to us. They did not understand that they had been outflanked, and not one of them realised this until we were about three hundred feet from the houses. Some of our bullets, which took them from behind, occasioned in them a rout that spread to the middle of the village. Unfortunately, we did not have a single squadron with us to exploit this, but it was still possible for us to capture some prisoners, who surrendered without difficulty. They were the Prussian Regiment of Ost. We saw more than 3,000 men run away in front of us. A few further shots made them run to the rear even quicker. At this point, Blücher, seeing this decisive movement, threw his black hussars forward to stop the cavalry of General Excelmans and General Pajol, who now advanced out of the village on our extreme right.

The vicious fighting in Ligny itself is described by a member of the 29th Prussian Infantry Regiment:[11]

> We fought with bayonets and muskets as clubs in the streets of the village. We seemed to be overcome with personal hatred; man fought against man. It seemed as if every individual had met his deadliest enemy and rejoiced at the long-anticipated opportunity to give vent to this. Pardon was neither given nor asked for. The French plunged their bayonets into the chests of those who had already been wounded, the Prussians swore loudly at the enemy, and killed anyone who came into their hands.

Another Prussian eyewitness, whose name is not known, writes about his perspective of the battle:[12]

> On 16 June, the enemy had dislodged the 4th Brigade out of Ligny village by sheer numbers. A battalion of the 3rd Westphalian Landwehr Infantry Regiment of the 3rd Brigade, which had been sent in support, was also pushed back to our side of the village. At this moment, Major-General von Jagow ordered both musketeer battalions of the 2nd West Prussian Infantry Regiment to attack, through both entrances of the village, the enemy which was advancing in masses along the main street of the village. These would, at the same time, be attacked on both flanks by the skirmishers of both musketeer battalions and the fusilier battalion of the same regiment advancing through the gardens and from behind the fences. Together they had to drive the enemy from the streets of the village with the bayonet. This so happened. The colours of both battalions remained at the head of these, and the attack succeeded in such a way that the enemy was pushed back to the far side of the village, only able to maintain a foothold in a single stone farm and inside the church. The latter, however, was occupied by only a few of the enemy.
>
> The battalions, however, lost in this attack a number of badly wounded and killed officers; among the former the commander of the 2nd [Musketeer] Battalion, among the latter the commander of the 1st [Musketeer] Battalion. The commander of the fusilier battalion was also slightly wounded. Despite this, the battalion held on against a renewed attack of the enemy, which was also reinforced by fresh

troops. Finally, the enemy broke through the village wall on the left side, and a number of enemy skirmishers attacked the flank and back of the 2nd Battalion. The battalion faced about and forced its way back through the village. Already during the advance, the colour [of the battalion] had received various musket holes and now again not only the colour itself, but also the casing and the flagpole. The enemy followed up on the column closely, with slightly less pressure however.

At this moment, NCO Rosenberg, who was with the colour party, was wounded and, because he could not keep up, he was bayoneted at fifty paces and in full view of the column. In order to secure the colour, the colour-bearer wanted to try to reach the head of the column now that the retreat route had been cleared. He was, however, not able to make his way through the column itself, and therefore he tried to pass the column through the gardens. The moment he tried to climb a fence, several French soldiers ran out of a shed. One of these immediately tried to grab the colour, but was shot down by Musketeer Schwencke, two more were bayoneted; one by Schwencke, the other one by Musketeer Putzke, several members of the colour party now rushed forward and provided the colour-bearer with their fire, this provided the time needed to secure the colour and to bring it to the head of the column, although not without a bullet grazing his leg and another one through his shako.

The two musketeer battalions reformed into close columns and counter-attacked, forcing their way into the village once again. Their skirmish platoons, under Captains von Witten and von Berg, were detached and sent to storm the churchyard which the French had now occupied. The West Prussians captured their objective, either killing or taking prisoner the French garrison. Both battalions were then preparing to advance south out of the village when they encountered the French battalions of the brigade of Le Capitaine (59th and 76th Line), which were now approaching Ligny in close columns. As the Prussians were caught in the narrow streets, and as the French did not have the time to deploy, they both halted to fire as they were. The ensuing exchange of fire lasted half an hour, with both sides suffering heavy casualties; General Le Capitaine was killed.

Major Stengel, commanding the 19th Prussian Infantry Regiment, writes:[13]

On the 16th, the army had drawn together at the heights of Fleurus and retreated behind Ligny and Saint-Amand, where it was placed in battle array. Here, Captain von Borcke with the 2nd Company came back to the regiment. As we had not yet heard anything from the enemy, food rations were distributed, and the troops allowed to cook.

Between noon and one o'clock, the enemy began to move and moved up to the village of Ligny and Saint-Amand. The 19th Infantry Regiment moved into the position of Ligny to repel the enemy attack that developed here.

Towards two o'clock began the attack, the enemy came to us with far superior forces to the village of Ligny, but was always thrown back at all points. Ligny was, between two and seven o' clock, alternately in the hands of the French, and in ours. Around this time, the enemy penetrated our positions with superior masses of infantry and the artillery bombarded Ligny with shells, and set it on fire: it was thus impossible to keep the village any longer. Now, the general retreat was begun. The regiment, incessantly in the fire, and was often isolated. It rallied on the 17th on the road to the town of Wavre in which the general rendezvous of the corps was arranged. We camped behind Wavre.

Franz Lieber recounts that his regiment, the Kohlberg Regiment, was sent forward to re-take the left side of the village of Ligny:[14]

The bugle gave the signal to halt; we were in front of the village of Ligny. The signal was for the riflemen to march out to the right and left of the column, and to attack.

Our ardour now led us to entirely beyond proper limits; the section to which I belonged ran madly, without firing towards the enemy who retreated. My hindman fell; I rushed on, hearing well but not heading the urgent calls from our sergeant. The village was intersected with thick hedges, from behind which the grenadiers fired upon us, but we drove them from one to the other. I, forgetting altogether to fire and what I ought to have done, tore the red plume from one of the grenadier's bear caps, and swung it over my head, calling triumphantly to my comrades. At length, we arrived at a road crossing the village lengthwise, and the sergeant-major now succeeded in his attempt to bring us somewhat back to our reason...If our whole company, which, on entering the engagement numbered about one hundred and fifty strong, at night only twenty or thirty combatants remained.

A Prussian officer wrote in July 1815 about his experiences of the aftermath of the battle:[15]

I have visited the field of battle. The sleep of the dead is sound. On this spot where this day a month ago, thousands thronged and fought, where thousands sank and bled, and groaned and died, there is now not a living soul, and over all hovers the stillness of the grave.

In Ligny, 2,000 dead were buried. Here fought the Westphalian and Berg regiments. The village of Ligny consists of stone-built houses thatched with straw on a small brook which flows through flat meadows. In the village are several farmhouses, enclosed with walls and gates.

Every farmhouse the Prussians had converted into a fortress. The French endeavoured to penetrate through the village by means of superior numbers. Four times they were driven out. They set fire to the farmhouses in the upper end of the village with their howitzers; but the Prussians still kept their ground at the lower end. A whole company of Westphalian troops fell in the courtyard of the church; on the terrace before the church lay fifty dead.

In the evening, the French surrounded the village. The Prussians retired half a league; the position was lost and it is incomprehensible why the French did not follow up the advantage they had obtained, and again attack the Prussians in the night.

After a protracted struggle, the Prussian garrison was on the point of falling back, but the French troops were exhausted and could not re-take the village, though they had succeeded in taking a farm complex. Only with the timely intervention of the Imperial Guard would the village be taken. Ligny had been the scene of terrible carnage, as Charles Philippe Lefol, aide-de-camp to General Lefol, graphically writes:[16]

At three o'clock in the morning, 17 June, I was awakened on the order of Vandamme to go to Ligny, a mile from us, to bring back to Saint-Amand our artillery battery that was detached the day before to help crush the Prussians and finish this struggle well. When I arrived at Ligny, I witnessed a horrible sight, and who has not travelled, like me, to this battlefield cannot imagine such a horror, let alone conceive the emotions to which one is exposed.

The village, which had been set on fire the day before, was still burning, grilling the wounded who had taken refuge in the houses. Piles of corpses completed a painting that has perhaps never presented the greatest wars, because here 4,000 dead soldiers were crammed into a very small area. The narrow lanes that led to Ligny were so congested that, without being accused of exaggeration, I can testify that my horse found difficulty in avoiding stepping on the corpses. It was much worse when it came to pass through with the guns and caissons to take them to Saint-Amand; I still have in my ears the sound produced from the wheels crushing the skulls of soldiers, whose brains, mixed with pieces of flesh, were spread out hideously on the road, perhaps among these men laying on the ground, and that we trodden under foot, were those whose hearts were still beating.

Losses sustained by the 12th Division at the Battle of Ligny are shown below:

Regiment	Killed		Wounded		Missing		Total
	Officers	Men	Officers	Men	Officers	Men	
30th Line Infantry[17]	0	18	0	140	0	60	218
96th Line Infantry[18]	0	25	0	151	0	0	176
6th Light Infantry	No data available						
63rd Line Infantry[19]	No meaningful data recorded						
Total	0	43	0	291	0	60	394

For the wounded, we are only seeing the returns for men still in hospital at the time of disbandment of the army on 15 September 1815. Captain François, of the 30th Regiment of Line Infantry, gives 700 men lost at Ligny, 482 more than actually recorded. The losses sustained on the day of battle are likely to be far higher than the recorded wounded. No doubt many men who were evacuated to the rear ambulances, or sent to hospital had recovered and joined the regiment again by September 1815. We are also not seeing the missing, as hundreds of men were written off in September 1815, and we have no idea when they had quit their regiments. The true losses, therefore, of wounded and missing men is not known. Totally missing are casualties for the 6th Regiment of Light Infantry and 63rd Regiment of Line Infantry. Total losses in the division are not known as a consequence of this. Losses of the 13th Division were as follows:

Regiment	Killed		Wounded		Missing		Total
	Officers	Men	Officers	Men	Officers	Men	
59th Line Infantry[20]	0	15	0	72	0	1	88
76th Line Infantry[21]	No data recorded						
48th Line Infantry[22]	0	12	No data recorded				12
69th Line Infantry[23]	0	13	0	67	0	55	135
Total	0	40	0	139	0	56	235

For the wounded, we are only seeing the returns for men still in hospital at the time of disbandment of the army on 15 September 1815. The true losses, therefore, of wounded men is not known. We are missing the casualty data for the 76th Regiment of Line Infantry entirely, and for the wounded men of the 48th Regiment of Line Infantry.

In comparison, the Prussian 4th Corps lost twenty-four officers, 149 subalterns, thirty-six musicians and 2,356 other ranks, of which:. killed were four officers, twenty-four subalterns, eight musicians and 606 other ranks; wounded were fifteen officers, twenty-four subalterns, four musicians and 479 other ranks; and missing were five officers, 101 subalterns, twenty-four musicians and 1,271 men.[24] The French, where data exists, sustained 629 men killed or wounded from four of the eight regiments from 12th and 13th Divisions which attacked Ligny. It seems the Prussians at Ligny lost far more men than the French, albeit based on incomplete data.

14th Division
The actions here on the French right wing and south-east of Sombreffe, towards Potriaux, are not clearly understood. It seems Hulot was involved in taking Togrenelle. In the fighting here, total divisional losses were as follows:

Regiment	Killed		Wounded		Missing		Total
	Officers	Men	Officers	Men	Officers	Men	
9th Light Infantry[25]	4	35	11	230	0	0	280
111th Line Infantry[26]	0	13	0	186	0	0	199
44th Line Infantry[27]	0	15	0	80	0	0	65
50th Line Infantry[28]	0	46	0	149	0	0	195
Total	4	109	11	645	0	0	769

For the wounded, we are only seeing the returns for men still in hospital at the time of disbandment of the army on 15 September 1815. Based on recorded casualties for other ranks, the division lost 18 per cent of effective strength at Ligny. The division, it seems, moved against the Prussian 2nd Brigade of Pirch. Here, the 6th Prussian Regiment lost a total of sixteen officers, fifty-seven subalterns, thirteen musicians and 868 men.[29] In total, the brigade lost 937 killed, 2,222 wounded and 1,393 missing—some 4,552 men, or a staggering 56 per cent of effective strength being lost to the French.

Crisis on the French left
d'Erlon's 1st Corps was marching to Ligny. Napoléon expected a body of troops to emerge on the left. However, his own men, it seems, were

not aware of this move. The sudden appearance of a large column of men on the French left caused panic to spread. Parts of General Lefol's command wavered, as Charles Philippe Lefol, aide-de-camp to General Lefol, writes:[30]

> It was, as far as I can remember, about six o'clock when there appeared among the soldiers of a regiment a movement of terror, which could have had fatal consequences without the extreme energy which was employed by General Lefol and other officers in attempting to stop this panic, caused first by the false news that a new enemy column had surprised the left of our division, and the painful impression caused in the 64th Line of the death of Colonel Dubalen they loved and believed in. Several soldiers left their ranks, threw down their guns and could undermine, and perhaps even lead the entire army corps back, when several officers, among whom was found General Corsin, commanding a brigade of our division, who ran forward, stopping the fugitives, and gathering them together and bringing them back into battle, which they sustained until the evening with the same intrepidity as at the beginning.

This column of the enemy was in fact the head of d'Erlon's 1st Corps, formed by the 4th Infantry Division under General Durutte, moving up to support Napoléon as ordered to do so. Napoléon had expected 1st Corps to move along the road from Namur to Brye, instead of a point to the north-west of Villers-Perwin on Vandamme's flank. For inexplicable reasons, the column halted rather than attacked, and the 2nd and 3rd Divisions then headed off back to Quatre-Bras, leaving just the 4th Infantry Division and 1st Cavalry Division. However, the story may be apocryphal. Given the terrain at Ligny, it is very unlikely that Durutte's column could actually be observed. General Dejean notes:[31]

> During the Battle of Ligny, I was instructed by the emperor to see what was happening to the left, firstly in the corps of General Vandamme, and then on the far left of the troops acting on this point: it was the cavalry, I believe, under General Subervie, at least he was there, and I vividly remember talking to him, there was in front of him either English or Hanoverian cavalry and I read the report to the emperor, and during the day I did not see any of the troops commanded by d'Erlon.

Subervie's 5th Cavalry Division had advanced to reinforce the wavering 3rd Corps. Dejean states he did not see Durutte's division. Napoléon had planned for 1st Corps to sweep around the Prussian right flank and rear; this did not happen. About what actually happened, Durutte's son explains:[32]

> General Durutte observed that an enemy column could emerge onto the plain which was between Brye and Delhutte Wood, and which would completely cut the emperor's wing of the army off from the command of Marshal Ney, he [General d'Erlon] concluded to leave General Durutte in this plain. Under his orders he left him, besides his own division, three regiments of cavalry commanded by General Jacquinot.
>
> General Durutte, when leaving General d'Erlon, asked him if he should march on Brye. d'Erlon replied that in the circumstances, he could give him no orders and that he relied on his experience and caution. General Durutte directed his cavalry towards the road running from Sombreffe to Quatre-Bras, leaving Wagnelée and Brye on his right, but still moving towards these villages. His infantry followed the same movement.
>
> General d'Erlon had told him to be cautious, because things were going badly at Quatre-Bras. This resulted in General Durutte thoroughly reconnoitring Delhutte Wood, for any retreat of Marshal Ney would place the enemy behind General Durutte.
>
> When General Jacquinot arrived, a cannon-shot away from the road between Sombreffe and Quatre-Bras, he was assailed by an enemy formation, with which he began an exchange of musketry and artillery fire which lasted for three-quarters of an hour. General Durutte advanced his infantry towards him in support. The enemy troops who were exchanging cannon fire with General Jacquinot retired and General Durutte, receiving no news about the left wing, marched on Brye.
>
> By the movement of our troops, he presumed that we were victorious on the side of Saint-Amand. His sharpshooters engaged Prussian light troops who were still at Wagnelée. He seized the village, and when the day began to end, and being assured that the enemy was in full retreat, he sent to Brye two battalions, who on arriving there found a few Prussian stragglers. During the night, General Durutte was ordered to move to Villers-Perwin.

Chapuis, of the 85th Regiment of Line Infantry notes:[33]

> The 85th, marching at the head of its division, followed the movement of other divisions of the 1st Corps, which on the morning

of 16 June, received the order of the emperor, brought by Colonel Lawrence, attached to the headquarters of the army, to change our direction of march to the right. It was made when we were marching towards Quatre-Bras.

We abandoned our movement from Marchienne-au-Pont, and we established ourselves on the new route with celerity, the column formed by divisions was to be established behind the right of the Prussian army. The position was one of great importance.

When the column had arrived at Wagnelée, Chapuis notes an officer from Marshal Ney ordered that the column was to march back to Quatre-Bras. It was now that General Durutte began a ponderous and slow attack on Wagnelée. Battalion Commander Rullieres, of the 95th Regiment of Line Infantry, notes:[34]

The voltigeurs of Durutte's division began to fire against Prussian scouts; it was about eight o'clock at night.

Chapuis continues his narration of the events witnessed by the 85th Regiment of Line Infantry:[35]

Located a short distance from the hamlet of Wagnelée, which was close to the village of Saint-Amand, we were waiting for the order that would have us march on Wagnelée, we were all convinced 1st Corps had been called to play a great part in the struggle that was engaged…Our position at Wagnelée gave us the absolute assurance that a few minutes would suffice to place the whole of the Prussian right wing between two fires, and not one of us there, soldier or officer, who could not see that acting with vigour and promptness, the safety of the enemy would be totally compromised.

This order on which we expected to gain such favourable results arrived, but it was not executed, as General Drouet d'Erlon had left to join Marshal Ney at Quatre-Bras, under whose orders were the 1st and 2nd Corps, and that General Durutte did not dare to give the order for such a movement, refusing the responsibility, as he was a divisional commander and not the commanding general of the 1st Corps. In consequence of this, he sent an officer to Quatre-Bras carrying this order and demanding instructions that others put in his situation would not have hesitated to carry out.

This can in no way be considered as the strong flank attack that Napoléon desired. If d'Erlon was guilty of splitting his command, then

Durutte was guilty for not attacking when he had the chance, and using his initiative rather than waiting for orders from d'Erlon, who, at Quatre-Bras, could make no valid contribution to the action at Ligny. d'Erlon should have issued clearer instructions to Durutte, but Durutte should have been able to judge the situation for himself. About the lack of action, Chapuis adroitly notes:[36]

> While this position was being taken, an angrier scene was taking place between our divisional commander, Durutte, and General Brue, our brigade commander. The latter was frustrated at the caution of his superior, and criticised him loudly. He shouted, 'it is intolerable that we witness the retreat of a beaten army and do nothing, when everything indicates that if it was attacked it would be destroyed'.
>
> General Durutte could only offer the excuse to General Brue 'it is lucky for you that you are not responsible!' General Brue replied, 'I wish to God that I was, we would already be fighting!'
>
> This episode was overheard by the senior officers of the 85th that were at the head of the regiment…for those that witnessed the scene and reflected upon it, that a major error had being committed in employing certain commanders, for whom, the words of glory and 'La Patrie' were no longer of the same significance as to their subordinates.
>
> This suspicion was further confirmed when we learnt that on the next day, 17 June, Colonel Gordon, the chief-of-staff of 4th Division, and Battalion Commander Gaugler, the first aide-de-camp to General Durutte, had passed to the enemy the previous morning and had been concealed from us for twenty-four hours…The desertion of these two men, in positions close to General Durutte and his hesitation a few hours earlier to execute orders, which should have been done quickly, produced such a bad impression on the 85th that it took all the efforts of the officers to restore the morale of the men.

Clearly, there was no trust between regimental officers and higher-ranking staff officers. General Brue commanding the 2nd Brigade of Durutte's division (formed by the 85th and 95th regiments of Line Infantry), notes:[37]

> We were ordered to capture the village of Wangenle [sic] This first order was transmitted to the 1st Army Corps when it debouched from Marchienne-au-Pont, by Colonel Lawrence of the artillery, attached to the staff of the emperor or to that of the major-general.

He adds:[38]

> If General Durutte had attacked the defeated and retreating Prussian
> army at Ligny, this army would have been annihilated; all those who
> were not killed would have been forced to lay down their arms and
> would have been captured.

He reproached Durutte for his actions as follows:[39]

> It is unheard of to march with shouldered arms in pursuit of a
> defeated army, when all indications were that we had to attack it and
> destroy it.

Brue further lambasted Durutte as a traitor, and that Durutte's failures
on 16 and 18 June led to the loss of the campaign—a fairly accurate
summary of Durutte's catastrophic failure to seize the initiative at
Ligny.[40] Napoléon's flank attack had been derailed by Ney, and then at
the vital moment when the 4th Infantry Division, with Jacquinot's
cavalry, could have dramatically intervened at Ligny, General Durutte
seemingly panicked and did nothing. Durutte was an experienced field
commander, but now, in 1815, he was timid and lacked the vital spark
of initiative that had driven hundreds of officers in the past. From
marshal down to private, the French army of 1815 lacked something
vital—it had no soul or desire to fight. The burning ambition to follow
the emperor to glory had, it seems, evaporated. Jean Baptiste Berton,
commanding the 14th and 17th Dragoons under the orders of General
Chastel (part of Excelmans's reserve cavalry), writes about these
operations as follows:[41]

> Orders were sent to the left wing and as instructed, the commander
> of the 1st Infantry Corps in reserve behind Frasné to move towards
> Villers-Perwin, and was already quite close to the village of Brye,
> when he received several orders to return to the left, which he
> unfortunately obeyed and fell back. A sergeant of the Gendarmerie
> d'Elite was sent with new orders that were dispatched for the
> second or third time to the left wing, the same as the first, and acted
> as a guide to Colonel Forbin-Janson, who was responsible for
> carrying the order. So that he could get there sooner, we gave him
> a fresh horse.
>   The French general was impatiently awaiting the first shots at
> Brye, the arranged signal, to move rapidly to Ligny, where the
> reserve was waiting...the prolonged delay of the signal cost the

French army precious blood … night had come, and the French general had not obtained the victory he had so well prepared for, the preparations for which the Prussian general had been ignorant of. The body of enemy troops which still held the heights between Brye and Saint-Amand retired from these villages. If Comte d'Erlon had taken possession of Brye, the corps of Ziethen, exhausted from a long struggle, and upon which we had inflicted great losses, would have been encircled and forced to lay down their arms. The Prussian army would have been largely destroyed and dispersed completely.

Michel Ordener, commanding the 1st Cuirassiers, concurs with Berton's assessment:[42]

> I commanded the regiment and the 7th Cuirassiers, where my brother was, and were part of the 4th Cavalry Corps of Milhaud's division Wathier Saint Alphonse.
>
> On the morning of 16 June, under the provisions adopted with the emperor, the corps which formed the reserve was placed in the second line, two or three hundred yards in front of Fleurus, near the village of Saint-Amand. We remained motionless for what seemed a long time, the wrong movements of d'Erlon prevented Napoléon from attacking at the time he had marked in his mind.

Durutte could and should have done more. Due to the blunderings of Ney, d'Erlon and Durutte, Ligny was far from the crippling blow to the Prussians that Napoléon believed it to be. Indeed, Adjutant-Commandant Janin, of 6th Corps, goes as far as to suggest that the appearance of the wandering 1st Corps drew reinforcements away from the central assault at a crucial time, robbing Napoléon of an all-out victory:[43]

> He [Napoléon] extended the line in one direction much more strongly than the other, and made the greatest efforts on the left and the centre of the enemy, which he simply could not sustain; he attacked timidly on the right. He was overthrown, and the attack stopped because an army corps appeared a league behind our left flank; he had to reinforce the whole of left wing and used part of the Guard to do so.

Janin notes that if 1st Corps had been an enemy column, then all of 6th Corps could have been destroyed due to the shortage of reinforcements.

As it was, the transfer of some of the Imperial Guard to the wing robbed the central attack of vital men, and robbed the operations on the right wing of troops to mount a cohesive attack.[44]

Attack of the Imperial Guard infantry

As dark masses of thunderclouds began to roll across the sky, the Imperial Guard artillery, together with the batteries posted along the front, unleashed a terrible bombardment from over 200 cannon. The smoke from the battery was dense, as an eyewitness narrates:[45]

> All the hills from Saint-Amand to Ligny were enveloped in a smoke similar to those thick fogs and white clouds of the morning which run through the undulating valleys of Savoy and cut in half their hills and mountains.

In support of this attack, numbers 1, 2 and 3 Companies of the Old Guard Foot Artillery, armed with 12-pounders formed a single massed battery. Also in action was number 5 Battery of the Old Guard Foot Artillery attached to Friant's grenadiers. They were armed with six 6-pounder and two 24-pounder howitzers. In support of the attack, the 6-pounders fired eighty standard rounds and eighteen rounds of canister shot.[46] Canister shot was a close-range weapon, with an effective range of 300 metres, compared to the 600 metres of cannon balls. The battery must have moved up with the Guard infantry in support, and fired at close range into the Prussian columns. The battery expended no howitzer shells, and each 6-pounder fired sixteen rounds. Contemporary drill manuals state a 6-pounder could fire one round a minute, so the battery had a frantic fifteen minutes of activity. Each 6-pounder had an ammunition box on the limber which held twenty-one rounds,[47] therefore the battery must have advanced forward without the cumbersome ammunition wagon (caisson), as the battery seems to have fired off all its munitions and then, we suppose, retreated, or was left in position while the infantry surged forward. The battery lost no men dead or wounded.[48] About their fire, Duuring, of the 1st Chasseurs, notes:[49]

> The balls of our batteries fell on the hill on the other side of the village, every moment they passed over the 1st Battalion without any harm to us, but struck some heavy cavalry. Some enemy infantry also fired on us. We lost not a man.

The artillery of the Guard went into action around 17.00 hours. Numbers 4 and 6 Companies of the Old Guard Foot Artillery seem to have been kept as a reserve. Also in action that day were numbers 3 and 4 Companies of the Guard Horse Artillery. The batteries were deployed at Saint-Amand.

The Prussian line at Ligny had been so heavily pummelled by the Guard artillery that it was close to breaking. Now all that was required was an injection of fresh troops to attack and decisively break through the Prussian centre. About the attack, Lieutenant Albert Rocca,[50] writing in 1816 (and a hard critic of Napoléon), says:[51]

> About seven o'clock, we were masters of the villages, but the Prussians still retained their positions behind the ravine. It was at that moment that Bonaparte, who from the beginning of the case had manoeuvred so that they could, when it was time, bring major forces beyond the ravine in order to expel from the heights of the mill of Bussy, the Prussian masses who occupied them, directed his Guard and all reserve on the village of Ligny. This bold movement, including what had happened to the left had been delayed until the last moment, was to fully isolate the rest of their army and the Prussian right that was behind Saint-Amand, and cut off their retreat to Namur.
>
> The entire Guard moved off to the charge, supported by numerous cavalry and a formidable artillery, crossed the village and rushed into the ravine it crosses amid a hail of bullets and shrapnel, while the fire that seemed to slow down a moment, again with an inconceivable violence; a terrible battle took place when, out of the ravine, approached the Guard with the bayonet who charged the Prussian squares determined in their charge. But nothing could resist the impetuosity of the French grenadiers, who all made their way through the village with the most horrific carnage; cavalry charges were executed at the same time by both sides, and determined a terrible melee.
>
> Finally, after the most obstinate resistance, and the most stubborn defence, the Prussians pressed on all sides, retreated abandoning the battlefield covered with dead, wounded, prisoners and some guns. The Guard immediately took possession of the heights they had just left, and the cavalry followed in pursuit.

Now, at approximately 19.30, to the accompaniment of peals of thunder and flashes of lightning, the massed ranks of the Imperial Guard cavalry and infantry advanced forward, with cries of *'Vive l'Empereur'*, in a deluge of warm rain to the attack. Sergeant de Mauduit narrates that:[52]

It was five o'clock in the afternoon, and our regiment had not yet moved from its last position, and finally at half-past five, Colonel Gourgaud was sent to the emperor, who was carefully following the attacks, in great haste from General Gérard, to announce that the 4th Corps reserves were all engaged, or about to be, without the possession of the village being finally decided. It was then that we took up arms and formed up our columns by divisions to take us on Ligny.

We marched to the left front, having before us the 2nd Regiment of Grenadiers; our four battalions formed a column by half-distances, along with a regiment of chasseurs à pied, the engineers and marines of the Guard.

Mauduit further notes that the attack was to be made by all three arms: cavalry, infantry and artillery:[53]

Only a few yards to the right of us the terrible artillery reserve of the Old Guard formed a third column of eight pieces facing the front.

Behind us came, two great columns: one on the right, composed of 1,700 mounted grenadiers, dragoon guards and gendarmes, the left column was composed of, 1,500 cuirassiers of General Delort; each of the two columns was sixty-four files wide.

Battalion Commander Duuring, of the 1st Battalion 1st Regiment of Chasseurs, narrates that on 16 June:[54]

The 1st Regiment passed through Fleurus in the afternoon; we rested for an hour. The whole division, as well as the grenadiers, took position on the right but slightly to the rear. All of the regiments were ordered to advance, except the 1st Regiment of Chasseurs, as well as the 1st and 2nd Grenadiers, which were to remain with the emperor.

These three regiments were ordered to follow the emperor, who marched to the right wing about one hour before dusk. We marched in column by division under a hail of balls, which wounded two men. Once the three regiments were through the village followed by the heavy cavalry, we debouched from the right side of the village into battle. We then formed squares by battalion. The grenadiers were to our front left, and withstood several charges by enemy cavalry, which suffered a considerable loss, because they thought, they were against the National Guard because they wore their hats.

General Christiani, commanding the 2nd Regiment of Grenadiers à Pied, recalls the Prussian cavalry attacks as follows:[55]

The battle of the 16th, while the corps of foot grenadiers remained in reserve, we crossed Fleurus and took a position on the left of the village, at a distance of perhaps half a mile from Ligny, which the enemy still partly occupied.

The regiments of grenadiers were ordered to advance. This movement was made without any resistance from the enemy, but while we were forming into squares by battalions to debouch from the other side of the village, we were surprised by a charge of Prussian lancers who passed through intervals of the squares, the result of which we could not open fire with musketry. The squares did not have time to form by echelons. The enemy would have been better received if they conducted a second charge, but they did not do so.

Clearly, for supposed seasoned troops to have been caught in the act of forming square, or not being aware of cavalry in the immediate locality, is indicative of poor command and control by the officers and sub-officers. It is also indicative of a lack of training and cohesion; the men being unable to change formation quickly and effectively as the situation dictated. If the regiments had not been able to mount some form of defence then no doubt the Guard would have been severely mauled by the Prussians in this encounter. Clearly a number of casualties taken that day by the grenadiers were no doubt due to this event.

It seems that also deployed here were the 3rd and 4th Grenadiers. During the battle, General Poret de Morvan, commanding the 3rd Grenadiers, had been:[56]

...ordered to cross the village and take a position on the heights. He executed this movement with shouldered arms, and not even the heavy fire of the enemy could stop his old grenadiers. General Roguet, who commanded the division, was ordered to march forward with a battalion and formed in square to oppose the Prussian cavalry. General Poret de Morvan took command of this battalion, and shut himself up in the square, which received two strong charges of cavalry, comprising lancers and cuirassiers, without letting them break the square; the enemy fell with great loss in these three charges.

Among the officers of the 3rd Grenadiers, one officer stood out from the rest: Lieutenant Goyard.[57] About the actions at Ligny, General Poret de Morvan writes:[58]

Plas-de-Mauberge 24 June 1831
In response to the request by M. Goyard (Claude Urbain) member

of the Legion of Honour, captain in retirement previously of the 3rd Regiment of Grenadiers à Pied of the Imperial Guard, who served under my command, I certify in all honesty, that M. Goyard at the Battle of Fleurus on 16 June 1815 distinguished himself in the capture of the village of Ligny and in the square of the 1st Battalion in which the general was, during the charges of the Prussian cavalry, which made multiple attacks and pressed on the square, but it held firm for which the general demands the presentation of the Officer of the Legion of Honour dated to 17 June.

First Lieutenant Jean François Bernelle, of the 2nd Battalion 3rd Grenadiers, writes about the savagery of the attack:[59]

> Our vanguard opened fire to take the village of Ligny, which was in the hands of the Prussians. We entered the village to drive them out, and in a moment the main street became littered with corpses from the two armies, we lost and re-took Ligny by slaughtering each other with fury, with dead bodies piling up for three hours in the horribly bloody ruins.
>
> Similar carnage took place at Saint-Amand-la-Haye, near Ligny. After six hours of fierce and terrible fighting the night would soon appear to cover the darkness of this human slaughter, the sun shone over the summit of the battle, which however was as yet undecided.
>
> The Old Guard had remained hitherto spectators quivering and eager to re-temper their arms in the blood of his cruel enemies of Leipzig; these old warriors had stopped biting their moustaches since the first gunshot was fired, their impatience was great. Silence of joy, or rather a dead silence, succeeded to the command given by Napoléon to charge and finish the battle.
>
> With the word of command they were set in motion, crossed a brook in which bathed numerous corpses of two nations. Once across the brook they re-formed their ranks under a hail of enemy musket balls, cannon balls and canister shot—they stood like a living wall that did not move. The Prussian cavalry rushed upon them with vigour, but due to the accuracy of their musketry, in a few minutes they covered the soil with their corpses, many horses of their dead riders flew in all directions.

Captain Antoine Nicholas Beraud recalls the operation of his regiment, the 4th Grenadiers:[60]

The 4th Foot Grenadier Regiment, commanded by the intrepid General Harlet, was the first to cross the village of Ligny under a terrible fire, and thus was the first to rush against the Prussian reserves.

At the entrance of the village the emperor alone, amid the bullets and shells, halted the regiment. 'Grenadiers', he said, 'you will pass the village, you will come across the Prussian reserve, and do not stop until you are established on the heights'. The brave 4th who, with only 600 men strong, did not hesitate; the village is crossed, the enemy pushed back, and for half an hour, the 4th stood against 15,000 men and repelled two cavalry charges.

About this event, Henri Niemann, of the 6th Uhlans, writes that it was his regiment that charged the 4th Grenadiers:[61]

On the morning of the 16th, we were ordered to change our position. It was a beautiful morning. Blücher's favourable position was turned later. Looking down the line at sunrise as far as the eye could reach, it appeared like silver mountains—regiments of muskets, artillery, and cuirassiers. About ten o'clock I was ordered to procure food in the city for the men and horses of my regiment.

In attempting this, the French marched in at the other gate, and of course I said 'good-bye' for the present. Immediately our 30,000 men were ordered to fall back at a slow pace, and thus Blücher's beautiful position had to be changed, and this day's dreadful slaughter commenced. No quarter given; Napoléon determined to crush Blücher first, because he feared him, and then finish Wellington, and therefore he attacked Blücher's corps with his whole army and 240 pieces of artillery. Foot-for-foot was disputed. The village of Saint-Amand I have seen taken and retaken several times.

At nine o'clock my light hussar regiment was ordered to break a French square, but we were received with such a rain of balls that we became separated. Lützow was taken prisoner. Blücher's fine charger was here killed under him, and an officer of my regiment—Schneider—gave Blücher his own horse and saved himself. The French cuirassiers drove us before them, but we soon rallied and drove them back. At this moment, Blücher was yet lying under his horse. Nastich, his aide-de-camp, had covered him with his cloak; after the French, driven before us, had passed, Nastich sprang forward, took the first horse by the bridle and Blücher was saved.

After eleven o'clock we left the field of this great battle and halted half an hour's distance from it. Exhausted, thirsty and hungry, I sucked clover flowers, halting in a large clover field. The French bivouac fires were before our eyes; neither party was conquered. Napoléon estimated our loss in the French bulletin as 15,000 men killed; since no quarter was given on either side we were not troubled with many prisoners. Several of our brave generals fell here wounded.

When the Old Guard got into Ligny the fighting was savage. The Prussian 2nd Westphalian Landwehr Regiment recruited in Minden and Ravensburg was slaughtered, loosing thirty-three officers and 1,986 sub-officers and men dead or wounded from a strength of 2,169 in three battalions. This represents a staggering loss of 93.1 per cent of the regiment's effective strength. All five Westphalian landwehr infantry regiments and the single uhlan regiment lost in total eighty-nine officers and 6,445 sub-officers and men.[62] In total, the Westphalian contingent, according to Peter Hofschröer had mustered some 11,348 men.

Thus, at Ligny the six Westphalian regiments lost 57.6 per cent of effective strength. It seems, therefore, that despite the shaky nature of the Imperial Guard in 1815—the regiments had only been together a matter of weeks before Ligny—they were still effective combat formations. We should note that the 2nd Westphalian Landwehr Regiment had been in action for most of the day and were probably exhausted by the time the Guard attacked. Therefore, the losses sustained in the action with the Imperial Guard cannot be ascertained, but the figures do show how brutal the fighting was in and around Ligny. One wonders what became of the civilian population. General Petit, commanding the 1st Grenadiers à Pied, continues that:[63]

> In the evening, all the corps of grenadiers (1st, 2nd, 3rd, 4th regiments) with the 1st Regiment of Chasseurs united on the hills behind the village and would soon take on the strength of the enemy, who defended the village with vigour against different corps line from the beginning of the battle. The 3rd and 4th Grenadier regiments formed the head of column: the 2nd marched in support. It was these three regiments, who after having driven the enemy infantry from its position on the other side of the village, received a rather brilliant cavalry charge that was repulsed by them with great loss of men and horses.
>
> The service squadrons comprising a squadron of horse grenadiers and a squadron of lancers and the half-squadron of elite gendarmerie emerged at Ligny around the same time as the 4th, 3rd and 2nd

Grenadier regiments emerged, they pursued the enemy cavalry and broke a square of infantry and retired in good order.

During this time the enemy cavalry rallied and charged in turn our service squadrons, but the enemy was arrested by the fire of three regiments of grenadiers (which was formed by squares of battalion), the service squadrons resumed the charge with great force, though outnumbered.

A French eyewitness, writing in 1816 from an anti-Napoléon standpoint due to the political correctness of the time (which he may not have had in 1815), recalls that:[64]

About seven in the evening, we were masters of the villages, but the Prussians still retained their positions behind the ravines. Buonaparte had all along manoeuvred so as to be enabled to make a sudden movement upon the rear of the ravine; he saw that the occasion was now at hand, and he instantly directed his Imperial Guard and all his reserve upon the village of Ligny.

This bold and most skilful movement had for its object to separate the right of the Prussians from the rest of their army, and thus to intercept it from making a retreat upon Namur.

The Guard moved forwards at the *pas de charge*, being supported, moreover, by a numerous cavalry and a most formidable artillery. It forced the village and, in despite of a shower of balls, cleared the ravine. The Prussians were for a moment daunted, and seemed about to flee, but, suddenly resuming their courage, recommenced a tremendous fire upon us while in the ravine. A sanguinary contest again began, until the Imperial Guard, rushing in front up the ravine, charged the Prussian squares with the bayonet.

The Prussians stood their ground for a time. But at length nothing could resist the impetuosity of the French grenadiers; they cut their way in every direction. The emperor finished the business at this moment by bringing up the cavalry to charge. The Prussians, thus pierced in every part, and seeing all their courage of no avail, now began their retreat, abandoning to us the field of battle, covered with the dead and wounded, and several dismounted cannons. The Imperial Guard took possession of the ground quitted by the enemy.

In the centre, the scene was now set for the *coup de grace* which was to be delivered by the cavalry reserve. On the left, the Young Guard assaulted Brye:[65]

Towards eight o'clock, the division was replaced by four battalions of the Young Guard, which debouched en masse and carried the position from the windmill of Saint-Amand to the heights of Brye.

The cavalry attacks

The French cavalry were mere spectators until around 17.30, when Subervie's 5th Cavalry Division had advanced to reinforce the wavering 3rd Corps. Also moved to the left were Milhaud's 4th Cavalry Corps and elements of the Young Guard.[66] Captain Aubry, of the 12th Chasseurs à Cheval, notes:[67]

> This is the day after the affair of Fleurus, a big and bloody battle for my squadron; we alone who were charged by a body of Prussian lancers who approached very close to us and where I and Commander Coffe, who was aide to General Gérard, was situated.
>
> During the heat of battle, we were in reserve behind the infantry and we got a few shots that killed three officers, but few of our men. One of the last balls came against my horse and it smashed my stirrup, but passed by my foot. It was incredible that I did not have my leg swept away by the ball. General Vino, who commanded us, was wounded at the same time as me, took me with him to his lodgings at Fleurus, and from the day after we heard the cannonade of Waterloo.

About the 12th Chasseurs à Cheval operations at Ligny, Colonel de Grouchy writes on 17 June 1815:[68]

> During the charge in the afternoon, a single squadron repulsed the charge of three squadrons of Prussian uhlans. Distinguished in the action were Chasseurs Schneiblein and Ferrad, who saved General Gérard[69] and his chief-of-staff who had become dismounted in the action. The avantguarde of the regiment charged an enemy artillery battery, captured a cannon and presented it to the emperor. The Sergeants Riss [Mathias], L'Homer, Schmitt and Chasseurs Bellot and Faur were particularly distinguished during the charge. During the day, the losses to the regiment were considerable from the fire of the enemy and from crossing sabres with them, despite this all actions were carried out with the utmost bravery.
>
> Colonel of the regiment
> Signe. A. de Grouchy.

Sergeant Mathias Riss was born on 30 October 1790 at Neuf Brisach, and was admitted to the 12th Chasseurs à Cheval on 30 October 1806, promoted to sergeant on 1 December 1811 and then to sergeant-major on 1 October 1813.[70] Henry Schneiblein was born in Bruges on 23 May 1794, and was admitted to the 16th Chasseurs à Cheval on 29 March 1812, serving until 16 July 1814 when he passed to the 2nd Company 2nd Squadron of the 12th Chasseurs à Cheval with the number 210. He was listed as 'in the rear' on 19 June 1815. Losses for the regiment were as follows:[71]

	Officers Killed	Officers Wounded	Other Ranks Killed	Other Ranks Wounded	Horses Killed	Horses Wounded
Total	1	4	1	14	8	17

On 10 June, the regiment mustered twenty-three officers with sixty-five horses and 273 men with 263 horses, along with six draught horses. In total the regiment had twenty-nine officers and 289 other ranks. Sixteen men were lost, and so were five officers: killed was Sub-Lieutenant Menzo and wounded were Captain Aubry and Sub-Lieutenant Remy. Corporal Bruguiere was killed.

In terms of other ranks, the regiment lost 5.5 per cent of its strength at Ligny. For their horses, some twenty-five were lost (9.5 per cent)—a ratio of almost two horses for every man.

Brigaded with the 12th Chasseurs à Cheval were the 4th and 9th Chasseurs à Cheval. General Domon notes at Ligny that the 9th Chasseurs à Cheval had two chasseurs mortally wounded, two wounded, three troop horses killed and one troop horse wounded.[72] The regiment's muster list records the following losses, confirming Domon's report: two men wounded in 1st Squadron, two wounded in 3rd Squadron and two men missing.[73] In the 4th Chasseurs à Cheval, General Domon records six chasseurs wounded and seven troop horses killed at Ligny, and one officer's mount.[74] Delort's cuirassiers charged into von Röder's cavalry, which lost the following:[75]

Regiment	Killed Officers	Men	Wounded Officers	Men	Missing Officers	Men	Total
5th Regiment of Brandenburg Dragoons	6	31	6	39	0	12	94
3rd Regiment Brandenburg Uhlans	134 killed or wounded from all ranks						
Total							228

The 5th Regiment of Brandenburg Dragoons lost 16.1 per cent of its effective strength, having mustered 585 officers and men at the start of the battle. What we are not seeing are losses for the horses, which could be as much as 300, or even more when dismounted men are factored in.

NOTES:

1. John Franklin, personal communication, 3 July 2014.
2. AN: LH 1225/8. Marie Theodore Gueulluy Rumigny was born on 12 March 1789. He was awarded the Legion of Honour on 20 August 1812, and made and Officer of the Legion of Honour on 28 September 1813 while serving as aide-de-camp to General Gérard.
3. Marie Théodore de Gueilly Rumigny, *Souvenirs du général comte de Rumigny, aide de camp du roi Louis-Philippe, 1789-1860*, Émile-Paul frères, Paris, 1921.
4. AN: LH 2442/29. Maurice Louis Saint-Rémy was born on 11 April 1769 and died on 31 October 1841. He served as the colonel chief-of-staff to 4th Corps.
5. SHDDT: Xc 192. Dossier 1815. Domon to Minister of War, 6 July 1815.
6. Rumigny.
7. Charles François, *Journal du capitane François (dit le Dromadaire d'Égypte) 1792-1830, publié d'après le manuscrit original par Charles Grolleau*, C. Carrington, Paris, 1904.
8. SHDDT: GR 21 YC 280 *registre matricule du 30e régiment d'infanterie de ligne 21 Juillet 1814 à 6 Juillet 1815*.
9. Gustave Schlumberger, *Lettres du commandant Coudreux, à son frère, 1804-1815 : soldats de Napoléon*, Plon, Nourrit et Cie, Paris, 1908.
10. Rumigny.
11. Wellmann, p. 99.
12. Anon., *'Muthvolles Benehmen zweier Musquetiere, am Tage der Schlacht bei Ligny'* in *Militair-Wochenblatt*, Berlin, 1816.
13. Wilhelm Ludwig Victor Henckel von Donnersmarck, *Erinnerungen aus meinem Leben*, Kummer, Zerbst, 1846, p. 641.
14. M. Russell Thayer, *The Life, Character and Writings of Francis Lieber*, Collins, Philadelphia, 1873, pp.8-9.
15. John Booth, *The Battle of Waterloo*, Booth, Egerton, London, 1816, p. LIV.
16. Lefol, pp. 59-60.
17. SHDDT: GR 21 YC 278 *30e régiment d'infanterie de ligne, 20 Février 1813-21 Juillet 1814 (matricules 12,577 à 16,020)*. See also: SHDDT: GR 21 YC 279 *30e régiment d'infanterie de ligne, 21 Juillet 1814-6 Juillet 1815 (matricules 16,021 à 16,744)*.
18. SHDDT: GR 21 YC 725 *80e régiment d'infanterie de ligne (ex 96e régiment d'infanterie de ligne), 7 Août 1814-2 Février 1815 (matricules 1 à 1,798)*. See also: SHDDT: GR 21 YC 726 *80e régiment d'infanterie de ligne (ex 96e régiment d'infanterie de ligne), 2 Février 1815-16 Août 1815 (matricules 1,799 à 2,414)*.
19. SHDDT: GR 21 YC 534 *59e régiment d'infanterie de ligne (ex 63e régiment d'infanterie de ligne), 25 Août 1814-5 Décembre 1814 (matricules 1 à 1,800)*. See also: SHDDT: GR 21 YC 535 *59e régiment d'infanterie de ligne (ex 63e régiment d'infanterie de ligne), 5 Décembre 1814-31 Juillet 1815 (matricules 1,801 à 2,197)*.
20. SHDDT: GR 21 YC 500 *55e régiment d'infanterie de ligne (ex 59e régiment d'infanterie de ligne), 28 Août 1814-22 Août 1815 (matricules 1 à 1,848)*.
21. SHDDT: GR 21 YC 614 *68e régiment d'infanterie de ligne (ex 76e régiment d'infanterie de ligne), 16 Août 1814-20 Juin 1815 (matricules 1 à 1,800)*.
22. SHDDT: GR 21 YC 416 *45e régiment d'infanterie de ligne (ex 48e régiment d'infanterie de ligne), 1 Septembre 1814-30 Avril 1815 (matricules 1 à 1,800)*.
23. SHDDT: GR 21 YC 580 *64e régiment d'infanterie de ligne (ex 69e régiment d'infanterie de ligne), 6 Septembre 1814-28 Mai 1815 (matricules 1 à 1,800)*.
24. See http://www.waterloo-campaign.nl/bestanden/files/notes/june16/note.3.pdf.

[25] SHDDT: GR 22 YC 81.

[26] SHDDT: GR 21 YC 798 *90e régiment d'infanterie de ligne (ex 111e régiment d'infanterie de ligne), 1 Août 1814-7 Mai 1815 (matricules 1 à 1,800).*

[27] SHDDT: GR 21 YC 381 *41e régiment d'infanterie de ligne (ex 44e régiment d'infanterie de ligne), 1 Octobre 1814-17 Janvier 1815 (matricules 1 à 1,800).* See also: SHDDT: GR 21 YC 382 *41e régiment d'infanterie de ligne (ex 44e régiment d'infanterie de ligne), 17 Janvier 1815-1 Septembre 1815 (matricules 1,801 à 2,358).*

[28] SHDDT: GR 21 YC 424 *46e régiment d'infanterie de ligne (ex 50e régiment d'infanterie de ligne), 24 Novembre 1814-3 Mai 1815 (matricules 1 à 1,800).*

[29] See http://www.waterloo-campaign.nl/bestanden/files/notes/june16/note.3.pdf.

[30] Lefol, pp. 59-60.

[31] Ney, p. 70.

[32] *La Sentinelle de l'Armée*, 4th year, No. 134, 8 March 1838.

[33] Chapuis, 'Waterloo' in *La Sentinelle de l'Armée*, 24 February 1838.

[34] SHDDT: GD 2 1135.

[35] Chapuis, 'Waterloo' in *La Sentinelle de l'Armée*, 24 February 1838.

[36] ibid.

[37] J. L. Brue, *'Lettre Addresse au Colonel Chapuis'* in *La Sentinelle de l'Armée*, 1 March 1838.

[38] Chapuis.

[39] A letter of 3 November 1837, published in the *Sentinelle de l'armée* of 24 February 1838.

[40] Letter of General Brue dated Tarbes 13 March 1838 published in *La Sentinelle de l'Armée*, 24 March 1838.

[41] Berton, p. 15.

[42] Henri Lot, *Les deux généraux Ordener*, R. Roger et F. Chernoviz, Paris, 1910.

[43] Janin, p. 25.

[44] Janin, p. 25.

[45] Georges Barral, *L'Épopée de Waterloo, etc*, Paris, 1895, p. 142.

[46] SHDDT: C15 5. Dossier 17 June. Chef-du-Bataillon Capelle to Friant.

[47] Ruty, *Observation sur la partie du system de l'an AXI*, 1814. SHAT 2w 84.

[48] SHDDT: C15 5. Dossier 17 June. Chef-du-Bataillon Capelle to Friant.

[49] D'Avout, *'L'infanterie de la garde a Waterloo'* in *Carnet de la Sabretache*, Volume 13, 1905, p. 115.

[50] Albert Jean Michel de Rocca (1788-1818) was a French lieutenant during the Napoléonic Wars and was also the second husband of Anne Louise Germaine de Staël. He was actually a Swiss national, born in Geneva. He served in the French army during the Peninsular War and was seriously injured. Back in Geneva, he had an affair with Germaine de Staël, who, exiled from Paris by Napoléon, lived in her chateaux at nearby Coppet. She had a son on 7 April 1812, whom his father legitimated as Louis-Alphonse Rocca. They separated when Mme de Staël started on a European tour to reach London through Vienna, Moscow, Saint Petersburg and Stockholm. Later they married and moved together to Paris after Waterloo. Germaine de Staël suffered a seizure on 5 January 1817 that left her paralysed, and she died on 14 July 1817, soon followed by her husband, who died in Hyères (Var) on 31 January 1818.

[51] François-Thomas Delbare, René Bourgeois, *Relation fidèle et détaillée de la dernière campagne de Buonaparte : terminée par la bataille de Mont-Saint-Jean, dite de Waterloo ou de la Belle-Alliance*, Brussels, 1816, p. 30.

[52] de Mauduit, Vol. 2, pp. 81-2.

[53] de Mauduit, Vol. 2, p. 82.

[54] D'Avout, p. 115.

[55] D'Avout, p. 111.

[56] Jean Baptiste Pierre Jullien Courcelles, *Dictionnaire historique et biographique des généraux Français*, Paris, 1823, pp 408-9.

[57] Claude Urbain Goyard was on born 22 January 1787 in the department of the Cote d'Or. He was admitted to the army aged twenty on 12 February 1807, as a soldier in the fusilier-

grenadiers. Due to his aptitude, he was swiftly promoted to fourier on 13 July 1807, as sergeant-major of the 1st Tirailleurs on 20 April 1810, and as sergeant-major of the newly raised 2nd Grenadiers à Pied on 1 July 1811. Following the Russian campaign, he was promoted to second lieutenant on 8 April 1813, to first lieutenant on 22 January 1814 and to captain on 1 July 1814 in the Corps Royale de Grenadiers à Pied des France. He was admitted to the 3rd Grenadiers on 1 April 1815.

[58] Author's collection.

[59] N. Cornevin, *Les Marchands de Vin de Paris*, Paris, 1869, pp. 64-5.

[60] Antoine Nicolas Béraud, *Histoire de Napoléon*, J. B. de Kock, Brussels, 1829, pp. 270-1.

[61'] The Journal of Henri Niemann of the Sixth Prussian Black Hussars' in *The English Historical Review*, Volume 3, July 1888, pp. 539-45.

[62] *Journal de Rouen*, 30 April 1815, citing The *Minden Gazette*.

[63] J. Petit, 'General Petit's account of the Waterloo Campaign' in *English Historical Review*, 1903.

[64] Anon, *The Journal of the Three Days of the Battle of Waterloo*, T. Chaplin, London, 1816, pp. 32-5.

[65] SHDDT: C15 5. Dossier 16 June 1815. Rapport 16 June 1815, dated 17 June 1815.

[66] Pétiet, p. 197.

[67] Aubry, p. 150.

[68] SHDDT: C15 5. Dossier 17 June.

[69] This is an error, it is actually General Girard according to Thomas Aubry.

[70] AN: LH 2337/47.

[71] SHDDT: C15 5. Dossier 17 June.

[72] SHDDT: C15 5. Dossier 17 June.

[73] SHDDT: GR 24 YC 299.

[74] SHDDT: C15 5. Dossier 16 June, Domon to Soult.

[75] See http://www.waterloo-campaign.nl/bestanden/files/notes/june16/note.3.pdf.

Chapter 5

Excelman's Dragoons

Rémy-Joseph-Isidore Excelmans joined the army as a volunteer in 1791, joining the 3rd Battalion of the Meuse. Thus, began a long and distinguished career as a cavalry officer of merit. After Napoléon's abdication, he was made inspector-general of cavalry of the 1st Military Division and a Knight of Saint Louis by the Bourbon government. In December 1814, he was arrested for communicating with the enemy, but managed to escape and fled to Lille, where he went before a council of war presided over by General Drouet d'Erlon. The council acquitted him unanimously on 23 January 1815. In March 1815, General Excelmans began to make contact with officers on half-pay, rallying them to Napoléon's cause. For his loyalty, Napoléon made him a Peer of France. In May 1815, he was placed in command of the 2nd Cavalry Corps. About Ligny, Excelmans writes:[1]

> The 2nd Corps of Cavalry supported the movement onto the plateau, when an entirely masked battery of thirty-five pieces opened fire. Excelmans had only twelve pieces with which to respond, and was commanded by Colonel Husson who worked wonders.
>
> At around five o'clock in the evening, eight or ten Prussian battalions advanced, supported by artillery on the right of the 2nd Corps, to gain two positions to pass the ravine and the river which separated them from us. Excelmans ordered a division supported by a battery of artillery to be deployed against this advance, but two enemy divisions retired on Sombreffe. He then moved to Tongrines to defend the place and the passage of the ravine.
>
> At the same time, General Hulot, from the corps of General Gérard, had arrived at the head of his brigade and stopped the enemy passing the river.
>
> The sun began to set when General Excelmans recognised a strong column of cavalry that was placed in front of him, located on the

heights which were south of Saint-Fiacre. He prepared his dispositions. As the column presented itself along the road it was met by the fire of canister shot from three pieces of artillery placed on the road, at the same time the fire was joined by the remainder of the artillery placed twenty-two metres to the rear. At that moment, the 5th Dragoons, placed in a fold of the terrain in support, deployed at the trot and then at the gallop under the orders of General Excelmans. The Prussian column was tumbled back; five artillery pieces were captured and were turned to fire upon the debris of the column.

A squadron under the orders of Commandant Letellier[2] filled with the ardour of pursuit, crossed the bridge and pursued the Prussians until they re-passed the heights.

The aide-de-camp to General Excelmans was Colin de Hams. He writes as follows:[3]

On 16 June at the Battle of Fleurus, I commanded in the capacity as aide-de-camp to General Excelmans. I lead a charge against Marshal Blücher and we gained the bridge at Sombreffe. There we captured six pieces of cannon. How we were not pushed back and managed to escape was nothing short of a miracle.

General Pierre Bonnemains, in his report of 17 June, confirms the capture of artillery and sequence of events as outlined by Excelmans:[4]

The brigade of General Bonnemains formed the first line on the far right, *vis-à-vis* Sombreffe, and was for all the action exposed to a murderous fire of artillery and musketry. Twice the Prussian cavalry tried to charge on it, but despite the overwhelming force, General Bonnemains's brigade managed to reject them beyond the defile to Sombreffe, causing considerable loss among them.

For a third time towards the end of the day, the cavalry marched forward again with yet more forces than on previous occasions, and supported by an artillery battery. They were attacked by General Bonnemains charging their front, and were charged in the flank by a brigade of the division of General Stroltz. These charges were, as the first two, successful and resulted in repelling the enemy beyond the Ligny brook, and we captured their artillery.

The brigade had about two hundred men killed or wounded. Among the latter is found Colonel Bouquerot des Essarts, of the 4th Dragoons, and Lieutenant de Tilly, an aide to the general. The 4th and 12th Dragoons maintained their former reputation.

General-de-Brigade Baron André Burthe writes:[5]

> The 5th Regiment, commanded by Colonel Saint-Amand, occupied
> the right of the first line of the corps, protecting at the same time its
> artillery, which caused losses among the enemy. The 13th Regiment,
> commanded by Colonel Saviot, was a gunshot away and observed
> a mass of Prussian cavalry preparing to charge. The movement had
> not escaped the vigilant eye of Comte Excelmans, who galloped to
> the head of the two regiments to better reconnoitre the enemy
> squadrons. The two enemy columns at the same time charged, one
> after the other with great intrepidness. The shock was violent and a
> melee ensued…the Prussian cavalry, despite their valour, slowly
> ceded ground and lost a good number of men and horses, and
> rallied behind their artillery for protection.
>
> The 5th and 13th Dragoons pursued with great impetuosity and
> fell like an avalanche on some concealed Prussian battalions, which
> could offer no resistance. Not content with these exploits, the
> dragoons silenced a battery and took five cannon. Sergeant Fremillot,
> of the elite company of the 5th Dragoons, was killed in the act of
> capturing a cannon. He was horribly mutilated by the discharge of
> canister that was fired at point-blank range. The virtuous soldier
> succumbed to his glorious wounds.
>
> Grenadier Brazé, of the same company, had the same fate. He
> crossed the enemy's first line in pursuit of a senior officer who he
> wanted to make prisoner, and was surrounded by thirty cavalry
> troops, who hacked at him and his horse. Despite this, he triumphed
> over these obstacles and Brazé endeavoured to escape, and was
> killed or wounded while trying to cross the Prussian line for a
> second time to re-join his regiment.

Burthe commanded the 1st Brigade of the 9th Cavalry Division under
General Stroltz. Also in action, it seems, was General Vincent's 2nd
Brigade, comprising the 15th and 20th Dragoons. The 20th Dragoons, led
forward by Colonel Comte Amand François, Baron Claude de
Bricqueville, attacked and destroyed a square of Prussian infantry and
carried away the accompanying artillery.[6]

Jean Baptiste Berton, commanding the 14th and 17th Dragoons under
the orders of General Chastel, who commanded the 10th Cavalry
Division, writes about these operations as follows:[7]

> We said above that the 4th and the 2nd Divisions of the corps was
> placed on the evening of the 15th at Heppignies, and was united with

the 3rd Corps to attack Saint-Amand. A division of the Young Guard was sent to be in reserve to the left of this village, along with the light cavalry of General Domon. A brigade of lancers, commanded by Marshal-du-Camp Colbert, was placed beyond these troops, to maintain communication with the left wing.

The 4th Corps was directed at Ligny with four regiments of cavalry, forming the division of General Maurin, to support the infantry to the right of Sombreffe, and to link with the corps of dragoons commanded by General Excelmans, which fell on Tongrénelle and opposite Tongrines; the corps of Pajol, which comprised six regiments of light cavalry, formed the extreme right of the army, to settle the affair along Orneau.

General François Toussaint was sent to examine the terrain and to occupy the right of the army in haste, where he only wanted to hold the Prussians, fearing that the enemy was in possession of the place. He deployed a battalion of the 50th Infantry Regiment, commanded by Colonel Lavigne (division under the command of Marshal-du-Camp Hulot), in a thicket on a small conical height, and between Tongrénelle and Tongrines beyond Ligny brook, to support the dragoons of Excelmans, who were, at all costs, to prevent the Prussians marching beyond Tongrénelle.

Their attempts to do so were rejected by several charges of the cavalry, took five guns, of which two were taken by the 5th Dragoons and three by the 13th Dragoons, which was commanded by Colonel Saviot.

The battalion of the 50th Infantry Regiment that had first seized Tongrines, which greatly alarmed the enemy, captured the village and then moved off to their left to Vilret, where there was a report of a large body of troops who had debouched at this point. The battalion commander had conducted himself throughout the day with so much intelligence and skill that I regret not knowing the name of the officer, for he was as brave and a good soldier. We could observe that the flanks of the first two points of attack were strongly directed against companies of the enemy.

So, on balance it seems that Stroltz charged to support 4th Corps.

Charge of the cavalry of the Imperial Guard

Sergeant de Mauduit, of the 1st Grenadiers, also mentions how the charge of the Guard heavy cavalry developed:[8]

A regiment of lancers went to attack the square of our 4th Regiment of Grenadiers, and took them to be a mobilised National Guard regiment as a result of their bizarre military uniform. A Prussian officer came forward and shouted at them that they should not risk to a useless defence against regular and seasoned troops, and finally he told them that they were to lay down their arms. But these proud soldiers were soon disillusioned, with their bodies and debris covering the approach to the square.

During this curious episode, which cost so dear to the Prussian Lancers...our regiment was halfway up the first hill, too busy to reform its divisions, when the horse grenadiers and the dragoon guards and the cuirassiers of General Delort defiled forward and re-formed at full speed, as if on parade, to complete the victory.

As these great squadrons passed us, we shouted 'long live the Guard! Bravo the Guard! Long live the grenadiers! Long live the dragoons!'

As the distance decreased, perhaps fifty yards off the square, the enemy executed a U-turn, and ran away under a hail of bullets.

The service squadrons, who that day were a squadron of horse grenadiers, a squadron of dragoons and a company of gendarmes, who had charged, almost at the same time as the grenadiers, began a continuation of the cavalry charge. A square of infantry tried to stop them, but was broken and cut up by the sabre. This attack allowed the pursued Prussian lancers to rally and to respond to the charge against our three squadrons, which, too few to sustain the shock, came to re-form behind our grenadiers who were always in front.

The Prussian lancers attacked them and, as the first time, turned around; the service squadrons resumed the charge with much vigour, and we never saw the enemy cavalry.

The Prussian cavalry was the 6th Uhlans, part of the 1st Corps cavalry brigade of General von Röder, under the command of Lieutenant-Colonel Baron Ludwig von Lützow.[9] Lützow attacked what he thought were mobilised National Guards, which were in fact the 4th Grenadiers. Two musket volleys fired at less than twenty metres dispersed the uhlans, killed or wounded seventy troopers, two sub-officers, eight lieutenants and three captains, and left Lützow a prisoner of the French after his horse was wounded.[10]

In support of the uhlans came a second wave of Prussian cavalry, comprising the 1st West Prussian Dragoon Regiment and the 2nd Kurmärk Landwehr Regiment.[11] Apparently stopped by a sunken lane and artillery fire, the attack was repulsed by a charge against their flank by the cuirassiers of French General Delort.[12] This incident made its way into the French official bulletin.[13] The grenadiers à cheval suffered the following losses:[14]

Squadron	Killed	Died of Wounds	Wounded	Missing
1st	0	0	2	0
2nd	1	0	2	0
3rd	0	0	1	0
4th	0	0	0	0
Total	1	0	5	0

The losses for the regiment were far lower than at Gilly, which implies the regiment did not see any major fighting on 16 June. The Empress Dragoons sustained casualties as follows:[15]

Squadron	Killed	Died of Wounds	Wounded	Missing
1st	1	0	8	0
2nd	0	0	4	0
3rd	1	0	1	0
4th	0	0	0	0
Total	2	0	13	0

The regiment lost fifteen men, far higher than the grenadiers à cheval. In the accompanying elite gendarmes, who also it seems participated in the charge, Captain Louis Joseph Dyonnet was promoted to squadron commander by the emperor for his valour in the action.[16] Killed in the elite gendarmes was Lieutenant Vienot.

Charge of the cuirassiers
The victory was decided by the attack of the cuirassiers. Michel Ordener, commanding the 1st Regiment of Cuirassiers, recounts the charge thusly.[17]

> When the sun began to fade on the horizon, we received orders to move. A total of eight regiments of cuirassiers began trotting to cross a portion of the battlefield, and turning towards the village of Ligny, we charged! The mass of Prussian infantry was in a moment overthrown and their cadavers filled the creek. However, Blücher reformed them and he put himself at the head of his last reserves of cavalry, and desperately attacked our squadrons. His efforts here came to nothing. Broken and prey to the most frightful disorder, his horsemen sought their salvation in flight, we pursued with our swords in their backs. Blücher fell under the feet of our horses: but

the night is dark, and unfortunately for France, this moment escaped our eyes. The loss of the division in the day at Ligny was about two hundred riders.

We have no further details for the operations of the 13th Cavalry Division at Ligny. Further archive research is needed to fully understand the role of the division in the days before Waterloo. Delort reported to General Milhaud, on 17 June 1815, that:[18]

The 14th Cavalry Division, after performing various movements, received the direct order of the emperor at about 6.30 in the evening to cross Ligny and pursue the enemy. Arriving on the heights overlooking the village, they met a large mass of Prussian cavalry, supported by infantry squares and several batteries of artillery.

Despite these obstacles, the 1st Squadron of the 5th Regiment, which had just arrived, headed by Marshal-du-Camp Farine and Colonel Frere, accompanied by their staff, charged with great vigour and, with all the impetuosity possible, the first line of enemy cavalry was quickly dispersed, leaving many dead on the battlefield.

A second line of cavalry came to the aid of the first. The 5th and 10th Cuirassiers charged and pushed back the second line with the same fearlessness, without being intimidated by the number of Prussian squadrons, three or four times greater than ours.

The enemy wanted to regain the plateau, on which I had just established myself on, to support the troops of the Imperial Guard. We became surrounded by the fire of musketry and artillery, and their cavalry threatened to charge us in front on the right flank and rear.

In this critical position, we charged in all directions: infantry squares were driven in, but my division came under a very deadly fire and were unable to enjoy all the advantages that we had obtained. Some prisoners, including a general officer of cavalry and a howitzer with horse team, remained in our power. This piece was captured by the 9th Cuirassiers. Colonel Frere and General Farine were seriously injured. I was wounded in the first charge, but with a slight sabre cut to the right arm.

I will send you, sir, by a special report, my losses in killed and wounded, and the names of officers, NCOs and soldiers who have distinguished themselves. I confine myself now to tell you that my division, in the midst of the keenest and well-sustained fire, remained steadfast, always facing the enemy and repelling them, whichever way it presented itself in the various charges executed at the end of the day.

General Delort continues, writing in 1820 that:[19]

> The village of Ligny was considered the crux of the battle, and had been taken and retaken four times. The French and the Prussians attached equal importance to the possession of it. It is in these bitter attacks, where so much blood was shed, that the brave General Girard found a glorious death. The French general was waiting, apparently, to deliver a decisive blow, his left wing was close to him, it was six o'clock, and the English army was assembled and already threatening our left.
>
> It was time to secure the victory by a vigorous attack. The infantry of the Guard, left hitherto in reserve, was ordered to take Ligny. The Guard, the elite of our heroes, had deployed at the entrance to the village and had seen the enemy off with all the valour that greatly distinguished them in battle. The division of cuirassiers of General Delort, composed of the 5th, 10th, 6th and 9th regiments, closely followed the fearless foot soldiers of the Guard.
>
> They quickly crossed Ligny, charged the Prussian squares posted on the heights overlooking the village and dispersed them. With the same momentum, they fell onto Blücher's cavalry, tumbling them back on all sides, covering the battlefield with their dead. The Prussian cavalry, led by Prince Blücher in person, returned several times to the charge. The cuirassiers moved forward and dispersed whatever troops they found. It is in these charges that Marshal Blücher was thrown from his horse, and he only escaped us as we did not recognise him.

Captain Descous,[20] of the 9th Cuirassiers, recounts the events of that day:[21]

> 16 June 1815, at Fleurus I served in the 5th Company of the 9th Regiment of Cuirassiers. After a forced march, we arrived on the field of battle and took position in front of our front line and faced the right wing of the Prussian army, commanded by Marshal Blücher. It was about eight o'clock in the evening.
>
> A while later, our regiment came under fire from enemy sharpshooters which were in front of a body of cavalry, which wounded men and horses. In an instant, we received the order to attack this cavalry. We charged the sharpshooters, which were in front of us, and the affair was decided in an instant, we then engaged in a charge, it was now when we came against two squadrons of hulans [sic Prussian lancers]. We began a serious melee, fought corps

to corps. In this action, the cuirassiers in my company's peleton fought with rare courage, and were commanded by the brave Sub-Lieutenant Gacon,[22] who showed prodigies of great valour. I was surrounded by a dozen hulans and had my horse killed under me from several lance thrusts, and I received several wounds, most of which were struck against my cuirass.

It seemed that I would inevitably succumb, being dismounted and without a horse and surrounded by hulans, when Cuirassier Combes[23] saved my life. He, with three of my comrades, allowed me to escape this terrible situation. They presented me with a horse taken from one of the dead Prussians, and in an instant I re-joined the charge.

The cavalry that remained before us, we tumbled back and they dispersed in a rout.

There remained in front of us several pieces of artillery, one of these, I can positively say, was captured by Cuirassier Combes, who killed the gunners who stood around the carriage.

Corporal Brig, of the 10th Cuirassiers, writes about his actions at Ligny:[24]

> I was admitted to the cuirassiers in 1811. I served with the 10th Cuirassiers during the campaign of 1812 in Russia, and that of 1815. At the Battle of Ligny I was promoted on the field of battle to sub-lieutenant, and made an Officer of the Legion of Honour by the Emperor Napoléon himself for capturing four artillery pieces.

The cuirassiers, it seems, captured either four or five pieces of cannon, and the 9th and 10th Cuirassiers had repulsed a body of Prussian lancers and light infantry. In the melee with the lancers, Captain Jean Claude Houdre, of the 10th Cuirassiers, was seriously wounded. He suffered some eleven wounds: seven lance thrusts and four sabre cuts.[25] About this action, the Prussian account is given by General Gneisenau:[26]

> Our soldiers fought with a bravery which equalled every expectation; their fortitude remained unshaken, because everyone retained his confidence in his own strength. On this day, Field Marshal Blücher had encountered the greatest dangers. A charge of cavalry, led on by himself, had failed, while that of the enemy was vigorously pursuing; a musket shot struck the field marshal's horse, the animal, far from being stopped in his career by this wound, began to gallop more furiously until it dropped down dead. The field marshal, stunned by the violent fall, lay entangled under the horse.

The enemy's cuirassiers, following up their advantage, advanced: our last horseman had already passed by the field marshal, an adjutant alone remained with him, and had just alighted, resolved to share his fate. The danger was great, but heaven watched over us, the enemy, pursuing their charge, passed rapidly by the field marshal without seeing him: the next moment, a second charge of our cavalry, having repulsed them, they again passed by him with the same precipitation, not perceiving him any more than they had done the first time. Then, but not without difficulty, the field marshal was disengaged from under the dead horse, and he immediately mounted a dragoon-horse.

Louis-Etienne Saint-Denis, otherwise known as the Mameluck Ali, narrates that:[27]

At nightfall, the emperor approached the village of Ligny. The artillery of the Guard had been, and still was, firing heavily at the other side of a ravine occupied by the Prussian army, when the head of the column of cuirassiers appeared. At the same moment, these brave troops plunged into the lane which divided the village in two, crossed the ravine, and fell upon the enemy. It had defiled before the emperor at a gallop. These gallant soldiers, whose squadrons followed one another rapidly, were full of enthusiasm and cried at the top of their lungs *'vive l'Empereur!'* which was heard far off. 'Spare your horses! Spare your horses!' the emperor never stopped telling them. 'You will need them later.' But the cuirassiers, paying no attention to the words which they heard, although they were repeated by Marshal Soult, still followed those who had preceded them. This march past the emperor, which took place to the light of cannon flashes and accompanied by their roar, was a magnificent spectacle. Brave cuirassiers! I still seem to see them brandishing their swords and rushing to the combat. How splendid you were! During the whole day, the enemy offered a strong resistance, but in the evening he was obliged to retreat, leaving many of his men on the field of battle.

Lieutenant Pontécoulant, of the Imperial Guard horse artillery, remembers the charge of the cuirassiers as follows: [28]

General Milhaud's cuirassier division crossed the brook separating the two armies, and attacked the village from the right and sabred both infantry and cavalry, who were advancing on Ligny, trying to unite with the troops already there. At the same time, another division of cuirassiers, supported by the mounted grenadiers of the Guard and the dragoons of General Excelmans, advanced to the left side of the village of Saint-Amand, crossed the ravine, forded the river, and then charged to their right, and swept away the Prussian masses that lined the slopes of the plateau of Brye, as well as the numerous batteries placed before both villages that had hitherto prevented our soldiers to advance. They made themselves masters of the guns. These charges were so impetuous and so well directed that several divisions of Prussian cavalry, which had been brought forward to try to stop them, were repulsed, and that Field Marshal Blücher, who had placed at their head, fell from his horse and was trampled under the horse's hooves of our cuirassiers…unfortunately, the night began to darken and it prevented us from recognising him. Though badly bruised he escaped on the horse of one of his escort of dragoons, who had dismounted to save his general.

About the cuirassiers, Prussian Lieutenant Hoeken wrote: [29]

We had been riding at a trot for some time when suddenly we saw a line of French cuirassiers about one hundred paces to our front. They greeted us with a salvo of carbine fire, and at that moment, our cavalry about-turned and rushed away. Although officers and men were screaming for everybody to halt, attempts to stop the flight were in vain, until all of us, myself included, got stuck in swampy ground.

Losses
Losses in Delort's cavalry were very low. The 5th Cuirassiers lost the following:[30]

	Killed	Died of Wounds	Wounded	Prisoner of War	Missing
Total	17	0	0	0	0

On 10 June, the 5th Cuirassiers mustered 469 other ranks. Of these, seventeen men are recorded killed, but we don't have any men listed wounded.

The losses of the brigaded 10th Cuirassiers are not known, as the regiment's muster lists seemingly included the losses of 16 June with those of 18 June.[31] However, losses for the 6th Cuirassiers were as below:[32]

Squadron	Killed	Died of Wounds	Wounded	Missing
1st	1	0	0	2
2nd	0	0	0	0
3rd	5	0	0	1
4th	1	0	2	0
Total	7	0	2	3

At Ligny, twelve men had been lost. On the morning of 10 June 1815, the regiment fielded twenty-two officers and 263 men. The losses, like with the 5th Cuirassiers, was minimal.

As with the 10th Cuirassiers, the losses of 16 June seem to be included in the losses for 18 June, assuming any men were killed or wounded.[33]

Aftermath of the battle
Marshal Soult wrote to Marshal Davout, the Minister of War in Paris, as follows about the victory:[34]

> Fleurus, 17 June 1815. Monsieur marshal, I announced yesterday, from the field of battle of Ligny, to His Imperial Highness Prince Joseph, the signal victory which the emperor has gained. I returned here with His Majesty at eleven o'clock in the evening, and it was necessary to pass the night in attending to the wounded. The emperor has remounted his horse to follow the success of the battle of Ligny. It was fought with fury and the greatest enthusiasm on the part of the troops. We were one to three.
>
> At eight o'clock in the evening, the emperor marched with his Guard: six battalions of the Old Guard, the dragoons, and horse grenadiers and the cuirassiers of General Delort debouched by Ligny, and executed a charge which separated the enemy's line. Wellington and Blücher saved themselves with difficulty: the effect was theatrical.
>
> In an instant the firing ceased, and the enemy was routed in all directions. We have already several thousand prisoners, and forty pieces of cannon. The 6th and 1st Corps were not engaged. The left wing fought against the English army, and captured some cannon and standards.
>
> Tonight, I will give you further details, for every instant prisoner are announced. Our loss does not appear enormous; since, without screening it, I do not reckon it at more than 3,000 men.

The official Prussian account of the battle notes:[35]

The battle began at three o'clock in the afternoon. The enemy brought up more than 130,000 men. The Prussian army was 80,000 strong. The village of Saint-Amand was the first point attacked by the enemy, who carried it after a vigorous resistance.

He then directed his efforts against Ligny. This is a large village, solidly built, situated on a rivulet of the same name. It was there that a contest began which may be considered as one of the most obstinate recorded in history. Villages have often been taken and retaken: but here the combat continued for five hours in the villages themselves; and the movements forwards or backwards were confined to a very narrow space. On both sides, fresh troops continually came up. Each army had behind the part of the village which it occupied great masses of infantry, which maintained the combat, and were continually renewed by reinforcements which they received from their rear, as well as from the heights on the right and left. About two hundred cannon were directed from both sides against the village, which was on fire in several places at once. From time to time, the combat extended through the line, the enemy having also directed numerous troops against the Third Corps; however, the main contest was near Ligny.

Things seemed to take a favourable turn for the Prussian troops, a part of the village of Saint-Amand having been retaken by a battalion commanded by the field marshal himself; in consequence of which advantage we had regained a height which had been abandoned after the loss of Saint-Amand. Nevertheless, the battle continued about Ligny with the same fury. The issue seemed to depend on the arrival of the English troops, or on that of the 4th Corps of the Prussian army; in fact, the arrival of this last division would have afforded the field marshal the means of making, immediately, with the right wing, an attack, from which great success might be expected: but news arrived that the English division destined to support us, was violently attached by a corps of the French army, and that it was with great difficulty it had maintained itself in its position at Quatre-Bras. The 4th Corps of the army did not appear, so that we were forced to maintain alone the contest with an army greatly superior in numbers. The evening was already much advanced, and the combat about Ligny continued with unremitting fury, and the same equality of success; we invoked, but in vain, the arrival of those succours which were so necessary; the danger became every hour more urgent; all the divisions were engaged, or had already been so, and there was not any corps at hand able to support them.

Napoléon's bulletin read:[36]

> The emperor's headquarters were at Charleroi, as were the Imperial Guard and the 6th Corps.
>
> The left wing had orders to march upon Quatre-Bras, and the right upon Sombreffe. The emperor advanced to Fleurus with his reserve.
>
> The columns of Marshal Grouchy were marching when they perceived, after having passed Fleurus, the enemy's army, commanded by Field Marshal Blücher, occupying with its left the heights of the mill of Bussy, the village of Sombreffe, and extending its cavalry a great way forward on the road to Namur; its right was at Saint-Amand, and occupied that large village in great force, having before it a ravine which formed its position.
>
> The emperor reconnoitred the strength and the positions of the enemy, and resolved to attack immediately. It became necessary to change front, the right in advance, and pivoting upon Fleurus.
>
> General Vandamme marched upon Saint-Amand, General Girard upon Ligny, and Marshal Grouchy upon Sombreffe. The 4th Division of the 2nd Corps, commanded by General Girard, marched in reserve behind the corps of General Vandamme. The Guard was drawn up on the heights of Fleurus, as well as the cuirassiers of General Milhaud.
>
> At three in the afternoon, these dispositions were finished. The division of General Lefol, forming part of the corps of General Vandamme, was first engaged and made itself master of Saint-Amand, whence it drove out the enemy at the point of the bayonet. It kept its ground during the whole of the engagement, at the burial-ground and steeple of Saint-Amand; but that village, which is very extensive, was the theatre of various combats during the evening; the whole corps of General Vandamme was there engaged, and the enemy there fought in considerable force. General Girard, placed as a reserve to the corps of General Vandamme, turned the village by its right, and fought there with its accustomed valour. The respective forces were supported on both sides by about fifty pieces of cannon each.
>
> On the right, General Girard came into action with the 4th Corps at the village of Ligny, which was taken and retaken several times.
>
> Marshal Grouchy, on the extreme right, and General Pajol fought at the village of Sombreffe. The enemy showed from 80,000 to 90,000 men, and a great number of cannon.
>
> At seven o'clock we were masters of all the villages situate on the bank of the ravine, which covered the enemy's position; but he still occupied, with all his masses, the heights of the mill of Bussy.

The emperor returned with his Guard to the village of Ligny; General Girard directed General Pecheux to debouch with what remained of the reserve, almost all the troops having been engaged in that village.

Eight battalions of the Guard debouched with fixed bayonets, and behind them, four squadrons of the Guards, the cuirassiers of General Delort, those of General Milhaud, and the grenadiers of the horse guards. The Old Guard attacked the enemy's columns with the bayonet, which were on the heights of Bussy, and in an instant covered the field of battle with dead. The squadron of the Guard attacked and broke a square, and the cuirassiers repulsed the enemy in all directions. At half-past nine o'clock we had forty pieces of cannon, several carriages, colours, and prisoners, and the enemy sought safety in a precipitate retreat. At ten o'clock the battle was finished, and we found ourselves masters of the field of battle.

General Lützow, a partisan, was taken prisoner. The prisoners assure us that Field Marshal Blücher was wounded. The flower of the Prussian army was destroyed in this battle. Its loss could not be less than 15,000 men. Ours was 8,000 killed and wounded.

On the left, Marshal Ney had marched on Quatre-Bras with a division, which cut in pieces an English division which was stationed there; but being attacked by the Prince of Orange with 25,000 men, partly English, partly Hanoverians in the pay of England, he retired upon his position at Frasné. There a multiplicity of combats took place; the enemy obstinately endeavoured to force it, but in vain. The Duc d'Elchingen waited for the 1st Corps, which did not arrive until night; he confined himself to maintaining his position. In a square attacked by the 8th Regiment of Cuirassiers, the colours of the 69th Regiment of English infantry fell into our hands. The Duke of Brunswick was killed. The Prince of Orange has been wounded. We are assured that the enemy had many personages and generals of note killed or wounded; we estimate the loss of the English at from 4,000 to 5,000 men; ours on this side was very considerable, it amounts to 4,200 killed or wounded. The combat ended with the approach of night. Lord Wellington then evacuated Quatre-Bras and proceeded to Genappe.

As the Battle of Ligny ended, odd pockets of Prussian troops that had not been totally disorganised in the fleeing mass of Prussian troops formed patches of resistance. The French had hoped to drive a wedge to separate the main Prussian field force and the command of Thielemann, located at Tongrénelle and Tongrines (to the east of Ligny itself), which had partially succeeded. The village of Brye, to the west of Ligny, was still in Prussian hands. Three battalions under the command of Jagow remained there until around 3.00. Between the two villages, Ligny was firmly in French control. Sporadic fighting, it seems, flared up during the early hours of 17 June. At Frasné, near Quatre-Bras, fighting broke out at around the same time as Brye was evacuated. The French outposts along the heights north of the Delahutte Wood exchanged fire with some Brunswick troops, and also at the Bossu Wood.[37]

Ligny: a summary

The combined arms operations of the Guard at Ligny had been superb. The Prussians had been forced back, but had not been annihilated. At 21.30, Lobau's 6th Army Corps passed through Ligny and took up position on the plateau of the Brye mill. On the battlefield, the band of the 1st Grenadiers of the Old Guard played *Victoire est a nous*. The Young Guard and the exhausted infantry of Vandamme and Gérard's corps set up bivouacs on the battlefield. The Prussian cavalry outposts were within range of the muskets of the French outposts guards. Some French battalions bivouacked drawn up in squares with one rank under arms.

However, General Delort notes that the battle was not a total victory for the French and claims that the attack on the centre of the Prussians was too late, and if all of Milhaud's division had attacked, then the outcome would have been more in the favour of the French. As it was, the 2nd Division of Milhaud's command was left in reserve, while Delort's command was left exposed with no support, and suffered greatly as a consequence.[38]

The view that Ligny was not a great victory for the French was shared by a general officer on Napoléon's staff, who writes the following about the battle, and the failure to cripple the Prussian army:[39]

> The Prussians abandoned their beautiful positions and withdraw in good order on the road to Namur; Marshal Grouchy followed them with his cavalry, but not strongly enough to cut off the road and their retreat.

Adjutant-Commandant Etienne Fulegence Janin, the serving assistant chief-of-staff of 6th Corps (commanded by General Mouton), reports the incident as follows:[40]

> They [the Prussians] remained at Gembloux and Wavre, we were advancing in that direction, and they fell back easily and without any

obstacles, and indeed on the 16th, after darkness had fallen, their army was still present: the dragoon guards, advancing on our right, were received by a brisk fire, and around midnight the Prussian cavalry tried to cut up our bivouacs, which, as at Lutzen, had no other purpose than to hide the movements of the enemy.

Ligny was not a clear-cut victory for the French, but it had badly mauled the Prussian army, which Napoléon believed was now in full retreat back to Namur and would take no further part in the campaign. Napoléon then turned his attention to the troops of Wellington. He was wrong in his summary of the results of the battle. The French army was as badly mauled as the Prussians, Girard's command taking no part in the remainder of the campaign due to horrific losses at Ligny—a high price to pay for a stalemate.

The recorded French wounded for Ligny were presented in a report made on the morning of 17 June by Marshal-du-Camp Antoine Joseph Claude Le Bel, who was assistant chief-of-staff serving under Lieutenant-General François Gedeon Bailly de Monthion. Le Bel writes:[41]

There exists in the town of Fleurus five ambulances, of which one is for the Imperial Guard.

Ambulance of the Imperial Guard:		
Officers	2	
Sub-officers and solders	55	57
In the four other ambulances:		
Officers	78	
Sub-officers and soldiers	1,521	1,599
Total		1,666
Evacuated to Charleroi:		
Officers	33	
Sub-officers and soldiers	387	420
Total wounded listed at this time		2,076

All the wounded listed here are those that have been taken in, more may be received during the morning.

The ambulances of the headquarters are missing doctors and infirmiers.

The marshal-du-camp

Commandant headquarters staff

Le Bel.

In a letter from Comte Daure, dated 17 June 1815, concerning the wounded, he noted that around 1,600 had been taken to the five ambulance posts, 800 wounded holders of the Legion of Honour had been sent to Charleroi, and a further 800 wounded at the time the letter was written to Soult were being taken to the ambulances.[42] This inflates the number of recovered wounded from Ligny to 3,676 men, which makes approximately 10 per cent of the men in the regiments.

The recovered casualties seem remarkably low. On 10 June 1815, 3rd Corps mustered 15,114 other ranks. A total of 2,964 men were killed, wounded or missing where the recorded data exists; 3rd Corps lost 19.6 per cent of effective strength at Ligny. In basic figures, 4th Corps lost 4,690 men from the 12th, 13th and 14th Divisions from 16 to 21 June— a loss of 40 per cent of effective strength. We don't know the breakdown for 16 and 18 June, but it seems likely that the vast majority were lost at Ligny, given 3rd Corps lost fewer than 500 men at Wavre.[43] Grouchy's command had lost around 7,000 men from 3rd and 4th Corps at Ligny. Theoretically, on 10 June Grouchy's command mustered 38,772 officers and men, of which 36,972 were infantry and foot artillery and 5,186 were cavalry and horse artillery. This gave Grouchy 29,869 infantry, of which 7,000 were lost on 16 June, leaving him with 22,869 infantry in theory.

Without more research, we won't be able to assess the total French loss in the battle. But based on the recorded losses for 3rd Corps, the Armée du Nord lost around 30 per cent effective strength. Conspicuous among the dead and wounded was the high number of officers. Lack of command and control due to dead or wounded officers and NCOs, as well as demoralised men, was to have a major contributing factor in the battlefield performance of the 3rd and 4th Corps over the days to come.

NOTES:
[1] Jean-Jacques Pattyn, personal communication, 16 October 2012, citing Touchot, *Personnalle Correspondence Au General Excelmans*.
[2] AN: LH 1620/22. Jules Letellier was born on 18 May 1777. He became adjutant of military transports on 28 September 1793, driver 2nd class on 28 October 1794, and administrator on 22 May 1795. He was admitted to the 5th Dragoons on 1 November 1798 and promoted to corporal on 30 June 1799, to fourier on 18 August 1799, to sergeant on 28 May 1800, to sergeant-major on 28 August 1800, to sub-lieutenant on 7 February 1803, to lieutenant on 24 March 1807, to captain on 29 June 1810, and to squadron commander on 19 September 1813. He was discharged on 5 December 1815. He was awarded the Legion of Honour on 1 October 1807 and made an Officer of the Legion of Honour on 18 May 1815.
[3] Jean-Jacques Pattyn, personal communication, 16 October 2012.
[4] SHDDT: C15 5. Dossier 16 June 1815. Extract of a letter dated 3 July 1815. Extract made 24 January 1845.
[5] de Mauduit, Vol. 2, pp. 204-6.
[6] AN: LH 367/78.
[7] Berton, p. 15.
[8] de Mauduit, Vol. 2, p. 94.

[9] Ollech, p. 160.

[10] Ollech, p. 155.

[11] Wagner, Vol. 4, p. 50.

[12] Andrew Uffindell, *The Eagle's Last Triumph: Napoleon's Victory at Ligny, June 1815*, Greenhill Books, London, 1994, p. 112. See also: Wagner, p. 50.

[13] John Booth, *The Battle of Waterloo, also of Ligny, and Quarter-Bras*, London, 1817, pp. 255-6.

[14] SHDDT: GR 20 YC 137.

[15] SHDDT: GR 20 YC 154 *registre matricule Dragons Garde Impériale*.

[16] AN: LH 887/64. Dyonnet was born on 27 August 1774 at Bourg-de-Peage. He enrolled as a volunteer in the 91st Regiment of Line Infantry on 8 July 1791 before passing to the 4th Regiment of Foot Artillery on 1 September 1792, and then to the gendarmes on 28 November 1793. He was promoted to corporal on 15 May 1798, to sergeant on 18 December 1799, to sergeant-major on 22 December 1800, to second lieutenant-quartermaster on 31 October 1801, to first lieutenant on 30 May 1805, and to captain on 28 September 1809. He was then admitted to the Paris gendarmes on 21 May 1813, then as captain to the elite gendarmes of the Imperial Guard on 23 April 1815. He was discharged on 16 April 1816, but re-admitted to the army on 16 October 1816, before retiring on 1 August 1821.

[17] Lot.

[18] Delort, '*Notice sur la batailles de Fleurus et de Mont Saint Jean*' in *Revue Hebdomadaire*, June 1896, pp. 371-3.

[19] Delort, pp. 370-1.

[20] Captain Joseph Henry Descous was born on 23 September 1767. He had enlisted into the 4th Cuirassiers on 3 February 1785, and was promoted to corporal on 1 January 1788. He was appointed as an officer in the National Guard on 1 October 1790 and passed to the mounted gendarmes on 11 June 1792. He became a gendarme d'ordonnance to Napoléon on 3 October 1806, and promoted to corporal on 6 December 1806 and to sergeant on 4 April 1807. With the force disbanded, he was admitted into the 2nd Regiment of Carabiniers with the rank of lieutenant on 22 May 1808 and then to the 9th Cuirassiers, when his squadron was disbanded on 16 August 1810, with the rank of lieutenant. He was promoted to captain on 9 August 1812.

[21] Author's collection, letter dated 30 September 1850.

[22] AN: LHJ 1050/30. Philibert Gacon was born on 27 March 1784 and admitted into the 11th Cuirassiers on 31 May 1805. He was promoted to corporal on 15 December 1807 and to sergeant on 13 April 1809. He was then incorporated into the 13th Cuirassiers on 1 January 1810 and promoted to sergeant-major on 1 March 1812, to sub-lieutenant on 27 August 1813, before being incorporated into the 9th Cuirassiers on 9 August 1814 with the rank of sub-lieutenant. He was taken into the cuirassiers du Dauphin on 21 May 1818 and awarded the Legion of Honour on 25 April 1821. He was discharged on 10 August 1821.

[23] Cuirassier Jean Combes was born on 2 October 1782, and had been admitted to the 7th Regiment of Cuirassiers on 1 December 1807. He was taken into the 13th Cuirassiers on 18 October 1808, and served with the regiment during the Peninsular War. With the disbandment of the regiment in 1814, he was admitted to the 9th Regiment of Cuirassiers on 9 August 1814. He remained in the army following the Second Restoration, and served in the cuirassiers until he passed to the grenadiers à cheval of the Royal Guard on 20 October 1821. When the Royal Guard was disbanded in 1830 he was placed on half-pay, and finally retired on 1 February 1839.

[24] Author's collection.

[25] AN: LH 1311/4.

[26] Ian Smith, personal communication.

[27] Mameluck Ali, *Souvenirs sur l'empereur Napoléon*, Ed. Christophe Bourachot, Arléa, Paris, 2000.

[28] Pontécoulant, *Souvenirs militaires*, pp. 103-4.

[29] Peter Hofschröer, *1815: The Waterloo Campaign*, Greenhill, London, 1998, p. 327.

30 SHDDT: GR 24 YC 36.
31 SHDDT: GR 24 YC 60 *Controle Nominiatif Troupe 10e Cuirassiers 15 Avril 1815-27 Juillet 1815 organisation 1814.*
32 SHDDT: GR 24 YC 41.
33 SHDDT: GR 24 YC 55.
34 *Cobbett's Political Register,* 24 June 1815.
35 Booth, *The Battle of Waterloo,* 1816, pp. 89-91.
36 Ian Smith, personal communication, 1 March 2012.
37 Peter Hofschröer, *Waterloo 1815 Quatre Bras and Ligny,* Pen & Sword, Barnsley, 2006, pp. 94-6.
38 Delort, p. 239.
39 *Nouvel Revue Rétrospective,* January 1896, p. 367.
40 Janin, p. 26.
41 SHDDT: C15 5. Dossier 17 June 1815, *Rapport du 17 Juin.*
42 SHDDT: C 15 5. Dossier 17 June 1815. Daure to Soult.
43 SHDDT: C15 35 *Situations Armée du Nord 1815. Dossier 4e Corps.*

Chapter 6

Morning of 17 June 1815

Napoléon's action plan for the morning of the 17th was to firstly find out where the Prussians had gone to, since contact with them had been lost during the night, and to drive them away from Wellington, and secondly, to find out how Ney had fared, and to send him help if he needed it.

Sometime after midnight, Pajol had been sent off in pursuit, as an officer on the general staff recounts the campaign to date:[1]

> This morning (the 17th) the cavalry of General Pajol is gone in pursuit of the Prussians upon the road to Namur. They are already two and a half leagues in advance of this place; whole bands of prisoners are taken. They do not know what has become of their commanders. The rout is complete on our side, and I hope we shall not so soon hear again of the Prussians, if they should ever be able to rally at all.
>
> As for the English, we shall see now what will become of them. The emperor is here.

Napoléon sent the following order to Ney at 9.00:[2]

> It is His Majesty's intentions that you take up a position at Quatre-Bras, as you were ordered; but if it is not possible, which seems unlikely, then send a detailed report immediately, and the emperor will manoeuvre in your direction. If on the contrary there is only a rearguard, drive them off and occupy the position.

Pursuit of the Prussians and containing Wellington were just two items occupying Napoléon's mind on the morning of 17 June. Care of the dead and wounded, it seems, was as paramount on that morning as finding Blücher. Marshal Soult wrote to Marshal Davout on 17 June 1815 that he spent the previous night:[3]

> Amidst the wounded as the ambulances were poorly organised, and that due to a lack of personal and other items that are indispensable and cannot be fully completed in time.

Indeed, the burial of the dead and treatment of the wounded was listed as one of the key objectives for the day by Napoléon:[4]

> Today is required for the completion of this operation [attacking Wellington's troops], filling up ammunition and gathering stragglers and detachments. Give the necessary orders, and see that the wounded are sent to the rear.

Napoléon's mind was also pre-occupied about a possible invasion into northern France, and noted that escorting prisoners was a major drain on his manpower in the field:[5]

> Our losses have not been that great, on the contrary they were slight, no more than 3,000 men killed, therefore at the moment it is only necessary to levee 200,000 troops. I therefore order that no more than ten battalions are to be used to garrison the 16th Military Division, the rest are to be sent to the camp at Avesnes to escort the prisoners.

In more mundane matters in Vandamme's 3rd Corps, men were promoted to new ranks to fill vacancies caused by battlefield losses. Early on the morning of 17 June, Vandamme was stationed at Saint-Amand. Assistant chief-of-staff, Battalion Commander Nicolas Marie Guyardin, wrote to General Berthezène with orders from Vandamme, which he received at six o'clock in the morning:[6]

> Saint-Amand 17 June 1815
> Monsieur the lieutenant-general,
> His Excellency General-in-Chief Comte Vandamme requests that without delay you send fifteen men to escort the convoy of rations to be at the disposition of the M. ordonnateur-in-chief. These men will go from Saint-Amand and will assemble at the church where the orders will be given for them to follow behind the convoy of rations and sundries from Charleroi, and will pass the heights of Fleurus.

During the day of 17 June, the staff of 3rd Corps was re-organised. In the battle of the 16th, Adjutant-Commandant Camille Alphonse Trezel was seriously wounded with a gunshot to the left ear during the capture of the village of Saint-Amand.[7] To this end, Battalion Commander Guyardin was named assistant chief-of-staff:[8]

> Order of the Day,
>
> The 3rd Corps which previously had M. Colonel Trezel as assistant chief-of-staff, has been grievously wounded, M. Lieutenant-Colonel Guyardin has replaced his functions until Marshal-du-Camp Revert arrives, as he has been delayed in joining us.
>
> Additional Order:
>
> The corps is to send to the staff their reports for the affair of the previous day.
>
> Additional Order:
>
> The army corps are to send their dispatches to the generals commanding their divisions, who will then send the letters to the chief of the general staff. They are to make sure that they are all collected and transmitted.
>
> The general headquarters at Saint-Amand 17 June 1815
>
> By order of the general-in-chief
>
> Lieutenant-colonel, the assistant chief of headquarters staff to 3rd Corps
>
> Guyardin.

The Prussians

As a result of the French breakthrough at Ligny, the Prussian 1st and 2nd Corps headed north, and had its bivouacs around the villages of Tilly and Gentinnes. At daybreak, around 4.00, the two corps began to move north towards Wavre. At the same time, the Prussian 3rd Corps which had remained on the field, together with 4th Corps, moved off east and reached Gembloux around 6.00. Clausewitz notes:[9]

> The 1st and 2nd Corps reached Wavre at midday on the 17th and then took their positions on both sides of the Dyle, having left part of their cavalry as a rearguard a few hours march behind them. The 3rd Corps remained at Gembloux until 2 p.m. and then proceeded towards Wavre, where it did not arrive until evening. The 4th Corps spent the night of the 16th in Haute- and Bas-Bodecé, two hours march behind Gembloux, and then during the 17th went to Dion-le-Mont, where it deployed to receive the other corps.

Captain Fritz, commanding a squadron of Westphalian Landwehr cavalry, attached to Jagow's infantry brigade, writes:[10]

> In very bad weather we set off again in the morning to cross the Dyle. The mood of the troops was certainly grave, but not in the least disheartened, and even if one could have detected that we were on a retreat rather than a victory march, the bearing of all but a few isolated units was very good. 'We have lost once, but the game is not up, and tomorrow is another day' remarked a Pomeranian soldier to his neighbour who was grumbling, and was quite right. The firm bearing of the army owed not a little to the cheerful spirit and freshness of our seventy-four year old field marshal. He had had his bruised limbs bathed in brandy and had helped himself to a large schnapps; and now, although riding must have been very painful, he rode alongside the troops exchanging jokes and banter with many of them, and his humour spread like wildfire down the columns. I only glimpsed the old hero ride quickly past, although I should dearly have like to have expressed to him my pleasure of his fortunate escape.
>
> Even my Westphalian Landwehr riders did not lose their good bearing. But in the rain many new saddles swelled, and the troops, as young riders often do, sat unsteadily and lolled about during the march, with the unfortunate result that I soon had a number of horses with saddle sores. I carried out a thorough inspection and anyone who had a horse in this condition was ordered to dismount and carry his portmanteaux on his back, and then go splashing through thick and thin on foot beside us.

Cavalry operations

When the Prussians were defeated at Ligny, the advantage of vigorous pursuit with all the available cavalry and Lobau's corps would have been enormous. The whole aim of Napoléon's strategy had been to crush the Prussians and to prevent them from interfering with his attack on Wellington. He had found Blücher ready to fight at Ligny and he had beaten him, but had not delivered the terminal knockout blow he needed due to the blundering of Ney and dithering of d'Erlon. To allow Blücher to retreat with fighting power left in his army was to be avoided at all cost. Vandamme's 3rd Corps, Gérard's 4th Corps, and Milhaud's cuirassiers were exhausted after a hard-fought contest in their vigorous attacks against the Prussians, and were in no condition to pursue. However, Excelmans and Pajol, with their two cavalry corps, and Lobau with the 6th Corps, were available for the pursuit.

Their troops were comparatively fresh; Lobau had only arrived on the field towards the end of the day. But no attempt was made to hinder the retreat of Ziethen and Pirch. Thielemann maintained a firm hold on Sombreffe, but he did not cover Brye or the roads to Tilly. Thielemann's rearguard did not begin to retreat until after sunrise, and when day broke the French were still in their bivouacs and the vedettes had not noticed any untoward movement by the Prussians. There seemed to be a fixed resolve to let the Prussians go free.

At Ligny, the Prussian right wing had not been crushed; it retreated because its position was dangerous as soon as the centre had given way after the assault by the Imperial Guard infantry, bolstered by the heavy cavalry of the Imperial Guard and Milhaud's cuirassiers. The left wing, formed by Thielemann's corps, remained in its position.

Sent off south was General Pajol with three regiments of hussars. Claude-Pierre Pajol was the son of a lawyer from Besançon and began his military career in August 1791, when he joined the 1st Battalion of Volunteers of Doubs.

At 3.00, Pajol sent a dispatch to headquarters about the movement of the Prussians. We are not sure when the dispatch arrived with Grouchy and headquarters, perhaps 5.00 or later, nor its exact contents as the original is now lost. We only know about its existence from a second dispatch from Pajol to Grouchy. In response to Pajol's information, General Teste's infantry division and artillery was sent to support him, along with it, seems, Berton's brigade of dragoons. Whoever ordered the cavalry to follow the Prussians south remains a mystery, as does why it was felt the Prussians were heading south, and only south. But the measure was clearly approved of by Napoleon. We must stress that the move to Namur was not part of Grouchy's mission. His mission was separate to that of Pajol's.

We must emphasise that although Pajol spoke of Prussian forces retreating upon Saint-Denis and Leuze, this information proved to be incorrect. Furthermore, in no way can Pajol's moves be considered a pursuit; its entire purpose was an attempt to locate the enemy rather than the pursuit of the defeated Prussians after a successful battle. Pajol's second dispatch has thankfully survived. At midday on 17 June, Pajol sent word to Grouchy:[11]

> In front of Massy, 17 June 1815 at midday.
> General Pajol to Marshal Grouchy
> I had the honour to send this morning at three o'clock my aide-de-camp, Dumoulin, to inform you that the enemy had evacuated their positions at half-past two, and in consequence I put myself in motion.

Since then, I am able to notify you I found the column before this village, and in consequence charged them. In doing so, eight pieces of cannon and a huge number of baggage carts, fodder wagons, etc. as well as their horses were captured.

The enemy continued their retreat towards Saint-Denis and Leuze to gain the road from Namur to Louvain and still have a great number of cannon and munitions despite what was left at the first town. They retired on the same road, along which I put in motion the division of Teste, which His Majesty had sent to me last night, to search behind Leuze and also along the Namur road to Louvain, which I think is where they are retreating.

If you please monsignour, send orders addressed to me along this road.

I have with me the artillery from Subervie's division; the remainder of the division is united and rests under the orders of Soult.

Please accept, Your Excellency, my assured respect

Signe Comte Pajol.

Clearly in the early hours of the 17th, Pajol and the infantry division of General Teste headed off in pursuit of the Prussians. Mazy stands almost due east from Ligny, a journey across country of around ten miles, about an hour ride from the field of battle. It is, however, likely that the Prussians retreated via Sombreffe to gain the Namur road to head south. We assume Pajol had sent off companies or squadrons in all directions to search for the Prussians, and only once contact had been made did he move the division towards Mazy in force. Pajol seems to be totally unaware that rather than heading east, the bulk of the Prussians had in fact headed north-east. This was to have a major impact on the day's events.

Due the emperor's fixation about Namur, Pajol's forces initially missed the Prussian forces near Gembloux and for that reason the action cannot be considered a real pursuit. Pajol had found some Prussians, but clearly not enough to be the defeated army of Ligny. With Pajol heading east and south, with three of the five light cavalry regiments assigned to Grouchy, as well as Berton's dragoons, Grouchy had no option but send out Excelmans's dragoons.

General Berton, commanding one of Excelmans's dragoon brigades, writes:[12]

From the morning of the 17th, the light cavalry of General Pajol began its advance on the road to Namur; they took ten guns and a lot of baggage belonging to the enemy, after having slashed and dispersed the hussars that escorted it.

I commanded a brigade of dragoons from Excelmans's corps and I was sent as head of the column behind the light cavalry for support when needed, I went past La Barrière, a village on the road, passing between Orneau and Gembloux, and I learned there, from the inhabitants, a large body of enemy cavalry had passed through along this road at night with wagons and in great disorder, but also that the Prussian army withdrew to Wavre, and there were still many troops in Gembloux. I reported this information, and in consequence I received orders to carry me onwards to Gembloux. I was before the town with my brigade, at nine in the morning, when, accompanied by the general, we saw a Prussian corps, which we judged to be more than 20,000 men bivouacked in the rear, with a line of vedettes in before him in the direction of Orneau. It was evidently the rearguard charged with protecting his retreating columns.

Berton marched from his position through Potriaux to the Namur road and there turned east. In front of Orneau, near La Barrière (400 metres west of Mazy), Berton learned from peasants that Prussian cavalry had passed there during the night and that a large Prussian force would be near Gembloux. As a result, Berton halted his troops in front of Orneau and, we assume, reported to Excelmans. Pajol was on the other side of Mazy, but it seems Berton was not aware of this.

Was Berton's information sent back to Grouchy? Houssaye thinks not. It would be an incredible lapse of judgement if headquarters were not informed, and yet Grouchy got no orders to move to Gembloux until after 13.00. By the time he set off, Gembloux was starting to be evacuated by the Prussians. From his position, south of Gembloux, likely to have been between the farm of Chênemont and the farm of Aimonts, Berton observed the Prussian 3rd Corps north of Gembloux and Sauvenière, having its outposts on Orneau. As soon as Excelmans was informed by Berton about the Prussian presence near Gembloux, he moved out to join him, and wrote to Grouchy. This dispatch is now lost, along with the bulk of material relating to Excelmans in the campaign.

Berton's observations were vital in helping to find the Prussians. Frederic Gautier, writing in 1827, presumably from talking to veterans or serving in the French army in 1815, concurs noting that:[13]

General Berton had found in the early morning that the bulk of the Prussian army had retreated to Wavre. He was ordered to pursue with his brigade of dragoons (14th and 17th regiments) to Gembloux, where he arrived about nine o'clock in the morning and was able to observe the army corps of Bülow, which was still in position behind Orneau. Shortly after, General Chastel arrived there with Bonnemains's brigade (the 4th and 12th regiments), and when about two o'clock the army corps of Bülow was seen to begin to retire towards Sart-a-Walhain and Tourines, Chastel's division crossed the town after the enemy.

Presumably Berton's report and Pajol's 12.00 dispatch made it clear that a body of the Prussians was heading south and another east to Maastricht. In response to this news, Napoléon now set in motion the pursuit. The emperor could not issue orders until he was sure in his own mind where the Prussians were going.

The facts of the case tell us that by midday Napoléon knew 40,000 Prussians were heading to Wavre, a point we discuss in detail later, and 40,000 were at Gembloux. Yet, he did not issue orders until after 13.00. A tragic mistake had been made by the emperor. If, upon receipt of Berton's report, infantry had been sent up with Excelmans, then the Prussian 3rd Corps would have been caught and destroyed. Yet on the morning of 17 June, as we shall see, pursuit was far from the emperor's mind.

About the movements of the cavalry reserve, Biot, aide-de-camp to General Pajol, relates that:[14]

> The general finally decided to send out a reconnaissance patrol, with orders to reconnoitre Sombreffe and push up the road from Nivelles to Namur. It is only the start of this discovery, it seems, we now knew the true direction taken by the enemy in his retreat. General Pajol immediately notified the emperor, noting he was riding to follow the trail of the Prussians. General Ameil, with the 5th Hussars, formed the vanguard. I was ordered to accompany him. We took the road to Namur, by which, presumably, the enemy had retired. We actually saw, at some distance, fragments of their artillery park that we captured. It consisted of twelve or fifteen cannon and ammunition caissons. We learned, from the prisoners, that the Prussians followed for some time after the Namur road, and then moved to the left, following a side road leading to Gembloux.

Confirming Pajol's operations is a short note written by Colonel Baron Jean Baptiste Liègeard, commanding the 5th Hussars, dated 2 July 1815:[15]

The 5th Hussars, on the day after the affair of Fleurus, captured from the enemy eight pieces of cannon as well as their ammunition wagons, which were magnificently harnessed, along with eighty or ninety baggage wagons, fifty prisoners. They also brought back numerous other munitions wagons and their horse teams, which were later deposited in the arsenal of Paris. The cannons were presented to the emperor at Fleurus in the afternoon of the 17th.

A note written by Squadron Commander Andre Louis Joseph Marie Brucco de Sordeval, of the 5th Hussars, further confirms this: [16]

17 June 1815, he was ordered with his squadron to charge an enemy column as it retired on the road to Namur. He fell on it with such impetuosity that he was able to put to them to flight. As a result, he captured many prisoners, captured six pieces of artillery, numerous ammunition caissons and more than a hundred baggage wagons, which earned him the praise of the general under whom he served.

So, it seems that the vanguard of the 5th Hussars did indeed capture the Prussian guns as Pajol says. However, Liègeard and Pajol mention eight cannon and de Sordeval six; the number of baggage wagons also differs. But, either way Pajol had found some Prussians. The Prussians admit to the loss of six field guns commanded by Captain Fritz.[17]
Biot, aide-de-camp to General Pajol, commanding the 1st Reserve Cavalry Corps, continues that:[18]

We moved to the left, and arrived at the wood of the Abbey of Argenton, where we encountered some Prussian cavalry scouts, who fled into the wood. We noted that on the other side of the wood, the enemy army was spread across the plain, it was not safe to cross the forest without infantry…we were then able to push forward, because we were now supported by the dragoons of the division of General Excelmans: and moreover, we saw the column head of the infantry division of General Teste (6th Corps), who had been made available to General Pajol.

All the day was spent in marches and counter marches; the evening we received the order to retreat and resume our positions of the morning. The next day, 18 June, we resumed our journey; it was the dawn of Waterloo!

The Abbey of Argenton stands about four miles south-east of Gembloux, approximately seven miles north-east from Mazy. Clearly, Pajol's men were spread out in an arc at least eight miles or so wide searching for the Prussians.

Grouchy's pursuit

Now some of the Prussians had been found, more troops would be needed to prevent them from linking with Wellington. Were all the Prussians heading to Namur and Maastricht, or were some heading north? Consensus seems to be that Namur and Liège or Maastricht were the main destinations.

What was the emperor to do? Ney, with 2nd Corps, three divisions from 1st Corps and the 1st Cavalry Division, were at Frasné. His lack of judgement on 16 June had resulted in the action at Quatre-Bras being a stalemate and had robbed the emperor of a total victory at Ligny.

At Ligny, 3rd and 4th Corps had suffered losses of perhaps 30 per cent of their effective strength. If a battle was coming with Wellington, the emperor needed as many fresh troops as he could. The 1st and 6th Corps had seen little action on 16 June, along with the bulk of 3rd Cavalry Corps, the Young Guard and the 1st and 2nd Grenadiers and Chasseurs à Pied. It made perfect sense to swing around to Quatre-Bras with 6th Corps, Milhaud's cavalry corps and the Imperial Guard, and then head north with 1st and 2nd Corps to face Wellington. Clearly, the emperor wanted to conduct any forthcoming battle against Wellington in person. Who could he trust to lead the pursuit against the Prussians? Ney had proved himself incapable of independent command. Given the major shortage of senior field officers, the emperor had no option but to employ Grouchy on this mission. As we have seen, Grouchy had served well on 15 and 16 June, and had proven his command capabilities to the emperor. Thus, fate dictated that Grouchy's first field command for a decade was to be of such momentous importance. The emperor, in sending Grouchy off, however, had seriously hindered the effective combat performance of the army under his command. Grouchy was commander of the cavalry reserve, with him heading north-east all command and control devolved to Ney. The emperor had no one other than Ney to personally direct attacks. The Imperial Guard had no commander-in-chief since Marshal Mortier had absented himself from the campaign. The lack of a commander for the 3rd and 4th Cavalry Corps, the Imperial Guard and a second field officer to deputise for the emperor at Waterloo to face down the Prussians was a major contributing factor to the loss of the battle. The Armée du Nord had a major shortage of field officers. As it was, Ney became filled with bloodlust to re-earn the emperor's favour at Waterloo, became myopic in his command and control responsibilities. Rather than remaining detached and objective to direct the massed cavalry charges, he was in the front rank hacking and slashing at the Allied troops. Exactly the same character flaw would be discovered in Marshal Grouchy at Wavre, where he became too focused on attacking rather than thinking laterally. Unlike Ney, Grouchy was jolted out of this by news from Waterloo, as shall see.

The emperor could not send Ney off to follow the Prussians; he had no option but to send Grouchy. The other candidates were Gérard or Vandamme. Both men barely tolerated each other, and Vandamme heartily disliked Grouchy. In either man, as with Grouchy, the emperor was taking a major gamble. With around a third of the army detached, against all common sense and the emperor's own maxims of keeping his forces concentrated, Grouchy was sent off. General Baudrand[19] explains how Grouchy was given his orders:[20]

17 June 1815, the day after the Battle of Fleurus, Napoléon mounted on horseback about nine o'clock in the morning, and went beyond the village of Ligny and alighted on the ground that the day before was occupied by the centre of the Prussian army.

Most of the people who accompanied the emperor also dismounted from their horse, I was of this number and found myself with three people, who unfortunately are no longer living, the two commanders of artillery and engineers. Generals Ruty and Rogniat and their Chiefs-of-Staff General Berge and myself.

There arrived in succession with the emperor several general officers of the staff, who probably came to report what had happened during the night or in the morning, and came to ask for orders or instructions.

Then you came, marshal, and after a few moments of conversation, as you became separated from Napoléon, he told you in a loud and clear voice, so as to be easily heard at the distance of twenty or thirty feet where we were: 'M. marshal, you will take the 3rd and 4th Corps, a division of the 6th, the cavalry...etc. and you will enter tonight in Namur' and when you were at some distance, the emperor added in a loud voice: 'I recommend to you, marshal, do not take many prisoners'.

You immediately departed, the emperor mounted his horse after travelling the battlefield which was covered in dead and wounded Prussians, by sending these words of consolation, Napoléon ordered that the headquarters be transferred from Fleurus to Marbais. He then turned quickly to Quatre-Bras, and taking with him the very small number of troops he had at hand, he began to pursue the English who withdrew on the Mont-Saint-Jean.

Of note, the writer says the order was given after 9.00, but gives no time of the conversation with the emperor. We have no idea how long the party were on the battlefield; thus, it is not impossible that the order was given at midday or event later. General Flahaut, aide-de-camp to Marshal Ney, recalled the episode as follows:[21]

> Towards ten o'clock we mounted our horses and, after having crossed the battlefield, we reached the highroad. There, the emperor left Marshal Grouchy by addressing him those words which I remember as if it happened yesterday: 'go, Grouchy, pursue the Prussians like a sword in their back, but always communicate with me from your left'.

For these two officers to recollect the same event but have the emperor saying totally different words makes us question the reliability of both supposed eyewitnesses, though of course the emperor may have said both phrases.

Many historians have speculated about this verbal order, but we cannot be certain as to its content. Therefore, we cannot use this hypothetical verbal order as a source of information about Napoléon's intentions for Grouchy. It is this ambiguity about the existence and the unknown contents of this verbal order, and the time it was given, which has been used to damn Grouchy ever since.[22]

NOTES:
[1] *Journal de l'Empire*, 22 June 1815, p. 2.
[2] SHDDT: C15 5. Dossier 17 June. Soult to Ney 17 June 1815, timed at 9.00.
[3] AN: AFIV 1939.
[4] SHDDT: C15 5. Dossier 17 June. Soult to Ney 17 June 1815, timed at 9.00.
[5] AN: AFIV 1939.
[6] SHDDT: C15 5. Dossier 17 June 1815. Guyardin to Berthezène.
[7] AN: LH 2628/33.
[8] SHDDT: C15 5. Dossier 17 June. Guyardin to Berthezène at Brye.
[9] Christopher Bassford, Daniel Moran, Gregory W. Pedlow, *The Campaign of 1815 Chapters 30-39*, On Waterloo, available at http://www.clausewitz.com/readings/1815/five30-39.htm [accessed 10 February 2013].
[10] Adrien Cuthbertson, personal communication, 17 June 2012.
[11] SHDDT: C15 5. Dossier 17 June 1815. Pajol to Grouchy timed at 12.00. Copy of the original made by du Casse in June 1865.
[12] Berton, p. 47.
[13] Frederic Gautier, *Relation de la Bataille de Waterloo*, Berthot, Brussels, 1827, p. 280.
[14] Fleury.
[15] *Journal des débats politiques et littéraires*, 4 July 1815, p. 3.
[16] AN: LH 377/15.
[17] Pierre de Witt, personal communication.
[18] Fleury.
[19] AN: LH 142/69. Marie Antoine François Henri Baudrand was born on 21 August 1774 and

was awarded Legion of Honour on 14 June 1804 as captain of engineers. He was then made an Officer of Legion of Honour as colonel of engineers on 29 July 1814. He was discharged on 26 February 1817 having been attached to Wellington's staff of the Army of Occupation.

[20] Grouchy, *Relation succincte de la campagne de 1815*, Vol. 4, pp. 146-51.

[21] John Franklin, personal communication, 7 November 2015.

[22] AN: LH 142/69.

Chapter 7

Grouchy's Orders

What were Grouchy's actual orders on 17 June? Many historians claim Grouchy received his orders well before noon. Indeed Siborne,[1] Morris[2] and Codman Ropes[3] all speak of an order by Bertrand that arrived with Grouchy around 11.30. Codman Ropes and most other historians present no historical basis for the time of arrival of the order to Grouchy. But what did the order say? Furthermore, they do not comment that orders could, and should, have been issued at daybreak if Grouchy was to catch the Prussians.

Searching in the French Army Archives at Vincennes has revealed not one, but two orders from Napoléon transmitted by Bertrand, as well as several other orders from headquarters to Grouchy about his course of action. Thus, the debate about what Grouchy's orders actually were is no longer open to speculation. It seems no historian since 1865 has bothered to actually consult the Army Archives to find out if missing orders actually exist. But, as we have said, Grouchy is always cast as the villain, and what Napoléon recalled years after the event has been good enough evidence for many about Grouchy's orders and his culpability in losing the Battle of Waterloo.

The following order is a copy made by Comte de Casse in June 1865, and may be an exact transcript of a now lost order to Marshal Soult that is also missing from the correspondence registers of both Soult and Grouchy:[4]

> Order of the emperor to Marshal Grouchy
> Order General Domon to return from the field of Marbais. He is currently under orders of Comte de Lobau and is to send a detachment, via Quatre-Bras, to traverse towards Brussels and to reunite with the troops of our left wing, the 1st and 2nd corps, which this morning are currently occupying the village of Frasné,

which are to march from there to Quatre-Bras against the English who are supposed to be there.

Order General Milhaud to move to Marbais. There he will find the light cavalry of General Domon. He will follow the movements of the corps of Comte Lobau and the Guard.

Ligny 17 June

Dictated by the emperor in the absence of the major-general

The grand marshal

Bertrand.

Here, the emperor makes provision for the attack against Wellington, but no provision at all concerning the Prussians. It was from Marbais that Milhaud observed Prussian troops retreating north from Gentinnes. Potentially written at the same time is the following order said to be a copy of an order sent to Marshal Ney on 17 June, written down in June 1865:[5]

It is His Majesty's intentions that you take up a position at Quatre-Bras, as you were ordered; but if it is not possible, which seems unlikely, then send a detailed report immediately, and the emperor will manoeuvre in your direction. If on the contrary there is only a rearguard, drive them off and occupy the position.

Here on the morning of 17 June, Napoléon's plans concentrated not on Blücher, but on Wellington and getting to Brussels. Clearly for Napoléon, the Prussian threat was not an issue at the time of dictating these orders. Concerning orders to Grouchy, the following was transmitted by Bertrand:[6]

Verbal order given by the emperor to Marshal Grouchy

Dictated when His Majesty was leaving the battlefield of Ligny to move towards Quatre-Bras 17 June at one hour after midday.

Pursue the Prussians, complete their defeat by attacking them as soon as you come up with them, and never let them out of your sight. I am going to unite the remainder of this portion of the army with Marshal Ney's corps, to march against the English, and to fight them if they should hold their ground between this and the Soignes Forest. You will communicate with me by the paved road which leads to Quatre-Bras.

Assuming that the order is authentic, it is very vague, but the phrasing of the first sentence is remarkably similar to that recorded by General

Flahaut, who we cited earlier. It also presumes that the headquarters staff knew where the Prussians were and where they were heading. Some historians, like John Codman Ropes, imply that this order was issued by Napoléon to Grouchy much earlier in the day, arriving with him at 11.30.[7] Codman Ropes does not give a source for this statement, and seems to have been totally ignorant of the order cited above timed at 13.00, and his whole thesis is written purely to slander Grouchy; the argument being that Grouchy got his orders earlier in the day and then did nothing until well after midday, therefore he could never catch the Prussians and thus lost the Battle of Waterloo. The truth is that Grouchy's first order was not issued until 13.00; the emperor could not issue orders until he knew where the Prussians were. Pajol reported in at 3.00 and again later in the day. Only then, once the Prussians had been found, could orders be given. With hindsight, we know where the Prussians were, but on 17 June 1815 the French headquarters had no idea. Even Grouchy falls into the trap of using hindsight to verify his line of argument, noting he asked for orders at daybreak to catch the Prussians—thus writing in 1818 he knew where the Prussians were, and tries to back-date this information to 1815. Yet, unless a now lost report from Pajol timed at 3.00 emerges, based on archive evidence, no orders could be given until the Prussians were found.

From the wording of the order, however, Grouchy was left entirely free by Napoléon to dictate his own best course of action. A second order to Grouchy was sent, it seems, after the one o'clock order, and read as follows:[8]

> Repair to Gembloux with the cavalry corps of Pajol and Excelmans, the light cavalry of the 4th Corps, Teste's division, and the 3rd and 4th Corps of Infantry. You will send out scouts in the direction of Namur and Maastricht, and you will pursue the enemy.
>
> Reconnoitre his line march, and tell me of his movements, that I may penetrate his designs.
>
> I shall move my headquarters to Quatre-Bras, where the English still were this morning; our communication will then be directed via the Namur road.
>
> Should the enemy have evacuated Namur, write to the general in command of the 2nd Military Division at Charlemont to occupy this town with a few battalions of National Guards.
>
> It is important to discover what Wellington and Blücher mean to do, and whether they meditate uniting their armies to cover Brussels and Liège by risking the fate of a battle.

At all events, keep your two infantry corps continually together, within a mile of each other, reserving several ways of retreat, place detachments of cavalry between, so as to be able to communicate with headquarters.

Sénécal, Grouchy's aide-de-camp, notes that the order was received by Grouchy sometime after 13.00, and that he immediately sent orders to Vandamme and Gérard to move out to Gembloux.[9] We can be sure that this second order *was* received by Grouchy and is an authentic document from 17 June, as Grouchy replies to its contents in detail at 6.00 on 18 June. The report read:[10]

Sire,

All my reports and information confirm that the Prussians are falling back on Brussels, either to concentrate there or to offer battle once united with Wellington. General Pajol reports that Namur has been evacuated. Regarding 1st and 2nd Corps of Blücher's army, the 1st Corps appears to be moving on Corbais, the 2nd Corps on Chaumont. Both are said to have moved off from Tourinnes and marched all night. Fortunately, the weather was so bad that they are unlikely to have gone far. I will move off to Sart-a-Walhain immediately, and intend moving on Corbais and Wavre. I will send you further reports from one or the other places.

I am with respect your humble servant.

Grouchy

P. S. Conforming to your orders, the general commanding the 2nd Military Division at Charlemont, de Loire, has occupied Namur with several battalions of National Guards and numerous artillery pieces have been transferred from Charlemont.

To ensure communication with Your Majesty, I have twenty-five horses at my disposal.

The corps of infantry and the cavalry under my command still have a full provision and a further half in reserve in the case of a major action. When we are close to using our reserve ammunition it will be necessary, Your Majesty, to make contact with the artillery depots you indicated to obtain replacements.

Important to our argument is the revealing fact that whenever this order has ever been published in full, the postscript is always omitted, presumed lost (which we know is not the case), as no historians had sight of the letter after Lettow-Vorbeck in 1904.

We see from the last paragraphs of the dispatch that Grouchy talks of garrisoning Namur with National Guards, just as Napoléon had ordered him to do so after 13.00 on 17 June. Therefore, we can be absolutely sure of what Grouchy's orders on 17 June 1815 actually were for the first time; no need for speculation. Grouchy was to go to Gembloux and then off to Maastricht.

This order, with more details, was logically sent after the one o'clock order, as it develops Grouchy's mission and objectives more fully. So far from being lost, two orders issued by Bertrand in the name of Soult and the emperor actually exist, albeit one is a copy. It is clear, however, that in both orders Grouchy was not allowed a considerable degree of flexibility. Only later on did Grouchy disregard his instructions in order to actually follow the movements of the Prussians. Furthermore, the order sent Grouchy's forces off in the wrong direction. Yes, the Prussians were heading north-east, but Maastricht was altogether in the wrong direction, as this would entail a more easterly line of march via Liège! The French headquarters had no idea where the Prussians were going and until Grouchy had found this out he could do very little.

With hindsight, we know the Prussians were heading to Brussels. But, based on the information that was known at 13.00 on 17 June 1815, all that the French headquarters knew was that Pajol, as we shall see, had found some Prussians at Namur and Abbey of Argenton. Had Grouchy not taken the initiative, which many historians claim he was not capable of, and sent out scouts both north and north-east, he would have happily marched to Namur or Maastricht and have been of no use at all on 18 June. In such a scenario, the defeat at Waterloo would have been even more total, as it would have freed up 19,000 Prussian troops. One cannot begin to imagine the impact that these troops could have had if Grouchy, who most historians like Hooper, A. F. Becke, Codman Ropes and Stephen Millar tell us lacked the vital skills for independent command and was mission-blind, had actually followed his orders! In reality, Grouchy was a far better field commander than historians allow him to be. Rather than rely upon a) Pajol's dispatch, and b) his orders, Grouchy did the obvious thing and sent out cavalry patrols to find the Prussians. We don't know who sent off Pajol south-east, but in doing so it meant that all future reconnaissance patrols had to be undertaken by Excelmans's dragoons—troops not ideally suited for this task, nor was it a task that many had experience of. Picket and patrol work were light cavalry duties, as Excelmans himself critiqued his commander for at the end of 17 June. Grouchy had no choice but to use Excelmans. Vandamme's light cavalry had been sent off to join Ney, and half of Pajol's command and Subervie's 5th Cavalry Division had also trotted off to Waterloo. Pajol's three remaining regiments had been sent off in the early hours of 17 June, and would not be seen again until late on 18 June; for twenty-four hours or more, Grouchy was robbed of his 'eyes and ears' provided by light cavalry. Little wonder then that Gérard's cavalry, commanded by Maurin, which had two chasseur regiments, was seconded to Excelmans. This being common sense to send the cavalry out on patrol, however, had a major drawback. It meant both Vandamme and Gérard had no 'eyes and ears' of their own. We know where the Prussians were, but on 17 June the field commanders had no idea at all. For all Vandamme and Gérard knew the cavalry screen could have missed a pocket of Prussians, who at any moment could attack their columns on line of march when the men were at their most vulnerable. Little wonder that Gérard, at the end of the vast column that would eventually move to Wavre, was slow. All he knew was that the Prussians were out there, and he had no idea where; proceeding with caution was the most sensible thing to do. But, it meant that when Grouchy needed a quick victory by concentrating his troops, Gérard was four hours behind Vandamme. Napoléon, in robbing Grouchy's vitally important light cavalry, made his task even harder. Napoléon and no other is to blame in not giving Grouchy orders until after midday, twelve hours after the battle ended. In sending Grouchy in the wrong direction, and stealing his light cavalry 'eyes and ears', Napoléon alone gave Grouchy an impossible task to perform.

Grouchy was acting upon the emperor's orders based on the reports he was receiving from men like Pajol, Vallin, Chastel, Vandamme and others. In hindsight, it is easy to say what Grouchy should have done. However, we must judge Grouchy's actions on the information he had to hand on 17 to 20 June 1815. His mission was vague, and in the first instance wrong. It is entirely due to his initiative that he found the Prussians heading to Wavre, and that he had to question his orders and also to ask critical questions about the reconnaissance reports sent to him. Pajol, as we shall see, found Prussians at Namur, but Grouchy was adroit enough to realise that the body of Prussian troops Pajol had found could not be the bulk of the army for Ligny, which he reasoned correctly was not heading to Namur or Maastricht as the emperor had told him, but must be heading towards Brussels. Yet Grouchy is always painted by historians as lacking this vital judgement so crucial in field commanders. He had the skill and ability to be a marshal of France, and indeed had more ability than Victor or Jordan. He was a highly capable field commander, whereas Ney, on 16 June, had been lacking in the same skills. Why did he dither at Quatre-Bras, a place he had been ordered to occupy on the previous day? Why did Ney spend the hours of 04.00 to

14:00 doing nothing in contradiction of orders? Of the two marshals with field commands with the Armée du Nord, Grouchy's star quality as a field commander was there for all to see, whereas Ney had bungled his orders on 15 and 16 June, unlike Grouchy, and had not kept his command concentrated, unlike Grouchy. In 1815, the better field commander was Grouchy, he showed the vital spark of initiative and intelligence that Ney had seemingly lost or had never had.

In all his later letters to the emperor, Grouchy informed him of his action. Therefore, Napoléon knew where Grouchy was and what he was doing, as we shall comment in later chapters. He knew that Grouchy was not heading to Waterloo, nor could he do so. It is this fact that Napoléon and his supporters, and men like Gérard, used to damn Grouchy for his failure of command and control on 18 June.

Grouchy begins his pursuit

Having received his orders, Grouchy writes with hindsight about an altercation with the emperor that may not have happened:[11]

> I was at his headquarters the next morning before sunrise, waiting for orders. Around 7.30 he sent word through the chief-of-staff that he was going to visit the battlefield and I should accompany him.

Meanwhile, General Pajol, who had been ordered to pursue the Prussians with his light cavalry and a division of infantry, was just then sending back several cannons which had been captured on the road to Namur. General Berton, like Pajol, reported a Prussian concentration at Gembloux.

This circumstance may have led to the belief that Blücher was retiring toward that town. General Bonnemains's dragoon brigade was ordered to Gembloux and to follow the Prussian line of movement. The Prussian 3rd Corps left Gembloux at 14.00, yet at 14.00 at Ligny, Grouchy was beginning to organise his move to Gembloux as ordered to do so by the emperor. Napoléon had known since the 4.00 dispatch from Pajol where 30,000 Prussians were (at Gembloux), confirmed by Berton's now lost dispatch sent around 9.00, that the Prussians were in force at Gembloux, yet he issued no order for Grouchy or any other general commanding an infantry corps to head to Gembloux, less than ten miles away, and attack. If, at say 10.00, when Berton's report got back to headquarters to attack, then he had four hours in which to assail the Prussians. Yet, Napoléon did no such thing. He let the Prussians slip away from him and then blames Grouchy for this lack of initiative. Grouchy could not attack at Gembloux until he was ordered to do so. Houssaye, like Hyde-

Kelly and Codman Ropes, lambasts Grouchy for not acting quickly upon orders issued at 11.00 or thereabouts. Yet no evidence can be found of any order being issued then, and the extant orders that do exist are written after 13.00, by which time only the Prussian rearguard was left at Gembloux. On the morning of 17 June, the Prussian army was ten miles from Ligny, yet Napoléon did very little to impede their march and attack. Clearly for Napoléon, the Prussians were a spent force and he had no need to pursue them with vigour and attack. Returning to the narration of the day:

> Between eight and nine o'clock in the morning, Napoléon left Fleurus in his carriage to go to the battlefield. The difficult condition of the roads across fields cut by ditches and deep furrows delayed him so much that he decided to mount his horse. Arriving at Saint-Amand, he had himself guided around the diverse avenues by which this village had been attacked the evening before. Then he walked on the battlefield, stopping to care for and question several wounded officers who were still there, and passing in front of the regiments who formed up without arms on the fields or who were bivouacked there, saluted them and received their acclamations. He spoke to almost all of the corps with interest, expressing satisfaction at their conduct the evening before. He then dismounted and spoke for a long time with General Gérard and myself about the state of opinion in the Parisian assembly, the Jacobins and diverse other subjects; all of which were extraneous to that which seemingly should have occupied his thoughts exclusively at such a moment.
>
> I am entering into such minute details because they serve to reveal how that morning was spent, the loss of which was to have such disastrous results. It was not until midday, after having received the report from a patrol that had been sent to Quatre-Bras, that Napoléon began to issue orders relating to the dispositions he intended to adopt. He then put into movement the corps of infantry and cavalry that he wanted to take with him and directed them toward the route to Quatre-Bras, and afterward gave me the verbal order to take command of the corps of generals Vandamme and Gérard and the cavalry of generals Pajol and Excelmans, and to pursue Marshal Blücher.
>
> I then commented to him that the Prussians had commenced their retreat at 10 p.m. on the night before, and that considerable time would be needed before the troops could be put into motion, for they were scattered across the plain and had disassembled their arms for cleaning and were making their soup and were not expecting to

march that day; also that the enemy were seventeen to eighteen hours ahead of the corps that were being sent after them; that although the reports of the cavalry did not give any more precise details on the direction taken by the mass of the Prussian army, it seemed that Marshal Blücher's retreat was in the direction of Namur, and that in pursuing him, I would therefore find myself isolated, separated from [the emperor], and outside the radius of his operations.

These remarks were not well received. He repeated the order that he had given, adding that it was up to me to discover the route taken by Marshal Blücher, that he was going to battle the English, that I was to complete the defeat of the Prussians by attacking them as soon as I had reached them, and that I was to communicate with him via the paved road which led from a point not far away from that on which we found ourselves at Quatre-Bras. The brief conversation that I then had with the chief-of-staff [Marshal Soult] concerned only the extraction, from the corps under my command, of the troops to be sent toward Quatre-Bras. These are word-for-word the only directions that were given to me, and the only orders I received.

Grouchy's aide-de-camp, notes:[12]

When the marshal had left the emperor, he sent me to General Vandamme, who was at Saint-Amand, to inform him of the order of the emperor, and tell him to go as quickly as possible, with his corps, to an inn called the Point-du-Jour, located at the junction of the roads of Namur and Gembloux.

I joined the marshal at Ligny, where he had visited M. General Gérard to give him his similar orders. I found him very unhappy with the reluctance of the general to move 4th Corps. He informed the marshal that his men were dispersed and said nothing was prepared for a speedy departure. The marshal, feeling the importance of following as quickly as possible the enemy that was more than twelve hours in front of us, he repeated the order to General Gérard to march, and went to Point-du-Jour to join Vandamme's corps on the road to Gembloux. Hardly had we begun to move off when a thunderstorm began: the rain fell in torrents, and soon the roads became impassable, therefore the corps of General Vandamme was forced to stop and bivouac in front of Gembloux where the artillery arrived quite late at night.

Gembloux is around ten miles north-east of Ligny, and had been the point of assembly for Grouchy's forces on 16 June, but they had never arrived there. From Gembloux, Grouchy could follow the Prussians on well-made roads.

Furthermore, in this report Napoléon tells Grouchy that he was to move off to Quatre-Bras with the Imperial Guard, the bulk of 6th Corps and what troops of 1st Corps he had to hand, along with the cavalry reserve, to engage Wellington. Thus, when Grouchy departed, he knew Napoléon was going to fight Wellington that day, as he sought to gain Brussels and, importantly, he did not know that a battle was to be fought on the 18th. Grouchy was ignorant of the fact that Napoléon had not engaged Wellington on the 17th and would not attack until mid-morning of 18 June. This important point will be looked at again when we come to look at Grouchy's operations on the 18th.

Major Hilaire Noël Taurin La Fresnaye,[13] of the 7th Dragoons, attached to the headquarters staff as officer d'ordonnance to Marshal Grouchy, notes:[14]

> On 16 June, I was with my regiment in the Battle of Fleurus, the next day you requested that I was to come back to you, I re-joined you towards one o'clock in the afternoon and found you on the battlefield of the previous day, with Napoléon. I do not know the orders you received, I just know that you were given the command of the infantry corps of generals Vandamme and Gérard and the cavalry of generals and Pajol and Excelmans to go in pursuit of the Prussians. As soon as you had left Napoléon, you transmitted these orders to the two generals.

Napoléon's first instruction to Grouchy was to concentrate all his forces at Gembloux. To enable both corps to arrive at Gembloux together, Gérard's should have marched off first and taken the cross-country road from Sombreffe to the old roman road, and thence along to Gembloux. Vandamme would then have had a clear road past Point-du-Jour undisturbed by Gérard's troops. As it was, Gérard's corps left after Vandamme, and had to traverse a road already cut-up by the Prussians and Vandamme's corps. Delayed by lack of orders and the time required to concentrate his troops, Grouchy's late departure was not helped by atrocious road conditions. With roads battered by heavy rains and turned into a quagmire, and not knowing exactly where the Prussians where, he was advancing slowly in a direction he assumed the Prussians were based on instinct rather than General Pajol's reconnaissance.

It is necessary to examine these events in further detail. Grouchy's primary mission objective was to find out what the Prussians were up to. Secondly, it was to pursue them. In his instruction to Grouchy to find out what the Prussians were up to, Napoléon saw only two possibilities: either move away from Wellington south-east towards the Meuse (Namur), or they could move north-east towards Maastricht in an attempt to link up with Wellington there. For that reason, Grouchy was to reconnoitre in both those directions, using Gembloux as a starting point. Napoléon was wrong. Furthermore, precise instructions for Grouchy concerning what he was to do when he confronted the Prussians are totally absent in the Bertrand order.

Excelmans's operations
That morning, Excelmans's men and horses were wet, hungry and had barely slept because of undertaking outpost duties during the night— a role traditionally conducted by light cavalry. Secondly, his corps had to manoeuvre without any infantry support or light cavalry 'eyes and ears', thereby limiting him in his actions. Grouchy, as a veteran cavalry commander, would have known all too well that dragoons were not light cavalry scouts or trained do these duties. But, he had no other choice than to employ dragoons as scouts. Subervie and Domon had been taken from him on Imperial orders. Time and again the lack of 'eyes and ears' was going to have a major impact on those June days of 1815. This situation explains Excelmans's caution for just observing rather than harassing the Prussians. General-de-Brigade Pierre Bonnemains narrates:[15]

> On the 17th, the army of Marshal Grouchy debouched on Gembloux. It was generally believed that the Prussian army defeated the day before at Ligny was in full retreat towards Liège. General Bonnemains, responsible for identifying the direction that they had taken, found in the village of Sart-a-Walhain the Prussian rearguard, which was forced to withdraw onto Wavre. Because of this movement and the information he had collected, he was convinced that the army of Blücher, which had rallied during the previous night, and had gone to take a position on the Dyle to be closer to the British army. General Bonnemains understood this and it was on his report that the movements of 18 June were based.

General Excelmans sent the following dispatch to Grouchy at 14.00 on 17 June:[16]

> General Excelmans to Marshal Grouchy, commander-in-chief of the cavalry of the army
> Monsignor,

I have the honour to inform you of the movement this morning I carried out towards Gembloux in order to follow the enemy that is massed there.

From what I have seen of the enemy so far, I have not seen him making a movement. His army is on the left of the Orneau; He has only on the right bank of the river in front of Lower-Bodecé a single battalion, which I believe will soon move, and I will follow it.

P. S. As I said this morning to you, my men are on their teeth [army expression for being exhausted]. The most fatigued are the dragoons which have been forced to do duty until tonight, and we can no longer ask them to do that as well as the light cavalry do, because they observe very little and their horses are entirely much faster. It makes me feel the need to attach to my corps of dragoons several squadrons of light cavalry.

Clearly, we are missing a report from Excelmans to Grouchy, the contents of which are now totally lost, beyond Excelmans saying his men and horses are tired. Of Interest, Excelmans does not acknowledge Grouchy's position as commander-in-chief of the right wing. His report has very little information beyond his grumbling that his dragoons should not be used as light cavalry, and had been sent off in the morning. So, is it possible that Excelmans went off at the same time as Pajol, or at midday? Perhaps the latter, supporting General Berton's hypotheses. But clearly, Excelmans did not know the Prussians were at Wavre. In reply to this dispatch, Grouchy ordered (the order being lost) that six squadrons were to move Sart-a-Walhain and three to Perwez. Excelmans had found the Prussian 3rd Corps. They had arrived here by 9.00. von Borcke's brigade, Thielemann's rearguard, left its positions here by 17.00, after which Excelmans entered Gembloux. von Borcke's 9th Brigade only reached the Dyle sometime by 7.00 on 18 June; it took this rearguard thirteen hours to cover a distance of about fourteen miles. Excelmans had moved off to Gembloux about 9.00, not to lead the way ahead of Vandamme, but to follow up General Berton's report. As he headed off to join Berton, the Prussian 1st and 2nd Corps headed to Wavre, and were spotted by General Milhaud, which we will return to later.

With hindsight, not sending off Excelmans with infantry now was a colossal mistake. If he had arrived in front of Gembloux with infantry support, no doubt action would have ensued that would have pinned down the Prussian 3rd Corps, and perhaps also sucked in the Prussian 4th Corps. If the Prussians had been caught at Gembloux, then the outcome of Grouchy's mission would have been utterly different. As it was, there was little Excelmans could actually do with his dragoons and two batteries of horse artillery. His presence did not result in an immediate evacuation of Gembloux, but surely Grouchy and Napoléon must have realised that as time passed the more chance the Prussians had of getting away, totally defeating Grouchy's primary mission objective (to find the Prussians). The emperor knew where the Prussians were, but tragically squandered the opportunity and the only chance Grouchy ever had of stopping them. Clearly, for whatever reason Gembloux was not a primary objective; Namur was, with catastrophic consequences. Namur was a concern for the emperor throughout 16, 17 and 18 June, making sure it was free of Prussians and garrisoned by the French. Clearly, he had his reasons, but we are not party to them in 2017. He never seems to have overcome his mission-blindness about Namur, and the Prussians not heading off deeper into the Netherlands until mid-morning on 18 June.

As Excelmans moved into Gembloux, the portentous dark sky let fall a deluge of rain. We forget amidst the Waterloo myths that not only did it rain on Napoléon and turn the ground into mud and prevent the men from lighting camp fires, it did so upon Grouchy. The need for shelter from the storm perhaps explains, as we shall see, Guyardin's draconian orders issued to 3rd Corps on 18 June. Grouchy's aide-de-camp notes:[17]

> Hardly had we begun to move off when a thunderstorm began: the rain fell in torrents, and soon the roads became impassable, therefore the corps of General Vandamme was forced to stop and bivouac in front of Gembloux where the artillery arrived quite late at night.

Charles Philippe Lefol, an aide-de-camp in 3rd Corps, writes:[18]

> The soldiers have never spent a night more dreadful. The day had been gloomy with intermittent rain. Towards evening the rain fell in torrents. So much so that when walking, our infantry had water up to their knees; the artillery advanced with the utmost difficulty and horses would barely tread on this wet ground, however our division was bivouacked around town deprived of shelter and food, so the next day our soldiers look like they had been dug up. Happier than they, were the officers of our staff who lodged in this city. I was sent out several times with orders during that cruel night.

The storm had another direct effect on Grouchy's mission. The Dyle and Orneau broke their banks, making the use of fords impossible, meaning the only river crossings were bridges. The marshy ground at Wavre, criss-crossed with a network of drainage dykes, flooded and forced Grouchy's men, once they had arrived here, onto the higher ground beyond the water-logged ground. This area is clearly marked on the 1777 map. It made the defence here far easier, as the water-logged ground funnelled the French onto the bridges, and they could not deploy along the banks of the river and open fire with musketry. Wavre was well chosen by the Prussians as a place to draw up a line of defences, which Grouchy marched straight into, just as the emperor was doing to his left. The Allies were dictating the place and terms of confrontation. In the past, the choice of place and time had been dictated by the emperor, and not too him.

Excelmans let Thielemann and von Borcke slip away in the torrential rain and thunder. The dragoons moved on to Bodecé, about half a mile south of Sart-a-Walhain; he clearly believed the Prussians were headed to Louvain to gain the Brussels road and not north to Wavre. With no infantry support and in torrential rain amidst a thunderstorm, we are happy to give Excelmans the benefit of the doubt that his inaction here was not malicious in not chasing Thielemann north and pursing von Borcke as closely as was needed to find the true destination of the Prussian 3rd Corps.

Vandamme's movements

Vandamme's 3rd Corps was to be the vanguard. It was first to assemble at the 'Cabaret Le Point-du-Jour', which was on the Sombreffe to Namur road. Here was a crossroads from where 3rd Corps could either turn north-east to Gembloux passing 'Cabaret Monti' or to continue to Botey and then turn towards Gembloux. Once off the paved Chaussee both roads were little more than trampled earth, which would be quickly broken down by the passage of thousands of hooves and boots. The best road for Vandamme and Excelmans to have taken was to head on the roman road just north of Sombreffe. But, the emperor was obsessed with the Prussians heading to Namur or Maastricht, and sent Vandamme on the indirect, cross country and much slower route placing him towards Namur, from whence, we assume, Napoléon's thinking was that he could head to the Namur area where Pajol had found some Prussians. At this stage, the troops at Gembloux were not important. Namur was the key place in Napoléon's mind, as his orders show. Battle should have been given at Gembloux, but when Vandamme set off it was too late for him to catch them. If he had moved on the roman road he would have intercepted the Prussian 1st and 2nd Corps heading north, which would have totally changed the outcome of the campaign. But, as the Prussians were off to Namur,

Excelmans and Vandamme had to swing south. Vandamme and Grouchy moreover, are damned for his slow rate of movement on 17 June. Napoléon overlooks the fact that his men moved on a paved road from Quatre-Bras to Genappe and thence Waterloo, whereas Grouchy's men were denied the roman road or paved roads to Gembloux, and instead had to contend with un-made roads and dirt tracks across fields. Napoléon ignores, or at least overlooks, this important fact. The Prussians knew the value of the metalled roads which is why the Prussian 4th Corps was heading to the Namur to Louvain road. Yes, time would be lost moving cross-country, but it would be made up for with the better road. It is also why Wavre was important. Departing the northern suburbs of Wavre was the chaussee de Brussels. Grouchy had no other paved road in his area, or for that matter precious few 'chemin' (dirt tracks with some metalling in the form of gravel), and mostly had unnamed dirt tracks to move upon. The lack of good roads was a major obstacle to any speedy movement. Yes, it is true that the Prussians moved on the same roads, but they were a good six hours in front, bar the small rearguards.

In returning to the narrative, we turn to Charles Philippe Lefol, aide-de-camp to his uncle, General Etienne Nicolas Lefol, who writes:[19]

> On the morning of June 17, 1815, the emperor confided to Marshal Grouchy the command of a corps of 35,000 men to pursue the Prussian army and to complete their defeat. Our division was among them. We made our departure around noon to Gembloux, where we arrived in the evening.

Lefol's figure of 35,000 men is rather suspect. Based on parade states of 10 June, Grouchy's command would have mustered 38,772 officers and men, but the actual figure seems to have been closer to 25,000 battle-weary and tired men. Lefol is also deeply critical of Grouchy, and it seems has gone out of his way to say that his division left the Ligny battlefield at noon—why? Simply to confirm the myth propagated by Napoléon that Grouchy's march was slow. Given Grouchy got no orders until after 13.00, and it would have taken at least two hours to get his orders issued and his command on the road, Lefol's division cannot have left the Ligny battlefield until at least 15.00. Here we have a textbook case of 'false memory'.

False memory is created by the eyewitness in two ways: firstly, having read material since the event described took place, their own memories have been overwritten. They then write down and recall what they have read since the event, rather than what they witnessed happened.

Secondly, false memory can be created by the mind recording memories of what it thinks ought to have happened. False memory is to play an important part in the historiography of 18 June. We must be vitally aware, however, of the limitations and failings of soldiers' memoirs as a source of empirical data. The written orders from 17 and 18 June are the real clues as to what did or did not happen, as we shall see in subsequent chapters.

Why did it take from 15.00 to perhaps 20.00 to travel ten miles? Did Grouchy really march very slowly? On good roads, this would take around two hours. This assumes, however, that Grouchy did indeed only need two hours to be assembled and leave Ligny at 15.00; it is possible he did not leave until 16.00, or much later. We don't know exactly when 3rd Corps left the battlefield. The torrential rain storm was a major factor, it seems, in Grouchy not progressing beyond Gembloux on 17 June; the rain would have made any cross-country marching virtually impossible, forcing both 3rd and 4th Corps on the Charleroi road. In his defence, he was ordered to go to Gembloux by the emperor, and it made sense, no doubt, to halt at Gembloux for him to get his command into some semblance of order. Furthermore, it was the ideal location, at the junction of three major roads, from which to move out from once the Prussians had been found.

Grouchy, at 20.00 on 17 June, still only knew the Prussians were roughly south of him, and clearly not the full force from Ligny. For him, it was better to wait for news to come in from Excelmans's dragoons, who, soaked to the skin and no doubt hungry and cold, were spread out in a great arc pointed north-east to try and find the Prussians. The slow rate of march on 17 June was beyond Grouchy's control, just as was the weather. Many historians, like George Hooper and A. F. Becke, castigate Grouchy for his tardy march to Gembloux and not going straight after the Prussians to Wavre—critically Grouchy, nor any other French officer, knew the Prussians were at Wavre until Excelmans's dragoons found them there. We must judge him and his plan of operations on what he knew on 17 June and not we know 200 years later.

Captain Jean Marie Putigny,[20] of the 2nd Battalion 33rd Regiment of Line Infantry (part of 3rd Corps), narrates:[21]

> Our regiment, the 33rd, was placed to escort an important convoy of food and munitions destined to the army corps of Marshal Grouchy. The horse teams only moved very slowly and it was not until night that we came to the village of Gembloux. On the orders of the marshal the bread was distributed to the soldiers and they prepared their soup in the last rays of the sun.

This places the ration distribution being around 22.00. The corps had been issued the following rations for the forthcoming campaign on 31 May:[22]

13,285 *quintaux*[23] 45 kilograms of grain
45 *quintaux* 32 kilograms of ride
87 *quintaux* 85 kilograms of dried beans
17 *quintaux* 78 kilograms of salt
1,950 litres of brandy
5,500 kilograms of meat
930 *quintaux* of straw
790 *quintaux* of hay
2,730 *quintaux* of oats

Due to lack of biscuits and bread, rice and beans had to be issued, but at least the men and horses had some food and, crucially, these men were fed during the course of the campaign.[24] However, it seems 4th Corps had no rations with them, and certainly had none issued by 5 June 1815.[25]

Sub-Lieutenant Gerbet, of the 37th Regiment of Line Infantry, notes that the 3rd and 4th Corps left Ligny at ten o'clock in the morning.[26] Again this is another instance of false memory.

However, Vandamme got to Wavre before Grouchy. The first authentic document from 17 June 1815 to identify Wavre as the place headed to by the bulk of the Prussians is a document sent from Vandamme:[27]

17 June 1815
General Vandamme to Marshal Grouchy
M. marshal
I have the honour to inform Your Majesty that the generals Thielemann and Borstel have passed here at the head of part of the army. They arrived here this morning at six o'clock, they were still here at ten o'clock this morning, and have announced that they have 20,000 casualties. They are heading in the direction of Wavre, Perwez and Hannut.
I have the honour, Your Excellency the marshal, to give you my humblest and devoted servant
Signe. D. Vandamme.

Undoubtedly the troops heading to Wavre was the Prussian 3rd Corps that finally evacuated Gembloux about 17.00, before Vandamme had arrived.

Gérard's movements

Captain François,[28] a veteran officer of the 30th Regiment of Line Infantry, narrates:[29]

> 17 June—from daybreak the army began to move and went on a forced march. the road was bad. The cavalry of General Excelmans, that of Marshal Grouchy, the army corps of General Vandamme and Gérard marched on Wavre, on Orneau and Beyle, the roads from Mont-Gembloux and Guibert. The other divisions of the army marched on different points, that of Marshal Ney on Quatre-Bras, to attack it again.
>
> We, in the army corps of Marshal Grouchy, marched against Blücher, who had crossed the Wavre, and to prevent his junction with Wellington and keep us on the road from Charleroi to Brussels, and to communicate with the emperor who had 68,000 men and 240 guns. Marshal Grouchy had approximately thirty-four thousand men and 200 guns.
>
> We made little progress, despite the forced march, but made a lot of unnecessary manoeuvres in the direction of Liège, to know the movements of Blücher, who was said to be 75,000 men marching to Wavre. Around 6 p.m. we reached Gembloux, where we found the dragoons of General Excelmans.

Captain François was writing to critique Grouchy and praise Gérard. It is clear his account is heavily biased, yet his account has often been cited as accurate, and proof that Grouchy marched slowly on 17 June, just as the emperor said he did. Again, François's testimony is overtly biased, and another case of false memory.[30]

Night of 17 June: reports come in

Grouchy arrived at Gembloux about 19.00 with the leading elements of 3rd Corps. Once at Gembloux, Vandamme's men began to run amok, no doubt seeking shelter and food rather than camp out in the rain in muddy fields. In the early hours of 18 June, Guyardin issued instructions to shoot looters. His order seems to say that there had been a major breakdown of discipline that night, and that officers needed to do more to prevent looting. Offenders, Guyardin recommended, should be shot as examples, and regimental commanders were to be held responsible for ensuring this happened as and when required.[31] Rogniat recounts:[32]

> The nuns of Gembloux came to us complaining that we had plundered their community. An officer was sent for. He found a non-commissioned officer of engineers who, taking advantage of a hole

in a fence, he and the sappers gained access to the convent and stole all the wine and provisions.

We took him prisoner, and the general, wishing to make an example, ordered him shot by a firing squad. This was executed without mercy against the convent wall, and an agenda announced that any act of plunder in Belgium, among our countrymen, would be punished with extreme severity.

Grouchy's command on 17 June had major issues of command and control, which was to present itself in a more disastrous way at Wavre, when men refused to obey orders.

Grouchy now awaited the reports from his subordinates to get a clear understanding of the Prussians' whereabouts. Pajol sent the following dispatch to Grouchy, timed at midday on 17 June. It was received by the marshal in the early evening. This reconnaissance report would inform Grouchy's moves against the Prussians; it read:[33]

> The enemy continued his retreat on Saint-Denis and Leuse, to gain the road from Namur to Louvain, and having been informed that a lot of artillery and ammunition has been left at this city, I plan to withdraw also by the same route, I will start with Teste's division that His Majesty has just sent me, to try to arrive tonight at Leuse, and cut the road from Namur to Louvain, and I understand that will be his route of retreat.

This route would take Pajol's command through Grand-Leez, and Sart-a-Walhain, travelling approximately north-west to arrive at Ottignies-Louvain-la-Neuve, a distance of twenty miles or so on good roads (over five hours marching for Teste's infantry), or still further if they travelled by Perwez as hinted at by Grouchy in the dispatch he sent to Excelmans. Leuze is due east of Saint-Denis, so it still seems that Pajol was convinced some of the Prussians were heading to Liège and Maastricht, or, as he says, to gain the Namur to Louvain road and head north to Brussels. Pajol's news about a move towards Brussels indicated that the Prussians were moving back into the Netherlands to regroup before fighting another action. Whatever troops Pajol was chasing, it was not the bulk of the army from Ligny. However, Grouchy still seemed under the impression that a large body of troops was heading that way, as well as seemingly east.

Still flung out in front were Excelmans's dragoons. At 19.00, Grouchy sent orders to Excelmans:[34]

Gembloux 17 June 1815 at seven o'clock in the evening

Marshal Grouchy to General Excelmans

My dear general, I have arrived here with the corps of Vandamme and Gérard. As soon as you make a halt, please inform me of your movements as well as on the movements of the enemy, importantly the direction they retire in and on which roads, I am assured that the Prussians have taken the road from Perwez-lez-Marche to the Leuze. I have ordered General Pajol to pursue them in this direction, and he will arrive this evening at Leuze.

Tomorrow morning you will pursue them.

I will order General Vandamme to march in your direction at daybreak tomorrow, when I shall write to you.

Despite our miseries, we must keep going until the end, since I command the right wing of the army and the dispositions of the infantry and light cavalry.

Please reply promptly to me, I am eager to hear your news about the movements of the Prussians so that I can transmit this to His Majesty who is now attacking Wellington again near Quatre-Bras.

Pajol captured this morning eight cannon, numerous baggage wagons and a good number of prisoners.

From this dispatch, we can see that Grouchy had been informed about the emperor's advance to Quatre-Bras, and also was party to the news that the emperor considered it a mere formality to brush Wellington aside and move on Brussels. Again, with hindsight, he was over-confident and badly mistaken. However, Grouchy did not know on the night of 17 June about Napoleon's planned battle on 18 June. For all Grouchy knew, the emperor was in Brussels. Grouchy had no news from the emperor till the early hours of 18 June. Napoléon never replied to Grouchy's dispatch. Grouchy was keeping in contact with head-quarters, but head-quarters did not talk to Grouchy – a situation that was to have fatal consequences. General Bonnemains reported to Generals Excelmans and Chastel that:[35]

General Bonnemains to General Chastel 17 June 10.15 p.m.

Sir, the enemy had occupied the village of Tourinnes until evening. There was, according to the saying of farmers, many infantry and some cavalry, who had passed along the road in a convoy. I watched until night and have retrograded to Baudecet, where I left a regiment, with the intent to accommodate my brigade, but I found there the 5th Dragoons were established here. I then

determined to come here, and I await your orders. I sent a peasant
to go from Sart-a-Walhain to Tourinnes to watch for the movement
of the enemy and said they quit the place a little before half-past
eight o'clock this evening.

Please be assured of my respect, general.

Signe Bonnemains.

The report arrived with Grouchy at 3.00 as he was making preparations
to move out.[36] He annotated the document, stating 'move with more
speed'.

Tourinnes-les-Ourdon and Tourinnes-Saint-Lambert are around ten
miles north-east from Gembloux, beyond Sart-a-Walhain and Libersat.
Baudecet is on the same road as he would have used to travel to Sart-
a-Walhain and thence to Tourinnes-les-Ourdon. Again, no news about
Wavre. So, what did Grouchy know? Pajol had some Prussians headed
to Namur and others either to Maastricht or to gain the Namur to
Louvain road. Bonnemains had Prussians at Tourinnes, heading off
perhaps to Brussels, again via the Namur to Louvain road. Grouchy
had been told to head towards Maastricht, yet now he was entertaining
the possibility that some of the Prussians were heading towards
Brussels.

Pierre Bonnemains adds more flesh to this narrative in the following
report he sent to Soult on 23 June, seemingly padded out with
hindsight:[37]

> We left late from Sombreffe, and after a long time we came near
> Gembloux without being able to determine any information about
> the enemy. General Bonnemains was finally sent to reconnoitre
> ahead of the corps and headed to Valhain [sic] and then onto
> Tourrinnes and Nil-Saint-Vincent, where he found some Prussian
> scouts with which his dragoons exchanged a few rifle shots, who
> then fled in the direction of Wavre. He had not been able to find a
> single soldier, but all the notable local inhabitants agreed that the
> army corps of Bülow had joined on the night of 16th to 17th near
> Gembloux with those who had fought at Ligny [sic] and as a result
> the whole Prussian army was in position to Wavre.
>
> General Bonnemains took up a position at Ernage as night began
> to fall, from where he sent his report to General Excelmans. About
> one o'clock in the morning a report came from a patrol that had been
> reconnoitring their outposts in the direction of Wavre, confirming
> again the information he had collected in his operations.

Crucially, did Grouchy know this? Using documents written on 17 or 18 June, so far he had not received any news that the Prussians were at Wavre. Nil-Saint-Vincent-Martin is at most eight miles due north of Gembloux. From Nil-Saint-Vincent-Martin, Bonnemains clearly headed back south to Ernage, a mere three miles north of Gembloux? What caused this major retreat? Did Bonnemains and his staff move back to join Grouchy, or did his entire brigade? Which troops were at Wavre? Why is Nil-Saint-Vincent-Martin omitted from the 17 June report? We simply do not know. Are both reliable? The dispatch to Excelmans and Chastel, however, is a copy made in 1865—has the original document been 'edited' by Comte de Casse? We have no evidence beyond the suspicion that, as it is so different to an authentic document written on 23 June 1815, that either Bonnemains withheld information from his direct commanders, or he forgot to add in to his report about moving to Nil-Saint-Vincent-Martin (which seems rather unlikely). Could he have moved from Tourinnes to Nil-Saint-Vincent-Martin after sending his dispatch? Yes, the two places are about two miles apart, and his command could have occupied the ground between Ernage and Baudecet. In this way, we can reconcile some of the differences between the two statements to an extent. We propose, therefore, that during the night of 17 June, the 5th Dragoons (Burthe's brigade of Stroltz's division) was at Baudecet. The brigade of Bonnemains was at Ernage, and the remainder of the corps (namely brigades of Vincent and Berton) was at Sauvenières. General Berton adds:[38]

> The dragoons from Chastel's division passed Gembloux, about an hour after the Prussians left, and received orders to halt at the mill, a little in front of the town, and to rest here for the night. All eight regiments were cantoned here to the right of Gembloux, except the 1st Brigade from Chastel's division, commanded by Marshal-du-Camp Bonnemains, who at the close of day sent reports back about the march of the Prussians to Wavre. The 15th Regiment of Dragoons was commanded by Colonel Chaillot,[39] this officer who was a good soldier had spoken with the peasants of the area and with prisoners, who announced the Prussian columns were dispersing towards Wavre where they would come to a halt.

What was the 1.00 dispatch? We don't know. The first authentic document from 17 June 1815 to identify Wavre as the place headed to by the bulk of the Prussians is a document sent from Vandamme, and is worth repeating again:[40]

17 June 1815
General Vandamme to Marshal Grouchy
M. marshal
I have the honour to inform your Majesty that the generals Thielemann and Borstel have passed here at the head of part of the army. They arrived here this morning at six o'clock, they were still here at ten o'clock this morning, and have announced that they have 20,000 casualties. They are heading in the direction of Wavre, Perwez and Hannut.

I have the honour, Your Excellency the marshal, to give you my humblest and devoted servant
Signe. D. Vandamme.

Based on the reports he had received, Grouchy believed three Prussian columns were in his immediate area: one, based on Pajol's intelligence, was moving to Namur in full retreat; a second column (presumably heading off north-east), which history illustrates was the Prussian 4th Corps; and a possible third directly north of Grouchy at Wavre—the Prussian 3rd Corps. This information did not help determine the plan of operations. The bulk of the reports indicated the Prussians were moving north-east to gain the Namur to Louvain road to then draw to Brussels. However, what of the troops at Wavre?

The column found by Pajol at Namur, however, was not one of the three columns, but a large body of troops accompanied by artillery and some cavalry that were indeed in full retreat. This body of men was misidentified and served to further confirm Napoléon and Grouchy's view that the Prussians were in full retreat and heading both to Brussels and Namur. Grouchy and his staff no doubt held a council of war. According to Sénécal, Grouchy's aide-de-camp, the consensus among the field officers was that the 'Prussian army was concentrated at Wavre, and the rest headed to Louvain'.[41] Wavre, when we consult the 1777 map, was the obvious point for the column heading from Gembloux to cross the Dyle and gain the Namur to Louvain road, or head east to gain the same road. In either case, the gathered data all suggested the Prussians were moving north-east. Grouchy, we recall, had had no news from the emperor. He had no idea where he was or what his plan of operations were. He did not know the Battle of Waterloo was to be fought, and therefore he had no need to worry at all about the Prussians heading west, because where were they going to? By now, Grouchy reckoned the emperor would be close to Brussels and had swept aside Wellington. Lack of communication from the emperor meant that Grouchy's plans were based on a dangerous assumption,

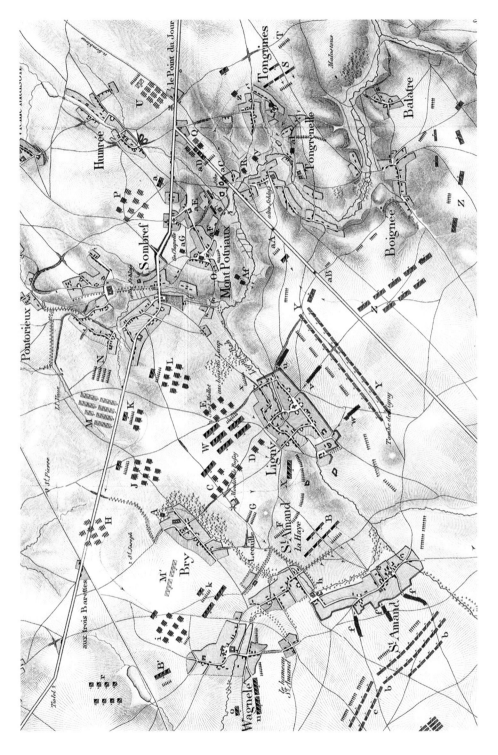

Map of the Battle of Ligny by Siborne. The troop depositions are accurate for the start of the battle.

Left: The Church at Saint-Armand, Ligny, the scene of bitter fighting on 16 June.

Below: Entrance to Saint Amand, Ligny. This narrow street witnessed the attack of the Grenadiers of the Old Guard on the evening of 16 June, as well as the death of General Girard.

Above: The farm at Ferm en Bas at Saint Armand was hotly contested by both the French and Prussians on 16 June; it was a Prussian strongpoint throughout much of the day. (Photo © D. Timmermans napoleon-monuments.eu)

Below: Blüchers headquarters at Sombreffe. (Photo © D. Timmermans napoleon-monuments.eu)

Above: Fleurus Chateau de la Paix. Napoleon's headquarters was located in this building on the night of 16 June 1815. It was from here that Napoleon set out to attack Wellington, and from here that Grouchy received his orders to attack the Prussians. (Photo © D. Timmermans napoleon-monuments.eu)

Below left: The Naveau Mill in Fleurus, which served as an observation post for Napoleon during the battle. (Photo © D. Timmermans napoleon-monuments.eu)

Below right: General Etienne Maurice Gerard was made Chief of the Army of the Moselle in 1815, which became the 4th Corps of the Army of the North.

Left: General Dominique Vandamme, commander-in-chief of III Corps.

Below: The mill at Bierge was the scene of bitter fighting on 18 June. (Photo © D. Timmermans napoleon-monuments.eu)

Bottom: La Haye. This farm was the centre of the Prussian defence against the Imperial Guard. (Photo © D. Timmermans napoleon-monuments.eu)

Left: Marshal Grouchy, the last of Napoleon's Marshals. His reputation has been tarnished by Napoleon and others for his supposed inaction at Wavre. However, Grouchy performed as well as he could given the terrain he had to fight the Prussians on.

Below: Moustier, now Mousty, has largely been subsumed into Ottignies. The church at Moustier stands on the west bank of the River Dyle, in the town square overlooking the bridge. General Domon came here on the night of 17 June 1815, and Captain Eloy, of the 7th Hussars, early on the morning of 18 June. The lack of Prussians here on 18 June convinced Napoleon that they had retreated towards Louvain and not could not therefore swing west to join Wellington.

Above: An early photograph of the bridge at Wavre.

Below: Rue Namur in Wavre. Vandamme attacked down this narrow street and got as far as the bridge before being stopped in his advance by Prussian musket and artillery fire.

Above: Wavre's hotel de Ville (town hall) at the end of Rue en Haute. Since 1815 the street has been very much widened.

Left: The church in Bièrge, located in the town square, stands on a ridge above the River Dyle.

and one that was wrong, directly due to poor communication from the emperor.

At 22.00, having assessed the contents of the reports he had received, Grouchy reported his intelligence to Napoléon:[42]

> Gembloux, 17 June, 10 p.m.
>
> Sire, I have the honour to report to you that I occupy Gembloux and that my cavalry is at Sauvenière. The enemy, about thirty thousand strong, continues his retreat. We have captured here a convoy of 400 cattle, magazines and baggage.
>
> It would appear, according to all the reports, that, on reaching Sauvenière, the Prussians divided into two columns: one of which must have taken the road to Wavre, passing by Sart-a-Walhain; the other would appear to have been directed on Perwez.
>
> It may perhaps be inferred from this that one portion is going to join Wellington, and that the centre, which is Blücher's army, is retreating on Liège. Another column, with artillery, having retreated by Namur. General Excelmans was ordered this evening to push six squadrons to Sart-a-Walhain, and three to Perwez. According to their reports, if the mass of the Prussians is retiring on Wavre, I shall follow them in that direction, so as to prevent them from reaching Brussels, and to separate them from Wellington. If, on the contrary, my information proves that the principal Prussian force has marched on Perwez, I shall pursue the enemy by that town.
>
> Generals Thielemann and Borstel formed part of the army which Your Majesty defeated yesterday; they were still here at ten o'clock this morning and have announced that they have 20,000 casualties. They enquired on leaving, the distances of Wavre, Perwez, and Hannut. Blücher has been slightly wounded in the arm, but it has not prevented him from continuing to command after having had his wound dressed. He has not passed by Gembloux. I am, with respect, sire, Your Majesty's faithful subject, Marshal Comte Grouchy.

What does the key phrase 'join Wellington' mean? Did Grouchy mean the Prussians were to head west to Quatre-Bras? Or, more likely, to head north-east, join the Namur to Louvain road and then head to Brussels and link there with Wellington? Based on his subsequent orders, this is what I believe he meant. If the Prussians were heading west, where were they going? A westerly move made no sense as far as he understood the situation, as he had no French troops to his west, or Allied troops to the immediate west, as they, surely, had been pushed aside by the emperor.

As we noted earlier, Napoléon did not keep Grouchy informed of his operations.

In later years, Napoléon generated a great deal of fake stories to cover his mistakes in the campaign and to blame everyone else, and it his story that many historians ardently believe, despite it not standing up to any scrutiny. We do wonder if this report ever reached the emperor. All Grouchy knew was that he was somewhere on the Brussels road between Quatre-Bras and Brussels itself. Napoléon never replied to the letter, yet about this report he, in later years, makes some fanciful claims about the dispatch. He even goes so far as to fabricate an order to show that Grouchy had disobeyed orders—he forgets that he ordered Grouchy towards Maastricht. Napoléon's 1820 version of the fictional 10.00 order to Grouchy was:[43]

> At ten o'clock in the evening, I sent an officer to Marshal Grouchy, who I supposed to be at Wavre, in order to let him know that there would be a big battle the next day; that the Anglo-Dutch army was in position in front of the Soignes Forest, with its left wing resting on the village of La Haye; that I ordered him to detach from his camp at Wavre a division of 7,000 men of all arms and sixteen cannon before daylight to go to Saint-Lambert to join the right of the Grand Army and co-operate with it; that, as soon as he was satisfied Marshal Blücher had evacuated Wavre, whether to continue his retreat in Brussels or to go in any other direction, he was to march with the bulk of his troops to support the detachment at Saint-Lambert.
>
> At eleven o'clock in the evening, an hour after this dispatch had been sent off, a report came in from Marshal Grouchy, dated from Gembloux at 5 p.m. It reported he was at Gembloux with his army, unaware as to which direction Marshal Blücher had taken, whether he had gone towards Brussels or Liège; that he had accordingly set up two advanced guards, one between Gembloux and Wavre and the other a league from Gembloux in the direction of Liège. Thus, Marshal Blücher had given him the slip and was three leagues from him! Marshal Grouchy had only covered two leagues during the day of the 17th.

Grouchy's report was sent at 22.00 and not 17.00, and he was not at Gembloux at 17.00. No evidence whatsoever has been found of the 22.00 order to Grouchy. Such an important order would have been logged by the major-general in his order book and by Grouchy. No historian since 1815 has ever found this order. It is fiction written to blame Grouchy for losing Waterloo. However, as we shall see, on 18 June 1815 the emperor was adamant that Grouchy had arrived at Waterloo—had he convinced himself beyond reasonable doubt that Grouchy could arrive in time, or was it a lie? Napoléon never seems to have replied to the news from Grouchy.

To get our story back on track, we must conclude that on 17 June 1815 Grouchy had found three Prussian columns: one heading to Wellington; one heading to Wavre (Thielemann); and a third that was apparently retreating. He informed headquarters of his operations. However, Napoléon did not do the same about his own to Grouchy. In reality, he had no idea where Napoléon and the bulk of the army was; his basic presumption was Quatre-Bras, as Napoléon had told him this, but equally he could have been further north towards Brussels.

The emperor's second major lapse of judgement was that the reconnaissance report he had received from Milhaud (commanding 4th Cavalry Corps) that a major Prussian column had been retreating through Saint-Géry and Gentinnes towards Wavre was not forwarded to Grouchy until 10.00 on 18 June, twenty-four hours after the news had come into headquarters. It is possible, of course, that the emperor did not acknowledge the importance of this news when he received it, as he was so convinced that the Prussians were heading to Namur or Maastricht that the column was clearly not a major force or a concern at all. The column's importance only seemingly grew throughout the day of 17 June and the morning of 18 June, when it became apparent that the Prussians Milhaud observed could have eluded Grouchy and were headed to Waterloo. He was of course correct in this, as neither he nor Milhaud had informed Grouchy of these troops, nor did the emperor inform Grouchy about his own operations.

Clearly on 17 June, the emperor was so convinced the Prussians were heading to Namur or Maastricht that he could not conceive of the reality of a Prussian link-up with Wellington in front of Brussels. He was sure in his own mind, as was Grouchy, that the next battle was going to be beyond Brussels.

When the emperor got Grouchy's 06.00 dispatch on 18 June he would have realised that: a) Grouchy was heading away from Waterloo; and b) a large Prussian force had come between him and Grouchy, ostensibly to link with Wellington.

If the emperor had informed Grouchy of this news, as soon as he had received it, and had the understanding of the true situation that the Prussians were able to give battle and were heading to Wellington, and that he (Napoléon) was facing the Allies at Waterloo on the night of 17 June, no doubt Grouchy would have swung north to Wavre and not headed, as Napoléon was convinced, in the direction of Louvain. If Grouchy had known the emperor was at Mont-Saint-Jean and that a Prussian column was between them, the obvious next conclusion was the Prussians were headed to Mont-Saint-Jean and not Louvain. But, in reality, the emperor was so unconcerned about this that he sent Grouchy further to the north-east, as we shall see in a later chapter.

These were the two greatest mistakes of the campaign. From now, the fate of the French army at Waterloo was sealed. Grouchy could not pursue a Prussian force he knew nothing about. A Prussian force had got between the two French armies. Napoléon had become mission-blind with his fixation on Namur or Maastricht and had sent Pajol off on a wild goose chase, tilting at phantoms in the night—which most historians wrongly ascribe to Grouchy; he had robbed Grouchy of Domon and Subervie's vital 'eyes and ears' (the light cavalry), and did not tell him he had taken Subervie's men; he withheld information from Grouchy which was vital for him to achieve his mission objective of finding the Prussians; he could not face the reality of a Prussian link with Wellington, because he was over-confident that his hollow victory at Ligny had damaged the Prussian army beyond repair. Yet Grouchy has been made, and is made by twenty-first century historians, the bad guy, the stooge, who was not fit for command and lost Napoléon the war. It is a tried and tested hypothesis repeated since 1815 which actually stands up to no critical enquiry. Napoléon's verbal instructions to Grouchy, as with the Bertrand order, must have made it clear to Grouchy that if the Prussians were not off to Maastricht then they were off to Brussels, and he was to give chase no matter what. Grouchy could not pursue a Prussian force he had no information about, and one that was specifically not in his theatre of operations. Yet Grouchy, despite this, did send off scouts to Wavre in the wake of Vandamme's news. Clearly, he had to follow up this information in case the Prussians were in a position to initiate a flank attack. So convinced was he by the emperor's orders and reasoning that he did not realise the Prussians were going to join Wellington until too late. Again, Napoléon blundered. On the morning of 18 June, Grouchy had no idea where the emperor was, or what he had done the previous day, or was about to do. Diligently, he had reported back to headquarters, yet Napoléon sent no news to him until 10.00 on 18 June. Grouchy could not conceive of a Prussian flank marching to Wellington, as he had no idea where Wellington was on the morning of 18 June. He could not plan his operations for an eventuality that he knew nothing about. Dammed by many since that fateful day for not marching to Wavre and then to Waterloo, he made a major mistake here when we look back at the day from 2017.

At no stage in the period between issuing orders on 17 June to 10.00 on 18 June did Napoléon inform Grouchy of his operations or his whereabouts. Grouchy did not know that a battle was to be fought at Waterloo. As far as he knew, the emperor had defeated Wellington at Quatre-Bras and was close to Brussels, assuming he had been made privy to the emperor's plans. Thus, for Grouchy, a Prussian link up with Wellington made no sense, as until he received news from the emperor that the Allies would draw back deeper into the Netherlands before another battle was to be fought, and he was to push the two Prussian columns in front of him away from the emperor's army. The more Bülow headed north-east, the more he became convinced of this, as the Prussians were moving as the emperor had anticipated; a logical conclusion, and one Napoléon seems to have acknowledged with the Bertrand order. For the emperor, the Prussians would only be moving to Maastricht or Brussels if a battle was to be fought anywhere but Waterloo in the immediate front of his forces, which could give Grouchy plenty of time to re-join him. Napoléon never planned to attack at Ligny and had the battle thrust upon him, nor did he plan the battle at Waterloo. Wellington dictated the terms of the battle. Thus, for both commanders, a Prussian link-up was not considered a reality until battle was joined on 18 June on the plain of Mont-Saint-Jean. This is why, as we shall see later, Napoléon ordered Grouchy away from Waterloo towards Wavre at 10.00, and importantly to keep moving east as the Prussians were not expected at Waterloo, since, for the French at least, no battle had been planned. In essence, Napoléon marched into a trap of his own making, and one he did not, or could not, see until the trap was sprung closed, just as had befallen poor General Mack at Ulm a decade earlier.

Returning back to the events of the fateful 17 June, Gérard's 4th Corps, we are told, did not arrive at Gembloux until approaching midnight on 17 June, as orderly officer to Grouchy, Captain Leguest, reports:[44]

> It is my understanding that the troops of the 4th Infantry Corps commanded by General Gérard did not arrive at Gembloux on 17 June until eleven o'clock at night, and that you were extremely unhappy with their inexplicable slow rate of march. To find the cause of the delay you sent several of your officers to inform you of the causes of the delay, which to you seemed incomprehensible, since, about two o'clock in the afternoon, you yourself had at Ligny

ordered the head of 4th Army Corps to go to Gembloux, which is only two leagues from Ligny.

Clearly Gérard marched far slower than Vandamme. Grouchy has been damned for the slow rate of his pursuit, but clearly his rate of movement was badly affected by Gérard's tardiness and reluctance in moving 4th Corps on 17 June, probably for good reason as it would, like 3rd Corps, need time to promote new NCOs and officers to fill vacancies caused by the battle on the previous day, re-supply munitions, and to try and rally the morale of the men. The same issues were faced by Vandamme—issues the emperor knew only too well about. The state of the roads that they had to traverse did not help either in allowing for a quick marching pace.

Napoléon, writing on Saint Helena, states that both 3rd and 4th Corps were at Gembloux at 18.00, and blames Grouchy for allowing the men to camp at this time and not pursue the Prussians.[45] Napoléon was probably mistaken in his timings, however Grouchy arrived some two hours later, around 20.00 with 3rd Corps, and 4th Corps arrived far later (around 23.00) if his aide-de-camp, Bella,[46] is accurate with his timings.[47] Therefore, Napoléon is attempting to blame Grouchy for his defeat by letting his men make camp rather than following the Prussians. While Napoléon might have planned for Grouchy to arrive at Gembloux around 18.00, he disguises the fact that his plans have come unravelled, with the French troops taking far longer on their march than he anticipated. Grouchy was an easy target. Ever loyal, General Gérard uses his former master's writing as evidence to condemn Grouchy in 1829 and 1830, writing a decade after Grouchy's own defence in 1818 and 1819. In fact, Gérard's writings were printed to demonstrate that he was a loyal subject of the saintly and liberal Napoléon at a time when his own political career was burgeoning with the Liberals in France.

NOTES:

[1] William Siborne, *History of the war in France and Belgium, in 1815, containing minute details of the battles of Quatre-Bras, Ligny, Wavre and Waterloo* (Vol. 1), Boone, London, 1848,.pp. 183-4.

[2] William O'Connor Morris, *The Campaign of 1815: Ligny, Quatre-Bras, Waterloo*, Grant Richards, London, 1900, p. 171.

[3] John Codman Ropes, *The Campaign of Waterloo*, C. Scribner's Sons, New York, 1892, pp. 248-9.

[4] SHDDT: C15 5. Dossier 17 June 1815. Bertrand to Grouchy. Copy of the now lost original order made by Comte du Casse in June 1865. We cannot corroborate this order since no other versions of the order exist. We have to trust that it is a direct copy of the original.

[5] SHDDT: C15 5. Dossier 17 June 1815. Soult to Ney 17 June 1815, timed at 9.00.

[6] SHDDT: C15 5. Dossier 17 June 1815. Bertrand to Grouchy, timed at 13.00. Copy of the now lost original order made by Comte du Casse in June 1865. We cannot corroborate this order

since no other versions of the order exist. We have to trust that it is a direct copy of the now lost original.

7   Ropes, pp. 209-10.
8   SHDDT: C15 5. Dossier 17 June 1815. Soult to Grouchy. This is the original, handwritten order from 17 June 1815.
9   SHDDT: C15 5. Dossier 18 June 1815. Sénécal to Grouchy, no date.
10 SHDDT: C15 5. Dossier 18 June 1815. Grouchy to Napoléon. Copy of the original order made in June 1863. See also: Hans Oskar von Lettow-Vorbeck, *Napoleons Untergang 1815*, Mittler, Berlin, 1904, p. 390.
11 Emmanuel Grouchy, *Observations sur la relation de la campagne de 1815 publiée par le général Gourgaud et réfutation de quelques-unes des assertions d'autres écrits relatifs à la bataille de Waterloo, par le maréchal de Grouchy*, Chaumerot Jeune, Paris, 1819, pp. 10-13.
1   Grouchy, *Relation succincte de la campagne de 1815*, Vol. 4, pp. 146-51.
13 AN: LH 1438/54. Hilaire Noël Taurin La Fresnaye was born on 3 September 1789 and was listed as a second lieutenant in the 2nd Cuirassiers on 1 June 1808. He left the regiment on 18 May 1810 and died in 1879.
14 Grouchy, *Relation succincte de la campagne de 1815*, Vol. 4, p. 136.
15 C. Mullié, *Biographie des célébrités militaires des armées de terre et de mer de 1789 à 1850*, Poignavant et Compie, Paris, 1852, p. 18.
1   SHDDT: C15 *Registre d'Ordres et de correspondance du major-general a partir du 13 Juin jusqu'au 26 Juin au Maréchal Grouchy*, p. 27. See also: SHDDT: C15 5. Dossier 17 June 1815. Excelmans to Grouchy.
17 Grouchy, *Relation succincte de la campagne de 1815*, Vol. 4, pp. 146-51.
18 Lefol, pp. 59-60.
19 Lefol, pp. 59-60.
20 SHDDT: GR 2 YB 232 *Contrôle Nominatif Officiers 32e régiment du Ligne 1 Juillet 1814 a 1 Mai 1815*. Jean Marie Putigny was born on 9 June 1774, and admitted into the regiment on 16 April 1792. He was successively promoted to captain on 22 June 1811 and wounded at Ligny and Namur.
21 Miot-Putigny, p. 245.
22 SHDDT: C15 35. Dossier 3rd Corps. Situation report 31 May, signed by Guilleminot.
23 One *quintaux* = 100 kilograms.
24 SHDDT: C15 35. Dossier 3rd Corps. Situation report 31 May, signed by Guillaminot.
25 SHDDT: C15 35. Dossier 4th Corps. Situation report 31 May, signed by Simon Lorrier 5 June 1815.
26 Gerbet, p. 13.
27 SHDDT: C15 5. Dossier 17 June 1815. Vandamme to Grouchy, 17 Juin 1815.
28 AN: LH 1026/31. Charles François was born on 19 June 1775 and volunteered into the 9th Regiment of Line Infantry on 5 September 1792. He was promoted to corporal on 3 January 1803, to fourrier on 9 January 1794, to sergeant on 17 November 1798, to sergeant-major on 8 April 1799, and to sub-lieutenant on 12 November 1803. He passed to the gendarmes in a reserve legion on 5 May 1807 and to the 30th Regiment of Line Infantry as lieutenant on 30 October 1810. He was promoted to captain on 8 February 1812. He had been wounded during the Egyptian Expedition and at Baylen on 19 July 1808, again on 6 September 1812, and again on 19 December 1812. He had been a prisoner of war from 19 July 1808 to 16 May 1810. He was awarded the Legion of Honour on 12 October 1812 and presented with the Order of the Lys by the Duke of Berry on 1 June 1814. He was discharged from the army on 28 August 1816. On his service papers, he totally omits his service and wounds in 1815.
29 François.
30 See Paul L. Dawson, *Memoires: Fact or Fiction? The Campaign of 1814*, The Napoleon Series, December 2013, available at http://www.napoleon-series.org/research/eyewitness/ c_memoires.html [accessed 28 February 2017].
31 SHDDT: C15 5. Dossier 18 June. Guyardin to 3rd Corps.

[32] Rumigny.

[33] SHDDT: C15 *Registre d'Ordres et de correspondance du major-general a partir du 13 Juin jusqu'au 26 Juin au Marechal Grouchy*, p. 27.

[34] SHDDT: C15 5. Dossier 17 June 1815. Grouchy to Vandamme.

[35] Grouchy, *Relation succincte de la campagne de 1815*, Vol. 4, pp. 60-1. See also: SHDDT: C15 5. Dossier 17 June 1815 Bonnemains to Excelmans.

[36] Grouchy, *Relation succincte de la campagne de 1815*, Vol. 4, pp. 60-1.

[37] SHDDT: C15 5. Dossier 23 June 1815. *Rapport Bonnemains to Soult, 23 Juin 1815.*

[38] Berton, pp. 48-9.

[39] AN: LH 468/64. Claude Chaillot was born in Dijon on 29 November 1768 and admitted to the 1st Volunteer Battalion of Paris on 1 September 1792. He was promoted to fourrier on 8 September 1792 (i.e. he must have been literate, as the rank of fourrier equates to company clerk) and to sergeant-major on 15 September 1792. Within the year, he was made sub-lieutenant on 26 December 1792 and then promoted to lieutenant on 12 May 1793, to aide-de-camp to General Rubell on 15 October 1795, to aide-de-camp to General Beguriot on 16 October 1796, to captain aide-de-camp on 12 April 1797. He was listed as aide-de-camp to General Druit on 20 June 1800, passed as a captain of the 7th Hussars on 27 June 1800, as aide-de-camp to General Boussart on 10 June 1802, as squadron commander of 21st Dragoons on 22 March 1807, transferred with the same rank to 22nd Dragoons on 14 November 1813, and then named as colonel of the 15th Dragoons on 15 March 1814. He was discharged on 20 February 1816 and died in 1837.

[40] SHDDT: C15 5. Dossier 17 June 1815. Vandamme to Grouchy.

[41] Sénécal, p. 10.

[42] SHDDT: C15 5. Dossier 17 June 1815 Grouchy to Napoléon, times at 22.00.

[43] Anon, *Memoires pour servir a l'Histoire*, pp. 100-1.

[44] Grouchy, *Relation succincte de la campagne de 1815*, Vol. 4, pp. 141-5.

[45] Anon, *Memoires pour servir a l'Histoire*, p. 99.

[46] AN: LH 168/59. Marie Joseph Auguste Bella was born in Strasbourg on 10 October 1777 and enlisted in the 7th Hussars in 1795, and rapidly promoted to sub-lieutenant in 1800. He was promoted to lieutenant in 1803, to captain on 14 July 1807, named as adjutant chief-of-staff to General Marchand on 8 January 1814, and promoted to battalion commander on 23 February 1814. He was made an Officer of the Legion of Honour on 20 November 1814. Following Waterloo, he was named as aide-de-camp to General Marchand on 4 August 1815 and discharged on 21 September 1816.

[47] Grouchy, *Relation succincte de la campagne de 1815*, p. 42.

Chapter 8

The Prussians

At nightfall on 17 June, while Grouchy was at Gembloux, the whole of Blücher's army (except two divisions—the 9th and 13th—and the reserve cavalry of Thielemann's corps, which were posted as rearguards to the 3rd and 4th Corps) had reached Wavre and its neighbourhood. The 2nd and 3rd Corps bivouacked on the left bank of the Dyle, beyond Wavre, and the 1st and 4th on the right bank. Pirch. was between Saint-Anne and Aisemont; Bülow was at Dion-le-Mont. The rearguards were posted at Vieux-Sart and Mont-Saint-Guibert; these troops fell back the next day as the French advanced. On Blücher's left, patrols scoured the country towards Namur and Louvain; on his right, they watched the Dyle and its approaches. Limale was held by a detachment from Ziethen's corps to protect the right flank, and cavalry patrols rode to and fro all over the valley of the Dyle. The reserve ammunition columns with supplies reached Wavre in the afternoon of 17 June, and thus munitions for the artillery and infantry was replenished, and it speaks well for the Prussian arrangements that these supplies should have reached Wavre at so important a moment when, on account of their unexpected retreat to Wavre, all previous arrangements had to be cancelled.

Bülow commenced his march from Dion-le-Mont at daybreak on 18 June, around 4.00, with Losthin's 15th Division as an advanced guard. Around 7.00, the division reached Wavre, but the crossing of the bridges over the Dyle occupied a long time, and a fire that had broken out in the main street of Wavre, through which the troops were marching, hindered the passage through the town. The advanced guard reached Saint-Lambert at about 10.30 and the main body arrived about midday, but the rearguard (Ryssef's division) did not arrive until 15.00. Ziethen, on the left bank of the Dyle, marched for Ohain at noon. Blücher was uneasy about Grouchy's strength, and was anxious to take his whole army towards Mont-Saint-Jean. He, however, appears to have been aware of the potential of an attack on his rear and flank. He therefore determined to leave Thielemann's corps at Wavre to await Grouchy's approach, and if the French were not in strength, Thielemann was to march to join the main body, leaving a small force in Wavre as a rearguard. Blücher himself, leaving Gneisenau to arrange matters at Wavre, rode on to Saint-Lambert at 11.00. Carl von Clausewitz sums up the faults he felt Napoléon committed that day with which the author is in agreement:[1]

> It is truly strange that on the morning of the 17th, the Prussian army was not pursued or sought at all in the direction of Tilly and Gentinnes, where two corps had gone, but only in the direction of Gembloux, where just one corps had gone, and in the direction of Namur, where none had gone. Virtually the only explanation for this astonishing fact is that when Bonaparte tasked Marshal Grouchy with the pursuit, his two cavalry corps were [already] facing toward Gembloux, because they had been fighting Thielemann all day. If Bonaparte had ordered the Guard cavalry and the 3rd Corps to conduct the pursuit, they would have picked up the trail more easily. The casual way in which Bonaparte did everything prevented him from giving Grouchy more detailed instructions. Furthermore, Bonaparte himself seems to have held so firmly to the idea that Blücher had to go to the Meuse that no thought was given to any other direction than Gembloux and the roman road. At any rate, we can see that a pursuit along the two roads to Gembloux and Namur must have been Bonaparte's intention, because they are mentioned in a message written by Marshal Soult to Ney from Fleurus on the 17th, and published by Gamot. These were obviously instructions to harass the Prussian army on its way to the Meuse, rather than to block its way toward Wellington. If Bonaparte had thought that Blücher was going to Wavre, it would have been more natural for him to send a strong force there via the left bank of the Dyle.
>
> There is still too little explanation for Pajol's movements—first in the direction of Namur, then towards Saint-Denis between Namur and Gembloux, and then back toward Mazy. Whether Grouchy or Napoléon ordered this strange movement remains uncertain, but the result was that after wandering around aimlessly on 17th June, Pajol and his corps, plus Teste's division, found themselves still near Mazy in the evening, thus more or less back on the battlefield of Ligny.
>
> Even Grouchy with the 3rd and 4th Corps was only able to reach the area around Gembloux by 10 p.m. where they had to spend the night, while Excelmans was sent forward to Sart-a-Walhain. But even this corps then sought quarters for the night and had only two regiments in front as an advanced guard.

The overall result of this day on the French side was that for all practical purposes they failed to pursue the Prussian army. Blücher was able to reach Wavre unimpeded and unite his corps there on the evening of the 17th.

While this seems to contrast strongly with previous French practices, we must also carefully consider the differing situations. The extraordinarily energetic pursuits that brought Bonaparte such spectacular results in his earlier campaigns were simply a matter of pushing far superior forces forward in pursuit of a totally defeated enemy. But now he had to turn his main force—in particular his freshest corps—against a new opponent who had not yet been defeated. The troops who were supposed to conduct the pursuit were the 3rd and 4th Corps, precisely the ones who had been engaged in a very bloody struggle until ten o'clock in the evening, and now needed some time to get themselves back into order, eat their rations, and replenish their ammunition. To be sure, the cavalry corps had not suffered and would therefore have been able to press the Prussian rearguard quickly. That they did not do so may well have been a mistake, but cavalry alone could not have produced results like those achieved in earlier victories by a general advance of the French army, because the terrain is too broken for cavalry alone to achieve much.

Grouchy issues orders

Grouchy, based on authentic documents from 17 June, did not know that all the Prussian forces were at Wavre. He suspected some where there, but had not yet grasped that all the Prussians were there, as he had clearly explained to the emperor. By mid-afternoon on 17 June, Grouchy had been informed by Pajol that the Prussians were moving towards Leuze; his latest information from Excelmans had been that a Prussian corps had been in the vicinity of Gembloux, but that it had moved off to an unknown destination. By the time he reached Gembloux, he must somehow have been informed, possibly by residents, that enemy columns had also been moving towards Perwez as well. When he sent his 19.00 order to Excelmans, it is abundantly clear that Grouchy was in a great hurry to acquire more definitive information about the Prussians. The order also makes clear that Grouchy regarded Excelmans's information as decisive for his further command decisions. It is unfortunate that Excelmans's report of the evening of 17 June cannot be found, as this contained the key information upon which Grouchy decided what to do during the following day. But the orders and reports written by Grouchy show that Excelmans most probably hinted towards a Prussian move towards Sart-a-Walhain, as this is where Grouchy directed his troops to. It was for this reason that he intended to halt here and upon new reconnaissance information either head further north or further east towards Perwez and Maastricht within the remit of his orders.

The orders Grouchy issued that evening make it very clear that he was not aware of the Prussian concentration at Wavre. Milhaud had observed the entire Prussian 1st and 2nd Corps heading to Wavre, yet Napoléon did not tell Grouchy this. Grouchy's idea about the Prussian whereabouts was based upon encounters with 3rd Corps, which drew his attention towards Gembloux and Wavre, and Bülow's 4th Corps likewise drew Grouchy's attention towards Perwez. The Prussian 1st and 2nd Corps were not spotted by Pajol or Excelmans, simply because the focus for this operation, as ordered by Napoléon, was to Namur and Maastricht. Finding the Prussian 3rd Corps at Gembloux only strengthened Grouchy's resolve that the Prussians were heading east, and he made plans accordingly. He never found the Prussian 1st and 2nd Corps, as he was ordered to operate in a different sphere of operations, and when he was told about the column moving from Gentinnes on 18 June, he was horribly aware that a major Prussian force was heading to Wavre and thence either to Brussels or Wellington. Grouchy had been ordered to stop the Prussians linking with Wellington, yet his sphere of operations was such, and the total failure by Napoléon to pass on vital information about the Prussians and his own operations, doomed Grouchy's mission to failure.

He issued orders to move some of Excelmans's squadrons back towards Wavre, as well as to send others towards Perwez.

The 3rd and 4th Corps was to move via Sart-a-Walhain; Grouchy's thinking, I feel, was that once the troops at Perwez had been found and their line of march established, he could either head to Wavre or to press on north-east on a more direct route to Brussels. Grouchy, judging by documents from 17 and 18 June 1815, thought that the Prussians were already at Wavre, and in the early hours of 18 June had already departed for Waterloo. Vandamme's orders for 18 June reads:[2]

> Gembloux 17 June
>
> I am writing to you, dear general, to inform you that tomorrow morning at six o'clock you are to march to Sart-a-Walhain. You will be preceded by the cavalry of General Excelmans. Behind you will be the corps of General-in-Chief Gérard.
>
> General Pajol has been ordered to march to Mazy on the Namur road, who is there at this moment, via Grand-Leez, and will move in

the new direction which I shall furnish to him. Accept, my dear general, the assurance I hold you in high regard. With sincere greetings

The Marshal Comte de Grouchy
To General Comte Vandamme.

A second order issued by Grouchy reads:[3]

Gembloux 17 June,
In case I forget to inform you, my dear general, you are to pass Sart-a-Walhain with your army corps, and that the 4th Corps of General Gérard will take up position in your rear. I will send you new dispositions when you arrive at Sart-a-Walhain; it will only be then that I can give you definitive dispositions. A thousand thanks
The Marshal Comte de Grouchy
To General Comte Vandamme.

This order was received by Vandamme's staff, and the following order was issued to all divisional commanders in direct consequence:[4]

Order of the day
3rd Corps Armée du Nord
There will be made tomorrow, the 18th, the distribution of water and bread to the troops of 3rd Corps. The distribution will take place at five o'clock in the morning under the instruction of the ordonnateur-in-chief.
At Gembloux, 17 June 1815
The battalion commander, assistant chief-of-staff of 3rd Corps
Guyardin.

According to an order from Grouchy to Gérard copied in June 1865 by Comte de Casse—and crucially which does not exist in Grouchy's correspondence register—reads:[5]

Gembloux 17 June 1815
At ten o'clock in the evening
I desire, my dear general, that you commence your march tomorrow morning, the 18th, instantly at eight o'clock. You will follow the corps of General Vandamme and will make provisions to move via Sart-a-Walhain. As soon as information is received from the scouts and the reconnaissance reports from Perwez and Sart-a-Walhain, I will alter the line of march accordingly.

Will you ensure, despite the bad weather, that the troops under your orders receive a double ration of water of life?

Marshal Grouchy.

A second order to Gérard, also copied by Comte de Casse, but that is also found in Grouchy's own register of correspondence, reads:[6]

Gemblousse [*sic*] 17 June 1815

My dear general, please order your cavalry, which is now resting at Borthey, that tomorrow at daybreak they will move to Grand-Leez. They are not to pass through Gembloux during their movement and will follow the left wing of the enemy which is retiring to Perwez. The march of your cavalry and yourself begins tomorrow morning and it is strictly necessary that your cavalry leave at a good hour, so that they arrive in good time for us to unite with them at the heights of Grand-Leez. At your pleasure, can you send me an officer from your staff so that I can transmit to him the movement orders for tomorrow. I expect that you will receive support from Excelmans.

Pajol had been at Grand-Leez since the evening of 17 June, yet apparently to Pajol, Grouchy sent the following order:[7]

To General Pajol, 17 June, 10 p.m.

Please, my dear general, tomorrow the 18th current at daybreak, depart from Mazy from where you will move with your corps and Teste's division to Grand-Leez, where I will send you new orders.

I will march in the wake of the enemy, who still had 30,000 men here at noon. I go on to Sart-a-Walhain, but according to the information that I will receive in the night and yours, perhaps I shall move on Perwez-Marché. As soon as you arrive at Grand-Leez, link with me by messengers and give me your news.

The emperor directs me to clear the road to Namur and find out if this city has been captured, and push towards it a strong, well-commanded reconnaissance patrol, he knows that there passed here infantry, cavalry and artillery and desires to know if Namur is evacuated.

We will meet you at the Grand-Leez by taking the shortest route without returning to Mazy. I also wish that you bear on Grand-Leez, without returning to pass Gembloux, which you will find crowded.

So, go by the direct route, which will be quicker, and the route we will follow on. Vandamme has ordered Subervie join you, did he not do so? Send me your two officers and news to me acknowledging this.

Grouchy desired that Pajol was to move in a large arc north-east from Mazy to Grand-Leez, which is about nine miles away. However, this order does not appear in Grouchy's register of orders. It conflicts with the reports Pajol had sent into Grouchy, stating he was at Grand-Leez. The order if genuine raises another question. Grouchy talks of Subervie's troops. History tells us when the order was written, Subervie was miles away at Waterloo. Had Grouchy been informed of this? We assume Vandamme had been, but clearly it had not gotten to Marshal. Was Vandamme being awkward in not passing on information? For fact, based on extant documents from 17 June 1815, Grouchy had not been informed Subervie's command had trotted off to Waterloo. He knew Domon's command had gone with the emperor. Surely Vandamme knew? Yet he chose not to tell his commander in chief. Vandammes personality was starting to impact on command and control decisions made by Grouchy.

If we look at Grouchy's register of correspondence, we find a letter from him to Pajol:[8]

> Gembloux 18 June 1815. Three o'clock in the morning
> Marshal Grouchy to General Pajol at Grand-Leez.
> Please, my dear General, on reception of this present order you are to move, with your cavalry corps, Teste's division to Tourinnes. I am at this moment heading to Tourinnes and will receive your news at my new address.
> A thousand thanks
> Signe. Comte Grouchy.

Among the boxes of documents at the Army Archives at Vincennes can be found this dispatch, sent presumably in response to the 22.00 order:[9]

> Mazy 18 June 1815, at four o'clock in the morning
> General Pajol to Marshal Grouchy
> Monsignor,
> I have the honour to report that Namur was evacuated yesterday and I pushed my troops beyond Temploux and Meux, I learnt that a body of 25,000 to 30,000 men had united in Gembloux, and not being supported, I thought it necessary to retire to Mazy.
> Respectfully
> Pajol.

If Pajol was writing on 18 June, Gembloux was occupied by the French and not the Prussians, so this order must have been sent on 17 June, long before Vandamme occupied the place in the evening. But, Pajol was clearly not at Namur on 16 June, so the date must be 18 June. Did Pajol not know Grouchy had occupied Gembloux? It seems very possible. The truth, however, must have dawned upon him when he got Grouchy's report from Gembloux. Had Pajol mistaken Grouchy's forces for Prussians? Perhaps. But if Pajol was back at Mazy, how do we ascribe the notes by his aide, Biot, that on the morning of 18 June he was at the Abbey of Argenton? Why did Grouchy think Pajol was at Grand-Leez?

Grouchy wrote the following order to General Louis Vallin, who had taken command of the division upon the wounding of General Maurin on 18 June:[10]

> Gembloux 18 June 1815.
>
> Marshal Grouchy to General Vallin at Grand-Leez.
>
> Please, my dear general, on receipt of this present order you are to move rapidly to Tourinnes via Sart-a-Walhain where you will join the cavalry corps of General Excelmans, which will also be my new address.
>
> From Grand-Leez detach twenty-five dragoons commanded by an officer and have them go to Gembloux, where they will receive new orders and will link me with the emperor, they are to march via Marbais on the four roads.
>
> Signe. Comte Grouchy.

Grouchy, sometime later, sent the following to Pajol at about 4.00:[11]

> Gembloux 18 June 1815, daybreak
>
> Marshal Grouchy to General Pajol at Grand-Leez.
>
> An opinion, which does not seem unfounded, tells me, my dear general, a large park of artillery of the enemy must be, in this moment, a league and a half from Grand-Leez. Carry out a reconnaissance, and if it is so, fall on them with your cavalry and Teste's division. If you could not attack, because of superior forces that escort this park, I will support you with troops that I shall send you via Sart-a-Walhain, which is where I am moving to.
>
> The retreat of the army of Blücher seems to be towards Brussels. Thus, in cases where the advice I give you is without foundation, move to Tourinnes in great haste, so we push ahead of Wavre as quickly as possible.
>
> Signe. Comte Grouchy.

Grouchy was still convinced that the bulk of the Prussians were heading to Wavre. He had made contact with two columns. Pajol estimated twenty-five thousand men and that a column was withdrawing via Tourinnes-les-Ourdons. But would they keep heading north-east or would they swing north? The most probable line of march was north-west to Wavre and then on to Brussels.

In accordance with the emperor's order dated 17 June, and which perhaps did not arrive with Grouchy until nightfall, instructions were issued to garrison Namur. Written at Gembloux in the morning of 18 June was the following order, sent presumably by Pajol:[12]

> The victory reported by the emperor at Fleurus has resulted in the evacuation of Namur, and His Majesty has instructed me to transmit to you the order to occupy Namur with several battalions of the National Guard, as well as a number of artillery batteries which you are to form, and to send them from Charlemont.
>
> Transmit this order to the marshal-du-camp of this place that His Majesty has authorised you to do so.
>
> Before you order the National Guard to leave for Namur in order to occupy this place, you are to make a reconnaissance to assure yourselves that the Prussians no longer occupy that place and the troops are heading to Liège.
>
> Please accept my highest regards and sincerest attachment,
> Signe Marshal Grouchy.

Grouchy reported the results of Pajol's intelligence, and his own logical reasoning of the situation, to Napoléon in a letter dated Gembloux, 18 June 1815 timed at 6.00. Again, Grouchy had to assume Napoléon was still somewhere between Quatre-Bras and Brussels. This document reached Napoléon around 9.30 to 10.00. The report read:[13]

> Sire,
>
> All my reports and information confirm that the Prussians are falling back on Brussels, either to concentrate there or to offer battle once united with Wellington. General Pajol reports that Namur has been evacuated. Regarding 1st and 2nd Corps of Blücher's army, the 1st Corps appear to be moving on Corbais, the 2nd Corps on Chaumont. Both are said to have moved off from Tourinnes and marched all night. Fortunately, the weather was so bad that they are unlikely to have gone far. I will move off to Sart-a-Walhain immediately, and intend moving on Corbais and Wavre. I will send you further reports from one or the other places.

I am, with respect, your humble servant.

Grouchy

P. S. Conforming to your orders, the general commanding the 2nd Military Division at Charlemont, de Loire, has occupied Namur with several battalions of National Guard and numerous artillery pieces have been transferred from Charlemont.

To ensure communication with Your Majesty I have twenty-five horses at my disposal.

The corps of infantry and the cavalry under my command still have a full provision and a further half in reserve in the case of a major action. When we are close to using our reserve ammunition it will be necessary, Your Majesty, to make contact with the artillery depots you indicated to obtain replacements.

Napoléon received the letter and dispatched a reply timed at 10.00, which arrived with Grouchy some hours later. Napoléon's version of the event differs from the hard facts of the time that the dispatch was sent and received, as recorded by Marshals Soult and Grouchy, in that the dispatch was timed at 2.00, and arrived with Napoléon at 5.00.[14] Here, yet again, Napoléon is setting up Grouchy as a fall guy for his own failure, and bending the truth to suit his own propaganda.

The mission of Colonel Marbot

Both General Berton and Colonel Marbot, of the 7th Hussars, state that reconnaissance patrols were sent out to link with Grouchy. No paperwork from 1815 exists at all to confirm this. However, it is not impossible that this did occur. The first reference to this was written in 1818, but it may very well be an elaborate case of false memory of what should have happened, rather than what did happen, as the author, General Berton, was writing to blame Grouchy for the loss of Waterloo. But his story seems to have a ring of truth about it, otherwise why would Grouchy have written to Marbot about the latter's own recollections of the day? Clearly Berton's writings had a grain of truth in them. Berton comments the following about the night of 17 June:[15]

Since Quatre-Bras, the division of Domon was detached to scout along the left bank of the Dyle, along to the Brussels road; the 4th Regiment of Chasseurs passed the bridge at Moustier, where his skirmishers opened fire with their carbines at the Prussian cavalry. With the onset of night, the division returned and bivouacked to the right of headquarters.

If this is correct, then Domon found the same column that Milhaud had spotted earlier that day. So clearly, if Berton is telling us the truth, headquarters now had intelligence of the Prussians still being on the right bank of the Dyle at Moustier. Was it in response to this news that Marbot was sent off? He writes:[16]

> The 7th Hussars, of which I was colonel, was part of the light cavalry division attached to the 1st Corps forming, on 18 June, the right wing of the army that the emperor commanded in person.
>
> At the beginning of the action, about eleven o'clock, my regiment was detached from the division, along with a light infantry battalion, which was placed under my command. These troops were established as a reserve at the far right, behind Frischermont facing the Dyle.
>
> Specific instructions were given to me from the emperor by his aide-de-camp, General La Bédoyère, and an aide, that I cannot remember the name of, specified that I was to leave most of my troop always in view of the battlefield, and I was to take 200 infantry into the woods of Frischermont, establish a squadron in Lasne, then move towards the positions at Saint-Lambert with another squadron, place half at Couture, and half at Beaumont, which were to send out reconnaissance patrols along the Dyle, and towards Moustier-Ottignies. The commanders of various detachments had to leave quarter of a mile between each outpost, forming a contiguous string along on the battlefield, so that by means of hussars, galloping from one post to the other, the officers on reconnaissance might inform me quickly before they met the vanguard troops of Marshal Grouchy, who were to arrive on the side of the Dyle. I was finally ordered to send directly to the emperor all the reconnaissance reports.
>
> I executed the order that I was given, it would be impossible, after a period of fifteen years, to determine which you ask for, the time at which the detachment arrived at Moustier. Especially as Captain Elon,[17] who commanded, had been instructed by me to proceed in his march with the utmost caution, but noting that he started at eleven o'clock from the battlefield, and had not more than two miles to go, one must assume that he did so in two hours, which would set his arrival in Moustier at one o'clock.
>
> A note from Captain Elon that I was promptly handed from the intermediate stations, told me that he found no troops in Moustier, nor at Ottignies, and the inhabitants assured him that the French left on the right bank of the Dyle were crossing the river in Limelette and Wavre.

I sent this letter to the emperor with Captain Kounkn,18 acting as adjutant major, he returned accompanied by an aide, who said to me, from the emperor, to keep the line at Moustier, and to send an officer and detachment along the defile of Saint-Lambert, and to dispatch the various parties in the directions of Limale, Limelette and Wavre.

I sent this order, and even sent a copy with my detachment chief at Lasnel-Saint-Lambert (his name is no longer in my memory, but I think it was Lieutenant Municheffer).[19]

One of our platoons, having advanced to a quarter of a mile beyond Saint-Lambert, encountered a picket of Prussian hussars, of which we took several men, including an officer! I informed the emperor of this strange capture, and sent him the prisoners. Informed by them that they were followed by much of the Prussian army, I advanced to Saint-Lambert with a squadron to act as reinforcements. There, I perceived a strong column heading to Saint-Lambert. I sent an officer at full speed to inform the emperor, and I addressed this advance guard; this company could be the corps of Marshal Grouchy moving from Limale, and driving before him the Prussians, some of which were among the prisoners that I had made.

I was soon convinced of the contrary: the head of the column approached, albeit very slowly. I threw back twice the hussars and lancers that preceded it, and tried to buy time by keeping at bay the largest number of the enemy, which had to advance on very difficult terrain, when finally compelled by superior forces, I beat a retreat. I ordered the adjutant-major to go and inform the emperor of the arrival of the Prussians before Saint-Lambert. He came back saying that the emperor ordered me to prevent this event and informed me that the head of the column of Marshal Grouchy was advancing at this moment by the bridges of Moustier and Ottignies, since they did not come by Limale and Limelette. I wrote to that effect to Captain Elon; but it having waited in vain without seeing any troops, and hearing the cannon at Saint-Lambert, and afraid of being cut off, and retiring by the successive small vedettes he joined the bulk of the regiment that remained in view of the battlefield, at about the same time that the squadrons returned from Saint-Lambert and Lasnes, pushed back by the enemy.

The terrible struggle that then began behind the wood of Frischermont. I was too absorbed in the action that I cannot specify exactly what time it was, but I think it could be nearly seven o'clock and as Captain Elon returned at the trot, and probably did not take more than an hour to get back, I think it will be about six o'clock that he left the bridge at Moustier, therefore he would have still been there around five o'clock. It is therefore surprising that there was not seen M. your aide-de-camp, unless he was mistaken about the name of the place where he crossed the Dyle.

We do know from material written on 18 June 1815 that the elite gendarmes of the Imperial Guard are said to have brought the Prussian prisoner from the 2nd Silesian Hussars to the French headquarters, who was then questioned by the staff. He revealed that he was carrying a dispatch from Bülow (commanding the Prussian 4th Corps) to Wellington, saying his command had just arrived at Chapelle-Saint-Lambert.

This intercepted letter is reported in the order Napoléon sent to Grouchy sometime between 13.00 and 13.30:[20]

> P. S. A letter which has just been intercepted, which says General Bülow is about to attack our right flank, we believe that we see his corps on the height of Saint-Lambert. Lose not an instant in moving towards us to join us, in order to crush Bülow, whom you will crush in the very act.

The news was also transmitted to Davout. Therefore, it does seem credible that Marbot is correct that such a document was captured. However, on closer examination Marbot's account has a lot of inconsistencies. Firstly, what order was Marbot sent off in response to? Was it the 10.00 dispatch to Grouchy? Possibly.

Secondly, he says he sent a squadron to Lasne with outposts at Chapelle-Saint-Lambert, a half-squadron went to Couture, and the other half arrived at Moustier and Ottignies by 13.00. Captain Elon says the local inhabitants had not seen any French troops in the immediate area and the French army was then crossing the Dyle. Given Excelmans was at Moustier about an hour earlier and at 13.00 was attacking the Prussians at La Baraque,[21] how could Captain Elon not have heard the fighting? How had the local inhabitants not heard or observed the Prussians and a division of French dragoons? Regardless, Marbot sent the squadron from Chapelle-Saint-Lambert to Limale, Limelette and Wavre, during which movement a small skirmish ensued with Prussian hussars, which were the vanguard of the Prussians heading to Waterloo. However, with more analysis, Marbot's account appears to fall apart.

Marbot cannot have occupied Chappelle-Saint-Lambert by 13.00, as it had been in Prussian hands since 10.30. If Captain Elon sent his dispatch to Marbot at exactly 13.00 it would not have got to Marbot until 15.00, and he may not have received them until 17.00, by which time the Prussians were now debouching at Waterloo and the 7th Hussars would be trapped behind the Prussians, thus the new orders to Elon cannot have existed if he ever got to Moustier at the times he presents. If Elon left Moustier to arrive back at Waterloo by 19.00, based on Marbot's testimony, he would have to have left Moustier by 17.00, by which time he and his men would have had no chance of moving back to Waterloo. Prussian sources are all of the same opinion that no fighting took place at Chapelle-Saint-Lambert at all and the fact that Lasne was not occupied by the French. Marbot's geography is also a little suspect. Moustier is ten miles from La-Belle-Alliance, an hour's ride from Waterloo. Yet Marbot makes this a two-hour mission. No other French source speaks of these orders to Marbot.

If Elon was at Moustier at 13.00, he would have heard Excelmans attack at La Baraque, and if there for two hours he would have heard Vandamme's guns at Wavre. The truth probably is that Marbot only operated to the south of Frischermont.

The possibility of course exists that Marbot got his timings very wrong. Did he in fact set off at first light and got to Lasne and Moustier before the Prussians, and that in reality, the Prussians he found were in fact the advance guard of Bülow's 4th Corps? If he encountered the Prussians heading to Saint-Lambert as he states, he must have been there before 10.30. Given the prisoner had arrived at headquarters by 13.00, he must have left Saint-Lambert an hour or more earlier. It is very likely, given the place names he gives, that Elon went via the rue d'Anogrune and thence to the rue de Lasne passing through Couture, Lasne, Chapelle-Saint-Lambert and then swung south-east along the rue des Ottignies—a journey of ten miles. Marbot infers it took two hours to get to Moustier. Chappelle-Saint-Lambert is midway, so for the prisoner to get back to Waterloo for 12.30, he must have been on his way to headquarters an hour or more earlier. It is very possible that Marbot was at Chapelle-Saint-Lambert as the Prussians arrived, and it was these Prussians he found at 10.30, from which he made a prisoner. If so, this places Marbot leaving Waterloo by 9.00 to get to Chapelle-Saint-Lambert before the Prussians, which means if Captain Elon got to Moustier he would have done so before Excelmans arrived, perhaps the same time as Pont Bellanger had done, as they both sent the same information back to their respective headquarters staff, and thus must have left by the time Excelmans went into action about midday. In this way, we can reconcile Marbot's account with the known events at La Baraque. In viewing the events that Marbot wrote about as real, but occurring a lot earlier, it helps to corroborate Berton's observations. If Domon had been at Moustier on 17 June and had spotted Prussians, it made sense for another patrol to be sent out, backed up with infantry to double check what Domon reported, to confirm the Prussian threat on the right wing. Clearly, by the time Napoléon had sent the 10.00 order to Grouchy, the Prussian prisoner had not been brought and the chance of a Prussian link-up with Wellington was not considered a major threat, which is why the emperor ordered Grouchy to attack at Wavre and keep heading east. It was now that the emperor told Grouchy about the column Milhaud and also Domon had observed. Despite telling Grouchy about the column, and the very real possibility of Prussians between the two forces and heading to join Wellington, the emperor, as we have noted earlier, rather than being fixated on Namur, was now obsessed with the notion of the Prussian withdrawal to Brussels. Given that on the night of 17 June Domon had found Prussians at Moustier, and by 10.00 on 18 June, if not earlier, no Prussians were at Moustier as reported by Captain Elon, the logical conclusion was that they had crossed the Dyle at Wavre and were heading to Louvain and onto Brussels. The idea of the Prussians going from Wavre to Waterloo was, therefore, not considered a real possibility, as Elon's report matched Grouchy's understanding of the Prussian line of retreat. Grouchy was correct that the Prussians were heading to Louvain, but doubled back to head to Waterloo and not Brussels. He could never have known this. For Napoléon, like Excelmans and Gérard in 1830, the obvious place to cross the Dyle was at Moustier and not at Wavre to head cross-country through wooded terrain to Waterloo. If Napoléon had considered a Prussian link-up with Wellington other than via Moustier as possible, he would not have sent Grouchy the order he had done so.

Only once the Prussian prisoner was brought into headquarters and interrogated was it now revealed that some of the Prussians were heading to Waterloo and not to Brussels. The Prussian 4th Corps was the strongest of the Prussian corps, as it had not been involved in the Battle of Ligny. Napoléon probably incorrectly assumed that the rearguard Grouchy had at Wavre was the rear-most men from Bülow's corps, and that Grouchy would be moving up behind.

Due to the heavy rain from the previous night the roads of the area were waterlogged. Because of this, Bülow's march was slow once he had passed through the congested streets of Wavre with accompanying artillery. Bülow was followed to Waterloo by 2nd Corps and then 1st Corps. Blücher and Wellington had been exchanging communications since 10.00. General Bülow reached Planchenoit about 16.30. In response to the Prussian arrival, the cavalry of generals Domon and Subervie was detached to defend the Paris Wood. Perhaps at the same time, 6th Corps was ordered to take up new positions. The division was placed in an L-shaped formation in front of the Chateau of Frischermont and Hannotelet Farm.

NOTES:

1 Bassford, Moran, Pedlow, *The Campaign of 1815 Chapters 30-39*, On Waterloo, available at http://www.clausewitz.com/readings/1815/five30-39.htm.

2 SHDDT: C15 5. Dossier 17 June 1815. Grouchy to Vandamme.

3 SHDDT: C15 5. Dossier 17 June 1815. Grouchy to Vandamme.

4 SHDDT: C15 5. Dossier 17 June 1815. Guyardin to 3rd Corps.

5 SHDDT: C15 5. Dossier 17 June 1815. Grouchy to Gerard, timed at 10.00.

6 SHDDT: C15 5. Dossier 17 June 1815. Grouchy to Gerard. See also: Grouchy, *Relation succincte de la campagne de 1815*, Vol. 4, p. 20.

7 SHDDT: C15 5. Dossier 17 June 1815. Grouchy to Pajol, timed at 22.00. Copy made by du Casse in June 1865. See also: Grouchy, *Relation succincte de la campagne de 1815*, Vol. 4, p. 18.

8 SHDDT: C15 5. Dossier 18 June 1815. Grouchy to Pajol, timed at 3.00. Copy made by Comte du Casse in June 1863.

9 SHDDT: C15 *Registre d'Ordres et de correspondance du major-general a partir du 13 Juin jusqu'au 26 Juin au Maréchal Grouchy*, p. 27. See also: SHDDT: C15 5. Dossier 18 June 1815. Pajol to Grouchy, timed at 4.00. Copy of the original order made in June 1865 by Comte du Casse.

10 SHDDT: C15 5. Dossier 18 June 1815. Grouchy to Vallin. Copy made by Comte du Casse in June 1863.

1 ibid. See Also: Emmanuel Grouchy, *Mémoires du maréchal de Grouchy*, Paris, 1874, Vol. 4, pp. 62-3.

1 SHDDT: C15 5. Dossier 18 June 1815. Grouchy to commander of 2nd Military Division at Charlemont. Copy of the order made in June 1865 by Comte du Casse. See also: Grouchy, *Mémoires du maréchal de Grouchy*, 1874, Vol. 4, p.27.

1 SHDDT: C15 5. Dossier 18 June 1815. Grouchy to Napoléon. Copy of the original order made in June 1863. See also: Lettow-Vorbeck, Vol. 8, p. 390.

14 Anon, *Memoires pour servir a l'Histoire*, p. 99.

15 Berton, pp. 49-50.

16 Grouchy, *Relation succincte de la campagne de 1815*, Vol. 4.

17 SHDDT: Xc 249. Dossier 1815. Captain Elon was appointed to the 7th Company, 3rd Squadron on 15 December 1814.

18 SHDDT: Xc 249. Dossier 1815. No officer of this name listed in the regiment.

19 SHDDT: Xc 249. Dossier 1815. Lieutenant of elite company.

20 SHDDT: C15 *Registre d'Ordres et de correspondance du major-general a partir du 13 Juin jusqu'au 26 Juin au Maréchal Grouchy*, p. 30. See also: SHDDT: C15 5. Dossier 18 June 1815. Soult to Grouchy, timed at 13.00. Copy of the original order made by Comte du Casse in June 1863. du Casse either copied Grouchy's version of the letter, or had access to a duplicate set of material. This order is missing from the correspondence register of Marshal Soult.

21 Etienne-Maurice Gérard, *Dernières observations sur les opérations de l'aile droite de l'armée française à la bataille de Waterloo*, Mesner, Paris, 1830.

Chapter 9

Pont Bellanger's Mission

As we noted in the previous chapter, Captain Elon, of the 7th Hussars, had arrived at Moustier, we think, by 10.00 on a reconnaissance patrol from Waterloo. Acting on Vandamme's news about Prussians at Wavre, Grouchy sent off a small force to follow up this report, and if Prussians were there, to find out where they were going.

Grouchy's aide-de-camp, de Blocqueville,[1] comments that at daybreak, Squadron Commander Bellanger,[2] with some of Grouchy's escort, headed north, ostensibly to follow up on Vandamme's comments about the Prussians moving to Wavre.[3] Bellanger, we are told, moved to the left of the main column of the army and arrived at Moustier. Here, he interviewed local inhabitants who told him that no enemy troops had been seen, other than a column heading to Wavre. Once sure of the fact he had found the Prussians, he reported the news back to Grouchy.[4] Sénécal, another of Grouchy's aides, reports the same story in 1829.[5] Officer d'Ordonnance Leguest writes that Bellanger was informed that several Prussian columns had passed through Moustier on the night of 17 to 18 June towards Wavre. He reported back to Grouchy, at Sart-a-Walhain.[6]

The news made the issues at hand much clearer for Grouchy. Firstly, he assumed that at Wavre was the Prussian rearguard behind the main army which was headed to Louvain. Secondly, he did not know Waterloo was to be fought, so did not consider that the Prussians might be heading west. In both cases, the receipt of this news resulted in Excelmans himself heading off with Stroltz's dragoon division. Vandamme and Gérard were now directed on to Wavre.[7]

Contrary to the myth about Grouchy lacking initiative, here, in sending off Bellanger, he was acting, it seems, on gut instinct developed by years of fighting that any reconnaissance report had to be followed up even if it suggested the Prussians were not where he was told to expect them. By having the initiative and lateral thinking to accept the possibility that the Prussian forces were not gathered at Perwez, but at Wavre, Grouchy found the Prussians. They had not yet crossed the Dyle. However, Vandamme was heading north-east and not north, and it would take time for the column to swing round towards Wavre. For whatever reason, the intelligence gathered on 17 June indicated that the Prussians were heading either to Brussels or Wavre. Grouchy, based on his orders, seems to have been of the opinion that both were possible and ordered his troops to move in the 'central position'—i.e. between the column moving to Wavre and the other heading to Brussels, and if indeed the Prussians were moving to Wavre, he could then turn towards Wavre as needed. So, Grouchy had found the Prussians at Wavre. It was this news that he transmitted to the emperor in his famous dispatch, as we shall see later. It had taken an inordinately long period of time to find the Prussians, however. If he had left Gembloux at 04.00 and headed north to Wavre, he would have caught the Prussians and stopped a far larger force getting to Waterloo. As it was, Grouchy was not aware that the Prussians were at Wavre in force. He could only issue orders based on what intelligence he received from his divisional and corps commanders, and all his intelligence pointed to the Prussians heading to Brussels or possibly Wavre on the night of 17 June, and he only learned the true situation about 10.00. With hindsight, Grouchy should not have camped at Gembloux and instead marched off to Wavre, or not sent Vandamme and Gérard to Sart-a-Walhain. But we must judge Grouchy upon his actions on those days of June 1815 from what he knew, rather than from what we know now.

The Prussians
On the morning of 18 June, Thielemann began his predations to head north in the wake of 1st and 2nd Corps. Carl Von Clausewitz notes:[8]

> The Prussian 3rd Corps arrived at Wavre on the evening of the 17th, where it was re-joined by the previously detached 1st Brigade of the reserve cavalry. Three brigades, the 10th, 11th, and 12th, as well as the reserve cavalry, went through Wavre and then encamped at La Bavette. The 9th Brigade remained on the far side of the river because it had arrived too late. Together with the 8th Brigade of the 2nd Corps it now formed the advanced guard against Grouchy. On the morning of the 18th, as the 4th Corps marched towards Saint-Lambert, General Thielemann received orders to form the rearguard for the other three corps. If no significant enemy force showed itself, he was to follow the others by taking the road via Couture, while leaving several battalions behind in Wavre to prevent any French patrols

from causing problems on the road to Brussels while the armies fought at Waterloo. But if a considerable enemy force showed up in front of Wavre, General Thielemann was to occupy the strong position on the Dyle there and cover the rear of the army.

The departure of the 2nd and 1st Corps from the position at Wavre took until around 2 p.m. Since nothing at all had been seen of the enemy up to that time, the Prussians were even more convinced that Bonaparte had turned his whole force against Wellington. General Thielemann, therefore, formed his corps into columns and was about to lead it down the Brussels road when a lively engagement began against the 9th and 8th Brigades, which were still on the left bank of the Dyle. General Thielemann, therefore, halted his troops until the situation became clearer. In the meantime, the 8th Brigade of the 2nd Corps left altogether. The 1st [Corps], which had stopped for a while, recommenced its march but left behind a detachment of three battalions and three squadrons under the command of Major Stengel at the village of Limale.

Movements to Sart-a-Walhain

Getting back to the events of the day at Gembloux, on the morning of 18 June the Prussians, as noted in a previous chapter, were too far ahead to be caught in time to stop them aiding Wellington and his allies. They had left Wavre at daybreak. Bülow had begun his march at 04.00 to go to Waterloo to attack Napoléon's right flank. He was followed by Pirch and Ziethen. At the same time as Bülow's men began to move off, Vandamme's 3rd Corps men began to leave their bivouacs and, marching by Saint-Denis and Grand-Leez, arrived at Tourinnes where they had been instructed to wait for further orders. At 08.00, Gérard was on the move. The aide-de-camp to General Etienne Nicholas Lefol writes:[9]

> The order of movement for 18 June, day of the Battle of Waterloo, was given about ten o'clock that morning. We were the head of the column of Vandamme's corps, and when we passed a league to the village of Saint-Martin where we remained, as far as I can remember, an hour or two to make soup, and eat our meals.

Lefol is again altering facts to suit his agenda. Nil-Saint-Vincent-Martin is roughly nine miles from Gembloux; around two hours' march on good roads. The road to Nil-Saint-Vincent-Martin was narrow, and would have entailed a lot of cross-country marching. However, owing to the rain, the road and fields were ankle-deep in mud which slowed progress.

The route which both Vandamme and Gérard followed was circuitous as well as inconvenient, the main roads being used by the Prussians. It led to Sart-a-Walhain, which forms the apex of an obtuse angle between Gembloux and Wavre, and could be preferred only because Grouchy did not know the exactly the direction or route of the Prussian retreat. The aide-de-camp to General Gérard notes:[10]

> Finally, around 10 a.m. after a feverish expectation, marching orders came, and they made us move in the direction of Wavre. We arrived near a farm; General Gérard was invited to lunch by Marshal Grouchy. The general, already displeased at our slow march, went with reluctance. The 3rd Corps of Vandamme was in front of Wavre; he met the Prussians and followed him fairly feebly.

However, we must note that the aide-de-camp to General Gérard is writing to blame Grouchy for the defeat of Waterloo and to exonerate Gérard, who claimed Grouchy lost the battle by not marching to the sound of the cannon of Waterloo or obeying the 13.00 order. Given Gérard marched behind Vandamme, and left his bivouacs at 08.00, the writer has altered the time to suit his agenda. Officer d'Ordonnance Leguest writes:[11]

> It is not possible for me to specify the time at which you left Gembloux on 18 June, but I know it was very early and it was only a mile or a mile and a half from this town you joined the head of the 3rd Corps, commanded by General Vandamme, which you had given the order of the day be set in motion early in the morning on the 18th, which he had done.
>
> I remember also that while your escort gathered near your accommodation in Gembloux, I heard several hussars say: 'Marshal Grouchy went forward with his staff, to prepare work for us; it will be a hot day to day!

The cannonade of Waterloo

Grouchy has been traditionally blamed for the loss of Waterloo for his supposed failure to 'march to the sound of the guns'. Indeed, the blame game and recriminations—largely to exonerate Napoléon—began almost immediately, led by the likes of General Gérard, the Baron Gourgaud and Napoléon himself. It is their version of history which has passed into myth (and even on the big screen) and has condemned Grouchy as a failure and for the fall of Napoléon. There are three problems with this theory, however: the first is whether Grouchy would actually have been able to hear the cannonade at Waterloo; secondly, even if he had been able to march to the sound of the guns, given how dispersed his troops were, and the ground conditions, whether he would have been able to have arrived to make any difference to the outcome; and finally, the validity of many of the sources used to condemn Grouchy.

Crucially, the majority of the supposed eyewitnesses to this event were officers who served under Gérard, or were part of his immediate entourage, and were his later political supporters. Marie Theodore Gueulluy, Comte de Rumigny (aide-de-camp to General Gérard), relates:[12]

Worried that our leaders had sat down to dinner in an isolated farm without troops to guard them, I left the room and walked to the garden, which was surrounded by a wall, with a kind of clerestory, painted green at the end. Some distance to the west was a wood. I was considering, when the thud of a gun made me more attentive yet. This explosion was followed by several others, I put my ear against the wall to better distinguish the sounds. I was alone and I heard many shots of various calibres. This could only be a simple fighting of the vanguard, I returned hastily into the farm. There they were properly seated, 'M. marshal, I say, there is in the direction where the emperor is a fierce battle. It may be a battle of the vanguard? Let me ask M. marshal down to the garden to judge'.

I conducted myself, the marshal and General Gérard at the end of the garden, where first we heard nothing about the noise of all these people together. I then put his ear to the ground, and I distinctly heard the cannonade the strongest. The marshal was then convinced and ordered to ride. At the executed order, we moved onto the road to Wavre. Leading the march, I heard the beginning of lively discussion between Marshal Grouchy and General Gérard.

By the time we reached the rearguard of General Vandamme, our two leaders entered a peasant's house, in which was a tiled stove, everyone was outside, except for M. Bellanger, aide of Marshal Grouchy, and me. We were both against the front door to prevent anyone coming to distract or interrupt them. I was, as you know, colonel, aide to General Gérard, and therefore the first of his officers. The general and marshal held open a map of a captain, and the marshal had supported his right hand on this map, suspended against the stove, the general supported it with his left hand.

The crux of the discussion was concerning the direction to give the army. Gérard wanted to move to the emperor, and Grouchy on the contrary, push the Prussians before him. The point where we were, there was no more to doubt that the fight was an intense and real battle, we saw the shells burst in the air again, we realised the left wing of the Prussian army and that it moved westward without our knowledge. It was now as clear as day. But the marshal hesitated, refused, piling on the reasons why. Finally, we heard General Gérard say with the utmost animation: 'Monsieur marshal, it is an axiom in war that we should march on the guns when you hear the cannon. General, you have to follow orders, not interpret them'. After these words, followed by a reflection that I did not hear, and some sharp words of the marshal, they separated. On reaching me, General Gérard was exasperated, he said 'there is nothing to do, it's awful!'

This account from an intimate of Gérard is rather exaggerated. It is highly doubtful that over a distance of around nine miles, in a direct line from Waterloo to Sart-a-Walhain, that howitzer shells could be seen, especially given the direct line of sight from Sart-a-Walhain to Waterloo is blocked by Mont-Saint-Gilbert. The account was written in the 1840s, decades after the event, so it is by its very nature going to be highly informed by what Rumigny has read, particularly the various writings of General, later Marshal, Gérard, and will be biased in favour of him. The writer was of course correct that the Prussians had moved to Waterloo.

Chief-of-staff of 4th Corps from 17 June, after the wounding of General Saint-Remy at Ligny, was Simon Loriere. He writes about the movements of 4th Corps as follows:[13]

The next day, 18 June, the 4th Corps left his position at seven in the morning, and although he had to go through all the long defile of Gembloux, we were obliged to halt in front of this city, to give time to the 3rd Corps to move through it (because, as before, we marched again on a single column). I do not know the reasons which had determined the marshal to put General Vandamme at the head, and at nine o'clock we were all marching to Wavre. At eleven, the 3rd Corps was fully deployed at Walin [sic]. Comte Gérard, who preceded the march of his corps, learned that Marshal Grouchy was stopped in a house in this village (belonging to M. Hollaert), he went with the officers of his staff, and he ordered me to follow: we found ourselves there for lunch.

I was walking around the garden of this house when I thought I heard (at about half-past eleven o'clock) the detonation of artillery on my left, the sound was muffled because the rain was falling heavily, yet I could not misunderstand this, and indeed, hastened to go and inform my general. He went immediately with the marshal to a high place in the garden, where I heard the noise; many officers were present, including the marshal, Comte Gérard, the aide-de-camp and orderly officers of generals Vandamme and Excelmans, and M. Denniee, our chief inspector of review. Everyone was convinced that I was not mistaken. The rain had stopped for a quarter of an hour, and the shots could be heard so distinctly that the earth trembled. The marshal himself supposed it to be another Battle of Wagram.

M. Hollaert, owner of the house where we were, was summoned by the marshal, who asked him where he supposed that terrible cannonade took place, he indicated the Soignes Forest, remote from the point where we were about three and a half leagues. General Gérard then opened the view to march immediately to the cannon, to put us promptly in connection with operations of the emperor. He suggested to the marshal to execute this movement with his corps and division of light cavalry of General Walin, observing that what we had before us could not do us much harm, because, since daybreak, we were informed that all we had before us was the army corps of Thielemann, responsible for supporting the retirement of the Prussian army that had gathered at Wavre; and in any case, our junction with the emperor became meaningful to both. The marshal did not seem to agree. He climbed immediately onto his horse to follow the road to Wavre.

This account is very different indeed to what Rumigny states. However, we must note that Grouchy did not know, based on his report to Napoléon, that he only had Thielemann's army corps in front of him. As the report states, he believed that all the Prussians were heading to Brussels. Therefore, the comment that 4th Corps could be detached with most of 3rd Corps (bar a small corps of observation to watch Thielemann) is informed by what the writer had learned subsequent to the actual event, ergo it seems unlikely that Grouchy would have willingly divided his force when he believed that he had in front of him at least 30,000 Prussians. He did not know Waterloo was to be fought, thus the Prussians were heading to Brussels to link with Wellington there, and a move to the west made no sense, other than to gain the Brussels road at Waterloo.

Another version of these events is from Captain François, of the 30th Regiment of Line Infantry, who we have noted already is far from a reliable eyewitness:[14]

18 June. General Gérard's division (to which I belonged), under the orders of Marshal Grouchy, left Gembloux with the other divisions at 10 a.m. The soldiers were impatient to engage the enemy. About one o'clock in the afternoon we arrived at Walhain, a village situated about halfway between Gembloux and Wavre, where we heard a brisk cannonade on our left in the direction of Mont-Saint-Jean and Waterloo, and we felt certain that the emperor was engaged with the enemy. Marshal Grouchy called a halt (we of the 30th were at the head of the column). He seemed anxious, and did not know what to do, whether to cross the Dyle, or march in the direction of the cannon, leaving one or two divisions on the left bank of the river, which they could cross, the bridge not having been cut, and the neighbouring positions of no importance, or the town itself either, which was surrounded by mud. Marshal Grouchy called a council of war. General Gérard voted for marching at once in the direction of the cannon; leaving a corps of observation on the right bank of the Dyle. This opinion did not prevail.

General Excelmans, who was much excited, said to the marshal: 'the emperor is fighting the English army, there can be no doubt about that. Marshal, we must march towards the firing. I am an old soldier of the army of Italy, and I have heard Bonaparte lay down that principle a hundred times. If we keep to the left, we shall be on the field of battle in an hour'. 'I believe you are right,' replied the marshal, 'but if Blücher comes out of Wavre and takes me in flank, I shall be blamed for not having obeyed my orders, which are to march against Blücher.'

General Gérard, who was glad to find General Excelmans of his opinion, said to the marshal: 'your orders state you are to be on the field of battle. Blücher has gained a march on you. He was yesterday at Wavre when you were at Gembloux; and who knows where he is now? If he has joined Wellington, we shall find him on the battlefield, and then you have executed your orders to the letter. If he is not there, your arrival will decide the battle. In two hours, we can be taking part in the fight, and if we have destroyed the English army, what can Blücher, who is already beaten, do?'

If Marshal Grouchy had followed the advice of these two brave men, the battle would have been won. I attribute the disaster of this unfortunate day to him.

General Vandamme's opinion prevailed. We marched forward at 3 p.m. crossed the three bridges and attacked Wavre. Horse and foot performed prodigies of valour. General Vandamme finally made himself master of the position. The battle was of little use to us, and we lost about 1,100 men. It did little honour to our generals who seemed to be groping in the dark; and all day long we heard the cannon on our left, in the direction of Waterloo. We ceased to hear it about 10 p.m. Nothing can describe the uneasiness this cannonade caused us. The soldiers were melancholy, and had the presentiment of a misfortune. They boldly declared that the emperor was beaten, because the sound of the cannon was always in the same direction. Contrary to my custom, I was sad also, but inwardly I was raging.

This account, written many years after Waterloo, is highly influenced by the numerous outpourings of General Gérard in the military press to damn Marshal Grouchy. The authenticity of the account has also to be questioned as to whether a lowly captain of infantry would have been present at a council of war and to have heard, or overheard, such a conversation. The timing of the event of the cannonade being heard and the late departure from bivouacs at 10.00 are in direct contradiction to reports from 18 June 1815 and the memoir cited previously. It is likely Grouchy had departed by 07.00, as ordered by Napoléon. The presence of Excelmans at this meeting appears to be a mistake, as according to his own orders written that day, he was miles away at Corbais. Clearly, Excelmans's presence and contribution is a misleading fabrication. Grouchy admitted to Napoléon in his 06.00 report that the Prussians had gained a march on him, a point he may have made clear to Napoléon at 08.00 on 17 June. Grouchy had little chance of catching up with the bulk of the Prussian army. In the three accounts, rather than blaming Napoléon for the late issuance of his orders, the escape of the Prussians is blamed on Grouchy, who could not start his pursuit until ordered to do so, by which time the Prussians were at least twelve hours in front of him.

The aide-de-camp to General Etienne Nicholas Lefol writes that Grouchy heard the cannonade at Saint-Martin:[15]

That hearing the sound of guns to our left, my general sent me thereby directly to Vandamme who, in turn, ordered me to leave, and gallop to Marshal Grouchy to inform him of the circumstances. I found the marshal at Sart-a-Walhain, in a castle belonging to M. [name omitted], and when I reached him, he was at a table, consulting maps, while the officers of his staff ate strawberries. I do not know if the marshal had already been advised of the news I brought him, but I can say is that immediately after hearing me, he gave the order to ride out. I remember that several officers ran into the garden and applied their ears to the earth to try and ascertain the direction of the cannon fire for a moment after the cannonade of Waterloo was heard then with such force that the earth seemed to be shaken.

We followed the marshal, who stood at the head of his army, and I re-joined our division which, in that time, was engaged with a large party of Prussians at a place called La Baraque between Sart-a-Walhain and Wavre.

We did not know which corps of enemy we faced, and neither did we know the number of our opponents, when a soldier told us that a man had fallen close to us. We proceeded immediately to the spot indicated, and we found a young Prussian officer, who had a terrible wound in the thigh. He was lost in the corn, which was very high at this time of the year, General Lefol asked him in German about the forces that were against us, and we were fully informed. We left this young man having directed him to the ambulance. I remained a little behind our staff to throw him my handkerchief which he seemed to accept with gratitude, and he used immediately to bandage his wound. What will become of this poor child? Was he found when they passed through the place the next day, or will he die without aid? This is what I know.

In this account, Vandamme was not present when Gérard and Grouchy had their altercation, which if true, casts more doubt on what we think actually occurred in the house and gardens that day. Neither Vandamme nor Excelmans, despite eyewitness testimony, seem to have been present. Adjutant-major to the artillery of the 4th Corps, Louis Etienne Thouvenin,[16] narrates on 21 May 1840 about the actions of 4th Corps on 18 June:[17]

I was captain in the 2nd Artillery Regiment, attached to the staff of the artillery of the 4th Corps, commanded by General M. Balthus.

On the 18, we arrived around 11 a.m. in Sart-a-Walhain, having behind us, between Sart-a-Walhain and Gembloux, marched the troops of 4th Corps. We dismounted near a large detached house, and from half-past eleven I was with several of my friends in the garden of this house, when we began to hear sharp gunfire on the left. Judging from the noise by putting my ear to the ground, the distance seemed to be about four or five leagues.

When we wanted to enter the apartments, an aide-de-camp told us that this was not possible, because the marshal was gathered in council with several generals. A few minutes later, he mounted his horse suddenly, and we followed the marshal galloping in the direction of Wavre. We could only speculate about the purpose of this rapid movement, and the opinion was that we would join the army of the emperor. Soon the cannon could be heard more and more, was moving closer, or by virtue of a greater number of cannon put into action? It was a serious commitment, a real battle, and with great emotion we did express regret to see that we did not march more directly on the cannon. M. General Balthus told us, with a kind of humour, that the ground being in the condition it was, being soaked by the heavy rain of the previous day, it was impossible to go through the fields, and our artillery could not to pass over them, meaning, I suppose, it would take a long time to join the emperor.

The myth about the Battle of Wavre states that Grouchy was at Sart-a-Walhain around 11.30 and heard the cannonade of Waterloo. We know Grouchy arrived at Sart-a-Walhain by 10.00 (that is the time given by Grouchy in his report to Napoléon). Given that time was not standardised in the period we are looking at, the time could have been within half an hour or so. Some authors state he arrived here at midday, two hours after Grouchy himself states, which coincided with the cannonade of Waterloo. Grouchy's time of 10.00, give or take thirty minutes, was a full hour before the action at Waterloo began; around 11.30. We must therefore question if the cannonade of Waterloo was actually heard. Certainly, Grouchy himself writing on 18 June 1815 states he was in a house, as eyewitnesses claim, when the cannonade was heard. His report, timed 10.00, informs Napoléon of his plans for the day, where he was to move, and makes no mention at all of the cannonade.

We must stress that Grouchy at this time did not know that Napoléon had planned to fight. He did not know on 18 June 1815 that the Battle of Waterloo was to be fought. Indeed, He was still of the opinion that Napoléon was moving to Brussels and that Wellington was still retiring to Brussels.[18] We know from hindsight it was, but importantly Grouchy did not know, despite Napoléon and Gérard's later protestations to the contrary, that a battle was to take place; he found out later in the day with the arrival of the 10.00 report.

Therefore, a cannonade would have been unexpected and may have raised a cursory question from Grouchy to Napoléon. Is the cannonade a nice invention of Gérard and Napoléon's supporters to blacken Grouchy's reputation, saying Grouchy should have marched to the sounds of the guns of a battle he did not know was happening, and thus his failure to march to the guns lost Napoléon the campaign and his throne? For this timeline to work requires Grouchy to have been at Sart-a-Walhain from approximately 10.00 to 12.00, a period of two hours which cannot be supported by eyewitnesses writing soon after the events or on the day, like Excelmans, who was nowhere near Sart-a-Walhain.

Also, we must ask what guns were actually heard. The Battle of Waterloo began with the moves of 2nd Corps against Hougoumont. The total number of French guns in action would be twenty-two, coming from the batteries of generals Piré, Foy and Jérôme. This is not the sound of a great battle, but more, as Grouchy is said to have noted, the sound of a rearguard action. The grand battery did not get into action until around 13.00 or later, and it is this famous cannonade that the supporters of General Gérard state that Grouchy heard and ignored. By this time Grouchy was at Wavre.

As stated earlier, Grouchy did not know that the Battle of Waterloo was to be fought until around 17.00, so any cannonade was likely to be a rearguard action, as Wellington withdrew to Brussels, and not a major battle, therefore there was no need to detach troops, as the bulk of the Prussians were thought to be directly in front of Grouchy. This, history shows, was incorrect, a point that has been seized upon by Marshal Grouchy's detractors since the event took place.

Of note concerning this cannonade, Grouchy, writing in 1819, makes no mention of this and states at 11.30 he was with General Excelmans close to Wavre. Grouchy in fact states he heard the cannonade of Waterloo as he was engaging the Prussians at Wavre, and not while having a meal at Sart-a-Walhain.[19] When he was writing in 1819, he was writing in objection to the writing of General Gourgaud. Indeed, General Berthezène also published, as did General Jamin, loud protestations about Gourgaud's narrative of events and the mistakes and slander he included in his work to exonerate Napoléon and blame others. Grouchy's publication is in defence of his action against Gourgaud. The issue, then, is absent from military journals until 1830 when General Gérard began his own campaign of publication against Grouchy. This was in part to vindicate his own actions and to serve his own political ends at that point in time. It seems likely that Napoléon's bulletin of 20 June, his later writings from the island of Saint-Helena, and of others such as Gourgaud, were all written to exculpate Napoléon and to point out the emperor lost the campaign due to the actions of traitors and incompetents. Because it was easier to believe the slander against Grouchy at a time of national tragedy and loss, and because Gérard, et al. published before Grouchy so that the latter was on the back-foot and writing in self-defence, led many to believe the Napoléon/Gérard version. It rapidly became an established myth, much as the famous words 'the Guard dies, it never surrenders' did, despite the event and words never being spoken, but filling a place in an emotional narrative of an army and a nation trying to come to terms with great loss. The myth of Grouchy eating strawberries and not marching to the sounds of the guns has to be interpreted in the light of this, and that it was probably simply invented by those wishing to further their own political ends by slandering Grouchy and exonerating Napoléon.

Grouchy chose to keep his force together and not detach 4th Corps, and pressed on to Wavre. No doubt his decision was informed by a dispatch from Excelmans. According to Houssaye, Major d'Estourmel[20] arrived with Excelmans's situation report from Neuf-Sart:[21]

> He announced that a strong Prussian rearguard was posted before Wavre. This officer was also charged to say that, according to all indications, the enemy's army had passed the bridge of Wavre during the night and morning, in order to get nearer the English army, and, consequently, that General Excelmans contemplated proceeding to the left bank of the Dyle via Ottignies. This fresh information and the opinion expressed by Excelmans, furnished additional reasons in favour of Gérard's opinions. However, to Grouchy, who was as convinced as ever that the Prussians had gained Wavre in order to retreat towards the Chyse, the presence of their rearguard in this town only confirmed him in his presumptions. He congratulated himself that he had resisted Gérard, because the emperor's orders were to follow the Prussian army and that at last he seemed on the point of reaching this army that had hitherto baffled him. He told d'Estourmel that he would himself give orders to General Excelmans and called for his horses.

Given that Excelmans was nowhere near Sart-a-Walhain to have written this order, eyewitnesses who place him with Grouchy are mistaken. General Bonnemains, in his report to General Chastel, places Excelmans at Limaile around 09.00, and so clearly cannot have been with Grouchy at Sart-a-Walhain.[22]

If these supposed eyewitnesses are mistaken about who was at Sart-a-Walhain, it is highly likely the event and time is an invention. Grouchy does admit he heard the cannonade in his after-action report of 20 June, but does not say where he heard it and when. Therefore, on balance, Grouchy has been made a scapegoat for Napoléon.

Grouchy's report

Grouchy's own narrative of the day makes no mention of the incident we have just discussed. Either he chose to ignore it to exonerate himself, or, more likely, it never existed. He narrates the period from 06.00 to 10.00 as follows:[23]

> I informed the emperor that at daybreak we were marching to Sart-a-Walhain. Indeed, at sunrise, Vandamme's corps was moving in this direction, following the cavalry of General Excelmans. Successive reports confirmed that several Prussian columns had passed in the area of Sart-a-Walhain.
>
> At this village I wrote again to Napoléon, to tell him that I thought at the time we had reached the Prussian rearguard, and I sent my dispatch by Major Frênaie. The officer was perfectly well aware of what I had collected of the enemy's movements, and reported promptly as ordered, as they were to give me the opinion of a former soldier decorated with the Legion of Honour, in whose house which I stopped at Sart-a-Walhain to write the letter reporting that the Prussians were concentrated in the plains of Louvain.

This is corroborated by one of Grouchy's aide-de-camps, de Blocqueville:[24]

> Upon leaving Sart-a-Walhain, where the marshal paused to describe the emperor and transmit the information he had collected and he had just received from the mouth of the owner of the house.

Grouchy's 10.00 report to Napoléon states:[25]

> Sire
>
> I will not lose a moment in sending you the information I have gathered here. I regard it as definitive, and so that Your Majesty receives it soonest, I am sending Major de la Fresnaye with it.
>
> Blücher's 1st, 2nd and 3rd Corps are marching in the direction of Brussels. Two of these corps marched either through Sart-a-Walhain or just to the right of it. They are marching in three columns more or less abreast. Their march through here lasted six hours without interruption. Those troops passing through Sart-a-Walhain are estimated as being at least thirty thousand men with fifty to sixty cannon. An army corps came from Liège and has joined up with these corps that fought at Fleurus. Enclosed is a requisition form which proves this. Some of the Prussian troops in front of me have headed in the direction of the plains of Chyse, which is on the road to Louvain, that is north of Wavre, and two and a half leagues from that town. They seem to want to mass there, either to offer battle to

186

any troops that pursue them there, or to join with Wellington—a plan about which their officers spoke. With their usual boasting, they maintain they only left the battlefield of the 16th to join up with the English army in Brussels.

This evening I will be standing before Wavre en masse, and in this way, be situated between Wellington, whom I assume is falling back before Your Majesty, and the Prussian army. I require further instructions, whatever Your Majesty chooses to order, as to what I should do. The terrain between Wavre and the plain of Chyse is difficult to pass; it is broken ground and boggy. I will be able to get to Brussels easily along the Vilvoorde road quicker than any troops who go over the plain of Chyse, especially if the Prussians make a stop there. If Your Majesty wishes to send me orders, I can still receive them before starting my movement tomorrow.

Most of the information in this letter came from the owner of this house where I have stopped to write to Your Majesty. He is an officer who served in the French army, and has been decorated and seems to support your interests. I attach some notes:

The rear of the corps that marches through Sart-a-Walhain is in Corroy. The entire army is moving on Wavre. The best route to Wavre is via Nil-Pierreux, Corbais, Baraque and Lauzelle. The wounded have been sent to Liège and Maastricht. The reserves and troops that did not participate in the Battle of Fleurus are marching to Wavre, some to Tirlemont. The bulk of the Prussian army is camping on the plain of Chyse. This is confirmed, and they seem to be massing there.

The letter to Napoléon is important for a number of reasons:

Grouchy still believed the Prussians were heading to Brussels to join with Wellington. With no news of the emperor, and with the Prussians still drawing back, the logical assumption to make was the emperor was at, or close to Brussels and the idea of a Prussian flank march made no sense, as where were they going to? Grouchy did not yet know Waterloo was to be fought;

He knew a rearguard was at Wavre. This must have come from either Bellanger or Excelmans reconnaissance;

Chyse is north-east of Wavre, and straddles the Namur to Louvain road, further convincing Grouchy that Brussels was the destination of the Prussians. To have spotted the Prussians here, a patrol must have travelled up the Namur to Louvain road. The patrol likely left the Tourinnes area and is presumed to have headed up the Chaussee de Saint-Wivienne passing through Saint-Barbe to Roux-Miroir, where they joined the Namur to Louvain road. The journey was about ten miles, or about an hour's ride. General Berton states his brigade was sent to the Namur-Louvain road via Nil-Saint-Vincent and that it approached the farm at 14.00.[26] Clearly, he had done so and reported back. Excelmans, therefore, only had one division with him at La Baraque;

He assumed the Prussians from Ligny had all moved east, and then from Gembloux north-east. He found three bodies of troops, likely to be the Prussian 1st, 2nd and 3rd Corps. It shows he had no information at all about the departure of the Prussian 1st and 2nd Corps from Ligny, via Sombreffe, heading north. He only learned this information later in the day on 18 June; and

Napoléon knew Grouchy was heading north-east and away from his position, but Grouchy did not know this, as he had no information about the emperor's whereabouts.

Upon consulting the 1777 map of the region, there is a notable lack of east-west roads from Sart-a-Walhain to Waterloo, a distance of twenty miles armed with a good horse and a good map. The most direct route would have been to head west to Blanmont, and thence Hevillers, and keeping west heading via Sart-Saint-Guillaume, crossing the river towards Le Feaux, heading to Bousseval, onto Genappe and thence to La-Belle-Alliance. On foot, that journey on good roads would take about four and a half hours, and perhaps a minimum of two on horseback. Allowing for bad roads and having to stop to ask the way, the dispatch perhaps took at least four hours to get to Napoléon. Certainly, the dispatch sent at 6.00 had taken four hours over better roads, so over worse roads, two hours could be an underestimate. For fact, the dispatch had not got to Napoléon by the time of the 13.00 order, and may have done so perhaps towards 15.00.

The dispatch was carried by Officer d'Ordonnance La Fresnaye. He recounts that:[27]

> I know that on the 18th we reached the head of the column of General Vandamme about a league from Gembloux. When we arrived at Sart-a-Walhain, a decorated officer came near you and informed you that Prussian columns were moving on Wavre, although he thought the army of Blücher was moving on Louvain. With this news, you [Grouchy] then wrote to Napoléon, and I was charged by you to carry your dispatches, orders and reports.
>
> I departed the place immediately, at the time when a cannonade that did not sound like a general engagement, was heard. I went to the sound of cannon, and after travelling for two long hours and a

half at trot and canter, I found Napoléon on the battlefield of Waterloo. I handed him the report you had entrusted to me, he read it, asked the point where you were and told me to stay with him. I remained there until evening. No orders were given to me to bring you, and it is not to my knowledge that other officers have been shipped.

The time of writing the order is awkward. The original is lost, and is variously stated to be written at 10.00 or 11.00. Either way, it did not arrive with headquarters at Waterloo until after 13.00. La Fresnaye says it took him two and a half hours to get to Waterloo from Sart-a-Walhain— departing at 10.30 would make for an arrival at 13.00 or thereabouts. If at about 11.30 if the cannonade was heard, then arrival would be closer to 14.00. In either case, the dispatch did not arrive until the 13.00 order had been sent to Grouchy, as Napoléon never seems to have replied to it. La Fresnaye seems adamant that he delivered the dispatch, so on balance it seems to have arrived with headquarters. Its contents, as we shall see, left Napoléon in no doubt whatsoever that Grouchy was not heading to Waterloo. However, in his dispatch to Davout, Soult makes no mention at all of Grouchy, but does admit to the Prussians:[28]

> The bivouac in front of La Caillou, 18 June at a quarter-past one o'clock
>
> Monsieur the marshal, the fighting has begun at this moment, the enemy are in position in front of the Soignes Forest, their centre placed on Waterloo. We are consuming a lot of ammunition; a great quantity of munitions was used in the Battle of Ligny.
>
> The emperor orders you that you send munitions from the citadels in the north to Avesnes with all speed in the midst of the battalions which I had ordered to be established there to escort the prisoners. The direction they will take from there will be to Beaumont and via Charleroi to join the army.
>
> You must, M. marshal, carry out these important orders of the emperor check that they are promptly executed and they will prevent the worst from happening in this regard.
>
> P.S. It is half-past two, the cannonade is joined all along the line. The English are in the centre, the Dutch and Belgians are on the right, the Germans and the Prussians are on the left. The general battle has begun, 400 cannon have opened fire at this moment.

These letters are of huge importance in our understanding of Waterloo. Clearly, Napoléon was concerned that his ammunition was running low, and needed to be urgently replenished, and that he also felt he needed an additional battalion of infantry with him in the field as soon as was practicable. With the arrival of Grouchy's 10.00 dispatch with Soult, and from the observations made by the headquarters staff at Waterloo cited earlier, clearly Napoléon, by 14.30, knew that some of the Prussian army had eluded Grouchy and had made contact with Wellington.

Either Napoléon believed that only a small portion of the Prussian army had eluded Grouchy (hardly surprising given the twelve to sixteen hour lead they had over the marshal), or Napoléon was over-confident in his chances of success against Wellington and the Prussians. As we shall see, Napoléon's judgement on both scenarios was horribly wrong.

However, Napoléon, writing in 1820, claims that this order timed at 10.00 was written at Gembloux, and that Grouchy was writing to inform him that he had not yet broken camp, and had not marched out at first light. It seems yet again Napoléon is twisting the known historical facts to meet his own ends.[29]

Officers under Grouchy and Gérard both states that they broke camp well before 10.00. The chief-of-staff to Gérard states that 4th Corps broke camp at 07.00.[30] Grouchy's dispatch, which left Sart-a-Walhain at 11.00 as he was departing, if not earlier to try and reconcile both times given as a compromise, caused little or no alarm at French headquarters. If Napoléon or Soult had any reservations about Grouchy's planned operations on 18 June, they did not immediately attempt to clarify the marshal's orders. Both men knew Grouchy's plan of operations but instead of clarifying what he was to do, sent a vague order written sometime between 13.00 and 14.00, which will be discussed later. The historian, Codman Ropes, surmises this lack of initiative by Napoléon thusly:[31]

> Napoléon and Soult, therefore, one would suppose, might have seen by the programme which Grouchy had marked out for himself in his despatch that in all probability he was not clearly apprehending the situation, and that it was therefore possible that he might make a serious, perhaps a very serious, mistake the next day. They ought, therefore, if they suspected this to be the state of the case, to have replied at once, giving him precise instructions as to his course in the event of the retreat of the Prussians on Wavre. They should have told him that, if he should find this to be the fact, he must at once march to cross the Dyle above Wavre, at Moustier and Ottignies, approach the main army, and act in conjunction with it. Yet although Grouchy told the officer who carried the 10 p.m. despatch to wait for an answer, none was returned. Grouchy was not even

informed where the army was, and that it was confronted by the English army in position. Nor was he advised, as he surely should have been, that Domon's reconnaissance had proved that a strong Prussian column, consisting, as we have seen, of the two beaten corps, those of Ziethen and Pirch, had retired on Wavre by way of Gery and Gentinnes. It is impossible to account for these omissions.

Excelmans's attack at La Baraque

While Grouchy's infantry was toiling through the mud, Excelmans's cavalry had overtaken the Prussian rearguards not very far from Wavre itself. Reporting this to Grouchy, General Excelmans notes that:[32]

> On 18 June, my troops were ordered to march in the morning. I was ready to move at about half-past seven o'clock, but with no light cavalry it was not until about nine o'clock I found behind Mazy the rearguard of the Prussian army, on the road to Wavre at the height of Moustier, and almost simultaneously observed a convoy escorted by a few thousand men near the tavern A Tous Vents, which appeared to be heading towards Louvain, but I was moving as to bring all my attention on the Dyle. I formed my troops in a wooded ravine to the left, near the farm of Plaquerie, and the right on Neufsar.

Some of Excelmans's dragoons were spotted at Mont-Saint-Guibert by the Prussians and were driven off. von Falckenhausen's men of the 3rd Regiment of Silesian Landwehr Cavalry took twenty-eight prisoners.[33] However, a wood and village would have blocked Excelmans's view of Cabaret A Tout Vent, so clearly it seems this information was passed to him from Bonnemains, as we shall see later. Berton's brigade was deployed on the Namur to Louvain road, with the 17th chasing Bülow's rearguard.[34]

Excelmans, without light cavalry, was yet again being used as 'eyes and ears'. What Grouchy needed for the task at hand was light cavalry, but the emperor had robbed him of the vast majority of his light cavalry. Mazy, in theory, is situated about six miles south of Gembloux. 'Neufsar' is Neussart and has hardly changed since 18 June 1815. Did he really swing south? It is very unlikely, and where Excelmans means by 'Mazy' is clearly not at Charleroi. Moustier, based on the Ferraris map, is just south of Ottignies. Cabaret A Tout Vent is on the outskirts of Dion-le-Mont, on its eastern side at the crossroads of the chemin de Tout Vent and chaussee de Huy. The building no longer stands. There is no wood to the right (east) of Neussart, assuming he was heading north, when we look at the Ferraris map of 1777. So, we assume he was on the flat ground between Vieux-Sart and the Sarats Wood. Louvain is to the north of Wavre and the Louvain road heads to Louvain, and thence heads west to Brussels. It also appears Louvain-la-Neuve, which appears on the 1777 map as Louvrange, which is south-east of Wavre, and the most logical direction for the troops at Cabaret A Tout Vent. But for Excelmans, the Prussians were seemingly heading north to Brussels or west to Wavre.

The farm of La Plaquerie was due east of Ottignes by less than a mile, and is clearly shown on the 1777 Ferraris map. Thus, it seems that Excelmans headed north through Helliers and Mont-Saint-Guibert, so to have the farm of La Plaquerie to his left and Neussart to the right. Perhaps he stood at the farm of De Biereux which was a few hundred metres due south of La Baraque.

Historian Tim Clayton states that it was now that Excelmans suggested to cross the Dyle here and advance to Saint-Lambert. He presents no new evidence beyond Gérard.[35] The endless repetition of the same myths of Waterloo does not make the study of those fateful days of June 1815 any easier for the historian. Excelmans is not only writing fifteen years later, but also seems to be writing the case for what should have been done, rather than what was done. His recollections are coloured by misgivings and hindsight that cannot be corroborated by any other source, seemingly yet more 'false memory'. The issue of Grouchy not getting to Waterloo is still so emotive for many historians that, as we have seen, moving away from the current paradigm is impossible for many. Hyde-Kelly[36] and A. F. Becke[37] failed in their analysis of Grouchy as they wrote tempered by hindsight and the genius of the emperor. It is easy to say, in 2017 (or 1830 for that matter), what Grouchy should have done, but we must judge him on what he knew on 18 June 1815 and how he acted upon what he knew.

It seems Excelmans only had with him Stroltz's division, as Bonnemains seems to have been sent off to Perwez. Clearly Stroltz's division had headed north from Gembloux and Bonnemains had headed to Perwez. Berton had headed even further north-east. General Berton claims the corps was initially sent to the Namur-Louvain road via Nil-Saint-Vincent and that it approached the farm at 14.00.[38] General Bonnemains's report notes:[39]

> The 18th, the corps of dragoons of General Excelmans was united at seven o'clock in the morning at Valhain [*sic*] and took the road to Wavre, around nine o'clock he found himself in the presence of many Prussian advance guards composed of all arms and we set in motion a movement to reconnoitre them. We had to withdraw about

a league from the place and wait for the arrival of Marshal Grouchy with the army corps of Pajol, Vandamme and Gérard. They joined us between one or two o'clock in the afternoon. At this moment, we heard a terrible cannonade from the direction of Waterloo before the Prussian avantguarde was attacked by the army corps of Vandamme that chased them into Wavre and beyond the Dyle. From that moment, and for the rest of the day, the corps of Excelmans remained in reserve.

However, another eyewitness states:[40]

The orders of the marshal were to march upon the army of the enemy, so as to prevent the junction between Wellington and Blücher. He arrived, to carry that object into effect at Gembloux on the 17th, which the Prussian army had quitted about noon for Wavre. The marshal left Gembloux with his army on the morning of the 18th to find the Prussians and to fight them. The 2nd Corps of cavalry, consisting of 4,000 men commanded by General Excelmans, discovered the rearguard of the Prussians near a place called Baraque at about ten o'clock in the morning. General Excelmans brought his cavalry to the Dyle, ready to pass that river when, at about twelve, the marshal arrived with General Vandamme's corps and gave orders to march upon Wavre; this he did, after Excelmans had defeated the rearguard of the Prussian army, which were from 8,000 to 10,000 men.

To the east were Vandamme and 3rd Corps, which we assume now swung north-west to head to Wavre once Grouchy had been made aware of this news. Clearly, Grouchy correctly now assumed that the Prussians that had been at Perwez had gone via Wavre to join Wellington instead of heading to Brussels. With the true line of Prussian movements only discovered towards midday, if not later, he could not have headed off to Wavre at daybreak, as all he knew for fact was of a body of Prussians at Wavre, some at Perwez and others moving from Namur.

Grouchy moves to Wavre
Having sent his report to Napoléon to inform him of his movements and new intelligence, Grouchy headed off with his staff to join Excelmans. He then describes his own subsequent movements as follows:[41]

I joined General Excelmans, who since morning had been close behind the extreme rearguard of the Prussian cavalry, and at half-past eleven, a league and a half from Wavre, finally we found a rearguard consisting of infantry with cannon. As soon as I had carried out my reconnaissance the cannonade began, and General Vandamme, arriving with the head of his infantry, marched to the Prussians, pushed them back, took the position of Limelette Wood, and there they were immediately attacked and overthrown: the cavalry of General Excelmans, by turning to the right and passing the wood, pushed on to Bas-Wavre. We followed the enemy strongly, and between one and two o'clock in the afternoon we were masters of that part of the town on the left bank of the Dyle.

This is corroborated by de Blocqueville, one of Grouchy's aide-de-camps:[42]

The marshal, having joined the dragoons of General Excelmans, who were in the presence of a Prussian rearguard, made the attack, pushed them back and they were forced to retreat to Wavre.

Napoléon, yet again in later years, states Grouchy did not arrive at Wavre until 16.00, whereas Grouchy and Excelmans *were* in Wavre by 14.00. Yet the Waterloo myth, fuelled by Napoléon's active propaganda machine, says Grouchy's supposed tardiness in not getting to Wavre, not attacking until 18.00, and disobeying an order, cost Napoléon the Battle of Waterloo.[43]

Coming from Sart-a-Walhain, Grouchy had joined the division of Habert—the vanguard of this corps—at Nil-Saint-Vincent by 13.00, where it had been awaiting further orders since midday. Grouchy himself notes that he re-joined Excelmans, who, since the morning, had been on the heels of the extreme rearguard of the Prussian cavalry.

Grouchy now ordered Excelmans to try and out-flank the enemy by moving through Dion-le-Mont to Dion-le-Val. From there, they moved to Bas-Wavre. But, looking at the 1777 Ferraris map, to get to Bas-Wavre the dragoons would have had to double back on themselves through a wood onto marshy ground. It is far more likely that they continued north-east to the hamlet of Gastuche. General Berton's brigade was certainly in the area. As a result, the 8th Regiment of Uhlans, from the brigade of von der Marwitz, detached its first squadron towards Laurensart to observe the French dragoons.[44]

Perhaps at 14.00, an officer from Pajol's staff presented himself to Grouchy. Pajol's forces had departed at dawn from their position at Mazy for Grand-Leez, and in accordance with his orders, had moved from there to Tourinnes in the expectation of finding Prussian troops.

With no Prussians in sight, Pajol had sent the officer to Grouchy to report this and to request new orders. Grouchy instructed the officer to tell Pajol to take up a position at La Baraque and to await further orders there.

After issuing orders, it seems that Grouchy now rode from l'Auzel, passing through the Warlembrout Wood to the heights of Limelette to see for himself the action here. While here he realised that a major battle was indeed taking place near the Soignes Forest, as General Bonnemains notes:[45]

> Between one or two o'clock in the afternoon. At this moment, we heard a terrible cannonade from the direction of Waterloo.

At this time, the guns heard must have been the massed batteries on the French right bombarding the Allied positions before d'Erlon attacked. Grouchy did hear the guns of Waterloo, but at Wavre and not at Sart-a-Walhain. He now knew a large battle was taking place.

Having reached the Prussians, whom he was ordered to pursue, and being already engaged with them, his duty was not to abandon them, but to attack them vigorously at Wavre, to prevent their undertaking anything on the side of Waterloo. He was not then, nor could he be, informed that at daybreak two of Blücher's corps had quitted Wavre, directing their march towards the British army, or that at about that moment the head of these corps were reaching the heights of Saint-Lambert, in sight of the French troops at Waterloo. Moreover, having reason to believe the Prussian force of 95,000 was concentrated before him, Grouchy was too weak to divide his forces and would have run the risk of being cut to pieces had he done so.[46] As it was he was outnumbered and would be until Gérard and Pajol arrived.

8th Division attacks at La Baraque

The troops that Excelmans had encountered, it seems, had not been totally repulsed, as the vanguard of 3rd Corps was drawn into the action at La Baraque, as the aide-de-camp to General Lefol notes:[47]

> We continued our march forward in pursuit of the enemy, when our general appreciated that many of our skirmishers had advanced too near a wood occupied by a party of Prussians, and sent me to warn them to turn back. As soon as I reached their place there came from this wood a brisk firing against four men around me, and which even wounded my horse, Sabol.
>
> Upon returning from this little expedition, I met General Corsin and head of our staff, Colonel Marion. I related what had happened,

when all of a sudden I saw him fall backwards. A bullet had seriously injured him, passing all the way through his body. The colonel, who had the strength to beg me not to abandon him, so I took with me four sappers who improvised a stretcher and carried him out of the reach of enemy fire. I wanted to give these brave soldiers a gold coin that I had removed from the pocket of General Marion, but they refused saying they had done their duty, the surgeon dressed the wound which had made a large cut on both sides of the body and, having been put in the cart of our *cantiniere* that had been emptied of all its goods, I took him to Walhain, precisely in the room where two hours before had been Marshal Grouchy. The house was already crowded with wounded, but that did not prevent the owner and his two charming daughters give all the care desirable to the colonel. In that place was also M. Foulques d'Oraison, then lieutenant-of-staff like me, now general, who was kind enough to help us aid our wounded...But, back to our day of June 18, believing that I had forever left Colonel Marion, I joined our division which was fighting at Wavre. The fighting had been going on since four in the afternoon, continued with equal violence from both sides until well into the night, the enemy General Thielemann put up a strong resistance, but was defeated, however, after we have lost many people.

Colonel François Marion (1774-1854) did not die, and he himself acknowledges that his speedy evacuation to Sart-a-Walhain saved his life:[48]

> Immediately transporting me after I suffered my terrible injury to Walhain, you saved my life. After your departure, I suffered a haemorrhage that required the greatest care.

About the action at La Baraque, General Pierre Berthezène, commander of 11th Division (part of Vandamme's 3rd Corps), notes:[49]

> On the 18th the army began to move at seven or eight in the morning, we marched to Wavre on the road from Sart-a-Walhain. Our movement was extremely slow. At Nil-Saint-Martin we made a long halt, during which the enemy occupied the hedges and open places in preparing the battlefield. It was only at La Baraque, arriving about two o'clock, we found that a rearguard that pretended to want to defend it, but a few musket shots quickly dispersed them.

NOTES:

1. AN: LH 2782/98. Edmond François Blocqueville de Coulliboeuf was born on 15 February 1789 at Falasie. He was awarded the Legion of Honour while a captain on Grouchy's staff on 31 January 1814 while serving in the 16th Chasseurs. He was then made an Officer of the Legion of Honour on 16 August 1823 while serving as squadron commander in the 5th Chasseurs. He was promoted to general-de-brigade on 30 April 1849 and died in 1861 aged seventy-two.

2. AN: LH 169/57. Didier Louis Ferdinand Bellanger Desboullets was born in Paris on 26 July 1784 and admitted to the 3rd Hussars in 1803. He was promoted to corporal and sergeant in the following year and to sub-lieutenant on 26 November 1806, before being listed as lieutenant aide-de-camp to Duc de Plaisance on 10 May 1807. He was promoted to captain on 28 December 1809, to squadron commander aide-de-camp to General Dupont on 23 August 1814 and dismissed on 25 March 1815. He joined Grouchy's staff on 22 April 1815 and was discharged from the army on 6 June 1817.

3. Grouchy, *Relation succincte de la campagne de 1815*, Vol. 4, pp. 141-5.

4. SHDDT: C15 5. Dossier 18 June 1815. Handwritten statement from Blocqueville to Grouchy, no date.

5. SHDDT: C15 5. Dossier 18 June 1815. Statement by Sénécal dated 1829 and copied by Comte du Casse in 1865.

6. Grouchy, *Relation succincte de la campagne de 1815*, Vol. 4, pp. 141-5.

7. Grouchy, *Relation succincte de la campagne de 1815*, Vol. 4, pp. 141-5.

8. Christopher Bassford, Daniel Moran, Gregory W. Pedlow, *The Campaign of 1815 Chapters 40-49*, On Waterloo, available at http://www.clausewitz.com/readings/1815/five40-49.htm [accessed 10 February 2013].

9. Lefol, pp. 59-60.

10. Rumigny.

11. Grouchy, *Relation succincte de la campagne de 1815*, Vol. 4. pp. 141-5.

12. Rumigny.

13. Etienne-Maurice Gérard, *Quelques documents sur la bataille de Waterloo*, Paris, 1829.

14. François.

15. Lefol, pp. 59-60.

16. AN: LH 2603/55. Louis Etienne Thouvein was born on 12 November 1791.

17. Gérard, *Quelques documents*.

18. Lettow-Vorbeck, Vol. 8, p. 391.

19. Grouchy, *Observations sur la relation de la campagne de 1815*, pp. 15-16.

20. AN: LH 910/54. Alexander Cesar Louis d'Estourmel was born in Paris on 29 March 1780 and in 1799 volunteered with the 'Legion Franks', serving in Egypt. He was promoted to sub-lieutenant in 1800, to captain of the elite company of the 27th Chasseurs à Cheval in 1806, to adjutant in 1808 to the headquarters staff, and to squadron-commander on 1 November 1814. He was attached to the Duke of Berry on 10 March 1815 and went with the king to Ostend on 25 March 1815. He was then attached to the staff of the 1st Military Division on 9 July 1815. He states he did not serve in the Hundred Days campaign, which if true, suggests he never carried an order to Excelmans.

21. Henry Houssaye, *1815 Waterloo*, Paris, 1903, p. 169.

22. Grouchy, *Mémoires du maréchal de Grouchy*, 1874, Vol. 4, pp. 60-1.

2. Grouchy, *Observations sur la relation de la campagne de 1815*, p. 15.

2. SHDDT: C15 5. Dossier 18 June 1815. Handwritten statement from Blocqueville to Grouchy, no date.

2. SHDDT: C15 5. Dossier 18 June 1815. Grouchy to Napoléon, timed at 11.00. Copy made by Comte du Casse in June 1865. See also: Lettow-Vorbeck, Vol. 8, p. 390, who states that the letter was sent at 10.00. In Grouchy's register, the letter has no time. See also: Grouchy,

Relation succincte de la campagne de 1815, Vol. 4, p. 28.

[26] Berton, p. 56.

[27] Grouchy, *Relation succincte de la campagne de 1815,* Vol. 4, pp. 136-7.

[28] AN: AFIV 1939, pp. 50-1.

[29] Anon, *Memoires pour servir a l'Histoire,* p. 122.

[30] Gérard, *Quelques documents.*

[31] Ropes, p. 246.

[32] Gérard, *Dernières observations,* pp. 25-6. See also: SHDDT: C15 5. Dossier 18 June. Excelmans to Gerard, 1 February 1830.

[33] Julius von Pflugk-Harttung, *Von Wavre bis Belle-Alliance (18 Juni 1815),* Berlin, 1908, p. 616.

[34] Berton, p. 64.

[35] Tim Clayton, *Waterloo: Four Days that Changed Europe's Destiny,* Little, Brown, London, 2014, p. 48.

[36] William Hyde Kelly, *The Battle of Wavre and Grouchy's Retreat,* John Murray, London, 1905.

[37] A. F. Becke, *Napoleon and Waterloo: the Emperor's Campaign with the Armée du Nord, 1815,* Greenhill Books, London, 1995.

[38] Berton, p. 56.

[39] Grouchy, *Mémoires du maréchal de Grouchy,* 1874, Vol. 4, pp. 60-1.

[40] Booth, *The Battle of Waterloo, also of Ligny, and Quarter-Bras,* London, 1817, p. 251.

[41] Grouchy, *Observations sur la relation de la campagne de 1815,* pp. 15-16.

[42] SHDDT: C15 5. Dossier 18 June 1815. Handwritten statement from Blocqueville to Grouchy, no date.

[43] Anon, *Memoires pour servir a l'Histoire,* p. 130.

[44] Damitz, p. 352.

[45] Grouchy, *Mémoires du maréchal de Grouchy,* 1874, Vol. 4, pp. 60-1.

[46] Grouchy, *Observations sur la relation de la campagne de 1815,* pp. 20-2.

[47] Lefol, pp. 59-60.

[48] Lefol, pp. 59-60.

[49] Berthezène, pp. 359-60.

Chapter 10

Napoleon's Orders

Vandamme arrived in Wavre around 15.00. The same time as Vandamme was pushing into Wavre, Grouchy received an order from Marshal Soult to press on in the same direction.[1] The order is timed at 10.00, and was written in response to the report sent to Napoléon at 6.00, having taken something like five hours to reach Grouchy. The order was carried by Adjutant Comte Zenowicz and states:[2]

> Monsieur marshal, the emperor has received your last report dated six o'clock in the morning at Gembloux.
>
> You speak to the emperor of only two columns of Prussians, which have passed at Sauvenière and Sart-a-Walhain. Nevertheless, reports say a third column, which was a pretty strong one, had passed by Gery and Gentinnes, directed on Wavre, reported by Milhaud's cavalry before they left.
>
> The emperor instructs me to tell you that at this moment His Majesty has decided to attack the English army in its position at Waterloo in front of the Soignes Forest. Thus, His Majesty desires that you are to continue your movement to Wavre, in order to approach us, to put you in our sphere of operations, and to make your communications with us, pushing before you those portions of the Prussian army which have taken this direction, and which may have stopped at Wavre, were you ought to arrive as soon as possible.
>
> You will follow the enemy columns which are on your right side with light troops, in order to observe their movements and pick up their stragglers. Instruct me immediately as to your dispositions and your march, as also to the news which you have of the enemy; and do not neglect to keep your communications with us. The emperor desires to have news from you very often.

The order is frustratingly vague, but however one reads it Grouchy was not ordered to Waterloo. Indeed, we suppose that the order from the emperor further confirmed in Grouchy's mind that the Prussians were making for Brussels. Napoléon also considered it very unlikely that the Prussian column Milhaud had spotted would be going anywhere else other than Brussels. He had not yet fully realised the situation he was in. Indeed, Grouchy was ordered to send out troops to the east and follow the Prussian forces at Chyse. He was ordered to attack at Wavre; he was not ordered to Waterloo. We say again, Napoléon, at 10.00 on 18 June, did not believe that the Prussians could link with Wellington and assumed that communication between the Prussians and Wellington were severed and they could not act in unison, as it assumed the Prussian army was a spent force heading to Brussels. This was a dangerous assumption to make and one that, with hindsight, was categorically wrong. Because Napoléon had lost contact with the Prussians he probably reasoned that Wellington had also lost contact.

Gentinnes and Saint-Gery are due north of Sombreffe and are clearly marked on the 1777 map. From Gentinnes, the troops would have headed to Vilroux, Hevillers and Mont-Saint-Guibert, heading towards Wavre or Louvain. From Mont-Saint-Guibert, the next point of destination would have been La Baraque. There is no doubt that this column, observed by Milhaud, was the Prussian 1st Corps which had had its bivouacs around the villages of Tilly and Gentinnes. It was followed by the Prussian 2nd Corps. This was vitally important information that could, and should, have been passed to Grouchy the day before. Prussian 2nd Corps had moved out at 06.30. Given Pajol's remit was to head to Namur, they had no chance of ever observing these two columns heading north. Why Napoléon did not transmit this news we can only guess at. The failure to pass on the information had catastrophic consequences. Indeed, not passing this crucial information onto Grouchy, or even considering the possibility that this column could link with Wellington rather than head to anywhere other than Maastricht, lost Napoléon the campaign. No blame at all can be assigned to Grouchy. It was a catastrophic mistake with calamitous ramifications.

To recap, Grouchy had no knowledge at all of the Prussian 1st and 2nd Corps and its movements. He never made contact with it, nor could he given the remit of his mission. By the time Excelmans left the battlefield of Ligny he could not have spotted the two Prussian corps heading north.

The troops that he did find at Wavre, Grouchy perhaps naturally assumed were the same troops as Milhaud observed. The troops at Tourinnes and Perwez were, based on Excelmans's reports, the body of troops from Gembloux that Excelmans had lost contact with on the night of 17 June in the pouring rain as he pressed onto Sart-a-Walhain. Another body of troops was at Namur. What Grouchy did not know, and could not have known on 17 or 18 June, was that the column Milhaud observed on 17 June was, by the time Grouchy got word of the column's existence, already at Waterloo. The Prussian 4th Corps under Bülow, which had been spotted heading to Perwez, had by now turned towards and passed Wavre and was heading to Waterloo, leaving 3rd Corps at Wavre. Grouchy, we think, supposed the troops at Wavre were the column Milhaud had observed, and he had now split the Prussian columns from one another to prevent their junction with Wellington. He was sadly mistaken on this view. It was Bülow that Excelmans spotted at Cabaret A Tout Vent, which had been Bülow's headquarters. It was Bülow that had been spotted at Tourinnes, who had not headed to Louvain, but was heading to Waterloo. Indeed, Napoléon had no idea what happened to these columns. He speculates they could have been at Wavre. Rather than press onto Wavre and Waterloo, Grouchy was ordered to keep moving north-east.

Napoléon clearly had no idea at this stage where the Prussians were. History tells us his illusions were soon to be shattered when Marbot's 7th Hussars made a Prussian officer prisoner carrying a letter from Bülow to Wellington, which told Napoléon in no uncertain terms that Bülow was heading to Waterloo. Napoléon perhaps assumed that Bülow was the body of troops Milhaud had observed. Given Grouchy's dispatch saying the Prussians were heading north-east, Napoléon, it seems, entertained the possibility of the troops spotted by Milhaud getting to Waterloo. At no stage did Napoléon ever think that the vast majority of the Prussians were linking with Wellington until it was too late, as Grouchy, it seems, had separated from Wellington two, if not three, Prussian columns. Of course, with hindsight we know he was grossly mistaken. Grouchy had found the Prussians, but he had only ever made partial contact with two separate corps, and he supposed that the troops at Wavre were a rearguard to cover the Prussian retreat to Louvain, and does not seem to have considered the Prussians were going to aid Wellington at this stage. The veil was only too cruelly lifted from his eyes in Napoléon's 13.00 order. Napoléon, in giving Grouchy a strict remit of heading north and east, shows how confident was in this assumption. Only too late did he realise his mistake.

By 16.00 at Waterloo, Prussian infantry had been massed in the Paris Wood. The cavalry of Domon and Subervie were ordered to reconnoitre the position, while Lobau and 6th Corps moved up. Prussian 1st Corps arrived by 18.00, followed by the 2nd Corps towards 19.30. The 1st Corps assaulted Frischermont, Papelotte and La Haye Sainte, 4th Corps attacked Planchenoit, with 2nd Corps in the centre. Three Prussian columns arrived at Waterloo and attacked hard; the Prussians won the Battle of Waterloo. Grouchy was never in a position to halt the Prussian 1st and 2nd Corps, and he never seems to have assumed that the troops at Tourinnes and Wavre were anything other than the same body of troops, drawn up as a rearguard to protect the Namur to Louvain road. The troops Milhaud spotted were presumably assumed to be the troops found at Wavre. As far as Grouchy was concerned he had found and stopped the Prussians, or at least a major part of the Prussian army, as he perhaps concluded some were at Namur and some were headed to Louvain, thus at least two-thirds of the Prussians had been sent off away from Wellington. Case closed as it were. Grouchy had no reason to believe that the Prussians were off to Wellington. He was acting according to his orders. He had sent scouts to Namur and towards Maastricht, and had found Prussians at Perwez, and then later at Wavre, and it was at Wavre and towards Louvain that Napoléon ordered Grouchy to attack, which is exactly what he did. He cannot be blamed for his actions, as he was carrying out Imperial orders from Napoléon. With hindsight he should have gone to Wavre and Waterloo, but he was not ordered to do so, nor did he have any reason to do so, based on what he knew on 18 June.

Waterloo had been thrust on the emperor by the Allies. He could not conceive of a Prussian link with Wellington. He, at 10.00 on 18 June, cannot have understood the importance of what Milhaud had told him. He failed categorically to acknowledge a strong body of Prussians were between him and Grouchy, and his own orders had sent Grouchy off further east.

Returning back to the narration of the day, the timing of the arrival of this order with Grouchy is in dispute. Grouchy gives a time of around 15.00, whereas Comte Zenowicz gives a time much later in the day. About the dispatch of this order, Zenowicz himself writes:[3]

> 18 June 1815, the day of the Battle of Waterloo, I was on duty as a senior officer in the Imperial Headquarters, and I was not allowed to leave for a moment. About nine o'clock, the emperor mounted his horse, and I followed him. Approaching to the lines of the army's right flank, after talking a few moments to Comte d'Erlon, he left his suite and returned, accompanied only by the major-general (Soult), he ascended a slight elevation, from hence we easily discovered various positions of the two armies. After reviewing some time with his glass without changing his position, he addressed a few words

to the general staff, and then when he came down from the plateau, the emperor beckoned me to come near to him, I obeyed; he then addressed those assembled near to him saying 'this is Comte d'Erlon on our right', he said, pointing to the corps of the general and continuing, after describing a circle with his hand to the right of the line, he added: 'Grouchy is marching in that direction, go to him, pass through Gembloux, follow in his footsteps, major-general will give you even a written order'. I wanted to point out to the emperor while he was talking to me that the road was too long, but without giving me time to finish, he said: 'it does not matter, you would be taken following the shortest route', and then pointing to the end of the right side of the line, he said: 'come back here and join me, where Grouchy will debouch on the line. It cannot wait; he must be in direct communication with us and come into the line of battle with us. Go, go!'

Immediately after I had received this order, I ran after the major-general, who at that time was at the farm of Caillou, where the Imperial Headquarters had spent the night. We arrived at ten o'clock at the farm. The major-general went to his room and sent for his secretary. The first thing to do is to log the date and time. It is easy to see that this time cannot be that for the departure of the dispatch, because before one leaves, it takes time to write it down, and it is also necessary to enter in the order register of the major-general. All this requires sufficient time and in an ordinary service, where the hours and minutes have no role to play, this observation is of no importance, but in a particular case, when counting the hours and minutes when we take a wrong bearer of an order, it must be possible to restore the facts as they occurred. I repeat, the time of the order which I was carrying was ten o'clock. I retired to the orderly's room. After half an hour of waiting, I joined the general staff.

Nothing yet other than the date was written, the major-general observed the map, and his secretary amused himself in cutting a feather. I returned to the living room where I found M. Regnault, chief officer of the 1st Army Corps who, learning that I had for twenty-four hours been in the saddle, I had not had anything to eat. He kindly sent from his wagon a piece of bread and water mixed with spirits. After my meal, I went back to the general staff, he was busy dictating the order I expected, and I went again to the orderly's room.

After half an hour I was asked for. Marshal Soult gave me the order that the emperor had told me. I departed and I arrived there, between three and four o'clock in the afternoon, a division of the rearguard which was part of the army corps I had been sent to locate. A quarter of an hour later, I joined Comte Grouchy; he was with General Gérard in a small room of a house where an ambulance had been established. I presented my dispatches to the marshal, and even told him verbally what I was charged with. After browsing through what I had given him, Marshal Grouchy communicated it to General Gérard, who after reading it cried, animated with energetic emotion, apostrophising Grouchy: 'I've always told you if we are f… it's your fault'.

However, an eyewitness states:[4]

> Several officers were sent before midday by Napoléon to search for Marshal Grouchy, but only one of them, Col Zenowicz, arrived at Wavre, and not until about six o'clock in the evening. The marshal then resolved to pass the Dyle at Limale with a part of his army, but it was then too late.

Based on Zenowicz and this account it is perhaps not impossible that the dispatch did not arrive with Grouchy until much later in the day. This, of course, is perfectly possible.

Grouchy was savvy enough to realise that the order, when it arrived, would have been out of date, but he had no course of action other than to press on. We have no accurate time for arrival of the letter. If it left at 13.30 to 14.00, and it took two and a half hours to get to Grouchy, the time would be 16.00 to 16.30 based on the time it had taken the 10.30 dispatch to get to the emperor. However, eyewitnesses say it arrived at 18.00. Given the large number of Prussian troops between Waterloo and Wavre, and the courier could not go 'as the crow flies', the order is likely to have arrived, in my view, in the 18.00 to 19.00 timeframe.

Grouchy was now committed to attacking the Prussians, and he had no easy way to break off the action. The remark from Gérard, here at Wavre, seems a more accurate recounting of Gérard's views than earlier in the day. Grouchy now had Imperial orders to attack at Wavre, and if he could, move towards Waterloo. Did Napoléon honestly expect Grouchy to be able to hold the Prussians at bay, and still have enough troops to send them to Waterloo? Seemingly so. Napoléon had clearly underestimated the strength of the Prussian columns, as well as the heavily wooded and undulating terrain between himself and Grouchy at Wavre. The other obstacle of getting across a river with the bridges, as we shall see, controlled by the Prussians, also seems to have slipped Napoléon's mind.

By the time that Grouchy received orders, Napoléon had already spotted the Prussians advancing from Saint-Lambert.[5] Clearly Napoléon by this stage must have known that some of the Prussian army had eluded Grouchy and had made contact with Wellington. Either Napoléon believed that only a small portion of the Prussian army had eluded Grouchy (hardly surprising given the lead they had over the marshal), or he was over-confident in his chances of success against Wellington and the Prussians. Napoléon's judgement on both scenarios was horribly wrong. Writing in 1820, and probably a true reflection of his own thoughts at the time, Napoléon felt 40,000 to 45,000 Prussians were inferior to 28,000 French.[6]

Napoléon, writing on Saint Helena, claims that the Prussians retreated in two columns; one on Tilly the other on Wavre. Clearly, directly contradicts himself.[7] Napoléon is one of the least reliable of eyewitnesses to the events of the campaign, as he is writing with hindsight to explain his errors away as the failings of others, who were traitors to him and France.

Regarding Napoléon's fabrication about his own actions, and those of Grouchy, Grouchy justifiably writes in 1820:[8]

I therefore declare the greater part of the assertions, which this work contains respecting me, to lie false and calumnious. I declare the greater part of the orders and instructions which it details so formally, to be invented or garbled. All those asserted to have been transmitted to me on the 17th, and during the night of the 18th, are suppositious. The amplest proof of this appears in the book of orders and correspondence of the major-general chief-of-staff, the organ of communication between the commander-in-chief and his general officers. This unquestionable document, given up to me together with the commander-in-chief of the army, by Marshal Soult, after the loss of the Battle of Waterloo, shows that no orders or instructions were sent to me, except those comprised in two letters, the one at ten o'clock in the morning, the other at one in the afternoon of the 18th. I challenge the production of a single note or minute of any other order, or of a single officer who will assert that during the evening or night of 17 June, he delivered to me a single instruction, dispatch, or even message from Napoléon or from the major-general.

Grouchy then describes his own movements as follows:[9]

While we fought in the Limelette Wood cannon fire was heard in the distance on my left. I moved in that direction and did not doubt that it was an attack on the British army by Napoléon. Having reached the Prussians that I was instructed to pursue, and, as I was already dealing with them, it was my duty not to abandon them and to attack strongly at Wavre, so that the troops here could not undertake operations against the army that fought at Waterloo.

I was not, and could not have been, informed that from the dawn two corps of Marshal Blücher had left Wavre to join to the English army, and at the time the head of column was only a few minutes away from the heights of Saint-Lambert to attack French troops at Waterloo. Moreover, having 32,000 men, and to believe the Prussian army 95,000 strong, was gathered in front of me, my force was too weak to divide and I ran the chance of being crushed if I had done so.

This is corroborated by de Blocqueville, one of Grouchy's aide-de-camps:[10]

The marshal ordered General Vandamme to continue his march towards Wavre, and to crown the heights overlooking the town, and to reconnoitre whether the Dyle bridges that were there were broken. The marshal always had attentive ears towards the gunfire and viewed that it had become much stronger, went a half-mile on the left at a gallop to better judge its position.

Having determined that the battle was general, he ordered General Pajol to move with his body and Teste's division to Limale, to pass the Dyle, to stand fast on the right flank of the Prussians, who were the left bank, and immediately get into communication with the emperor. These orders were executed with vigour and success, but the enemy, who appreciated the importance of his possession, reoccupied Limale with superior forces.

As noted by de Blocqueville, Grouchy ordered Pajol and Teste to take the Sart-a-Walhain road, advance to Limaile and cross the Dyle and to attack the enemy.[11]

Also, it is worth pointing out again that as the Battle of Waterloo did not commence until around 11.30, no cannonade could have been heard at Sart-a-Walhain between 10.00 and 10.30, whereas in all probability it was heard at Wavre, as Grouchy makes clear later. If gunfire was heard at Sart-a-Walhain it cannot have been the opening salvos of the Battle of Waterloo, therefore Grouchy was not only correct to keep heading to Wavre, but also in his assessment of the situation that the cannon fire was a minor skirmish. It could be Gérard did hear cannon at 11.30, which were probably the opening shots of Excelmans's attack on Wavre.

The point about Grouchy hearing the cannon of Waterloo and not marching to the guns has been seized upon by his detractors without endeavouring to establish where Grouchy actually was when the Battle of Waterloo began. It seems when the cannonade was heard, Grouchy knew a battle was to take place and had just received orders to attack at Wavre, therefore the cannonade was expected and Grouchy, in attacking Wavre, was acting upon orders and, it seems, had no need to move to Waterloo. As stated before, Napoléon, with a similar force, had defeated the Prussians two days earlier (without 1st and 2nd Corps), so it seemed reasonable that with a similar strength force, with the fresh 1st Corps of over 20,000 men, Napoléon could easily overcome the already defeated troops under Wellington, which he did not know would be significantly re-enforced by the Prussians.

According to Sub-Lieutenant Gerbet, of the 37th Regiment of Line Infantry (part of 3rd Corps), the corps broke camp at 4.00 at Gembloux, where they had arrived on the 17th at around 19.00, and arrived at Sart-a-Walhain at 12.00 on 18 June.[12] The 37th Regiment of Line Infantry and, presumably, its division arrived at 16.00 in the vicinity of Wavre. The bridge, a key objective to capture, was defended by a row of houses which were occupied by the Prussians.[13] Gerbet's division may have been at the rear of Vandamme's column, so would have arrived after the head of the column had done, given that Vandamme began his attack sometime around 14.30 to 15.00, and not 18.00 as Napoléon states in 1820.[14]

Grouchy's march on Wavre has been condemned by Napoléon and others as slow and a cause for the defeat of Waterloo. Carl von Clausewitz, who served on Thielemann's staff during the action at Wavre, notes:[15]

> There can be no doubt that in the morning Grouchy had no clear idea of the direction that Blücher had taken with his army. Grouchy himself says this, and when he departed Gembloux, his march was directed only toward Sart-les-Walhain, not yet toward Wavre. This explains the sideward move of Pajol and the way the French were tapping blindly around, which slowed the march. It was only the encounter with the rearguard of the Prussian 2nd and 3rd Corps in front of Wavre that drew Grouchy toward that place.
>
> This failure to recognise the true line of retreat of the Prussian army borders on the incomprehensible, because it requires an

assumption of the highest degree of clumsiness and negligence on the part of the French generals, which is not at all easy to make.

On the other hand, we do not find the slowness of Grouchy's movement toward Wavre as astonishing as most others do. In recent wars, we have become accustomed to rapid movements and marches of twenty, twenty-five, or thirty miles in a single day and therefore feel justified in demanding them, since great speed may be very valuable. But such speed results more from favourable march conditions than from the urgency of the requirement. This is all too clear to anyone who has had to deal with such matters and has had to struggle with all of the difficulties that can arise. Weather and the state of the roads, lack of rations and quarters, fatigue of the troops, lack of information, and so forth, may—despite the best intentions— reduce a march to one-half or even one-third of what was thought possible on paper. Let us take the example of the French after the battles of Jena and Auerstädt, when they were completely victorious and had the greatest reason to hasten their movements. Although they were at that time at the peak of their military efficiency, they did not exceed an average of ten miles per day during their pursuit.

If we assume that Grouchy's corps did not leave the field of battle at Ligny before 2 or 3 p.m. [on 17 June], then it is not surprising that these corps did not reach the neighbourhood of Wavre before 2 or 3 p.m. [on 18 June], that is to say, twenty-four hours later, since Wavre is twenty-five miles from the Ligny battlefield on the road that Grouchy took, [which passed] through a range of hills; plus, the conditions were very unfavourable, as we have already seen. The cavalry might certainly have begun the pursuit much sooner, but while this would not have been completely useless, it still would not have achieved the results that some commentators argue could have achieved by Grouchy with respect to the Battle of Belle-Alliance. The only reproach that can clearly be made against General Grouchy is that he sent his whole force down a single road, which naturally resulted in the last divisions of the 4th Corps arriving only around evening.

Thielemann's preparations

As soon as Vandamme's corps began to deploy to attack, Prussian General Thielemann immediately started to organise the defence. Wavre was afforded favourable means for defence in that the Dyle, which ordinarily was a shallow stream, was in full flow due to the torrential rain of the night of 16 and 17 June. In order to cross the flooded valley, the French had to capture and control the vital bridges, which were heavily defended by the Prussians. Carl von Clausewitz notes:[16]

General Thielemann now occupied the Wavre position as follows: the 12th Brigade was placed behind the crossing at Bièrges, the 10th to the right behind Wavre, the 11th to the left behind Wavre on the main road. Wavre itself was occupied by three battalions of the 9th Brigade, and the remainder of this brigade, as well as the reserve cavalry, were designated as the reserve and placed in the vicinity of Bavette.

The three forward brigades kept as well concealed as possible in brigade assembly areas, with the greater proportion of their force in columns, and employed only individual battalions or half-companies of skirmishers for the defence of the bridges and the river itself. Meanwhile, all of the artillery—with the exception of one battery (totalling twenty-seven guns) kept in reserve—was spread along one side of the valley and immediately went into action against the enemy coming down the other side.

The position of the 3rd Corps extended 2,000 paces from Bièrges to Lower-Wavre, so it was not too extensive for a corps of 20,000 men. There were four bridges across the river—one near Lower-Wavre, two at Wavre, and one at the mill of Bièrges. The Dyle itself was fordable if necessary. On the other hand, the left bank of the river valley was rather high, perhaps fifty to sixty feet, and so steep that it could be considered a significant obstacle to any approach, while still offering full fields of fire. Since the countryside in the vicinity of the right and left wings was open, and some strongpoints presented themselves farther to the rear, the position could certainly be considered among the strongest that could be occupied immediately without much preparation.

General Thielemann's directions were designed to expose as few troops as possible, to maintain the firefight with the smallest possible numbers of infantry, and to rely mainly on artillery, so that if the enemy troops attempted to break out of the valley by storm, he would be able to send a mass of fresh men against them. The actual reserve was to be used to attack the flank of any enemy that attempted to envelop one of our flanks. Misfortune caused one of these arrangements to fail.

The 9th Brigade, which had withdrawn via Lower-Wavre after the enemy had deployed in strength, had occupied Wavre with two battalions and placed a third behind it. Owing to some unexplainable misunderstanding, the brigade then failed to keep its remaining six battalions, two cavalry squadrons, and eight guns in reserve near La Bavette, and instead followed the other corps going via Neuf Cabaret to Couture, which had been the original destination for the whole corps. No one noticed this mistake, because at the moment when General Borcke withdrew through the lines at Lower-Wavre, everyone's attention was focused on the deployment of the enemy's force in front of the lines. It was not until about 7 p.m. when it was realised that the reserve might be needed, and a preparatory order was sent that it was discovered that General Borcke had marched away instead of remaining with the reserve cavalry. Officers were sent out to see whether he had taken up some other position in the area, but when they returned without having found out anything General Thielemann let the matter rest, because, as he said, the place where the heavy cannonade of a great battle could be heard was the place where the whole affair would be decided, and whatever might happen at Wavre would have no effect on that; so perhaps it was even better that another [brigade] would be there.

Thus, it was that on 18 and 19 June General Thielemann had only twenty-four battalions of infantry, twenty-one squadrons of cavalry, and thirty-five guns, for a total of about 15,000 men, to oppose Marshal Grouchy, whose total strength could not be seen because of the woods, although about 10,000-12,000 men were visible by around 3 p.m.

On the left bank of the Dyle, about three-quarters of a mile upstream, to the south-west of Wavre, was the mill and bridge of Bièrges, destined to be the scene of the fiercest fighting. At Limale, a village two miles upstream from Wavre, was another vital bridge over the Dyle. The mill at Bièrges, houses at Limale and Wavre were loopholed, and the two bridges at Wavre were barricaded.

NOTES:
[1] Sénécal, p 10.
[2] AN: AFIV 1939, pp. 49-50. See also: SHDDT: C15 5. Dossier 18 June 1815. Soult to Grouchy, timed at 13.00. Copy of the original order made by Comte du Casse in June 1863. du Casse either copied Soult's version of the letter, or had access to a duplicate set of material. A third version exists, published in 1826. This order is missing from Marshal Grouchy's correspondence register, however.
[3] Georges de Despots de Zenowicz, *Waterloo: déposition sur les quatre journées de la campagne de 1815*, Ledoyen, Paris, 1848.
[4] Booth, *The Battle of Waterloo, also of Ligny, and Quarter-Bras*, London, 1817, pp. 251.
[5] AN: AFIV 1939, pp. 50-1.
[6] Anon, *Memoires pour servir a l'Histoire*, pp. 119-20.
[7] Anon, *Memoires pour servir a l'Histoire*, p. 95.
[8] *Monthly Magazine and British Register*, Volume 49, 1 July 1820, pp. 408-9.
[9] Grouchy, *Observations sur la relation de la campagne de 1815*, pp. 15-16.
[10] SHDDT: C15 5. Dossier 18 June 1815. Handwritten statement from Blocqueville to Grouchy, no date.
[11] SHDDT: C15 *Registre d'Ordres et de correspondance du major-general a partir du 13 Juin jusqu'au*

26 Juin au Maréchal Grouchy, p. 27.

[12] Gerbet, p. 15.

[13] Gerbet, p. 18.

[14] Anon, *Memoires pour servir a l'Histoire*, p. 130.

[15] Bassford, Moran, Pedlow, *The Campaign of 1815 Chapters 40-49*, On Waterloo, available at http://www.clausewitz.com/readings/1815/five40-49.htm.

[16] Bassford, Moran, Pedlow, *The Campaign of 1815 Chapters 40-49*, On Waterloo, available at http://www.clausewitz.com/readings/1815/five40-49.htm.

Chapter 11

The Battle of Wavre

Von Borcke's division had been pushed back onto Wavre by 15.30,
and Vandamme proceeded to attack without waiting for orders
from Grouchy. Excelmans, behind Vandamme's 3rd Corps at Dion-le-
Mont, and Pajol with his cavalry and Teste's division, were miles further
behind at Tourinnes. A Prussian publication of 1825 notes the following
about the attack at Wavre:[1]

> Colonel von Zeppelin had hastily occupied the houses on the banks
> of the Dyle, and fitted the houses with loopholes, and sought to
> barricade the great bridge, but all the doors were locked and the
> residents were all hidden or fled, he was only able to bring together
> the three wagons he had found for the barricade; his preparations
> were not yet completed when the gunfire began. The smaller bridge
> was completely free. Major von Bornstadt was sent with two
> companies to defend the bridge at Lower-Wavre.
>
> It was the corps of General Vandamme which arrived at about
> four o'clock at Wavre, and the cannon fire was from his two batteries,
> one of which were 12-pounders, who had left the road to set up, they
> were joined later by a third battery, which reinforced the battery
> standing on the left. General Excelmans stood with his dragoons on
> the right in reserve. General Gérard was behind more than half a mile
> with his corps, and General Pajol had just arrived at Tourinnes.

Marshal Grouchy notes:[2]

> In possession of a part of Wavre, we had in front of us on the other
> side of the Dyle, a Prussian army, of which it was difficult to assess
> the strength due to the terrain. The Prussians crowned the heights on
> the other side of the town, occupied the village of Bièrges and the mill
> of the same name, situated at the foot of this place, and extended in

212

the direction of the village of Limelette. It was clear from one side of the river to the other. A severe cannonade began from General Vandamme's battery of 12-pounders and the enemy batteries opened fire: our infantry exchanged fire with the Prussian infantry, but they could not cross the river, whose passage was defended by a murderous fire of musketry and artillery.

As Vandamme fought his way into Wavre, officers on his personal staff were wounded. Aide-de-Camp Captain of Engineers Jean Pierre Christian Willmar was wounded on the road to Wavre.[3] First Lieutenant Bonaventure Jean Baptiste Gustave Loir de Lude, attached from the 10th Cuirassiers as an aide-de-camp, was killed at Wavre. Captain Marie Joseph August Bella, aide-de-camp to Marshal Grouchy, recounts:[4]

> General Vandamme had the whole corps down in the suburb of Wavre, probably hoping to cross the river and march against the enemy. But finding the bridge over the Dyle strongly barricaded, our troops could not win, and were forced to seek refuge in the streets parallel to the river to escape the enemy's fire. A single Prussian battery played variously along the banks did us little [damage], unlike the bullets of the enemy infantry who ambushed us from the houses along the river.

Bella's summary of events was correct; Vandamme could not fight his way over the bridges. Why Excelmans's command was not sent off to reconnoitre a ford seems a major lapse on the part of Grouchy.

10th Division

The attack on the bridge at Wavre commenced around 16.30.[5] Vandamme seems to have caught the Prussians off guard, pushed them back off the heights above Wavre and chased them into the town with his cavalry, infantry and preliminary bombardment by his artillery batteries. He then launched the whole of Habert's 10th Division, consisting of the 22nd, 34th, 70th and 88th regiments of Line Infantry, against the village and its bridge. General Pierre Berthezène, commander of 11th Division (part of Vandamme's 3rd Corps), notes the following about the preliminary moves of 3rd Corps:[6]

> Wavre was occupied by the Prussians; houses were filled with sharpshooters, the bridge was barricaded and defended by numerous artillery batteries, which established on the heights overlooking the left bank of the Dyle. When he arrived before the

town, General Vandamme ordered the attack immediately, without taking any measure to ensure the success of his operation: he simply ordered Habert's division to enter in column. Despite the murderous fire of the enemy, this division came to the bridge, but General Habert was wounded, and they retired in disorder and came to reform the city gates. This crazy attack cost us 500 or 600 men and several senior officers were wounded, and Colonel Duballen, an officer of great promise, was killed. Yet it would have been easy to take control of the position with little loss: he had only to cross the river at the front of the town, or rather above, at the bridge of Bièrges, and take the enemy from the rear. Moreover, the occupation of Wavre could have no influence on the fate of the campaign.

Wavre was defended by the Kurmärk Landwehr, commanded by Major von Bornstadt, who writes:[7]

> The defence of the town of Wavre witnessed us occupy part of it—that is the suburb, which was away from the enemy, with sharpshooters—and the great bridge was barricaded meagrely due to a lack of material to do so. The houses of the Dyle were provided with loopholes and occupied. The Kurmärkischen Landwehr Battalion was drawn into Wavre, and its commander, Major v. Bornstedt, detached two companies to occupy the bridge of Lower-Wavre, the remainder being were distributed close to the still unoccupied village and its bridge.

Louis Stranz, of the 1st Battalion Kurmärk Landwehr, writes:[8]

> On 17 June 1815, after the Battle of Ligny, the 3rd Army Corps (Thielemann) pulled out at daybreak, in well-ordered retreat, to Sombreffe thence to Gembloux, and from there over to Wavre. Our Battalion v. Bornstedt (Fusilier Battalion of the 1st Kurmärkischen Landwehr Infantry Regiment, Berlin) formed the rearguard in this retreat. We arrived before Wavre after all the troops had passed through the town already, our battalion was stopped in the market place, from here Major v. Bornstedt with his usual circumspection, made his own dispositions to defend the crossing of the Dyle in and around the town.

Kohlheim, of the 3rd Battalion Kurmärk Landwehr, adds some more details:[9]

On 18 June 1815, about six o'clock in morning, we, the 3rd Battalion of the 1st Kurmärkischen Landwehr Infantry Regiment, under the command of Major von Bornstedt, arrived above Wavre from Gembloux. We were the last troops from the battlefield of Ligny to retire. We bivouacked on the heights near Wavre, where for meat some cattle were slaughtered, as, since early on 15 June, nothing had been delivered to us to eat, but unfortunately after about two hours later the vanguard of the French forced us to leave everything we had prepared.

Due to some houses in the main street of Wavre being on fire, the powder carts had to drive around the town. We marched into the city and stationed ourselves on the left bank of the Dyle, and the artillery was established on the heights of the same bank. We had heard that General Field Marshal Prince Blücher had ordered the commanding general of the 3rd Army Corps, von Thielemann, that he should be on the defensive, and not to behave aggressively; nevertheless, Major von Bornstedt ordered his battalion to line up for battle, which happened, and it deployed en masse and established a line of skirmishers on the left bank of the Dyle stationed from inside the town to the bridge at the town hall and Lower-Wavre. For the defence of the bridge, about eighty men of the 1st Company (v. Eickstedt) from v. Bornstedt's battalion (under who the undersigned served) were established, which the major commanded in person.

Over this bridge several Prussian regiments moved to the left bank, the 30th Regiment, the 1st Battalion of the 1st Kurmärkischen Landwehr Infantry Regiment (9th Brigade), as well as the generals, their aides and some cavalry. Since we had no carpenters to barricade the bridge, the retreating regiments were asked to pass them over to us, and if I'm not mistaken, this was done by the 30th Regiment.

We marched the eighty men on the right bank of the Dyle after Major von Bornstedt had said these words: 'children, we each take our leave of life', inviting us to 'defend the bridge unto the death', and occupied the village of Lower-Wavre.

No sooner had this happened when we saw at a little distance from the village (on the northern bend of the road) French cavalry regiments moving upon us. We were ready for battle, the militia men Jannot and Schlei made the proposal to occupy the houses of the village which were empty and had the thatched roofs on fire, which was approved by the commander and soon set to their task. Either one or two men occupied the houses with burning thatch and we shot out of the windows and doors of the houses, at the same time the battle began in the town and the skirmishers and the artillery began its fire. The bridge was barricaded behind us, a cannon was brought up to the bridgehead.

The battle took place when the firing spread. So, we were, it seemed, in v. Bornstedt's battalion going from the defensive to the offensive. The battle began at about four o'clock in the afternoon and lasted until the evening after nine o'clock. The survivors of the eighty men retired to a small hill on the left bank, where at half-past nine o'clock French cannon balls destroyed our bivouac fire. It was a heavy, hot battle: about 1,500 Prussians against almost thirty thousand Frenchmen.

So clearly, the Prussians that had occupied the right bank of the Dyle on the early morning of 18 June had been surprised by Grouchy's vanguard, and had retreated into the town of Wavre under French artillery fire. A barricade was hastily thrown up on the stone bridge, but not until the French had stormed the bridge, as Captain Nachtigal, of the Kurmärk Landwehr, notes. Captain Nachtigal, again like Kohlmein, notes that Vandamme's supposed rash attack was not rash and mindless as the myth of the battle implies, and he notes that Vandamme pushed the Prussians back from right bank of the Dyle through to Wavre, as opposed to commencing a headlong and headless attack against the Prussians in well-defended positions:[10]

> I had the command over a portion of the left wing outside the town, and hardly had the last Prussian passed the bridge when the French, following them almost on their heels, made an attack. However, it was to be in vain, for though French were probably three times stronger than we were, I held it with my musket volleys for one hour alone, holding the position that my commander, Major von Bornstedt, and I had pledged to hold until we received support.

This first assault was conducted by the brigade of General Louis Thomas Gengoult, with the 34th and 88th regiments of Line Infantry. The 34th Regiment of Line Infantry formed the vanguard. The regiment mustered three battalions, and at the start of the campaign had mustered 1,384 other ranks and fifty-five officers. The 88th Regiment of Line Infantry was also of three battalions, and had mustered on 10 June 1,265 other ranks and fifty-seven officers. The strength of the two regiments on the 18th is hard to establish after the hard fighting of the 16th; each regiment perhaps totalling under 1,000 men.

The 34th Regiment of Line Infantry advanced in column with a skirmish screen from its voltigeur company flung out in front, and supported by a furious cannonade from two batteries of 12-pounders placed to the right of the Brussels road. The voltigeurs, their yellow coat collars and jaunty green and yellow plumes, bobbed over the broken ground down towards the bridge. They quickly cleared the few Prussian sharpshooters from the buildings on the French bank of the Dyle, and pressed on to the main bridge. As the voltigeurs stepped onto the bridge they were met with close-range and deadly musket fire. The Prussians had loopholed the buildings flanking the far end of the bridge, and also lined hedges and walls. To make things worse for the voltigeurs, the Prussian artillery batteries fired into the French attacking columns, and on the whole of the ground behind them. Wounded leading his regiment, the 34th Regiment of Line Infantry, was Colonel Jean Antoine Augustin Mouton, who suffered a gunshot wound to his left thigh. He had only been in command since 14 April 1815.[11] Also wounded was Lieutenant Antoine Chancenotte.[12] Two officers were killed in the action. The eagle part of the 34th Regiment of Line Infantry came under fire. Third Porte-Aigle Jean Grenier was wounded at Wavre and evacuated to the ambulances the same day.[13] Clearly the rear area services of the army with Grouchy were operating effectively to be able to evacuate wounded men. On 18 June, the regiment lost three men killed and fifty-eight men wounded, all bar two being evacuated to ambulances.[14] The 70th Regiment of Line Infantry lost four men killed and sixty-seven wounded, all of which were taken to ambulances;[15] the 88th Regiment of Line Infantry had five men killed, four deserted and ninety-four wounded, all of whom were evacuated to ambulances.[16]

Undaunted, the French crossed the bridge and entered Wavre. Captain Göhren, of the Kurmärk Landwehr, writes:[17]

> I was with the 2nd and 3rd Companies of the fusilier battalion of the 1st Kurmärkischen Landwehr Infantry Regiment, whose commander was Major von Bornstedt who commanded all the troops above the bridge, which marked the entrance of Wavre on this side of the Dyle. In ordinary circumstances our troops would have retreated against the attacks of approximately nine hundred attacking enemy, instead we defended to the utmost and complied with our orders as best we could, so that the enemy had not been able to penetrate this part of town.
>
> Because as soon as the last Prussian troops retired across the bridge, it also let the enemy occupy rapidly this bridge, which led to Namur.

Vandamme's brash attack had captured the stone bridge at Wavre and Habert's men surged forward, capturing houses in the lower part of the town. In the close confines of the village streets, vicious house-to-house and room-to-room fighting developed as the French fought for every inch of ground.[18]

Vandamme's gain was to be short lived. The 34th Regiment of Line Infantry was dispersed among the village streets, and the 88th Regiment of Line Infantry seems to have been pinned down on the far bank waiting to cross the bridge. It was perhaps now that Fusilier Louis Bapt was wounded. At Wavre, according to the regimental muster list, he was wounded by a canister shot to the left leg and two gunshot wounds, one of which took away two fingers from the right hand, and the other entered his right leg.[19]

A timely counter-attack from the Prussian 30th Infantry Regiment and the 1st Battalion of the Kurmärk Landwehr drove the French back over the bridges. The French, who had not had chance to evacuate the houses, were bayoneted and in the retreat General Habert was wounded. He had led the 34th Regiment of Line Infantry forward in person and was wounded in the lower part of his stomach.[20] Baron Paul Marie Rapatel, chief-of-staff to General Habert, who, on the 16 June, had contributed to the capture of a Prussian 12-pounder, was wounded in the firefight that saw Habert's men retreat from Wavre.[21]

Vandamme's rush against Wavre had succeeded, but due to the bottleneck caused by the narrow bridge was not able to bring up reinforcements. In consequence of this, the attack was beaten back.[22] Vandamme could not get enough men across the bridge to have numerical superiority on the far bank. Despite having a larger force, he could not bring this overwhelming advantage to bear against the Prussians, who were able to deploy troops as and where they were needed, and it seems likely that in the fighting the Prussians had more troops engaged than the French. With loopholed buildings and numerical superiority, the attacks by Vandamme were checked. For Vandamme to break out, he needed to get more troops across the river, and for that he needed to occupy both the bridge at Wavre and Bas-Wavre and create a bridgehead. Both, it seems, were un-obtainable goals.

Captain Göhren, of the Kurmärk Landwehr, continues about the Prussian counter-offensive but does not mention the Prussian 30th Infantry Regiment:[23]

> I had ordered the lieutenants Nachtigal and Britzke already, with two platoons, to proceed in close order, throw the enemy back, which

they executed with the utmost bravery, for a time, partly occupying the neighbouring houses, sometimes setting fire to them. But the resistance was hardly possible for much longer and fortunately there reached us the reinforcements of the fusilier battalion of the 30th Regiment. This allowed us to withdraw, but for some time the bridge was contested.

After some time, Lieutenant Nachtigal went forward with new volunteers and showed at the repeated attacks of the enemy great heroic determination, which admirably helped him earn the praise of his very anxious commander. I myself was during these operations employed by the bridge on the other points where the enemy sought to penetrate—partly by forming a chain of skirmishers, partly passing through the gardens, where the Sergeants Knack and Friedrich behaved very admirably, especially the former. The repeated attacks continued on into the late evening, when the enemy tried to storm a place about two hundred steps to the left of the bridge. Thus, the town which marked, in my opinion, the left wing of the army was happily kept in our possession.

During this fight back by the Prussians, Captain Pierre Etienne Roz, of the French 88th Regiment of Line Infantry, was wounded. He was born at Villers-Robert on 9 June 1777 and had served with the regiment since 5 August 1792. He had been wounded at Ligny with a gunshot wound, and at Wavre a musket ball shattered his left thigh, with the ball and bone splinters passing through his right thigh. He was left for dead and made a prisoner of war, until being returned to France on 16 February 1816.[24] Also captured was Sergeant-Major François Mary.

Gengoult's brigade had been bloodied in the costly assault on the town, and was withdrawn to allow the division's 2nd Brigade to move up and attack.

As the Prussian eyewitness notes, further attempts by Habert's men to force the bridge were beaten back with frightful loss, and the division was placed in a very serious position. If they retreated they came under the heavy fire of the Prussian batteries on the opposite heights; if they remained where they stood the enemy's sharp-shooters would annihilate them—to advance was impossible. Gradually, they found shelter, company-by-company, under the walls of the buildings along the bank whence they had just driven the Prussians. Vandamme was now deeply committed to the fight and could not withdraw.

Vandamme then threw into the fray the 2nd Brigade from Habert's division, which comprised the 22nd and 70th regiments of Line Infantry under the orders of General Dupeyroux. Fantin des Odoards, colonel of the 22nd Regiment of Line Infantry, adds more detail to these later futile assaults in a letter dated 23 July 1815, highly influenced by hindsight:[25]

> In the night, some information came in that the Prussians were moving to Brussels; we marched in this direction at daybreak. Upon reaching Wavre, a town on the Dyle, we found there in position and immediately we went into action. Instead of crossing the Dyle above or below Wavre, where it is fordable in many places, General Vandamme ordered us to cross over to dislodge the enemy, who were walled up in the town, to capture a barricaded bridge which was protected by thousands of sharpshooters who were posted in the houses on the other bank. He should have outflanked this strong position, but the general persisted in approaching in lines abreast en masse which engaged in a long road which was parallel to the bridge, received all the fire of the Prussians without being able to utilise their own. We lost many of our men for little purpose.
>
> The 70th Regiment of Line suffered similarly, and having been disconcerted two days earlier, was not ordered to charge and clear the bridge. Under a hail of bullets they were driven back. Rallied by their colonel, it hesitated, when the brave Maury, seizing the eagle, cried 'why you scoundrels, you dishonoured me the day before yesterday, and you repeat the offence today! Forward, follow me'.
>
> With the eagle clasped in his hand he dashed forward over the bridge, the regiment followed him with the charge being beaten by the drummers. Scarcely had he arrived at the barricade than this worthy man fell dead, and the 70th Regiment of Line fled rapidly away. Without the help of the 22nd Regiment of Line, the eagle, which was on the ground in the middle of the bridge at the side of my poor comrade spread out lifelessly on the ground, would have become the prize of the enemy sharpshooters who were ready to seize it.

In the attack the 70th Regiment of Line Infantry lost one officer, Captain Emperor, and two were wounded, namely Lieutenant Faure and Second Lieutenant Jean Baptiste Desire Thirou, who took a gunshot wound to his left arm.[26] In this incident the 22nd Regiment of Line Infantry lost Andre Felix Germain, at the head of the 1st Battalion, who was wounded with a musket ball to the right arm.[27] Captain Jean François Prevot was also wounded,[28] as were Captains Pierre Guillaumont and Jean Baptiste Rigollot and Second Lieutenants Petit and Pierre Mercier. Killed that day, according to Martinien, was Lieutenant Conte. Wounded in the accompanying 2nd Swiss Regiment, advancing with the grenadier company of 1st Battalion, was First Lieutenant Charles Antoine Louis

Schwich, a native of Corsica, so too was Second Lieutenant Jean Baptiste Roy. Wounded in the 1st Company of Fusiliers were Lieutenant Charles Magetty and Second Lieutenant Pierre Messonnier. At the head of the 3rd Fusilier Company, Captain Barthelemy Varenna was wounded, as was First Lieutenant Thomann. At the head of the voltigeur company, Captain Charles Edouard Augustin Tagloretti was wounded, along with First Lieutenant de Martinet. Also wounded was Captain-Adjutant-Major Joseph Xavier Huber, with a gunshot to the lower part of his stomach, and Captain d'Ernest.[29] About the day's actions, Fantin des Odoards writes:[30]

> On all other points, our attacks from one side to another of the Dyle had no more success, because they were ill-combined and feebly executed, poorly studied field. Toward night, however, we managed to cross the river above Wavre.
>
> It was too late. General Vandamme agreed, the next day, he had committed a fault here, but the fact unfortunately is all the more regrettable that we have also misused valuable time that loss of the Battle of Waterloo has no other cause. While the Prussians amused us by a screen of skirmishers and kept us in check, their principal masses, favoured by a hilly and wooded area that eluded us, marched to the aid of the English.

The attack against the bridge continued to around 19.00. Bornstedt notes the French attacked with courage, but little wisdom.[31] Losses for the division were as follows:

Regiment	Killed		Wounded		Missing		Total
	Officers	Men	Officers	Men	Officers	Men	
34th Line Infantry[32]	2	3	2	58	0	0	65
88th Line Infantry[33]	1	8	2	94	0	4	109
22nd Line Infantry[34]	2	1	6	93	0	540	642
70th Line Infantry[35]	1	4	2	67	0	0	74
2nd Swiss	0	0	12	0	0	0	12
Total	6	16	24	312	0	544	902

The division lost 902 men at Wavre, a huge number. For the 22nd Regiment of Line Infantry, of the missing, 271 were listed as prisoners of war, and the wounded comprised of one man sent to hospital, seven wounded but remained with the regiment, and eighty-five men wounded who had not been seen since 18 June 1815. The huge number of prisoners suggests that the 22nd Regiment of Line Infantry did indeed surge across the bridge, and these men were not able to re-cross and join the regiment.

11th Division attacks

Realising the French 11th Division was approaching, and that the barricade on the bridge of Lower-Wavre would not stop them, Major Bornstedt sought to demolish the bridge before the French arrived:[36]

> …the French lined up to attack on the opposite bank of the Dyle in Lower-Wavre, shortly before the last Prussian troops had crossed the bridge to the left bank. Major v. Bornstedt, when he noticed the enemy arrangements, and that the promised material to make the bridge un-usable had not arrived, he called for a team of volunteers from the 9th and 12th Companies of his battalion, which he had stationed there under the command of Captain von Gikstedt, and by speaking in front of the team of volunteers as a doting father would, and spoke a few words on the need to stop the passage of the enemy from crossing by not drawing his attention. There came immediately from the 9th Company the Militiamen Schley (a carpenter) and Jannot, who were followed by the master-sergeant (carpenter), the Militiamen Grohmann (butcher), Friebel and Wolff, also of the 12th Company, who were experts in dealing with construction material, and as before they volunteered at the request of the major to destroy the bridge by hand. Notwithstanding that the enemy's vanguard sought to prevent the operation so that the bridge could remain passable to people, with constant encouragement of Major v. Bornstedt and Captain v. Eickstedt, who was once an artillery officer in Szczecin, who was particularly astute, the details set about their work. They succeeded, with the small hand-axes and picks to break several boards, some of which fell down into the water.

As the Prussians were attempting to remove the roadway of the bridge, the French voltigeurs swarmed forward under enemy fire. They retrieved some of the planking from the river by fishing for the planks and piercing the timbers on the ends of their bayonets. As the French were endeavouring to salvage the bridge timbers, von Bornstedt ordered a counter-attack:[37]

> These bold enemies fished for the planks and carried them back to the bridge, and they were accompanied by thirty to forty men; however, the enemy's courage was in vain, because with the aide of the major, Lieutenant Coburg, and Lieutenant Jaeckel, of the 9th Company, who, along with the company, immediately advanced and opened fire on the voltigeurs. They gave way and left hurriedly.

222

After numerous attacks and counter-attacks, the French gained the bridge at Lower-Wavre. After a murderous firefight in the town, fought building-to-building as Berthezène sought to link up with Habert, a counter-attack by the Prussians forced Berthezène to withdraw.[38] The attacking French seem to have been the 56th Regiment of Line Infantry, the only regiment in the division to record officers dead or wounded on 18 June. In the attack, Battalion Commander Andre Enders, leading his 1st Battalion, was shot in the right buttock, presumably in the retreat.[39] Also wounded was Second Lieutenant Allinquan. Sergeant Ambroise Marc Senel, a native of Evreux, who had served in the 56th Regiment of Line Infantry for twenty years by the time the Battle of Wavre was fought, was wounded. He was later wounded in front of Soissons during the retreat.[40]

With the French attack checked, the bridge at Lower-Wavre was barricaded once more and an additional infantry battalion, three squadrons of cavalry and several artillery pieces were moved to bolster the defence against Berthezène's efforts. The sharpshooters of the 1st Kurmärk Landwehr were deployed to the right of the bridge and those of the 30th Infantry Regiment to the left, those of the 8th Infantry Regiment were placed in reserve. A detachment of hussars was sent to screen another wooden bridge further downstream. The assaults on Lower-Wavre ended in the early hours of the 19th, the French successfully holding some houses in the village which acted as strongpoints.[41]

About the futile attack at Lower-Wavre, Captain Jean Marie Putigny, of the 2nd Battalion 33rd Regiment of Line Infantry, narrates:[42]

> At Wavre there began an affair over the river, which was difficult to cross and had marshes on both sides. We removed the wagons which barricaded the bridge. We were faced with a well-supported fire from the houses in front of us, ten men of my company were killed and we re-grouped in the suburbs without further incident from the Prussians, from where we made another tentative move on our part.

Regiment	Killed		Wounded		Missing		Total
	Officers	Men	Officers	Men	Officers	Men	
12th Line Infantry[43]	0	0	0	18	0	14	32
56th Line Infantry[44]	0	1	0	16	0	6	23
33rd Line Infantry[45]	0	1	0	1	0	0	2
86th Line Infantry[46]	No data recorded						
Total	0	2	0	35	0	20	57

Seemingly only the 1st Brigade was in action; however, we cannot be sure as the muster list for the 86th Regiment of Line Infantry does not list what happened to the men who were in the regiment in 1815.

8th Division attacks once more

With the assault at Wavre repulsed, Marshal Grouchy divided 3rd Corps so that Lefol's division shifted south-west and assaulted the mill at Bièrges, with what remained of Habert's division (as well as the uncommitted battalions of Berthezène's divisions) being sent to Lower-Wavre. Excelmans's dragoons were brought up, but were of little use in this infantry struggle. Lefol's division had lost heavily at Ligny, losing 30 per cent of effective strength; this, however, does not seem to have dampened the ardour of the officers and men.

The mill at Bièrges is a large, three-storey, brick building and was built in 1767. The machinery inside was powered by a water wheel in the River Dyle. Attacking the mill was never going to be an easy option. Garrisoned by Prussian troops, the building became a strongpoint that was easily defendable by the nature of the approach from the south through water meadows cut by drainage ditches. The approach road through a wood ended abruptly on the marsh edge. The Prussians in the mill buildings and across the Dyle, separated by a good hundred yards or more, could easily pick off the French as they emerged through the wood. The French had no space to deploy, and the wood edge was the killing ground.

Perhaps one of the best-known analogies as to how difficult attacking such a strongpoint could be is perhaps the tillery at Aspern, where Marshal Masséna, in 1809, held of Austrian attacks for two days. The chateau and farm at Hougoumont is another good example, as indeed La Haye Sainte. The approach to the tillery at Aspern was not as tortuous as the approach to the mill of Bièrges, so one can see how this naturally defended bulwark became a major stumbling block for the French if they were to capture the bridge. It seems, however, that much later in the day the 44th Regiment of Line Infantry forded the river downstream towards Limale and out-flanked the position, but not before many hundreds of officers and men lay dead or wounded after attempting to storm what had become a small fortress. Why no artillery appears to have been brought up to bombard the place is a mystery to the author. Vandamme had a battery of 12-pounders, which, despite not being siege guns, could have battered down the walls of the mill and make the position untenable. As with the chateau at Hougoumont, the idea of an artillery bombardment was not considered or the gunners were shot down at their pieces before the guns could open up. The lack of Prussian and

French sources mentioning a French bombardment suggests that the option of a bombardment was not considered.

The mill was garrisoned by one company from the 31st Infantry Regiment, supported by the 2nd Battalion 6th Kurmärk Landwehr and six guns from Horse Battery Number 20.[47]

In the vanguard of Lefol's division was the brigade of General Billard, latterly commanded by Colonel Vernier, of the 23rd Regiment of Line Infantry. The 15th Regiment of Light Infantry, commanded by Colonel Brice, was deployed in skirmish order in front of the accompanying 23rd Regiment of Line Infantry. As the 15th Regiment of Light Infantry moved forward, Captain Nicolas Charpentier, commanding a carabinier company, was hit by a musket ball in the right leg.[48] A similar fate befell Captain Jean Baptiste Joseph Pringuet, who was hit in the left arm by a musket ball.[49] In the assault, Lieutenant Ambroise Dubarry, a native of Cologne, took a musket ball to the left hand.[50] When the assault failed, Lieutenant Louis Gay, who was wounded, was left behind and captured by the Prussians. He writes:[51]

> I declare that I was promoted to the rank of lieutenant by the Minister of War on 24 January 1814, and I lost my papers of promotion in 1815 when I was made a prisoner of war at the Battle of Wavre. I was returned to France after the disbandment of the army.

The eagle of the regiment was carried at Wavre by Lieutenant-Porte-Aigle Pierre Alexis Lieffroy,[52] who was wounded in the attack.[53] Also wounded was Lieutenant François Sardine, who suffered a gunshot to the head.[54] Sub-Lieutenant Edme Nicolas Noel Renvoye was wounded at Ligny on 16 June, and took a musket ball to the heel of his left foot at Wavre.[55]

In the accompanying 23rd Regiment of Line Infantry, Lieutenant Ondelin and sub-lieutenants Latour, Josse and Pillet were killed. Wounded in the action was Captain Augustin Theodore Blin de Mutrel with a gunshot to the thigh.[56] Sergeant-Major François Paillard, also of the 23rd Regiment of Line Infantry, was wounded. He was born at Breugnon on 13 April 1783 and had joined the regiment on 24 December 1804. He was promoted to corporal on 21 October 1808, to corporal-quartermaster on 21 May 1809, sergeant on 15 July 1813 and to sergeant-major a day later. About his involvement in the Battle of Wavre he writes:[57]

> I was wounded with two gunshots to my left arm at the Battle of Wavre in Belgium on 18 June 1815.

Two days earlier, at the Battle of Ligny, he had captured a Prussian 12-pounder field gun. Sergeant Jean Baptiste Courtouis had his right arm fractured by a musket ball.[58]

In the 2nd Brigade of Lefol's division, the 37th and 64th regiments of Line Infantry, were commanded by General Corsin. Sub-Lieutenant Gerbet, of the 37th Regiment of Line Infantry, notes that the attacks of Vandamme were costly in dead and wounded, but had no success:[59]

> Grouchy, who had by this time arrived on the scene, unaware of the strength of the Prussians at Wavre, and unaware, too, of Blücher's march on Saint-Lambert, made arrangements to support Vandamme's attack by two other attacks on either flank. For this purpose he ordered Excelmans to move his cavalry from Dion-le-Mont to the front of Bas-Wavre, and General Corsin's division to make an attempt to cross at the mill of Bièrges.

About the operations of the 37th Regiment of Line Infantry, Sub-Lieutenant Gerbet notes that they arrived at Sart-a-Walhain at 12.00 on 18 June and at Wavre around 16.00. He notes the regiment stood idle until the early evening:[60]

> Our regiment, the 37th, was occupied in the evening of 18 June with the assault on the mill at Bièrges, which was located at the bottom of the valley, where the enemy were firmly entrenched and their musket balls were murderous to us, which when conjoined with the fire from numerous sharpshooters firing at us in front from the place they occupied. We deployed as skirmishers and returned the enemy fire until about six or seven o'clock in the evening, there suddenly appeared General Gérard, the commandant of the 4th Corps. He was on foot and passed close to us, his face coloured with rage. He then exclaimed 'we must capture the mill' then an enemy ball came and hit him in the left shoulder.

In this action, Sergeant-Major Letivaut and his company were detached as skirmishers from the main body of their battalion. The skirmishers surprised a Prussian picket, killed two Prussians and made six prisoners. Letivaut was wounded with a sabre cut in this action.[61]

It seems that while the 37th Regiment of Line Infantry was pinned down in front of the mill at Bièrges, the 64th Regiment of Line Infantry endeavoured to out-flank the mill and capture the bridge which was hard by the mill. Battalion Commander Jean François Charles Collignon[62] writes:[63]

> I participated in the campaign in Belgium in June 1815. I was wounded with four gunshot wounds at the affair of Wavre on 18 June in endeavouring to force a passage across the bridge at the head of four companies from the regiment.

Wounded in the assault was Captain Bernard, as well as Captain Claude Rigaunaud, who took a musket ball to this left thigh.[64] First Lieutenant Nicholas Mollerot took a gunshot wound to the left side of his head.[65] Lieutenant Charles Balthazar Charpentier had his right thigh fractured by a gunshot. A similar fate befell Second Lieutenant Jean Pierre Truffier, who had a musket ball pass through both his thighs,[66] while Sergeant-Major Jean Louis Gudin took a gunshot to his left arm.[67]

The position was virtually impossible to attack, as Captain Marie Joseph August Bella, aide-de-camp to Marshal Grouchy, recounts:[68]

> I do not myself remember the number of the regiment which attacked the mill at Bièrges; but I well know that a very wide ditch and a muddy swamp made the approach very difficult and that it was perhaps impossible to overcome obstacles of this kind. No criticism of the regiment should be made.

A similar view was held by Aide-de-Camp de Blocqueville, who writes that:[69]

> General Vandamme attacked the mill at Bièrges, in order to cross the river, but his efforts were without effect. This mill was defended by ditches and swamps which made the approach impossible.

Losses experienced in the division were as follows:

Regiment	Killed		Wounded		Missing		Total
	Officers	Men	Officers	Men	Officers	Men	
15th Light Infantry[70]	1	34	14	210	0	0	259
23rd Line Infantry[71]	1	10	4	71	0	3	89
37th Line Infantry[72]	0	8	1	49	0	2	60
64th Line Infantry[73]	0	13	8	93	0	37	151
Total	2	65	27	423	0	42	1,559

The division lost very heavily in the attack. The Prussians were no easy pushover for the French. The losses here were higher than those suffered by 5th or 6th Division at the Battle of Quatre-Bras, which helps to demonstrate the scale of the fighting the 8th Division faced on 18 June.

The operations of 4th Corps

With Vandamme's 3rd Corps separated and ineffective after thirteen assaults against the Prussians, Grouchy had to wait for 4th Corps to arrive. So far Grouchy had only achieved troop parity with the Prussians, as he was unable to bring all his forces into action.

Adjutant-major to the artillery of the 4th Corps, Louis Etienne Thouvenin, narrates on 21 May 1840 about the actions of 4th Corps on 18 June:[74]

> We could not consistently follow the marshal to Wavre, and when we arrived about five o'clock, the troops of the 3rd Corps had already been for some time without success engaged in the attack on the bridge of Wavre. These troops occupied the portion of the town which is on the right bank of the Dyle: we are told that the bridge was cut. The Prussian artillery on the left bank occupied positions that dominated ours, but at a relatively great distance (1,200 to 1,600 metres).

General Gérard confirms that 4th Corps was slow in its movements due to mud, poor terrain and also that Vandamme had a two-hour lead over 4th Corps:[75]

> These troops arrived as quickly as humanly possible: on the 17th they entered into their bivouacs at ten o'clock at night, and all day they had had to withstand a rain that fell in torrents, and which had made the roads terrible, they slept below Gembloux, which is a steeply hilled country, and the next day, the 18th, they had to defile through the town: there had never been in this march a mingling between the corps of Vandamme and mine due to the distance between our respective corps, that is to say, Vandamme, who had his troops a league or a league and a half in front of Gembloux, and since the 18th always had his troops two leagues ahead of me.

General Hulot also notes the difficulties he had in marching to Gembloux and Wavre:[76]

> The 18th, about seven o'clock in the morning, I received orders from the commander-in-chief, which required all troops from the 4th Corps to be able to begin its march at eight o'clock in the morning, in the same order as before, to move to Sarra-Walin [sic], following the corps of General Vandamme. I immediately ordered my division to take up arms, and started to march along the defile of Gembloux, whose roads were awful. Having found the city crowded with troops of all

arms, who came for distributions and then marched on again, I took over an hour to reach the general rendezvous of the 4th Corps, which was about a quarter of a league in front of Gembloux. Here, all the divisions were united and made a long halt to wait until the road was cleared. As soon as the rear of the 3rd Corps had left, the commander-in-chief of the 4th Corps resumed the march, and recommended to me to close up the gap with the 3rd Corps, which is exactly what I did, for all the roads we had to march on were extremely bad and we advanced very slowly, very painful, requiring the 3rd Corps to make frequent halts, as always happens in a country with defiles, and when a column is as long as the one that preceded us.

With 3rd Corps split between Wavre, Bas-Wavre and Limale, the arrival of these troops was the only force really disposable and capable of being marched immediately towards Saint-Lambert. While these matters were in progress, Grouchy returned with Gérard to Wavre, hoping that Vandamme could have passed the Dyle, and that he might direct his corps towards Saint-Lambert by the left bank.[77] Marshal Grouchy notes about the attack he ordered to be carried out by Gérard:[78]

> The head of the column of General Gérard, arriving in the meantime, was ordered to attack the mill of Bièrges to pass the Dyle on this point. The cavalry of General Excelmans was at Bas-Wavre, and that of General Pajol moved as directed, as I have already said, on to the village of Limale to put me in communication with Napoléon, and be able to cut off the retreat of the Prussians as they withdrew to Brussels, where I would have driven them from the position of Wavre. General Pajol would have been on this road before them, and would have greatly hindered in their movement.

Grouchy was now realising that he had better make a new plan to cross the River Dyle. The attacks at Wavre had failed, and in this regard Grouchy had become too involved in the attacks. Yes, he had stood back from being in the frontline, but he could not, it seems, think beyond repeating the same mistake over and over again in attacking Wavre. At least he seems to have realised this. Gérard notes how his troops were to be used to replace Lefol's division at Bièrges and how a division was left at La Baraque:[79]

> M. Grouchy wished that I was to relieve the troops of the 3rd Corps that were at Bièrges mill, though I should have proposed to shorten the time to replace the troops of General Vandamme by the number

of mine he deemed proper to force the passage of Wavre. M. de Grouchy also claims that the attack was carried out feebly on Bièrges mill was by my troops, he speaks of the attack as if it had occurred before we had come together at Baraque when it was very late when General Hulot, who had been sent with a battalion to La Baraque, returned. It is only in that moment when I was wounded in the attack started by the troops of the 4th Corps.

About this movement leaving troops at La Baraque, Captain J. M. J. Deville, of the 111th Regiment of Line Infantry, gives the following narration which suggests that his regiment took no part in the fighting on 18 June, and was the only one of Grouchy's regiments to try and march to Waterloo as Napoléon had ordered:[80]

18 June, in the morning an orderly officer arrived from the Imperial Headquarters of the emperor on the left of our regiment, and asked where he could find Marshal Grouchy, for whom he carried orders. We indicated where he could be found and he went in that direction. During our movement at the moment when the cannonade shook the earth, a second orderly officer arrived from the same place escorted by some lancers, and turned to me and said 'I bring an order to the marshal, to tell him to march to his left. Send this order to your colonel to commence this movement to be followed and executed without delay by the other corps until I can talk to the marshal'.

I went immediately to Colonel Sauzet and I passed the order to him that I had received. Colonel Sauzet left the line of battle and ordered his column to march to its left. Whether the other corps had followed us or had received a counter-order I do not know exactly, but the movement was stopped. We remained immobile in this position until three, four or five o'clock. We then decided to march, albeit hesitantly, moving towards the gunfire, which had greatly decreased, after an hour of marching we stopped and after half an hour later we occupied the positions we had done during the day, and where we spent the night.

It seems the regiment was at La Baraque, but oddly the order for the movement is said to have come from the emperor and not Grouchy, if indeed the eyewitness narration, as we shall discuss later, is reliable or a fiction to slander Grouchy. We should note, however, that the 111th Regiment of Line Infantry is recorded as having no officer casualties, which may support the idea that the regiment was detached and witnessed no fighting on the 18th.

Regiment	Killed		Wounded		Missing		Total
	Officers	Men	Officers	Men	Officers	Men	
59th Line Infantry[81]	4	14	5	36	0	7	66
76th Line Infantry[82]	0	11	10	4	0	8	33
48th Line Infantry[83]	No data recorded						
69th Line Infantry[84]	No data recorded						
Total	4	25	15	40	0	15	99

For the wounded, we are only seeing the returns for men still in hospital at the time of disbandment of the army on 15 September 1815. The losses sustained on the day of battle are likely to be far higher than the recorded wounded. No doubt many men who were evacuated to the rear ambulances, or sent to hospital by September 1815 had recovered and joined the regiment again. The true losses, therefore, of wounded men is not known. The data for the 48th and 68th regiments of Line Infantry are totally missing.

14th Division attacks

General Hulot's division formed the head of column of 4th Corps, and was the first of Gérard's troops to arrive, after detaching a battalion at La Baraque. The division comprised the 1st Brigade under the orders of Hulot (the 9th Regiment of Light Infantry and 111th Regiment of Line Infantry), the 2nd Brigade (the 44th and 50th Regiments of Line Infantry), commanded by General Jean François Toussaint. Gérard notes how the attack developed:[85]

> The first attack made on the Bièrges mill were by the troops of the 3rd Corps, but it was not until half-past four or five o'clock in the evening that Comte Grouchy ordered me to replace the troops General Vandamme had at the mill of Bièrges with some battalions of my troops. I pointed out that this movement would be brought about very slowly, and to shorten the time, I sent a message to General Vandamme to enquire the number of my troops he might need at his disposal to force the passage of Wavre. However, the commander-in-chief insisted I was to execute his order, that's when I charged General Hulot, a clever and brave officer, to go with a battalion of the 9th Regiment of Light Infantry to renew an attack already attempted without success by the troops of the 3rd Corps. This new attack, and another that followed, took place in the presence of Comte Grouchy and did not succeed any more than the first attacks. One cannot assign fault to the troops, and they showed a lot of courage on several occasions, but the nature of the foot of the

231

heights overlooking the valley, the distance of a gunshot from the Dyle, along with marshy meadows that make up this area which were cut with lines of very deep ditches which were parallel to the river, but were too deep, too large to be overcome; they were filled with four, five and even six feet of water. These ditches prevailed throughout this part of Limale to Wavre.

The banks of the Dyle were forested, besides the Prussian infantry which ambushed us from the mill itself, it adorned the left bank of the river and dominated the hillsides. The fire from numerous artillery pieces, together with the firing of the infantry from the mill and the left bank, carried into the meadows we had to cross to get to the bridge, before we could take it. These barriers alone foiled all attempts on this point, I repeat; I cannot without the greatest injustice to blame the troops for the failure, and especially not those of the 4th Corps nor those of the 3rd Corps. Moreover, all these attacks were always head on, always lethal. It would not have occurred if we had passed our troops on to the left bank of the Dyle by the bridge at Moustier.

Excelmans had been at Moustier with its vital bridge over the Dyle. Here, he could have sent a part to his left (west) to out-flank the Prussians that were in front of him at La Baraque. But this thought does not seem to have occurred to him. Gérard is correct in this observation, one we note that neither he nor Excelmans seems to have actually made on 18 June 1815.

Marie Theodore Gueulluy, Comte de Rumigny (aide-de-camp to General Gérard), relates:[86]

> Meanwhile, Vandamme had arrived at Wavre and he had hoped to make the point without difficulty. A little hesitation caused the failure of his attack: the Prussians had at first little artillery and then the resistance was organised, formidable artillery finally allowed them to repel all attacks. Gérard's corps had spread to the left of Vandamme, having before him a small bridge and a mill on the River Dyle, which covered his front. The troops were massed, awaiting orders. Upon arrival on this point, the Prussians were still before them, with only a few sharpshooters along the river.

General Hulot himself notes:[87]

> Shortly after, almost at the same time, the head of the third body was committed in front of our direction, which did not check the progress

of our march, the enemy had held La Baraque and its contest lasted for a short time. From this latter point, the head of the column of the 4th Corps was ordered to move to the left of Wavre on the steep height which is vis-a-vis the Bièrges mill, that position was occupied by several pieces of artillery belonging the 3rd Corps. The head of the 4th Corps arrived at half-past three or four o'clock in the afternoon at a time when all the troops of 3rd Corps that were involved in Wavre had withdrawn. I received the order to halt behind and beside the artillery, the other divisions came to deploy to our rear between two woods, half an hour after my arrival at this height.

The artillery is perhaps that of Lefol's division, namely 7th Company 6th Regiment of Foot Artillery and comprised six 6-pounder field guns and two 24-pounder howitzers. These guns were ideal for close infantry support and did not have the hitting power to bombard the mill to rubble or offer sufficient fire power to make garrisoning the mill a viable proposition. By this time, both banks of the Dyle, from Bièrges to Bas-Wavre, were lined with skirmishers and sharpshooters, pouring a terrific fire into each other. Hulot's division had great difficulty in moving through the swamps and mud to the bridge at Bièrges, and suffered severely from the Prussian batteries. The battalion which relieved Lefol began at once to make a fresh attempt to force the bridge, but was beaten off with loss. In the attack, the 9th Regiment of Light Infantry lost a number of officers and men dead or wounded.

Only the 9th Regiment of Light Infantry appears to have been involved in this attack, as the 111th Regiment of Line Infantry appears to have been left at La Baraque. General Vichery formed the rearguard.[88]

12th Division attacks
Somewhere between 18.00 and 18.30, General Pecheux arrived with the 12th Infantry Division and commenced to attack the bridge at Bièrges, but with little or no success due to the wet ground. Pecheux's division comprised the 1st Brigade commanded by General Rome (the 30th and 96th regiments of Line Infantry), and the 2nd Brigade of General Schaeffer (the 6th Regiment of Light Infantry and the 63rd Regiment of Line Infantry).

NOTES:
[1] Wagner, p. 100.
[2] Grouchy, *Observations sur la relation de la campagne de 1815,* pp. 15-16.
[3] AN: LH 2758/3.
[4] Grouchy, *Relation succincte de la campagne de 1815,* p. 42.

5 Sénécal, pp. 10.
6 Berthezène, pp. 359-60.
7 Major von Bornstedt, Louise von Bornstedt, *Das Gefecht bei Wavre an der Dyle am 18 und 19 Juni 1815*, Heinicke, Berlin, 1858, p. 16.
8 ibid, pp. 118-20.
9 ibid, pp. 105-6.
10 Major von Bornstedt, Louise von Bornstedt, *Das Gefecht bei Wavre an der Dyle am 18 und 19 Juni 1815*, Heinicke, Berlin, 1858, pp. 50-1.
11 AN: LH 1959/46.
12 AN: LH 479/47.
13 SHDDT: GR 21 YC 309.
14 SHDDT: GR 21 YC 309. See also: SHDDT: GR 21 YC 310.
15 Fantin des Odoards, pp. 403-10.
16 SHDDT: GR 21 YC 681.
17 Bornstedt, pp. 40-4.
18 Bornstedt, p. 18.
19 SHDDT: GR 21 YC 309.
20 AN: LH 1256/7.
21 AN: LH 2267/29.
22 Bornstedt, p. 18.
23 Bornstedt, pp. 40-4.
24 AN: LH 2421/2.
25 Fantin des Odoards, pp. 433-5.
26 AN: LH 2595/11.
27 AN: LH 1123/3.
28 AN: LH 2226/19.
29 See http://www.3rgtsuisse.be/PDF/etranger1815.pdf/.
30 Fantin des Odoards, p. 435.
31 Bornstedt, p. 18.
32 SHDDT: GR 21 YC 309. See also: SHDDT: GR 21 YC 310.
33 SHDDT: GR 21 YC 681.
34 SHDDT: GR 21 YC 197 *21e régiment d'infanterie de ligne, 18-20 mai 1815 (matricules 1 à 1,800).*
35 SHDDT: GR 21 YC 590.
36 Bornstedt, p. 18.
37 Bornstedt, p. 18.
38 Bornstedt, p. 18.
39 AN: LH 897/41.
40 AN: LH 2500/53.
41 Bornstedt, p. 19.
42 Miot-Putigny, p. 245.
43 SHDDT: GR 21 YC 111 *12e régiment d'infanterie de ligne, 9 Septembre 1814-11 Décembre 1814 (matricules 1 à 1,824).* See also: SHDDT: GR 21 YC 112 *12e régiment d'infanterie de ligne, 11 Décembre 1814-29 Juillet 1815 (matricules 1,825 à 2,453).*
44 SHDDT: GR 21 YC 471 *52e régiment d'infanterie de ligne (ex 56e régiment d'infanterie de ligne), 5 Août 1814-2 Mai 1815 (matricules 1 à 1,800).* See also: SHDDT: GR 21 YC 472 *52e régiment d'infanterie de ligne (ex 56e régiment d'infanterie de ligne), 2 Mai 1815-28 Juillet 1815 (matricules 1,801 à 1,910).*
45 SHDDT: GR 21 YC 301 *32e régiment d'infanterie de ligne (ex 33e régiment d'infanterie de ligne), 13 Août 1814-14 Mars 1815 (matricules 1,801 à 2,253).*
46 SHDDT: GR 21 YC 673 *74e régiment d'infanterie de ligne (ex 86e régiment d'infanterie de ligne), 19 Août 1814-9 Août 1815 (matricules 1 à 1,751).*
47 Bornstedt, p. 21.
48 AN: LH 494/74.

49 AN: LH 2228/47.

50 AN: LH 809/37.

51 AN: LH 1101/66.

52 Pierre Alexis Lieffroy was born at Salins, in the Jura, on 1 June 1786. He was conscripted into the regiment on 12 October 1806 and promoted to corporal on 17 February 1807, to corporal-quartermaster on 15 March 1807, to sergeant on 21 February 1809, and to sergeant-major soon after on 1 October 1809 following the Battles of Aspern-Essling and Wagram. He was subsequently promoted to adjutant-sub-officer on 26 April 1812, and was wounded on 7 September 1812 at the Battle of Borodino. Promotion to second lieutenant came on 25 March 1813, to porte-aigle on 15 May 1813 and to lieutenant on 29 September 1813. At Wavre, the regiment came under both musket and artillery fire. Lieffroy was unlucky enough to be hit by a canister shot which hit his left knee. He was discharged from the army on 30 October 1815, and had his leg amputated on 8 May 1815 at the hospital at Besançon due to his wound received at Wavre. Presumably, the eagle was picked up from his prone body and saved.

53 Ian Smith, personal communication.

54 AN: LH 2459/56.

55 AN: LH 2302/45.

56 AN: LH 258/5.

57 AN: LH 2035/60.

58 AN: LH 616/28.

59 Gerbet, p. 18.

60 Gerbet, p. 15.

61 Charles Sébastien Faivre D'Arcier, Auguste Henri Royé, *Historique du 37e Régiment d'Infanterie, etc*, Paris, 1895, p. 210.

62 Collignon was born on 6 January 1775 at Beuville. He had joined the army as a volunteer in 1793 and was one of the few men in the army in 1815 to have fought at both Battles of Ligny. He had served with the 64th Regiment of Line Infantry since 1 October 1813 and was discharged from the regiment on 20 October 1815.

63 AN: LH 568/79.

64 AN: LH 2330/17.

65 AN: LH 1900/46.

66 AN: LH 2636/49.

67 AN: LH 1214/28.

68 Grouchy, *Relation succincte de la campagne de 1815*, p. 55.

69 SHDDT: C15 5. Dossier 18 June 1815. Handwritten statement from Blocqueville to Grouchy, no date.

70 Le Musée Napoléonien in Ligny.

71 SHDDT: GR 21 YC 215 *23e régiment d'infanterie de ligne, 16 Juillet 1814-13 Décembre 1814 (matricules 1 à 1,800)*. See also: SHDDT: GR 21 YC 216 *23e régiment d'infanterie de ligne, 8 Décembre 1814-11 Août 1815 (matricules 1,801 à 2,358)*.

72 SHDDT: GR 21 YC 336 *36e régiment d'infanterie de ligne (ex 37e régiment d'infanterie de ligne), 4 Août 1814-8 Avril 1815 (matricules 1 à 1,800)*. See also: SHDDT: GR 21 YC 337 *36e régiment d'infanterie de ligne (ex 37e régiment d'infanterie de ligne), 14 Avril 1815-11 Juillet 1815 (matricules 1,801 à 2,233)*.

73 SHDDT: GR 21 YC 541 *60e régiment d'infanterie de ligne (réorganisation de 1814), 9 Août 1814-21 Janvier 1815 (matricules 1 à 1,800)*. See also: SHDDT: GR 21 YC 542 *60e régiment d'infanterie de ligne (réorganisation de 1814), 21 Janvier 1815-11 Juillet 1815 (matricules 1,801 à 3,274)*.

74 Gérard, *Quelques documents*, p. 12.

75 ibid, p. 8.

76 Gérard, *Quelques documents*, p. 47.

77 Grouchy, *Observations sur la relation de la campagne de 1815*, pp. 28-32.

78 Grouchy, *Observations sur la relation de la campagne de 1815*, pp. 15-16.

79 Gérard, *Quelques documents*, p. 10.

[80] George Deville, *'Grouchy a Waterloo'* in *Revolution Français*, No. 53, 1907, pp. 281-4.
[81] SHDDT: GR 21 YC 500.
[82] SHDDT: GR 21 YC 614.
[83] SHDDT: GR 21 YC 416.
[84] SHDDT: GR 21 YC 580.
[85] Gérard, *Quelques documents*, pp. 41-2.
[86] Rumigny.
[87] Gérard, *Dernières observations*, pp. 51-2.
[88] Gérard, *Dernières observations*, pp. 51-2.

Chapter 12

Wounding of General Gérard

Marshal Grouchy writes in 1819 that he led an attack at the mill upon his return from Wavre to check on Vandamme's progress:[1]

> I found things in the same state, a fusillade of cannon and musketry continued without results from one side to the other. Impatient, I jumped down from my horse to lead a battalion myself on a new attack at Bièrges mill, where the shooting was not having much result. General Gérard was then wounded by a bullet in the chest, and the projected movement had no success.

General Gérard was wounded near Bièrges. Officer d'ordonnance to Marshal Grouchy, Leguest, notes:[2]

> I was with your escort, on the heights of Wavre, when you dismounted to lead the attack yourself against the mill of Bièrges, but when General Gérard, who also dismounted to follow you, was wounded near you a report came to you. I was not close enough to hear what he could say; I only know that it was reported in the regiment, and your officers, that it was for you to engage and to save the country.

About this event, Comte de Rumigny, aide-de-camp to General Gérard, further details Vandamme's movements and notes he was wounded with an attack carried out by the 30th Regiment of Line Infantry, under the orders of General Rome:[3]

> Gérard's corps had moved to the left of that of Vandamme, having before him a small bridge and a mill on the River Wavre. The troops were massed, awaiting orders. Upon arrival on this point there were only a few Prussian sharpshooters along the river. General Gérard

sent me to Grouchy telling him he could march by the left, cross the bridge and head towards the emperor. The marshal replied, very impatiently, despite always being polite: 'in a moment General Vandamme will be master of Wavre and the whole army will follow'. Alas! This illusion ended the misfortune of the army. General Gérard went to warn marshal and again had a heated discussion with him; he came back to us even more exasperated.

Finally, he sent two or three officers, one after another, to tell the marshal that the Prussians were seen with divisions on the right bank heading to the battle. Battalions succeeded the battalions, and a whole corps walked briskly in front of us to attack the right wing of Napoléon. The marshal persisted, refusing to come to the aid of the emperor. It was getting late, and it was high time to decide. The general went again to find the marshal, then back to us he said: 'when after twenty-five years of war do we see such nonsense, a general officer who respects himself should be killed'. So, despite our objections, he took off his coat, which was a frock-coat after the fashion of the time, and advanced towards the Prussian skirmishers, who directed their fire on him immediately. He appeared in blue coat, with the neck collar of the Order of Dannebrog in diamonds, several other decorations, and the badge of the Legion of Honour. The bullets were falling very thickly, an officer of staff was wounded, a sapper with the 30th Line was killed, and suddenly a bullet, which was in striking range, laid down the general.

We seized him and, wrapping him in my coat, we took him back and placed him on a farm wagon. There we waited anxiously for the prognosis of Dr Cuttinger, chief surgeon of the corps. The bullet had hit the third button of his coat, and had taken with it a part of the frill from his shirt in the wound and then had lodged in the left lung.

The news of the day did not reassure us. We knew the attack on Wavre by Vandamme had been repulsed and he remained on the left bank. We could no longer hear the cannonade in the direction of the emperor.

At eight o'clock, General Gérard called me. Here are his words, I wrote them in my diary which I kept because of the importance of the subject. After a few words uttered with difficulty, the general, drawing me near his bed, said 'my dear Rumigny, it is likely that I will die, my heart fills with blood, but before I die I want to make a last service to the emperor. Go to Brussels where he should be now, tell him that I hate nor have ill will against Grouchy, but every single corps left in his hands are lost for the French army'. He made me repeat his words: 'I count on you', he added engraving them on my mind without adding or subtracting any word. I swore to him I would and, after saying farewell with tears in my eyes, I mounted my horse and I went to the outposts to get to my destination. I found [along] the way M. Souci, who commanded a company of voltigeurs. He told me that the Prussians at Wavre had not retreated and the bridge and the mill were still in their power. I went down the river, with some horsemen, to find a way to go and fulfil my mission. I finally discovered a ford, and crossed the creek with fifteen of this cavalry. I was going towards the Soignes Forest when I saw horsemen in pursuit of a trumpeter of ours without a cap, which fell in our midst. His first words were: 'the emperor is defeated, I just got away, we are done, the Imperial Guard is defeated. I ran all night without knowing where I went, pursued by the enemy'.

These comments and the scared look of this man seemed to me suspicious, I had his bridle taken by a dragoon and I told him I was going to take him to the headquarters of the emperor. However, I saw some Prussians coming out of the woods [which] made me think and I approached the river, it was almost a quarter of a mile away. At a certain distance, I was charged by a squadron and we had only time to swim. Two of our men were taken. I hastened to return to the army of Marshal Grouchy, taking my musician (the trumpeter). We had just learned at that instant the terrible disaster of Waterloo!

If Rumigny is correct, this event took place when General Rome's brigade was attacking at approximately 18.00, as opposed to when General Corsin's brigade from Lefol's division was attacking Bièrges. However, for Gérard to have seen the Prussian columns he would have needed a periscope from a submarine or a helicopter! Bièrges is, and was, in a valley, surrounded by woodland according to the 1777 Ferraris map. Therefore, it is highly unlikely that the Prussians were observed. Here we have Rumigny inventing, it seems, tall tales to slander Grouchy and to praise Gérard. It's a good story, which no doubt contains some truth about Gérard being wounded, but all else is likely to be false memory. Also, if Bièrges mill was defended only by a few sharpshooters, why did Gérard not take the initiative and attack? Given in other accounts of the action at Bièrges, it seems very unlikely that Gérard could have easily succeeded as Rumigny suggests, compared to the attacks here earlier in the evening.

With Gérard wounded, Vandamme was now placed in command of both corps and seemingly promoted by Marshal Grouchy to marshal-du-camp. General Vichery took command of 4th Corps. Captain Marie Joseph August Bella, aide-de-camp to Marshal Grouchy, recounts:[4]

The attack of the mill of Bièrges met with little success. You had to dismount to lead this attack. Comte Gérard was wounded at your side and was forced to move to the rear. General-of-Artillery Balthus refused to replace Comte Gérard, which caused a scandal in the army.

Napoléon's summons

It was now, according to Marshal Grouchy, at 19.00 that a message arrived from Napoléon (sent at 13.30), saying that Bülow's corps had just been seen at Saint-Lambert.[5] Did this message come in response to Grouchy's 10.00 dispatch? Clearly it did not, as the reply is obviously in response to the 6.00 letter. In the message, Napoléon ordered Grouchy to lose no time in moving to join the emperor's right, where he would crush Bülow in the flank:[6]

> Monsieur marshal, you wrote to the emperor this morning at six o'clock, saying that you were marching on Sart-a-Walhain, and that you planned then to move to Corbaix and to Wavre. This movement conforms with the dispositions of the emperor which have been communicated to you.
>
> However, the emperor orders me that you should manoeuvre in our direction and try to get closer to the army, so that you can link with us before another corps can come between us. I do not indicate a direction of movement. It is for you to see the place where we are, to govern yourself accordingly and link with our communications, and to always be prepared to fall upon any of the enemy's troops who seek to annoy our right and crush them.
>
> At this moment, the battle is won on the line of Waterloo, in front of the Soignes Forest; the centre of the enemy is at Mont-Saint-Jean, and manoeuvre to reach our right.
>
> Marshal Duc de Dalmatie.
>
> P. S. A letter which has just been intercepted, which says General Bülow is about to attack our right flank, we believe that we see his corps on the height of Saint-Lambert. Lose not an instant in moving towards us to join us, in order to crush Bülow, whom you will crush in the very act.

The order is of importance on a number of points:

In the first portion of the letter, Napoléon clearly felt the Prussian force that was between him and Grouchy was going to Brussels and not Waterloo. Otherwise he would not have said 'before another corps can come between us'. He was totally ignorant of the true destination of the column spotted by Milhaud and its importance. He was fixated with the idea that Brussels was the true destination of the Prussians and could not conceive of the idea of Prussians moving to his position to link with Wellington;

In the post script, written sometime later, once the Prussian prisoner had been brought into headquarters at an unknown time, Napoléon now realised that the Prussians were between him and Grouchy;

Grouchy was initially not ordered to Waterloo. He was ordered to 'try and get closer to the army', a very different thing to be ordered directly to Waterloo;

Grouchy was free to choose his own line of movement, but the emperor told him to contain the troops at Wavre. Containing the Prussians at Wavre had to be achieved before the second objective of moving to Waterloo was possible;

Napoléon, since he received Grouchy's 06.00 and 11.00 dispatches, knew that Grouchy was going into action at Wavre and could not easily break off action. A look at his campaign map would have told Napoléon that from Wavre the route to Waterloo was neither quick nor direct, and was likely to be controlled by the Prussians, and Grouchy would have to fight his way to Waterloo; and

Napoléon wrongly assumed that the order would get to Grouchy quickly enough to be acted upon in sufficient time to get to Waterloo. He must have known that it had taken four hours for Grouchy's 06.00 dispatch to get to him, and a similar length of time had been taken for his 11.00 dispatch to arrive, therefore, Napoléon must have realised that Grouchy may not get his orders until early evening at best *if* it was not intercepted by the Prussian army which was placed on the line of movement from Waterloo to Wavre. He had failed to take to into consideration the length of time needed to get the order to Wavre, and for Grouchy to be able to act upon it and get to Waterloo.

Of interest, this order does not appear in the register of orders and correspondence of Marshal Soult, so we cannot be sure of its authenticity. However, the 6.00 message from Grouchy to Soult does exist and can be found in both the correspondence registers of Grouchy and Soult. However, Vaudoncourt presents the order in full.[7] The original document was later cited by Houssaye in 1906. In 2009, the authenticity of the order was questioned by Bernard Coppens, and soon after by Michel Damen. Damen states that because the order was found in 1906 makes it a fake. Neither Coppens nor Damen are aware of the publication of the order in 1826. Gareth Glover considers the document to be doubtful and uses the orders non-existence, ignoring

Soult's letter to Davout which is undoubtedly authentic, to explain Napoléon's astonishment about the Prussians arriving to try and explain the fact why Napoléon did nothing to counter the Prussian threat until the Prussian forces reached the battlefield. This is totally incorrect. The order existed in 1826 and must have been obtained from Grouchy, and therefore the order does seem genuine. Indeed, if it did not exist, then Soult writing to Davout about the Prussians arriving and not telling Grouchy would be an incredible lapse of judgement, one that is totally unbelievable, but it panders to those who see Soult as the traitor at Waterloo who lost the campaign through his officially sanctioned sabotage from his royalist paymasters.[8] Of course, not giving Grouchy the vital information about the column observed by Milhaud plays into this idea, which seeks to exonerate the emperor, overlook his mistakes and blame anyone but the emperor for his own blundering.

If this order was indeed written in response to the 06.00 report, clearly Napoléon had not by this time received Grouchy's report of 11.00, which clearly seems to have arrived after this order we are discussing was sent. If the order *was* written in response to the 11.00 message, surely Soult would have acknowledged it so. Thus, Napoléon was not informed at the time the 13.00 order was dispatched of Grouchy's movements that were then taking place as outlined in Grouchy's 10.00 dispatches. When Grouchy received the order is not known, but clearly *after* the 13.00 order had been sent on its way to him.

This second order to Grouchy is again vague. He was ordered to be 'prepared to fall upon any of the enemy's troops' which is exactly what he did at Wavre. Until Grouchy had fought his way past the Prussians at Wavre and Limale, he could not move to Waterloo. Of critical comment is that the 13.30 order to Grouchy was sent in response to the 6.00 report and not the 11.00 report. This implies that Grouchy's dispatch had not yet reached Napoléon. When it did arrive with Napoléon, he would have certainly been aware of where Grouchy was, and how it was impossible for him to arrive at Waterloo. Alas, we do not have a time when the dispatch was received by headquarters at Waterloo.

By 14.30, Napoléon, at Waterloo, acknowledged that the Prussians had linked up with Wellington, as Soult notes in a letter to Marshal Davout:[9]

> It is half-past two, the cannonade is joined all [along] the line. The English are in the centre, the Dutch and Belgians are on the right, the Germans and the Prussians are on the left. The general battle has begun, 400 cannon have opened fire at this moment.

In the 11.00 letter to Grouchy, cited earlier, Napoléon spoke of three columns of Prussians, only one of which was in the area of Grouchy's operations. Thus, Napoléon knew by 14.30 (if not sooner if the 13.00 order is genuine) that at least one column of Prussians had managed to link with Wellington. This left two columns heading either to Waterloo or to Wavre.

Napoléon had also known with Grouchy's dispatch timed at 10.00 that he was fighting, or was about to engage, the Prussians in accordance with his own order of 10.00. Did Napoléon honestly believe that Grouchy, once committed to action, could quickly break the action off and move to Wavre without having to leave a rearguard against what we now know to be Thielemann's forces and get to Waterloo? Napoléon now seems to have set in motion in his own mind, and the minds of his subordinates, that Grouchy would respond to the summons, and indeed even announced Grouchy had arrived several hours later to bolster the flagging French army. He was failing to acknowledge his own errors, as it must have been clear to him once then 10.00 dispatch arrived that Grouchy could not get to Waterloo. Grouchy has gone down in history for disobeying orders and also for not marching to the guns of Waterloo. The blame, however, must fall with Napoléon. For fact, Napoléon knew he faced both Wellington and Blücher and that Grouchy was not marching to his aid regardless of what later French and Anglophone writers have stated. Grouchy's own actions at Wavre were a major concern for the Prussians. Rather than as traditional history tells us, Grouchy's attacks were not feeble. At Wavre and Limale, Lieutenant-General von Thielemann was finding himself hard-pressed by Grouchy's force. Such were the veracity of the attacks headed by General Vandamme that Thielemann sent General Gneisenau a dispatch, stating that if he was not sent reinforcements, his force would be overwhelmed by Grouchy. No reinforcements were sent, as Gneisenau clearly understood the need to get every man that he could to Waterloo, and not to allow men to be drawn back south to Wavre.[10] Had Prussian troops been sent back to Wavre then Waterloo may have had a different outcome. As it was, Grouchy tied down all of Thielemann's command, a force equal in size, if not larger, than that of Grouchy. Grouchy's actions at Wavre prevented the defeat at Waterloo being far worse than it was. That Grouchy, outnumbered until around 18.00 when Gérard and 4th Corps arrived, managed to pin down the Prussians and prevent full Prussian concentration at Waterloo is of great credit to him and Teste's division; Grouchy could not have marched to Waterloo. Gérard's 4th Corps could have been sent to Waterloo by the time it arrived at Wavre, but it stood no chance of getting there in reality. Gérard, robbed of his eyes and ears with the removal of Vallin's cavalry division, acted prudently and cautiously in his approach to Wavre, plus coupled with the nature of the roads after the passage of 3rd Corps, his arrival was many hours after Vandamme. The troops Grouchy did have to hand, and did not commit to fighting, were Excelmans's 2nd Cavalry Corps. Dragoons were of little use in the fighting at Wavre or Limale. But where was Excelmans on 18 June? What did his division actually do? His twelve guns and nearly 3,000 men seem to have managed the impossible and disappeared on 18 June, and only appeared once more on 19 June at Namur. If Grouchy had sent Excelmans to harry Bülow from the rear, maybe events could have turned out rather differently at Waterloo. Excelmans appears to have spent 18 June inactive. The 17th Dragoons followed the Prussian 4th Corps, but without artillery or infantry, what could they actually achieve? Grouchy, on the day of the battle, must have had good reason, and more research may indeed find out why. But in hindsight, this was a failure by Grouchy in not using his resources as effectively as he could. Grouchy above all else was a veteran cavalry officer, and he knew very well indeed that dragoons were of little use at Wavre, and yet he did not, it seems, take the initiative to send the dragoons off in pursuit of Bülow. As it was, Excelmans was at Bas-Wavre, deployed against von Borcke's Prussians. The latter moved on the night of 18 June to Limale, but where was Excelmans? He attacked at La Baraque around midday on 18 June, and by the morning of 19 June was at Limale. Seemingly, Bonnemains's brigade had reached as far north as Ottenbourg by the morning of 19 June. Berton's brigade may still have been on the Namur to Louvain road. What Excelmans's corps did in the intervening period we have no information; without further research, we simply do not know. Excelmans is also to blame for not taking the initiative; the key may well lay in the muster lists for the officers and men of Excelmans's corps.

Given that it had taken four or more hours for Napoléon's dispatches to get to Grouchy, Grouchy could not have arrived for at least eight hours, by which time the battle was lost.

We know that Soult dispatched an order to Grouchy around 13.00, which was in direct response to Grouchy's 06.00 dispatch and not to his report timed at 10.00. Had La Fresnaye arrived after this order had been sent, as he implies? Yes. Clearly, Napoléon did not know of Grouchy's operations after 06.00 at the time he was writing the 13.00 order. When La Fresnaye arrived with Napoléon around 13.00 to 14.00, Napoléon was far better informed of the movements of the Prussians, which by this time had already started to arrive at Waterloo. Why did Napoléon not send a reply to the report of 10.00?

With the arrival of this dispatch, Napoléon now knew that Grouchy was heading off to Wavre, and did not issue an immediate order to directly call him back, and he also knew that due to the nature of the terrain (one glance at his campaign maps would tell him) that Grouchy's movements and communication would be correspondingly slow. Indeed, he must have already recognised this, as the 06.00 report from Grouchy took a full four hours to reach him; so too did the 10.00 report. We do not know why Napoléon did not issue an order to Grouchy once the 10.00 report had reached him. This was a major error on his part, or he truly believed that his 13.00 order was specific enough for Grouchy to arrive at Waterloo.

We also need to assess if Grouchy could have marched to Waterloo as many claim he could and should have, as he was ordered to do so. The answer is yes; he could get to Waterloo, but not for many hours and had no chance at all of intervening in the battle. The historian, Edward Horsburgh, citing Edgar Quinet, the French historian, share the same view that it was impossible for Grouchy's regiments to have interceded in the fighting at Waterloo:[11]

> M. Quinet induced two friends of his to traverse the whole journey on foot. It took them five and a half hours. Thus, they walked at a rate of a little more than 3 mph. An army corps could not advance at anything like that rate, more particularly when the state of the roads is taken into account. Two mph is a fair rough estimate for the march of an army corps under such circumstances as then prevailed. Grouchy's leading columns would therefore have debouched on Planchenoit at 9 p.m. assuming that he started from Sart-a-Walhain at twelve. This calculation is based entirely upon the assumption that his march would have been unimpeded by the Prussians. Such might have been the case, but at the same time it is most improbable that it would have been so. If the Prussians disputed the passage of the river, it is clear that Grouchy could not arrive on the field of Waterloo that night. If they did not do so, he could not arrive until the battle was over.

The distance from Gembloux to Wavre is eighteen miles; from Fleurus to Wavre in a straight line is some twenty-four miles. The distance from Wavre to Chapelle-Saint-Lambert is nine miles, and from Wavre to the field of Waterloo is twelve miles. At 2 mph this would have taken six hours to march from Wavre to Waterloo, more if one factors in a rearguard from the Prussians. Unless summoned at 10.00 to march directly to Waterloo, Grouchy could not have been expected to arrive there.

Thus, from midday onwards on 18 June, Grouchy was unable to intervene at Waterloo. By the time the 10.00 report arrived with Napoléon, he was fully aware that Grouchy was heading off to Wavre and planned to take a stand there, and on the following day. Napoléon must also have realised that because Grouchy was engaged he could not fully or quickly withdraw his troops. The idea that he could arrive in time to affect the outcome of the battle cannot, therefore, have been on Napoléon's mind; there is overwhelming evidence that even if Grouchy had 'marched to the sound of the guns' that he would never have been able to arrive in time. Napoléon, it seems, deluded himself into thinking Grouchy would arrive. Grouchy became the scapegoat for Napoléon and many later historians.

Grouchy has been damned for not obeying this order. Indeed, former officers suggest that he issued orders to countermand Napoléon's. One such officer was Captain J. M. J. Deville, of the 111th Regiment of Line Infantry, who seems convinced that Napoléon ordered Grouchy to march to his left, and that Grouchy issued orders to halt this movement by 4th Corps.[12]

The 111th Regiment of Line Infantry was brigaded with the 9th Regiment of Light Infantry, under the orders of General Hulot. Hulot had taken command of the 14th Infantry Division (part of 4th Corps) on the morning of 15 June upon the defection of its commander, General-of-Division Bourmont. The writer alludes to the two dispatches from Napoléon to Grouchy which suggested Grouchy was to march back to Waterloo, as have been noted in earlier chapters. Did one of the couriers have a better understanding of the order Napoléon intended, but only passed this vital information onto a single regiment from 4th Corps and not to Marshal Grouchy? It seems very unlikely. Was the 111th Regiment of Line Infantry detached from the 9th Regiment of Light Infantry? Again, this seems unlikely and that the author is writing to blame Grouchy for not marching to Waterloo, and countermanded the emperor's orders.

NOTES:
[1] Grouchy, *Observations sur la relation de la campagne de 1815*, pp. 15-16.
[2] Grouchy, *Relation succincte de la campagne de 1815*, Vol. 4, pp. 141-5.
[3] Rumigny.
[4] Grouchy, *Relation succincte de la campagne de 1815*, p. 55.
[5] Grouchy, *Observations sur la relation de la campagne de 1815*, pp. 15-16.
[6] SHDDT: C15 *Registre d'Ordres et de correspondance du major-général a partir du 13 Juin jusqu'au 26 Juin au Maréchal Grouchy*, p. 30. See also: SHDDT: C15 5. Dossier 18 June 1815. Soult to Grouchy, timed at 13.00. Copy of the original order made by Comte du Casse in June 1863. du Casse either copied Grouchy's version of the letter, or had access to a duplicate set of

material. This order is missing from the correspondence register of Marshal Soult.

7   Frédéric François Guillaume Vaudoncourt, *Histoire des campagnes de 11814 et 1815, en France* (Vol. 5), Chez A. de Gastel, Paris, 1826, pp. 201-2.

8   Stephen M. Beckett, *Waterloo Betrayed: The Secret Treachery that Defeated Napoleon*, Mapleflower House Publishing, 2015.

9   AN: AFIV 1939, pp. 50-1.

10   Ian Smith, personal communication, 9 December 2016.

11   E. L. S. Horsburgh, *Waterloo: A Narrative and a Criticism*, Methuen, London, 1895, pp. 171-2.

12   George Deville, *'Grouchy a Waterloo'* in *Revolution Français*, No. 53, 1907, pp. 281-4.

Chapter 13

Waterloo

Unbeknown to the French throughout the late afternoon, Ziethen's 1st Corps had been arriving north of La Haye Sainte. About the arduous march the corps had under taken, Neimann, of the Prussian 6th Uhlans, writes:[1]

> At two o'clock in the morning of 18 June we broke up and marched towards Wavre, where Blücher's corps concentrated itself. After a long and dreadfully hard march the whole day, in spite of the great battle of the 16th, and only one day's rest, and privation for men and horses, we arrived at last in full trot at the field of battle at Mont-Saint-Jean towards four o'clock. Our brigade of four regiments of cavalry was commanded by the brave Major-General von Folgersberg, Lützow having been taken prisoner on the 16th.
>
> Hard work for the Prussian army again. Wellington was almost beaten when we arrived, and we decided that great day. Had we arrived an hour later, Napoléon would have had Wellington surrounded and defeated. At about nine o'clock in the evening the battlefield was almost cleared of the French army. It was an evening no pen is able to picture: the surrounding villages yet in flames, the lamentations of the wounded of both armies, the singing for joy; no one is able to describe nor find a name to give to those horrible scenes.

The Prussian official account of the start of their operations at Waterloo notes that:[2]

> It was half-past four o'clock. The excessive difficulties of the passage by the defile of Saint-Lambert had considerably retarded the march of the Prussian columns, so that only two brigades of the 4th Corps had arrived at the covered position which was assigned to them. The decisive moment was come; there was not an instant to be lost. The

generals did not suffer it to escape. They resolved immediately to begin the attack with the troops which they had at hand. General Bülow, therefore, with two brigades and a corps of cavalry, advanced rapidly upon the rear of the enemy's right wing. The enemy did not lose his presence of mind; he instantly turned his reserve against us, and a murderous conflict began on that side. The combat remained for a long time uncertain, while the battle with the English army still continued with the same violence.

Napoléon had been aware of the Prussian 4th Corps since 13.00. Based on Grouchy's intelligence contained in his 10.00 dispatch, Napoléon knew that the Prussian 1st, 2nd and 3rd Corps were heading to Louvain to gain the Brussels road, and a rearguard was at Wavre. Therefore, he no doubt reasoned, that it was the only body of Prussian troops likely to arrive at Waterloo. To make matters worse, Napoléon probably incorrectly assumed that the rearguard Grouchy had at Wavre were the rear-most men from Bülow's corps, and that Grouchy would be moving up behind as ordered to do so, ergo the next troops to arrive at Waterloo would be his.

Napoléon knew, or thought he knew, where the bulk of the Prussian army was. His reasoning was based on a lot of assumptions:

It assumed Grouchy had found the Prussian 1st, 2nd and 3rd Corps, the bulk of it heading north and not able to fight, leaving a weak rearguard;

It assumed the Prussians were heading to Louvain en masse;

It assumed the column observed by Milhaud and Domon had not already crossed the Dyle, and Grouchy indeed had three Prussian corps in front of him;

It assumed Grouchy could act quickly on the orders sent; and

The next body of troops to appear at Waterloo would be Grouchy.

The sad truth was Napoléon was wrong. The Prussians that Grouchy was chasing were indeed heading to Louvain. Grouchy's intelligence was spot on. Some Prussians were at Wavre, and others were heading to Louvain, which history tells us was what actually happened. His reconnaissance reports were reporting back to the emperor exactly where the Prussians say they had troops. The problem was Grouchy thought he had *all* the Prussian army in front of him.

History shows us that Grouchy never made contact with the Prussian 1st and 2nd Corps, only ever minimal contact with 4th Corps and only ever all of 3rd Corps. He assumed that the Prussian army had entirely moved north-east, leaving 4th Corps at Namur, which Pajol had found. Grouchy was never in a position to accurately identify the Prussians he had before him. All he knew was three Prussian columns were at Ligny, and he found three bodies of Prussian troops, discounting the column at Namur. He assumed he had the 1st, 2nd and 3rd Corps, as it was these corps that were at Ligny.

When he got Napoléon's dispatch about a column heading to Wavre, Grouchy naturally assumed that the men he found at Wavre were also the same men reported to him by Vandamme and the emperor; a logical conclusion to make. The truth is that when Bellanger found the Prussians at Moustier, these were the troops that had retreated from Gembloux and were not the same body of troops. Grouchy could never have known otherwise. He assumed that these were the same men as Milhaud and Domon had found. Marbot's reconnaissance failed to find the Prussians at Moustier on the morning of 18 June, it led to the belief that they had gone north-east once over the Dyle and not north, totally evading French observation until they appeared at Waterloo. Grouchy was never in a position to not assume that the column the emperor told him about heading to Wavre was ever anything but the troops he found. Nor was the emperor ever in any position other than to assume the same thing.

Only when Grouchy learned that 4th Corps was at Waterloo did he realise that his assumption was wrong.

The truth is, as we said earlier, that the column found by Milhaud and Domon was the Prussian 1st and 2nd Corps which, given the remit of Pajol on the morning of 17 June, were never observed by Pajol's command, nor when Excelmans headed off; the column had already left the area and was therefore not observed by him either. As far as Grouchy knew, he had all the defeated army from Ligny in front of him heading to Louvain. He did not know the 1st and 2nd Corps were not in front of him. The Prussian 1st and 2nd Corps, although spotted by the French, had crossed the Dyle and taken up position on Wellington's left. The French never knew this until too late.

Napoléon only understood that Bülow was on his way to Waterloo and the bulk of the army was elsewhere. No one realised until too late that the Prussian 1st and 2nd Corps had evaded the French totally, and were poised to descend on Napoléon's right flank. So, sure of the fact that Grouchy would be the next body of troops to arrive on the field, he could not consider it possible that they could in fact be more Prussians. Renee Bourgeois, of the 12th Cuirassiers, commented in 1816 that:[3]

> At the moment in which all his enterprises had completely miscarried, he received the intelligence of the advance of the Prussian

columns against our right flank, and of their menacing our rear; but he would attribute no faith to these reports, and repeatedly answered that they had been deceived in their observations, and that these pretended Prussians were nothing more than the corps of Grouchy. He even abused and angrily dismissed several aide-de-camps who successively brought him this information. 'Be gone,' he said to them, 'you have become afraid; approach these columns with confidence, and you will soon be satisfied that they are those of Grouchy.'

After so positive an answer, several of them, indignant at such treatment, approached the Prussian sharp-shooters, and in spite of a hot fire by which they were assailed, advanced near enough to be either slain or made prisoners—it was, however, necessary to yield to evidence. It was indeed impossible to disparage any longer the truth of this intelligence, when at length these columns, which severally on their coming up had formed themselves in line, actively attacked our right. One detachment of the 6th Corps was sent to sustain this new shock, in expectation of the arrival of the divisions under Marshal Grouchy, on whom we always reckoned. The report even prevailed, that his troops were already in line…It is evident that this operation had been concerted between the two generals-in-chief, and that the English only defended their position with so invincible a tenacity, in order to allow time for the Prussians to effectuate this combined movement, on which depended the whole success of the battle, and of which the first demonstrations were every moment expected.

Buonaparte, who in spite of all that happened, seemed to harbour no doubt of the speedy arrival of Marshal Grouchy, and who, without doubt, persuaded himself that he would immediately hold the Prussians in check.

For this eyewitness, Napoléon clearly believed the Prussians were not moving to his position. But the possibility is that this assumption had some basis in fact.

Found among the paper archive at Vincennes is the muster list of the 22nd Regiment of Line Infantry. The muster lists contain a story about Waterloo that has never been spoken about: the regiment had men at Waterloo, namely:[4]

MAT no. 397 Dominique Moreau. Adjutant-sub-officer attached to regimental staff. Wounded with a sabre cut to the right hand and one to the head on 18 June 1815 at Waterloo;

MAT no. 407 François Lepers. Adjutant-sub-officer on the regimental staff. Left leg amputated following the Battle of Waterloo;

MAT no. 494 Sergeant Philippe Joseph Bruner, 3rd Company 1st Battalion, wounded with a lance thrust to the left arm on 18 June 1815 at Waterloo;

MAT no. 980 Jean Pierre Sitrain, private, 1st Company 2nd Battalion, made prisoner 18 June 1815 at Waterloo;

MAT no. 1023 Sergeant-Major Jean Baptiste Etienne Faglain, grenadier company 3rd Battalion, wounded with a bayonet thrust, lance wound to the left hand and to the right leg at Waterloo 18 June 1815; and

MAT no. 1741 Jean Renee Beillard, private, 1st Company 2nd Battalion, wounded with a gunshot to the left leg at Waterloo 18 June 1815.

Did Vandamme order a detachment of the 22nd Regiment of Line Infantry to head for Waterloo once the news of the battle had been passed to Grouchy in order to take news about the action at Wavre? If they did, Vandamme says not a word, nor does Grouchy. Did these half-dozen or so men evade the Prussians and get to the French headquarters? Was their appearance at Waterloo further proof that Grouchy was on his way? Did they carry a message? We simply do not know. All we do know is that these men are recorded by the regiment as being at Waterloo and are the only men wounded on 18 June 1815 at a specific location. All other casualties are listed merely with a date. These are the only men who are recorded with details of their wounds. Therefore, someone got back to the unit with their story. But does Waterloo actually mean Wavre? We simply do not know, but the prospect is that Vandamme, in his rush into Wavre once he knew what was happening with the emperor, ordered some men to find Napoléon and tell him what was happening, and perhaps also to say that Vandamme believed he could quickly brush the Prussians aside and get to Waterloo. We have no idea what message the men carried, or if they got to Waterloo. But if they did, their appearance probably further confirmed to the emperor that the next body of troops to emerge on his right would be Grouchy. When he did not arrive, but more Prussians did, the emperor's plans collapsed and Grouchy was now the villain of the day. This is all rampant speculation of course. Vandamme, Grouchy or any other French observer never mention dispatch of men to Waterloo, let alone the arrival of news from Grouchy during the battle. It leaves us with a very tangible 'what if' scenario that we cannot answer.

In reality, what was spotted was the Prussian 1st and 2nd Corps, which Grouchy had never known anything about. The troops Grouchy had followed since 17 June from Tourinnes were heading to Louvain, but at no stage had any of the pursuing troops witnessed the corps turn west. As far as Grouchy knew he had the Prussian 1st, 2nd and 3rd Corps in front of him. Even when Napoléon knew beyond reasonable doubt about the Prussians had arrived in force, he chose to spread the lie to the army that the troops were in fact Grouchy's. It had a cataclysmic effect on the army.

Grouchy had found and pursued the Prussian 3rd and 4th Corps. Napoléon's men had found the Prussian 1st and 2nd Corps, but so convinced was Napoléon that the Prussians were heading to Louvain (based on Grouchy's reports), that he never considered the possibility that they were anything other than the 4th Corps.

Grouchy's new plan of 0perations

Meanwhile at Wavre, totally unaware of the what was happening at Waterloo, Grouchy endeavoured to achieve Napoléon's orders, and the plan he came up with was masterful and the best that fitted the circumstances. He cannot be blamed for the time it took to dislodge the Prussians. His forces only ever exceeded Thielemann's on the night of the 18th, as his forces arrived piecemeal, firstly with 3rd Corps and then sometime later 4th Corps arrived, but due to the nature of the terrain, Grouchy could not press his numerical advantage until he had crossed the Dyle at Limale on the night of the 18th. Only then could Grouchy deploy his full force. Aide-de-Camp de Blocqueville writes:[5]

> The marshal expressed his displeasure, because the congestion of troops was so great that there was no way at the moment to deploy all his corps.

Grouchy himself notes at the moment of receiving this letter that all his troops were engaged—Vandamme's corps could not be drawn from its position without the danger of the enemy re-passing the river, and preventing, or at least retarding, his movements. It was the same with the part of Gérard's corps engaged at the mill, which had not yet been carried; but about half of the latter corps was in the rear and nearer to Saint-Lambert than the troops at Wavre.

As it was, for most of the action at Wavre, Grouchy had roughly equal strength with Thielemann, and not superiority. As we shall see, Grouchy could only feed his troops into the action, rather than deploy both infantry corps to swamp the Prussians. To do so he had to cross the Dyle. A major obstacle in this movement was the mill at Bièrges. Aide-de-Camp de Blocqueville writes that the mill at Bièrges was an impossible position to assault:[6]

> The position of the 3rd Corps did not allow the marshal to disengage easily. Having on hand a brigade of the 4th Corps, who had just arrived on the heights of Wavre, and wanting to march as quickly as possible on Saint-Lambert, with the support of the cavalry of General Pajol and Teste's division, he marched them back to the front of the other divisions of the 4th Corps, to direct them to the point where he would join them at Limale, instead of letting them get to Wavre, where they were further away from Saint-Lambert.
>
> The marshal, arriving at Baraque and not finding the 4th Corps, the marshal dispatched Bella to locate the commander and to order him to move on Limale and Saint-Lambert, while he, the marshal, returned in person to Wavre where things were still in the same state as before, and we could not cross the Dyle. He therefore found it appropriate to renew the attack on the mill of Bièrges, to create diversion and draw the Prussian forces from Limale. If this second attack had succeeded, we would have gained the direct route from Wavre to Mont-Saint-Jean.

It was now that Gérard, we are told, was wounded in very different circumstances to those presented by Rumigny.

Grouchy, as noted above, knowing that he could not now disengage Vandamme, sent orders to Pajol to hasten his march on Limale, and ordered Gérard to lead the 4th Corps towards that village at once. He conceived the idea of assaulting and carrying Wavre with Vandamme's corps, aided afterwards by Excelmans's cavalry, while he sent the remainder of his army on Chapelle-Saint-Lambert, via Limale.[7] About this plan, Grouchy writes on 20 June 1815:[8]

> ...being impatient to debouch on Mont-Saint-Lambert, and co-operate with Your Majesty's army on that important day, I detached to Limale Pajol's cavalry, Teste's division and two divisions of Gérard's corps to force the passage of the Dyle and march against Bülow.
>
> Vandamme's corps, in the meantime, maintained the attack on Wavre and on the mill of Bièrges, whence the enemy showed an intention to debouch, but which I did not conceive he was capable of effecting, the position and courage of our troops being pledges that he could not.

My movement on Limale required time in proportion to the distance: I however arrived, executed the passage, and the heights were carried by Vichery's division and the cavalry. Night did not permit us to advance farther, and I no longer heard the cannon on the side where Your Majesty was engaged.

This was a skilful plan of operation, as the movement on Limale would have had the double effect of turning Thielemann's left flank, while it allowed 4th Corps, Teste's division, as well as the cavalry of Pajol, Vallin and Excelmans, to move towards Napoléon's right. Vandamme and the remaining half of Excelmans's corps were to be left as a rearguard at Wavre. But it was now too late for Grouchy to catch Bülow and attack him in the flank.[9] For Grouchy's plan to work he had to push back the Prussians at Limale, capture the bridge and break out.

He has been damned with hindsight for not marching to the sounds of the guns earlier in the day, vindicating Excelmans and Gérard's thesis, and for not obeying the 13.00 order by those wanting to shift the blame of defeat at Waterloo from Napoléon to other scapegoats, namely Marshals Ney and Grouchy, as well as General Guyot and others. In the event, Grouchy, in pinning down Thielemann's 19,000 men, helped prevent the defeat at Waterloo being far worse than it was to be. Grouchy, with the 13.00 order, knew where the Prussian 4th Corps was, which vindicated his own reconnaissance reports that he had the rearguard of the Prussian 1st, 2nd and 3rd Corps before him. It was his duty to both contain the Prussian rearguard and stop more troops moving to Wellington, and to also aid Napoléon. This is what he sought to achieve. With hindsight, Grouchy should have put the plan into operation sooner, but until 4th Corps, Teste and Pajol had arrived he had insufficient troops. Moreover, until he received the 13.00 order, he was not aware of the possibility of a Prussian link-up with Wellington, as the emperor had ordered him to keep heading east and attack Wavre.

Pajol's operations at Limale
About his movements at Limale, Marshal Grouchy writes in 1819:[10]

Seeing that they neither succeeded at Wavre or Bièrges, and desperate to get to Napoléon, I determined to leave the corps of Vandamme and Excelmans's cavalry before an army whose forces were necessarily superior to mine, and march those troops I had to hand under Gérard's orders to Limelette, to re-unite them with the rest of the corps and march via Baraque. I went there in person at speed, but unfortunately the country on the right side of the Dyle is cut by ravines and streams, following the river.

Furthermore, practicable communication could not be utilised between Wavre and Saint-Lambert which is on the left bank occupied by the enemy, so that the movement of the troops required a lot of time. However, the cavalry of General Pajol and an infantry division cross the Dyle, and that night we were masters of the first hills of the other side, the positions which the Prussian artillery had fired from. We arrived in the valley through which flows the Dyle, on the plateau overlooking the villages of Limale and Limelette, by a steep and rugged road, which the darkness of the night made the climb slow and difficult: there was extreme congestion on the road, the terrain being masked and proximity of the enemy being such that his balls reached the head of the defile, I felt the danger of such a position, I stayed until nearly midnight on this point busy placing my men personally, as they gained the part of the plateau that we were masters of. The cavalry of General Pajol was on the left, with the Dyle behind them, their situation was not much better than the infantry and artillery that I had on this side of the river. The Prussians continued to occupy half of Wavre, as well as the mill and the village of Bièrges. I moved to the right and through the woods with the troops. It is likely that if we had been vigorously attacked, we would have been pushed back, with much loss, to the other side of the Dyle.

Written sometime on 18 June is the following order to Pajol:[11]

18 June 1815
Marshal Grouchy to General Pajol
Order the division of Teste and your corps, with much haste, to Bièrges. Cross the River Dyle and attack the enemy which will face you there.
Signe. Marshal Grouchy.

Thus, Grouchy left Vandamme and Excelmans to carry on the fight at Wavre, while he himself led the remainder of Gérard's corps to Limalette. Pajol had arrived in front of the Limale Bridge shortly before dark with Teste's division and his own cavalry. About the operations as they unfolded at Limale, Carl von Clausewitz notes:[12]

When the French 4th Corps (Gérard) arrived, a part of the [14th] Division (Hulot) was also sent to Bièrges. After having been repulsed at Wavre, the French generals placed great hopes on the attack at the Bièrges mill and were, therefore, present in person, but they were not able to gain control of this crossing. Hulot's division later—that is to say between 8 and 9 p.m.—moved to Limale, where it was joined by the other two divisions, which arrived considerably later after having been directed there from La Baraque. Pajol also proceeded in that direction with his cavalry corps and Teste's division of the 6th Corps.

All these troops reached Limale just as darkness fell. They found the town and the river crossing undefended, probably because Colonel Stengel was already withdrawing to follow the 1st Corps. The French, therefore, crossed over the Dyle in the dark and pushed forward in thick masses up to Delburg on the rim of the Dyle valley, facing the right flank of General Thielemann.

It was not until around 10 p.m. that the 12th Brigade reported that the enemy had crossed the river at Limale. General Thielemann thought that it was a detached column, consisting perhaps of just one division, and ordered Colonel Stülpnagel to go there with all the forces he could collect and drive the enemy back over the river. A brigade of the reserve cavalry was sent at the same time. General Thielemann hurried over to the threatened point himself. The attack took place in the dark, but it was not successful, in part because the attacking battalions were thrown into disorder by a sunken road, and in part because the enemy was already too strong.

Colonel Stülpnagel was therefore forced to take up a position very close to the enemy in order to tie them down and prevent them from spreading out. The first cannon shots began at dawn, at a distance of 500 paces. A violent struggle now commenced, during which the French methodically pushed their four divisions forward under the protection of a large line of skirmishers. The 3rd Corps resisted in three different positions. The first was in the low ground near the small wood, with the 12th Brigade and Colonel Stengel, who was still nearby. The next position was between Bièrges and the Rixansart Woods, with fourteen battalions of the 12th, 10th, and 11th Brigades and the reserve cavalry, while six battalions remained behind Bièrges and Wavre, and four remained in Wavre.

By 19.00, the small Prussian garrison had been easily swept aside by the French cavalry. Limelette was captured a short time later. Gérard was ordered to send two divisions to Limale. To counter this new threat, Thielemann sent a brigade to Limale, but Grouchy was able to drive them back at about 21.00. General Berton caustically notes about the failure of the attacks at Wavre as follows:[13]

We all marched on Wavre without even acknowledging the bridge of Moustier, we remained for a part of the day to throw ourselves back and forth, against a formidable position beyond a river, where anywhere else we should have already been able to cross without having to fire a single shot. But we led successive attacks of infantry against the bridge of Wavre and the mill of Bièrges, where we lost a lot of people unnecessarily against the only two points that the enemy could defend with advantage. Four-fifths of our infantry could not be brought into action before Wavre, and eighteen regiments of cavalry were doing nothing, and partly thrown to the rear right where there was nobody, because, independently of the corps of Pajol which was in Tourinnes, I received orders to send a regiment of my brigade (the 17th Dragoons, Colonel Labiffe), to reconnoitre the road from Louvain to Namur, and the means to properly ensure the right and rear of this Prussian corps had crossed the Dyle.

But where was the rest of Excelmans's corps? Why had Grouchy issued him no orders? Why had Excelmans not shown initiative and asked for orders? This was the biggest failing by Grouchy on 18 June—not using his resources more effectively. Clearly, some of the dragoons had been at Chyse, where they reported Prussian troops, which was in reality the Prussian 4th Corps, which we know the French followed towards Ottenberg. He further notes that:[14]

> The cavalry division, commanded by General Vallin, passed the bridge of Limale at six in the evening, without meeting any resistance, and was followed an hour later by the division of General Vichery, and finally the entire 4th Corps.
>
> Orders were sent to General Pajol in Tourinnes at about four o'clock in the afternoon, thus he did not reach Limale until about eight o'clock with his cavalry. Teste's division, which was close behind, went across the same bridge over the Dyle and occupied the heights to the right to support the attack on the village of Rosierne, which was captured from the enemy between nine and ten in the evening, which made us masters of the road from Wavre to Brussels. Vandamme's corps was still in Wavre and had brought one of its divisions vis-a-vis to the mill of Bièrges; the headquarters were established at Limale.

About the movements of the cavalry reserve, as noted by General Berton, Colonel Biot, aide-de-camp to General Pajol (commanding the 1st Reserve Cavalry Corps) relates that:[15]

We moved out from Gembloux and moved to our left and marched on a road boarded by heather. As we arrived we encountered the division of General Maurin. This general officer had been wounded at the Battle of Ligny and was replaced by General Vallin. The division was composed of two regiments of light cavalry and two regiments of dragoons and was placed under the orders of General Pajol. General Pajol received, inexplicably, two orders from Marshal Grouchy, both written at the same time: one was to march on Wavre, and the other was to march to the emperor. The general reflected, it was decided that a day of battle when there is uncertainty, the best thing to do was to carry ourselves to the cannon, but we had ceased to hear them from the morning.

Marshal Grouchy, in leaving Gembloux, had followed the road of Wavre with the body of Vandamme, while the body of Gérard, [the] intermediary between us and Wavre, to march also on the Dyle. As General Pajol debouched onto the heather of Baraque, we could see arriving at full speed Bellanger, first aide-de-camp of Marshal Grouchy. He cried from a distance that the emperor had been successful and that the enemy had fled, and that is just waiting for the cavalry to pursue and complete their rout. He added that the order of the marshal urges us to pass the Dyle on the spot, the Limale Bridge and harass the enemy in his retreat. We were formed for battle in the heather, it was necessary before arriving in the basin of the Dyle to pass through a defile extending down to the bridge. Noticing a peasant, I ran to him: this man told me the road. But my request to march with us, he said he assumed that the French had won and wanted to return to where he had come from, fearing that in his absence harm had come to his family. It was a shame that the peasant could not have come with us, but he had shown me the way down to Limale Bridge.

So, I returned without a guide, but on my affirmation, that I recognised the country and the road, the general ordered me to march in front of the column and to direct it. The division of Maurin was at the head of the column. Hardly had we gone 200 yards in a defile when the words 'who goes there?' struck my ear. In my response: 'France', it replied 'none shall pass'. At the same time, two bullets came to greet our arrival. I felt very isolated at the front, but I quickly found myself in the presence of a sergeant of infantry of the corps of Gérard. He tells me that the Prussian infantry are posted in the mill and houses that are to the right and left of the bridge, defending the passage of the river, and it was also supported by artillery which was installed on the heights of the left bank of the Dyle.

259

The rout of the enemy announced by Bellanger, the report of the sergeant of voltigeurs, the musket shots that had been fired at us, all seemed such a contradiction that without listening to the sergeant, I pushed my horse onto the bridge. As I did so, the enemy opened fire at me from the houses, and I had to stop my advance.

I made sure, however, of the width of the bridge, which we could not pass by column of four, I recognised that on leaving the road made a curve to the left, hugging the houses, since it shared, fifty paces farther on, the right fork down on to Wavre along the left bank of the Dyle, the other fork, the left, through the village, which was one long street. I went to report to the general of the obstacle that I had met and of the places I had just reconnoitred. We had been in a similar situation at the Battle of Montereau. I knew that the bridge was not barricaded, we could carry it by a vigorous charge, being supported by cavalry and followed by infantry, we would take the whole village, but he remained unsure. If the enemy had a force strong enough to oppose us at the other side of the village, the column would be put into disorder once advancing down the defile.

When I had explained the entire movement thus, the general thought for a moment. Then, according to one of those inspirations that were so natural to him in war: 'we must go there. Tell General Vallin to give us the 1st Squadron of the 6th Hussars, and you capture the bridge. But do not stop; take immediately the road to the right of which you spoke, and debouch onto the plain. I will support you as needed'.

I ran to transmit the order to General Vallin. The Prince of Carignan, brave and excellent officer, who was near him, asked to charge with his squadron. We set off at full gallop; the rest of the column followed us at a trot. We took off the bridge, after suffering a shooting that did us no harm. Then taking the right path and opening into the plain, we found ourselves in front of a Prussian battalion. The charge was successful, and we entered the square, from the houses laid down their arms. We had to regret one officer killed from the 6th Hussars. As we passed on the road then going to Wavre, between the left bank of the Dyle and the hill, we perceived the corps of Gérard, who had taken position between Wavre and Limale...The enemy, at the end of the plateau where we debouched opened fire on us with artillery. The dragoons followed the same route; the 75th Line was marching as best they could. A young drummer of the regiment, to whom I ordered to beat the charge, was shot in the hand; he continued nevertheless to tap on the drum with the hand that remained. And we came onto the plateau, the enemy had entirely disappeared. This plateau, covered with heather and wooded in places, led in the direction of Saint-Lambert, the direction taken by the enemy. A skirmish ensued in the heather, but, at nightfall, it stopped. The skirmishers were recalled, and established their bivouacs. The division of Maurin and that of Pierre Soult, and the infantry division of General Teste had passed the Dyle: they settled on the plateau beyond the left bank. The dragoons of the division of General Excelmans and the 4th Corps, that Marshal Grouchy had reminded with, bivouacked on the right bank. Thus, ended for us on the 18th, the day of Waterloo.

What document did Bellanger carry? By its description that it contained news that the Battle at Waterloo was won, it was the 13.00 order to Grouchy. Major Stengel, commanding the 19th Prussian Infantry Regiment, writes:[16]

Major Stengel, commanding the regiment occupied with the fusilier battalion the village of Bièrges and its surroundings, and placed 1st and 2nd Battalions on the right of Bièrges to stop the attack of the enemy, which being well concealed, burst forth and attacked, but was thrown back. The enemy, about a quarter of an hour later, then made a strong attack again on the right, and captured both places. Instantly, the 19th Infantry Regiment was commanded to the leave the positions assigned to them and to occupy, as speedily as possible, Limale, and upon arriving immediately faced the enemy in a tough battle. In the very unfavourable terrain, he nevertheless, with his regiment and a squadron of the 6th Lancers under the orders of Colonel Count Lertum, to prevent the advance of the enemy which was six times his own number, and prevented the union of both of Napoléon's armies. At midnight, they withdrew to the wood, the moonlight favoured continuous heavy fire and it was only when all the ammunition had been fired, and after attempting again a bayonet charge, did the utter wearing of the soldiers result in a retreat of 800 paces. Without having any food brought to them and only having two to three hours sleep, the enemy was again bombarded at daybreak with balls and howitzer shells.

The passage had been forced, and Teste's division sent across; Stengel, finding himself very much outnumbered, abandoned Limale and took up a position on the heights above the village. Grouchy had now crossed the Dyle, and Pajol's cavalry was surging up the road to Neuf Cabaret.

21st Division attack

Teste's division, as well as General Vichery's division that had marched at the rear of 4th Corps, were the closest troops to Limale and led the attack.[17] About this plan, Grouchy wrote on 20 June 1815:[18]

> I detached to Limale Pajol's cavalry, Teste's division and two divisions of Gérard's corps to force the passage of the Dyle and march against Bülow.
>
> Vandamme's corps, in the meantime, maintained the attack on Wavre and on the mill of Bièrges, whence the enemy showed an intention to debouch.

As both Grouchy (above) and Biot note, moving up behind the cavalry came the division of Teste, Vichery's division and Toussaint's brigade from the 14th Infantry Division of General Hulot. Captain Bella, aide-de-camp to Marshal Grouchy, recounts that the attack by Teste and Pajol was successful:[19]

> The Prussians had evacuated Limale, but they occupied a very strong position vis-a-vis, on the left bank of the Dyle, they put up a strong resistance and you had a lot of trouble to approach them. The climb to get there was very rapid and swept by enemy cannon fire, you and your staff had to dismount, and you placed yourself at the head of the troops to increase their momentum, with your own hands you helped to push the artillery pieces. Your efforts succeeded, and the Prussians were overthrown, but they lost little ground and reformed soon, it was eleven o'clock at night, the night was dark and there was so little distance between your troops and theirs that enemy bullets reached some men of your escort.

Officer d'Ordonnance Leguest notes that Grouchy dismounted and led 4th Corps and Teste's division in a frontal assault on the Prussian positions:[20]

> You and your officers dismounted, to encourage the soldiers, and you helped us to even reach the Prussian cannon that were in front of us, and made a plunging fire on us, which made it very difficult to ascend the heights. We finally gained the height and the enemy were swept away by your troops, but the enemy took position half a cannon-shot away, and you judged the situation of the 4th Corps to be so critical that you determined not to leave the position during the night, and camped in one of its squares.

General Teste, commanding the 21st Infantry Division (part of 6th Corps) comprising the 8th Regiment of Light Infantry, the 75th Regiment of Line Infantry and 1st Battalion of the 65th Regiment of Line Infantry, writes in his memoirs, published in 1912 in the *Carnet de la Sabretache*:[21]

> The 18th at five o'clock in the morning, the division moved out with the cavalry to Saint-Denis, Grandley at Tourinne, and took up position. It was about a quarter-past twelve that we moved in the direction of Baraque, where we arrived about eight o'clock in the evening. We had passed the valley of Limale and passed through the village of the same name, where Marshal Grouchy gave the order for us to march to Rosierne on the road to Brussels. Here we encountered the Prussian troops under General Thielemann. The strength of their attack forced us to abandon the heights of the village.

Prussian counter-attack

Hearing of Stengel's difficulties, Thielemann sent the 12th Division (Stülpnagel's) and Hobe's cavalry to reinforce him. It was now that Thielemann realised that the goal of the French forces to was cross the Dyle at Limale, and not Bièrges or Bas-Wavre. In consequence of this, he moved all the troops he could spare towards his right. Four battalions of the 10th Division took up Stülpnagel's former position, leaving three battalions of the 12th Division to defend Bièrges; the remainder marched to join Stengel. About this, Colonel Stülpnagel writes:[22]

> About eight o'clock in the evening, Major von Stengel, of the 19th Regiment, reported to me that he had been given three battalions and three squadrons to maintain a line of communication between his corps and the 3rd Corps. Shortly after that, Major Simolin, of the hussar regiment, reported to me that there was no infantry at Limale, and a strong enemy column had been seen moving towards it. I immediately requested Major von Simolin to occupy Limale and sent the two squadrons of his brigade there.
>
> However, I believed that the enemy had already passed the Dyle at Limale. I reported this fact to the commanding general, and that I was marching with the brigade on Limale and requested cavalry support. General Thielemann ordered the reserve cavalry to support me and ordered me to prevent the French breaking out of Limale. I then marched off leaving all my sharpshooters on the Dyle, one battalion between Wavre and Bièrges, and to protect my left flank, two battalions were left in Bièrges.

> I found Limale and the heights in front of it already occupied by the enemy, and Stengel's detachments retiring to these heights. The darkness prevented a judgement of the enemy's strength. As Limale was an important position, I was of the firm belief that I should do everything to recapture it.

It was in this attack that perhaps Teste's division was forced to retreat. The Prussian 31st Infantry Regiment was part of the Prussian 12th Brigade of Oberst von Stülpnagel. Commanding the skirmish company was Second Lieutenant Mannkopff, who writes:[23]

> On the morning of 18 June, we broke out of the bivouac again and marched forward against the Dyle, so that Wavre was to our left front. However, we made several times a prolonged stop. During the afternoon, the French (Grouchy and Vandamme) debouched on the opposite valley edge of the Dyle with considerable forces, and it developed gradually into a violent struggle in Wavre, over who controlled the town and particularly the passage of the Dyle there, with the troops of the 9th Brigade. General von Borcke, of our corps, defended the place doggedly.
>
> The French deployed on the opposite side of the valley, which was terraced, some artillery batteries and maintained a lively fire from the place upon the town and our troops. During this time in the gardens around the town and on the banks of the Dyle, a fierce battle commenced and the French threw grenades into the town and in many places fires were started. Until the evening we were only spectators of this struggle for the possession of Wavre and the passage over the Dyle. Only a few stray bullets reached our brigade and were reciprocated with our artillery.

In order to face down Stülpnagel, the remaining regiments of Hulot's division, and also Teste's division from 6th Corps, were ordered to attack.

General Toussaint attacks Bièrges

Here, between Limale and Bièrges, the counter-attack against Stülpnagel was led by the 2nd Brigade from Hulot's 14th Infantry Division, comprising the 44th and 50th regiments of Line Infantry. About operations here, we have to rely upon a statement made by Colonel Paolini.[24] About the action, he writes:[25]

> At the Battle of Wavre on 18 June 1815, the 44th Line was ordered to pass the Dyle. This passage was defended entirely by Prussian

artillery, whose bullets and shrapnel made a dreadful havoc in the ranks.

Colonel Paolini, seeing a moment's hesitation among his men, he seized the eagle of his regiment, and threw it like a spear onto the other side of the bank. Jumping in the water, shouted to his soldiers 'my friends, would you let your eagle come into the possession of the enemy?'

The regiment followed its colonel, who was by now already on the other side.

Was this attack at Bièrges or at Limale, or mid-way between the two where a ford is suggested on the 1777 Ferraris map? Perhaps we won't know for sure, but it does seem that the 44th Regiment of Line Infantry crossed the River Dyle by fording it to out-flank the Prussian positions at Bièrges. The fate of the regiment after this point is vague. Martinien lists no officers killed or wounded on either 18 or 19 June, so presumably the resistance to the regiment once it had captured the Prussian guns melted away. However, given how strong the natural defences of Bièrges were, the only logical way to assault the place and capture it was by a holding action in front of the place, perhaps that of the 9th Regiment of Light Infantry or the 30th Regiment of Line Infantry, with the 44th and 50th Regiment of Line Infantry sent to the west to ford the River Dyle between Limale and Bièrges, and attack Bièrges in the flank. Presumably, this attack at Bièrges occurred concurrently with, or after, the attack at Limale and the Prussian troops there, mentioned earlier, being contained in order for the flank attack to Bièrges to have been successful. In the brigaded 50th Regiment of Line Infantry, a single officer, Sub-Lieutenant Lemaire, is listed as wounded.

By 21.00, the 44th and 50th regiments of Line Infantry were apparently at Neuf Cabaret after successfully repulsing the counter-attack lead by Stülpnagel, who were pushed back into the woods beyond the place.

Vichery attacks
Stülpnagel's attack seems to have been pushed back by General Vichery's 13th Infantry Division, which so far, it seems, had taken no part in the fighting.

It was now dark, but the battle continued with vigour. Grouchy posted his battalions from Vichery's division in front of Limale, and, considering the darkness of the night, it is surprising how he managed to place them without confusion. Stengel's men kept up a harassing fire on his columns as they wound their way through the muddy lanes from the village to the height above the Dyle, and deployed to receive Stülpnagel's attack. Pajol moved his cavalry to the French left flank. Commanding the skirmish company of the Prussian 31st Infantry Regiment was Second Lieutenant Mannkopff:[26]

> Gradually, the French developed more and more forces along opposite the Dyle, and especially for us, and with the onset of darkness, we were also drawn into the struggle, the French having managed to pass over the Dyle through Wavre and at Limale. Our skirmishers advanced in front, and there ensued with the enemy voltigeurs a long and stubborn fight in the darkness and in the man-high corn with which the fields were covered. This soon degenerated quickly into a chaotic mess of single combats, so I made several attacks with my skirmishers to defend ourselves against enemy cavalry or voltigeurs both to our front and back. About midnight, our skirmishers, where possible, pulled back to the columns, and now at the double made a general bayonet attack, but as due to the darkness and the high corn, it was not easy to survey the terrain, as well as battle conditions made a uniform line impossible. The action was equally without significant results and continued as a battle of skirmishes.
>
> My battalion to which I had re-joined with my skirmishers again came suddenly, and during this attack stumbled into a deep ravine or ditch, and at the same moment on the opposite edge a strong volley of small-arms fire struck us. However, probably because of the other edge of the ravine (or trench) was higher, chiefly over the heads of our soldiers and officers who were not on horseback, the shots mostly missed and its effect only manifested itself primarily by the violent rattling our bayonets gave. In contrast, all the mounted officers were hit, namely the regimental commander (Major v. Kestelloot) and the battalion-commander (Major von Tiedemann) were wounded and the battalion adjutant (Lieutenant von Aderkas) was shot dead. Soon after this general bayonet attack, we broke off from our part of the battle, and we withdrew without being pursued by the enemy into a nearby pine forest (partly large trees, sometimes young, dense coniferous) behind us.

In the attack, the Prussian 19th Infantry Regiment was pushed back and the bridge at Limale captured, Grouchy's objective to be seized in the morning was taken in the early evening. Vichery's infantry and Pierre Soult's cavalry forced the Prussians back, and resulted in Prussian General Thielemann ordering troops to concentrate at Limale, to try and drive the French back across the river. About the events of that night, Second Lieutenant Wehmeyer, of the Prussian 31st Infantry Regiment, writes:[27]

> The outposts were standing so close to the enemy that you could hear every word that was spoken over there. Many of the wounded were close and lay in front of the line of outposts, partly in the line, and all night long you could hear their wailing tones. Every moment we clashed with the enemy patrols. Standing on the right wing with a cordon of vedettes was the landwehr cavalry, who were chased back with every shot fired at them, and also led the retreat of the outposts, so that the whole chain remained in constant motion. No one had a bit of food, and even water to clear the burning thirst was nowhere to be found. For the French, it was a very lively night. Late at night they beat their usual retreat, and slaughtered some pigs they had found, whose cries accentuated our hunger, as they seemed to be very good to eat. With us, there was dead silence, interrupted only by the sentries with their calls. Everything else was resting on the bare earth, musket in hand, awaiting the new battle that was to begin at dawn.

The night of the 18th at Limale was one of an un-easy truce. In the attack, the 59th and 76th regiments of Line Infantry, which formed Vichery's 1st Brigade, temporarily commanded by Colonel Laurain (of the 59th Regiment of Line Infantry), lost heavily. Colonel Laurain himself had been wounded at Ligny with a gunshot to the left shoulder and was again wounded at Wavre with another gunshot.[28] At the head of a grenadier company, Captain Jacques Auguste Masson was wounded.[29] Also wounded were Lieutenant Soyer, who would be killed fighting under the walls of Paris on 2 July 1815, and Second Lieutenant Voirin. Wounded in the early hours of the 19th were lieutenants Bosset, Guignoux and Vanneroy. Sergeant-Major Andre Olagnier was wounded with a gunshot to the right leg and was made prisoner of war, being returned to France on 30 January 1816.[30]

In the brigaded 76th Regiment of Line Infantry, Captain Ferrand de Missole was wounded, as were captains Nicolas Gumbelot and Jean Louis Vedel and lieutenants Bizanet and Blauwe. Pierre Joseph Constantin de Blauwe was born on 16 November 1777 at Gand. He was wounded at Wavre and made a prisoner of war.[31] Second Lieutenant Fabrice Jules Reau was wounded.[32] Furthermore, second lieutenants Chameroy, Naigeon and Rousselot were mortally wounded. Total recorded losses for 4th Corps at Wavre are shown below:

Regiment	Killed		Wounded		Missing		Total
	Officers	Men	Officers	Men	Officers	Men	
12th Division							
30th Line Infantry[33]	0	0	0	0	0	0	0
96th Line Infantry[34]	0	4	0	29	0	1	34
6th Light Infantry	No data available						
63rd Line Infantry[35]	No meaningful data recorded						
Division Total	0	4	0	29	0	1	34
13th Division							
59th Line Infantry[36]	3	14	5	35	0	7	64
76th Line Infantry[37]	No data recorded						
48th Line Infantry[38]	0	1	5	No data recorded			6
69th Line Infantry[39]	0	1	0	1	0	2	4
Division Total	3	16	10	36	0	9	74
14th Division							
9th Light Infantry[40]	0	2	0	12	0	0	14
111th Line Infantry[41]	0	0	1	0	0	0	1
44th Line Infantry[42]	0	0	0	4	0	0	4
50th Line Infantry[43]	0	0	2	2	0	0	4
Division Total	0	2	3	18	0	0	23
Corps Total	3	22	13	83	0	10	131

Losses on the day were no doubt a lot higher, as all we are seeing are the numbers of men still in hospital in September 1815 when the army was disbanded, and furthermore, four regiments record no casualty data for the campaign as a whole. Without a total breakdown of losses, we can say very little about the fighting at Wavre. Of interest, the 9th Regiment of Light Infantry took minimal casualties, but due to shaky morale and cohesion was no longer capable for further action. It seems this was true of a number of regiments, which took small losses at Wavre, and no longer took part in offensive operations. No doubt the effect of the losses from Ligny upon morale, as well as fighting a battle after a march of fifteen miles or so through deep mud had had a major impact on the fighting capacity of the corps.

Tactical summary
After the initial success of Habert and Berthezène, Wavre had proved too hard a nut to crack, so Grouchy had changed his plans in reference to Napoléon's summons to march to Waterloo. He would hold the Prussians at Wavre and then send all his available force via Limale to cut off the Prussians at Wavre and fall on the rear of the Prussians, and affect a junction with Napoléon. This plan was put in action, but took longer

to execute than hoped, Limale and its brigade not falling until the evening of the 18th, by which time Grouchy would not have been able to reach Waterloo in time. Grouchy notes in 1819:[44]

When Napoléon ordered me on the 17th at noon, to pursue the enemy and, in consequence of the delays of the generals under my orders, their troops did not leave the plains of Fleurus until about three o'clock of that day, the Prussian army was already collected near Wavre. When I reached Wavre between one and two o'clock of the 18th the Prussian columns were already on the heights of Saint-Lambert, and in sight of the French army, which was engaged at Waterloo.

I have just shown that the late hour of the arrival of my troops at Gembloux, and the weather, still more than my slender information as to the real movements of the Prussians, had hindered me from pushing my infantry beyond that town on the 17th. But on the 18th, before sunrise, it was in motion in the direction of Sart-a-Walhain and Wavre, at which place the head of the column did not reach until between one and two o'clock, though it marched without halting for an instant. To assert that then I could have paralysed, by a flank movement which my proximity to the enemy did not permit me to make, the attack of General Bülow on the right wing of the French at Waterloo shows ignorance of the position of the Prussian army, which was at this time in echelons between Napoléon and me—and shows a forgetfulness of distances, of the state of the roads and the nature of the country; for the Prussian corps which decided the fate of the battle had marched from Wavre at daylight, and were on the march from four in the morning until one in the afternoon, before they reached the head of the defile of Saint-Lambert. (See the report of M. Blücher). Thus then, unless I could have given wings to my soldiers, it was impossible that they could have arrived in time to be useful at Waterloo.

To hold in check, as it is asserted I could have done, an army 95,000 strong with a corps of 32,000 men was a very difficult task, and it is publishing an erroneous opinion to advance that I could have accomplished it. On the evening of the 17th, my troops had scarcely reached Gembloux. On the evening of the 17th, Marshal Blücher had all his army, except a rearguard, collected near Wavre—at sunrise on the 18th, Blücher detached from Wavre a part of his troops for the purpose of forming a junction with the Duke of Wellington. At sunrise on the 18th, I was seven hours march from thence. How could I hinder the detachment and prevent the junction?

It cannot be said, with more justice, that Marshal Blücher had deceived me, or had concealed from me the movement of a part of his army, as some writers have advanced:

First, because, not only I was not in position before M. Blücher, when he commenced his movement towards the left of the English army, with the design of turning the right of the French at Waterloo, but, as I have remarked, my troops were at a great distance when this movement was executed.

Second, because I did not reach the Prussian rearguard until the 18th, about noon, a league and a half from Wavre, that town having been occupied during the night by the enemy's corps, which effected, at daybreak, the movement in question.

Grouchy had done the best he could in the difficult circumstance he found himself in. His plan to reach Saint-Lambert was masterful, what was lacking was its rapid execution, for which Grouchy is partially to blame, but also his senior commanders in their own attacks to gain both Wavre and Limale. Grouchy, it is true, had lost some focus by continuing with the attacks of Wavre, he also failed to utilise Excelmans's dragoons effectively. His performance at Wavre was in contrast to the myopic blindness Ney suffered at Waterloo at the head of the cavalry reserve. Ney could not see the larger tactical position at Waterloo from the front ranks of the cuirassiers. Grouchy did see the larger picture, and developed a plan that was very effective, if somewhat delayed. That Grouchy failed to use Excelmans's corps was a major mistake in hindsight. He could have sent them to look for fords to cross the Dyle, but he chose not to. We do not know why he made this command decision. Was it the poor state of the corps which was exhausted? Perhaps.

Night of 18 June

That night, Grouchy made his preparations for the following day's attack, and hoped to join Napoléon at Brussels. At midnight, he ordered General Vandamme:[45]

My dear general,

You are to debouch at Limale, that the dark night has not allowed you to do, so we are beak-to-beak with the enemy. Since you have not been able to pass the Dyle, please go immediately to Limale with your corps, leaving at Wavre the number of troops needed to defend the bridge.

At daybreak, we will attack the troops that I have in front of me [at Limale] and we will succeed, I hope, to join the emperor as ordered to do so. They say he beat the English, but I have no news of him and I'm going to send him ours.

In the name of the country I pray, my dear fellow, you carry out this order. I see that this is the way out of the difficult position we are in, and the salvation of the army depends on it.

I also put under your command the whole corps of Gérard.

A thousand thanks

Marshal Comte Grouchy

Limale, 18 June 1815 midnight

P.S. A report has been received that tells us the Prussians of Bülow and Blücher are in front of us.

Vandamme received this order, we are told, at midnight on 18 June.[46] Grouchy sent the following dispatch to Napoléon in the early hours of 19 June:[47]

Sir, yesterday, when I was attacking Wavre, I received the letter which Your Majesty told me to move to Saint-Lambert and attack Bülow. The canon of Your Majesty made me hasten my movement, but by then I had already committed strongly all the corps of General Vandamme. I had great difficulty in passing the Dyle.

However, I managed to make the crossing at Limale, but it was now night and I could not make much progress, especially since the passage of Wavre and that of Bièrges had not succeeded. In attempting the latter, General Gérard was shot in the chest and it is hoped, however, that he will not perish.

Not hearing the guns this morning, and believing Blücher and Bülow before me, I felt compelled to attack, they would have avoided punishment by retreating on all points.

NOTES:
[1] 'The Journal of Henri Niemann of the Sixth Prussian Black Hussars' in *The English Historical Review*, Volume 3, July 1888, pp. 539-45.
[2] Booth, *The Battle of Waterloo*, 1816, p. 321.
[3] Delbare, *Relation circonstanciée*, pp. 69-72.
[4] SHDDT: GR 21 YC 197.
[5] SHDDT: C15 5. Dossier 18 June 1815. Handwritten statement from Blocqueville to Grouchy, no date.
[6] Grouchy, *Relation succincte de la campagne de 1815*, Vol. 4, pp. 146-51.
[7] Grouchy, *Observations sur la relation de la campagne de 1815*, pp. 18-19.
[8] Grouchy, *Observations sur la relation de la campagne de 1815*, pp. 18-19.
[9] Grouchy, *Observations sur la relation de la campagne de 1815*, pp. 18-19.
[10] Grouchy, *Observations sur la relation de la campagne de 1815*, pp. 15-16.
[11] SHDDT: C15 5. Dossier 18 June 1815 Grouchy to Pajol. Copy of the original order made in

June 1865 by Comte du Casse.

12 Bassford, Moran, Pedlow, *The Campaign of 1815 Chapters 40-49*, On Waterloo, available at http://www.clausewitz.com/readings/1815/five40-49.htm.

13 Berton, p. 64.

14 Berton, pp. 66-7.

15 Fleury.

16 Donnersmarck, p. 642.

17 Gérard, *Dernières observations*, pp. 51-2.

18 Grouchy, *Observations sur la relation de la campagne de 1815*, pp. 18-19.

19 Grouchy, *Relation succincte de la campagne de 1815*, p. 55.

20 Grouchy, *Relation succincte de la campagne de 1815*, Vol. 4, p. 145.

21 *Carnet de la Sabretache*, 1912.

22 Lettow-Vorbeck, pp. 455-6.

23 Bornstedt, pp. 106-8.

24 Colonel Jean Dominique Paolini was born on 25 October 1762 on Corsica, and had entered the 2nd Battalion of the Royal Corsican Regiment on 1 March 1782. Promotion to sergeant came on 1 October 1790 and to sub-lieutenant on 21 October 1791 while serving with the 4th Battalion of Light Infantry, which was formed from the Corsican Light Infantry Regiment. He was promoted to captain on 6 October 1795, served as aide-de-camp to General Rey and from 23 September 1802 he was aide-de-camp to General Gouvion Saint-Cyr. For this service, he was promoted to battalion commander on 4 January 1805. From 19 April 1806 he was attached to the 52nd Regiment of Line Infantry and listed as major of the 60th Regiment of Line Infantry on 27 July 1809. He was promoted to colonel of the 44th Regiment of Line Infantry on 28 January 1813, retaining his position under the Bourbons in 1814 and was retained by Napoléon in 1815.

25 Lécrivain, *Histoire des généraux, officiers de tous grades et de toute arme, sous-officiers et soldats qui se sont distingués dans les différentes campagnes des armées française*, 1817.

26 Bornstedt, pp. 106-8.

27 Max Gottschalck, *Geschichte des 1. Thüringischen Infanterie-Regiments Nr. 31*, E. S. Mittler und Sohn, 1894, p. 95.

28 AN: LH 1498/10.

29 AN: LH 1783/8.

30 AN: LH 2013/2.

31 AN: LH 256/15.

32 AN: LH 2276/52.

33 SHDDT: GR 21 YC 278. See also: SHDDT: GR 21 YC 279.

34 SHDDT: GR 21 YC 725. See also: SHDDT: GR 21 YC 726.

35 SHDDT: GR 21 YC 534. See also: SHDDT: GR 21 YC 535.

36 SHDDT: GR 21 YC 500.

37 SHDDT: GR 21 YC 614.

38 SHDDT: GR 21 YC 416.

39 SHDDT: GR 21 YC 580.

40 SHDDT: GR 22 YC 81.

41 SHDDT: GR 21 YC 798.

42 SHDDT: GR 21 YC 381. See also: SHDDT: GR 21 YC 382.

43 SHDDT: GR 21 YC 424.

44 Grouchy, *Observations sur la relation de la campagne de 1815*, pp. 15-16.

45 This order exists in three forms:
SHDDT: C15 *Registre d'Ordres et de correspondance du major-general a partir du 13 Juin jusqu'au 26 Juin au Maréchal Grouchy*, p. 27.
SHDDT: C15 23 C15 23 *Registre d'Ordres et de correspondance du major-général à 3e Corps d'Armée*, p. 32. This is a transcript by Vandamme noting he received the order.

SHDDT: C15 5. Dossier 18 June 1815. Grouchy to Vandamme. This is the original order sent from Grouchy to Vandamme.

46 SHDDT: C15 23 p. 32.

47 Grouchy, *Mémoires du maréchal de Grouchy*, 1874, Vol. 4, p. 291.

Chapter 14

19 June 1815

On the morning of the 19th Grouchy, who was still ignorant of Napoléon's defeat, prepared an attack on his part. About the operations planned for the day, Grouchy writes:[1]

> I spent most of the night to get everything ready for an attack at daybreak, and yet I had few troops and resources united. When the dawn appeared, the enemy saved me the trouble of marching to them, and advanced against me. They were pushed back and as the number of my troops available to me was increasing, I ordered Teste's division to take the village of Bièrges. This attack forced the Prussians to evacuate, as well as the part of Wavre that they occupied. General Vandamme then passed the Dyle without obstacles and the enemy was pursued to Rosierne in the direction of Brussels, as I was convinced that Napoléon, victorious yesterday, was already master of this city.

Grouchy's troops vastly exceeded Thielemann's thin forces, and included Gérard's corps (three divisions), Teste's division and Pajol's cavalry. Vandamme, it seems, had not obeyed Grouchy's orders of the previous night to march with his corps to Limale and was still at Wavre.

Grouchy now formed three divisions—Teste's, Vichery's and Pecheux's—in first line, divided into three columns of attack. Teste's division formed the right column and was to attack Bièrges and the mill; Vichery's division in the centre to attack the Prussian centre; and Pecheux's division against Stülpnagel's right flank. Lefol's division had also crossed the river. Each column was provided with a battery of artillery, escorted and preceded by skirmishers. The remaining division—Hulot's—was in reserve behind the centre column. Pajol's cavalry was to turn the Prussian right flank, which rested on the

Rixensart Wood. Twenty-eight French battalions were arrayed against ten Prussian battalions.

Thielemann perceived the coming attack, and reinforced his line with one battalion, which he posted on his left, which were all the troops he could spare. The French columns now hopelessly out-numbered the Prussians, and the 12th Division gave way. In consequence of this, Grouchy's men now occupied the Rixensart Wood. Stülpnagel was forced to fall back on his reserves, namely the three battalions of the 11th Division and two attached artillery batteries, and took up a new position behind the wood.

At Bièrges, Teste's attack on the mill was slowly taking its toll on the two Prussian battalions there, and four battalions of the 10th Division were brought up in support. On the Prussian extreme right, the cavalry brigades of Marwitz and Lottum—in all twelve squadrons—occupied Chambre and secured the flank.

Grouchy was pushing the Prussians back on all points. Success was short lived however.

At 08.00, definite news arrived of the French rout at Waterloo and the Prussian's flagging morale was no doubt raised, and they redoubled their efforts and recaptured the Rixensart Wood. Stülpnagel's counter-attack was, however, short-lived. Due to the lack of reinforcements when Grouchy renewed the attack, the Prussians were again driven out of the wood.

Commanding the skirmish company of the Prussian 31st Infantry Regiment deployed at Limale was Second Lieutenant Mannkopff. He writes about the operations on the early morning of 19 June:[2]

> We were up at daybreak of 19 June having rested a few hours under arms. With the start of the day the skirts of the forest occupied by the enemy clashed with our skirmishers, while the battalion in column remained in reserve behind us to make a stand. No sooner had we taken up our positions [when] the French voltigeurs attacked. They were very skilled and knew to use the high corn to sneak up close and unseen on our skirmishers with a very superior firepower. As it might have been of importance for us to maintain this forest, so our fire line on the skirts of the forest was gradually reinforced by the greater part of our battalions and so we maintained our position, and the forest, for several hours.
>
> Suddenly we found ourselves attacked violently in the left flank and rear by the enemy. They had captured a village [Limale], which formed an extension of our left flank and was occupied by a landwehr battalion from our brigade, thus taking the key point to our

defence, and passing round the left flank. After a determined and confused battle in the forest which cost us a lot of people, we had to yield to superior numbers. The signal was given for a general retreat, which was all the more welcome as we had fired most of our ammunition. I even had to leave my skirmishers during the battle in the forest to go to the same landwehr battalion that stood behind us to get a small quantity of cartridges, because most of my men had fired all that they had.

The French, after they had come into possession of the forest, halted and did not pursue us beyond the forest, so that the debris of the three battalions of the regiment were able to rally beyond the forest without being disturbed by musket fire. We formed only a single battalion column. The remainder of the troops, who had taken part in the combat at Wavre, were already falling back in the direction of Louvain, so we too joined the withdrawal in this direction. The enemy did not pursue, but merely lobbed some shells at us.

Captain Deville, of the 111th Regiment of Line Infantry (part of 4th Corps at Limale), writing to damn Grouchy for his slowness and laziness, and in direct contradiction to French and Prussian eyewitnesses, suggests that:[3]

Around noon, we were still at camp when an orderly from the general staff ordered us to clean our pantalons and muskets. This order was executed, but barely had we got our pantalons wet and our muskets dismantled, then the enemy, who had manoeuvred before us throughout the morning, attacked us.

The inference here is that Grouchy cared more for the appearance of his soldiers than addressing the enemy. The historical record, as we shall see below, tells us that by midday Grouchy was already making plans to retreat and that the Prussians had attacked in the early hours of the 19th, and not at midday. Most French narrators were writing to pass the blame for the defeat of Waterloo to others, and here Deville endeavours to show that the 111th Regiment of Line Infantry did their duty, but were failed by Grouchy. A more truthful narration of 19 June follows.

Teste's operations
General Teste, commanding the 21st Infantry Division (part of 6th Corps), writes about his activities on 19 June as follows:[4]

19 June, at three in the morning the enemy attacked. The fire from his sharpshooters was well supported. He showed forth three pieces of cannon in battery that threatened our infantry squares, which retreated only a few paces backwards. The artillery of the division began to fire and made that of the enemy force to change their position several times and dismounted two of their guns.

The enemy deployed to our right. M. the marshal began to use our forces to repel him, and he pursued the enemy into the ravine; many sharpshooters were detached from the 1st Brigade of the division, which soon chased them away and soon seized the first houses of Bièrges which stands on a very steep escarpment and is cut up by several sunken roads.

As a result, due to this advantage, our skirmishers took possession of the church, which dominates the village, and carried on to attack the mill. Here, they were ordered to halt. Marshal Grouchy was waiting for the corps of Vandamme to debouch on our right. This is the moment when the General Penne, urging his horse to follow the movements of our brave voltigeurs, has his head blown off by a cannonball. This general officer, full of bravery and merit, was generally regretted. Captain Le Roux, his aide, became mine for the rest of the campaign. The masses of the 3rd Corps soon debouched on the left of Bièrges, our skirmishers, supported by the 1st Brigade, continued their success against the troops of General Thielemann, who retired with great confusion.

Clearly, Teste's men had taken the village, and then doubled back onto the mill from the north, thus encircling the position. Teste's losses that day were as follows:

Regiment	Killed		Wounded		Missing		Total
	Officers	Men	Officers	Men	Officers	Men	
8th Light Infantry[5]	2	Not known	4	58	0	Not known	64
65th Line Infantry[6]	0	2	0	74	0	1	77
75th Line Infantry[7]	0	8	0	55	0	1	64
Total	2	10	4	187	0	2	205

The losses may include men lost on 18 June; indeed two men are listed as deserted on the 18th during the march to Wavre. It seems that the 65th Regiment of Line Infantry bore the brunt of the fighting in the action. The division had a twenty mile march ahead of it on the morning 18 June, but it does not seem to have impacted greatly on the effectiveness of the battle.

12th Division's operations

The troops of General Pecheaux stood to the north of Limale, facing towards Bièrges. In the early hours, the outposts were attacked by the Prussians. François, of the 30th Regiment of Line Infantry, also recounts the same early morning attack:[8]

> 19 June. We, of the 30th at the outposts, were attacked at three in the morning by the troops of the Prussian General Thielemann.
>
> General Pecheux sent us forward, and we surprised a Prussian avantguarde of about three hundred men, some of whom we bayoneted, and the rest we took prisoners.

Here, too, were parts of General Berthezène's 11th Infantry Division from 3rd Corps. Captain Jean Marie Putigny, of 2nd Battalion 33rd Regiment of Line Infantry (part of 3rd Corps) narrates:[9]

> At dawn at the bridge of Limale, we entirely pushed back their positions and with the sword in their backs, we drove them on the road to Brussels.

Lefol's division, which had attacked at Bièrges, had also crossed the Dyle. Charles Philippe Lefol, aide-de-camp to his uncle, General Lefol, during the Hundred Days writes:[10]

> The fighting had been going on since four o'clock in the afternoon and continued with equal violence from both sides until well into the night, the enemy General Thielemann put up a strong resistance, but was defeated, but not until we had lost many men.
>
> On the 19th, after taking some rest, we were again attacked vigorously at three o'clock in the morning, and our troops fought so bravely so that we were still masters of the ground, but without the success we might have benefited from with the junction of our army corps with the army commanded by Napoléon.

Clearly, it seems from the previous accounts that the attack at Limale was a success. Captain Marie Joseph August Bella, aide-de-camp to Marshal Grouchy, notes that the attack by Teste and Pajol was successful:[11]

> As you expected, the Prussians came to attack you at daybreak. But the necessary arrangements for good reception were taken, so that their attack, as you planned, was rejected back to the other side of the Dyle, and we became masters of all the artillery that passed to the left

bank of the river, many of the enemy troops were killed, and leaving them no time to rally, you pursued them to Rosierne village, on the road from Wavre to Brussels, the Prussian corps, which had until then been at Wavre and defended Bièrges, outflanked by your movements hastened to retreat, heading also to Brussels.

At 09.00, Bièrges and the troublesome mill had fallen into the hands of Teste, who had had a very hard task to drive out the two Prussian battalions defending the place. The capture of this point was a serious blow to the Prussians, as Grouchy's forces had now broken through Thielemann's defensive line in two places: the centre having been broken and the right was now seriously threatened by overwhelming numbers. Thielemann had no other option other than to withdraw. Grouchy's objective for the previous evening had been gained, but over twelve hours later than planned. The way was now open at long last to march to Napoléon at Waterloo. Carl von Clausewitz notes about the action at Limale and Limalette:[12]

> The resistance in this second position lasted the longest, and it was here that General Thielemann learned that the battle [Waterloo] had been won and that the Prussian 2nd Corps had been ordered to take his opponent in the rear by advancing via Galbaix and La Hutte.
>
> These places were so far from the field of battle that General Thielemann could expect no assistance, so he could only hope that his opponent had also heard of the outcome of the great battle and would quickly begin to retreat out of fear of being cut off. General Thielemann, therefore, had his troops shout loud hurrahs and show signs of rejoicing. But this hope was in vain. The enemy continued to press forward, and General Thielemann was forced to retire further, and finally to begin a general retreat in which he also ordered Colonel Zeppelin to withdraw from Wavre.
>
> General Thielemann withdrew in the direction of Louvain as far as Saint-Achtenrode, three hours march from the battlefield, and lost only a few thousand killed and wounded. The 3rd Corps 9th Brigade had continued its march towards Saint-Lambert, spent the night of the 18th in the woods there, marched back towards the cannon fire of Wavre early on the 19th, and finally reunited with the rest of the 3rd Corps at Gembloux on the 20th after passing through Limale.

Operations at Wavre

Vandamme, as ordered by Grouchy, had sent what troops he could spare south to cross the Dyle at Limale and join with Grouchy. General

Vandamme, with Habert's 10th Infantry Division, had remained encamped above Wavre on the night of 18 to 19 June 1815. Captain Göhren, of the Kurmärk Landwehr, writes about the defence of the bridge at Wavre:[13]

> Where we were to make every effort to hold this position…We had to give up the position when the skirmishers and the fusilier battalion of the 30th Regiment, which covered our flanks, had to retreat. I feared that the enemy would pursue our troops and cause a rout. I went with Lieutenant Nachtigal and 150 men and again returned to the bridge where the enemy was, but were unable to recover it. The whole place had suffered terrible devastation.

As soon as Zeppelin withdrew from Wavre, Vandamme pushed his men across the Dyle, both at Bièrges and Wavre, and advanced up the Brussels road running north out of Wavre. Two battalions of the 4th Kurmärk Landwehr Regiment fell back to La Bavette. Upon reaching a small wood to the east of La Bavette, the Prussians re-formed and opened fire against the squadron of pursuing French cavalry. It was now the turn of Marwitz's cavalry to advance, and pushed the French cavalry back towards Wavre. Vandamme's infantry was moving up both the Brussels road (having forded the Dyle to the north-east) and moved men up from Bièrges, and by sheer weight of numbers forced the Prussian infantry to retreat towards Louvain, through the villages of St Achtenrode and Ottenberg; but behind Saint-Achtenrode, Thielemann halted and took up a defensive position.[14]

Operations at Neuf Cabaret

To the north of Limale stood Neuf Cabaret, where General Borcke's brigade of Prussians was stationed; they had taken no part in the fighting on the 18th. He notes that he witnesses the French cross the River Dyle on the 19th at some point after daybreak, and observed a strong column of French cavalry heading towards Genappe. Against the French he deployed his artillery, which resulted in the French retreating back to Limale, crossing the river. However, his aide-de-camp contradicts this account, saying Borcke's men confronted the French at Neuf Cabaret, that the cavalry took little notice of the artillery, that the French moved off to Chambre, and that it was only at 17.00 that the French abandoned Limale. The truth was no doubt part-way between the two accounts. This body of cavalry could have been one of four formations, but likely to have either been Maurin, from 4th Corps, or Pajol.[15] On balance, the troops were likely to be the latter. About the movements of the cavalry reserve, Biot, aide-de-camp to General Pajol (commanding the 1st Reserve Cavalry Corps), relates that:[16]

> The following day, 19 June, as dawn broke, the bivouacs of the 1st Hussars were rained upon by a hail of bullets. It was the Prussian corps of Tauentzin, forming the rearguard of Blücher, who had been left there to defend the bridges and Limale and Wavre; we appeared to be cut off by them and we sought to join the main body. At first shot, I went directly to the attacked party, and returned to warn General Pajol of what had happened: he went himself to the scene. Our troops were already formed, but not across the river.
>
> There was a danger that they would strongly advance down the defile and fall onto the divisions of Gérard and stop their line of retreat. General Pajol instructed me to express thoughts to the marshal, and I asked him to pass immediately, in front, the 4th Corps, which was done. We also recalled the 3rd Corps, which had forced the bridge of Wavre. The latter came to pass the River Dyle at Limale. When the reinforcements arrived where we were, the enemy decided to retire, but then abandoning his first line at the defiles of Saint-Lambert, we began marching towards the woods of Rixensart, leading to Rosierne. In this clash, we had the misfortune to lose General Penne, of Teste's division, carried away by a cannonball. This general officer had received a shot in the leg at the Battle of Ligny. I was ordered to accompany General Ameil, charged with 4th and 5th Hussars, to pursue the enemy and to accelerate his retirement, by passing through the Rixensart Wood.

General Berton narrates the day as follows:[17]

> 19th, at three o'clock in the morning, General Thielemann wanted to restore communication with Brussels, attacked the French troops at Rosierne and Bièrges; the small force he used was easily repulsed, Vandamme then proceeded to advance one of his divisions by the mill of Bièrges, the enemy had to stand and defend his right. It was the same day, on the heights of the village of Bièrges, that General Penne, who commanded a brigade of Teste's division, found a glorious death: it was regretted by all the braves. The corps of dragoons had also crossed in front of Limale.

At Wavre around 10.00, General Thielemann ordered the retreat. Thielemann knew that Grouchy must himself either attack or retreat sooner or later, but to hold on to Wavre too long would mean his own destruction. By retreating, he would gain time, and when the opportunity occurred he would again advance, and possibly convert Grouchy's retirement into a rout. Under the protection of Marwitz's cavalry, which comprised the 7th and 8th Uhlans and the 3rd and 6th Landwehr Cavalry with three batteries of horse artillery, the infantry retired, and Zeppelin evacuated Wavre.

Hollow victory

By now, on Grouchy's left, the Prussians had defeated the emperor, the bulk of the Armée du Nord was heading south in a panic-ridden mob. Soult and Napoléon arrived at Philippeville in the morning of 19 June. One of the first acts Napoléon did was to write to Marshal Davout, the Minister of War in Paris, from Philippeville as follows:[18]

> Monsieur the marshal, I have the honour to write to you for the first time since I wrote to you on the field of battle of Waterloo at half-past two o'clock when the battle was begun and we had experienced great success, however at seven o'clock a false movement was carried out with the orders of the emperor, all was changed, the combat continued until night fell and a retreat was effected, but it was in disorder.
>
> The emperor rallied the army at Philippeville and Avesnes and began to organise the corps and to tend to their needs. You can well imagine that the disaster is immense.
>
> I have written to the commandants of the 2nd and 16th Military Divisions so that the enemy may not profit from any advantage over them.

Marshal Soult sent the following dispatch to Grouchy, dated Philippeville 19 June:[19]

> Dear Comte,
> There has been fought a great battle at Waterloo in the front of the Soignes Forest, the army was not favoured and the army is retiring to France.

History tells us that the fighting capacity of the remnants of the Armée du Nord with Marshal Soult was nil in the immediate aftermath of the battle. The men only regained something of their former vigour and enthusiasm as they got closer to the walls of Paris. Marshal Soult was in command of a spent military force that could no longer defend itself. All that was left was Grouchy's forces.

At about 11.00 on 19 June, Grouchy received word of the emperor's defeat. He writes as follows about this event:[20]

> About eleven o'clock, an officer sent by the major-general announced the disaster of Waterloo. His report was only verbal; he was carrying no orders or instructions that indicated the points on which Napoléon withdrew, nor where I should direct myself. However, the details he gave were so detailed that it cast no doubt on the inevitability of events of the day: my first thought was to march on the rear of the enemy, but with too few troops for such a movement in which I would have been followed by the Prussian troops I had in front of me, I decided to retire on the Sambre and the Meuse, where based on that information I would judge my movement to be the most useful in difficult circumstances. I effected my retreat in two columns, in the directions of Temploux and Namur, with my light cavalry at Marc-Saint-Denis, and my dragoons on the last of these towns.

Aide-de-Camp de Blocqueville writes:[21]

> The 19th, at ten o'clock in the morning, the marshal, having learned of the disasters of Waterloo, informed his generals, and that this fatal event forced him to retreat.

The officer who carried the dispatch was Pierre Jean Baptiste Aube Demonceaux.[22] The news of Napoléon's defeat at Waterloo must have come as a shock for everyone, but for Grouchy most of all.

About 12.00, Soult's second messenger brought orders for Grouchy to retreat towards Laon:[23]

> Marshal,
> I give you the state of the location of the various army corps which formed the column commanded by the emperor in person.
> The army corps under your orders is not listed. His Majesty wishes, but does not give you a destination, that you are to arrive at either Philippeville or Givet. I am instructed to inform you that as soon as you arrive at one or the other of these places you will operate in the direction of Laon to join the army and inform me immediately so that I can send commands: the headquarters are moving to Laon.
> Marshal of the empire, Major-General Duc de Dalmatie.

A third order was sent by Soult to Grouchy:[24]

Philippeville 19 June 1815

Marshal Duc de Dalmatie, the major-general to Marshal Grouchy.

The army is withdrawing on numerous places, this evening we will be crossing the Sambre, you are to execute a movement, despite the bad weather, so that you will move via Philippeville to Givet, where we shall be reunited.

In the name of the emperor

Duc de Dalmatie.

The order outlined that General Reille was commanding 1st, 2nd and 6th Corps and was heading to Laon, the artillery was to move to La Fere, the engineers to Laon, the 1st Cavalry Division to Marie, the 2nd Cavalry Division to Saint-Quentin, the 3rd Cavalry Division to Rhefel and the 5th Cavalry Division to Hervins. The Imperial Guard was to march to Soissons.[25]

About this movement to retreat, Fantin des Odoards, of the 22nd Regiment of Line Infantry, writes:[26]

About eleven o'clock, our commander-in-chief finally learned the fatal news by a staff officer who had miraculously escaped the enemy.

The retreat from Wavre

General Excelmans was ordered by Grouchy to march to Namur and occupy the vital bridges over the Sambre as quickly as possible. He set off just after midday. Pajol's cavalry and Teste's infantry division were to act as the rearguard to give time for 3rd and 4th Corps to break off action and head south. General Vichery, who had been placed in command of 4th Corps, was ordered by Grouchy:[27]

At Nil-Perreux 19 June 1815

Marshal Grouchy to General [Baron de] Vichery, commandant of the 4th Corps of the army

My dear general,

The disorder is great at this point in the march, making it necessary that you take your position with the rearguard for some time at La Baraque, to let pass your artillery park and other vehicles. I first wanted you at the front, but I prefer you now to follow the column, to try to overcome the disadvantages of the march.

General Vandamme will keep Wavre until ten o'clock at night, so it is necessary that you take the position of La Baraque (by carefully monitoring the defile at Limale) long enough so that the enemy cannot stand between you and him.

Put in your centre your artillery divisions and they are to be kept close and at a distance, so that the 4th Corps can give a new proof of the good spirit that animates it, deploying a lot of energy in these difficult circumstances.

My intention is that we push without stopping until Temploux and Gembloux have been passed: you will only make stops from time to time.

I ordered one of your divisions to move to Baraque so it can support the cavalry, and is head of the column.

Be reassured, general, of my high consideration of yourself

Signe. Grouchy.

An officer from either 3rd or 4th Corps writes in 1816 or 1817 a letter that was published in London in 1817 by John Booth:[28]

It was about eleven o'clock in the morning of the 19th that the marshal learnt that Napoléon had been beaten. The attack which he intended to make on the road from Brussels to Louvain was therefore given up and the army passed the Dyle at four points: Wavre, Limale, Limilette, and Oittigny. General Excelmans, with his corps, pushed on to Namur where he arrived in the evening, and where the marshal arrived the next day. The Allies attacked the rearguard, commanded by Vandamme; the conflict was very obstinate, but the Allies suffered so much that the retreat of the French was afterwards unmolested.

Grouchy began his retreat. His troops had reached the line La-Bavette-Rosierne in their pursuit of Thielemann, and now Excelmans's cavalry was sent off with orders to make all speed to Namur and secure the bridges over the Sambre at that place. Excelmans reached Namur at around 16.30, a little more than five hours to cover thirty miles by devious lanes and byways in a terrible condition after the rains. General Bonnemains's report notes:[29]

The 19th at nine o'clock in the morning, Marshal Grouchy, being master of the defiles, made the corps of Excelmans, with the brigade of General Bonnemains forming the head of column, to debouch and to charge the enemy. It was at this moment when the commander-in-chief received the sad news of the loss of the Battle of Waterloo. He ordered the movement to be stopped and ordered General Bonnemains to move with the 4th and 12th regiments of Dragoons and two batteries of light artillery to Namur and leave no stone unturned to get there and hold the place before the enemy could.

Passing near Gembloux, General Bonnemains learned that beyond the city a column of enemy cavalry had appeared, headed to Genappe onto Namur.

It was here that General Bonnemains deployed his ten squadrons. General Bonnemains, after a reconnaissance, with some men hastened to gain Namur where he was welcomed by all the people and authorities of this city. He asked them to prepare for our wounded and provide emergency supplies for the army. General Bonnemains, having been relieved in the evening by the other brigades from the corps of Excelmans, marched for the same purpose on to Dinan [sic]…and was happy to get there before the enemy did, which was that night about a league off in the direction of Charleroi on the 20th.

Gérard's corps, preceded by the 7th Cavalry Division (six squadrons under Vallin, who had taken Maurin's place), re-crossed the Dyle by the bridge at Limale, and moved by a narrow lane to the main Namur-Brussels road. Vandamme's corps withdrew from La Bavette and marched through Wavre, Dion-le-Mont, Chaumont, Tourinnes, Sart-a-Walhain, Grand Leez, Saint-Denis and then to Temploux on the Namur-Nivelles road, where it arrived at 23.00. Gérard's corps had reached Temploux an hour earlier.

Pajol, in command of the rearguard, which was composed of the 4th Cavalry Division—twelve squadrons under Baron Soult—and Teste's infantry division operated against Thielemann to keep him occupied until Wavre had been cleared, and then retreated by Corbaix, Sart-a-Walhain, Sauvenière to Gembloux, where he bivouacked for the night.

This retreat was largely unhindered by General Thielemann's Prussians, many of whom had been routed after Grouchy's action at Wavre. But General Pirch's 2nd Corps was on its way to cut of Grouchy's line of retreat. He arrived at Mellery at about 11.00, but his troops were so exhausted that he had to let them rest. Namur was not gained until the early hours of 20 June.

NOTES:

[1] Grouchy, *Observations sur la relation de la campagne de 1815*, pp. 20-2.

[2] Bornstedt, pp. 106-8.

[3] George Deville, 'Grouchy a Waterloo' in *Revolution Français*, No. 53, 1907, pp. 281-4.

[4] *Carnet de la Sabretache*, 1912.

[5] Lieutenant Pitot, *8e Demi-Brigade Legere 2e Formation 1796-1803 8e Regiment d'Infanterie Legere 1803-1815*, Ancestramil, 2012, available at http://www.ancestramil.fr/uploads/01_doc/terre/infanterie/1789-1815/8_ri_legere_historique_1803-1815.pdf.

[6] SHDDT: GR 21 YC 550 *61e régiment d'infanterie de ligne (ex 65e régiment d'infanterie de ligne)*,

1 Août 1814-22 Mars 1815 (matricule 1 à 1,800).

[7] SHDDT: GR 21 YC 607 *67e régiment d'infanterie de ligne (ex 75e régiment d'infanterie de ligne), 1 Septembre 1814-2 Janvier 1815 (matricules 1 à 1,800).* See also: SHDDT: GR 21 YC 608 *67e régiment d'infanterie de ligne (ex 75e régiment d'infanterie de ligne), 2 Janvier 1815-5 Août 1815 (matricules 1,801 à 2,187).*

[8] François.

[9] Miot-Putigny, p. 245.

[10] Lefol, pp. 59-60.

[11] Grouchy, *Relation succincte de la campagne de 1815*, p. 55.

[12] Bassford, Moran, Pedlow, *The Campaign of 1815 Chapters 40-49*, On Waterloo, available at http://www.clausewitz.com/readings/1815/five40-49.htm.

[13] Bornstedt, pp. 40-4.

[14] Bassford, Moran, Pedlow, *The Campaign of 1815 Chapters 40-49*, On Waterloo, available at http://www.clausewitz.com/readings/1815/five40-49.htm.

[15] Lettow-Vorbeck, pp. 460-1.

[16] Fleury.

[17] Berton, p. 67.

[18] SHDDT: C15 5. Dossier 19 June 1815. Soult to Davout. This is the original order sent to Davout, Minister of War. See also: AN: AFIV 1939, pp. 54-5.

[19] SHDDT: C15 23, p. 333.

[20] Grouchy, *Observations sur la relation de la campagne de 1815*, pp. 20-2.

[21] Grouchy, *Relation succincte de la campagne de 1815*, Vol. 4, pp. 146-51.

[22] AN: LH 62/73.

[23] This order exists in a number of original transcripts:
SHDDT: C15 5. Dossier 19 June 1815. Soult to Grouchy. This is the original order in Soult's handwriting.
AN: AFIV 1939, p. 52.
SHDDT: C15 *Registre d'Ordres et de correspondance du major-general a partir du 13 Juin jusqu'au 26 Juin au Maréchal Grouchy*, p. 30. This is Grouchy's receipt of the order.
SHDDT: C15 23 p. 32. This is a transcript by Vandamme noting he received the order.

[24] SHDDT: C15 5. Dossier 19 June 1815. Soult to Grouchy. Copy of the original order made by Comte du Casse in June 1865.

[25] SHDDT: C15 *Registre d'Ordres et de correspondance du major-general a partir du 13 Juin jusqu'au 26 Juin au Maréchal Grouchy*, p. 27. See also: SHDDT: C15 23, p. 32.

[26] Fantin des Odoards, p. 446.

[27] SHDDT: C15 *Registre d'Ordres et de correspondance du major-general a partir du 13 Juin jusqu'au 26 Juin au Maréchal Grouchy*, p. 32. See also: SHDDT: C15 5. Dossier 19 June 1815. Grouchy to Vichery. Copy of the original order made in June 1865 by Comte du Casse.

[28] Booth, *The Battle of Waterloo, also of Ligny, and Quarter-Bras*, London, 1817, p. 251.

[29] Grouchy, *Mémoires du maréchal de Grouchy*, 1874, Vol. 4, pp. 60-1.

Chapter 15

Grouchy's Action at Namur

At daybreak on 20 June, Grouchy's rearguard left Gembloux and marched on Namur via Saint-Denis and La Fallise; his infantry left Temploux about 9.00. A short distance beyond Temploux, the column was attacked by Prussian cavalry which had been sent off in pursuit by Thielemann at daybreak that morning. At the same time, more cavalry was seen coming against the rear, along the Nivelles-Namur road.

On arriving near the village of La Fallise, about three miles from Namur, the Prussians found Vandamme's rearguard posted on the brow of the hill, below which lay the town in the valley of the Meuse. About this, Charles Philippe Lefol, aide-de-camp to General Lefol, writes:[1]

> About three-quarters of a league from Namur, close to a village called Fallise, the general, suspecting that we would be charged by a strong column of cavalry which followed us closely, immediately made the regiments form square in the midst of which we took refuge, but the square was barely formed when the cavalry attacked with great advantage. If it had not been for the small wood close at hand, into which our disordered troops ran for safety, although we were slashed by sabres severely, the Prussians would have had far more success.
>
> By rallying the other side of the wood, we realised we had abandoned two cannons in our flight, and we were left stuck in the middle of a thicket. The general immediately ordered that we should recover them, and I was appointed to accompany the men called to this expedition. After strenuous efforts, despite the Prussian cavalry firing their pistols at us, we were able to return these two pieces to the cries of joy from our brave soldiers.
>
> We always fought, and the resistance was obstinate, we were pursued at the point of the bayonet to Namur, where the engagement

was very fierce, and where we lost a lot of people. Forced to defend ourselves we were pushed into the suburbs with great vigour until we reached the gate of the city, this was more a flight than a retreat. They had surrounded the gate with huge chunks of wood lined with straw and coated with pitch, which was set on fire at the arrival of the Prussians.

About the retreat, as he remembered it, General Berton writes:[2]

Seven regiments of dragoons from Excelmans's corps, with the wounded and the reserve artillery, marched quickly to capture the bridge at Namur, over the River Sambre, and entered the city the same day at four o'clock. The infantry had remained in position in front of Wavre until midnight, supported and enlightened, on his right by the cavalry corps of General Pajol, on his left by the division under General Vallin; the 20th Regiment of Dragoons, from the corps of Excelmans, marched with the central columns.

The infantry reached Namur on the 20th in the morning, after having fought several bloody battles with the very Prussians who were following them with ardour, and against which the 20th Dragoons, commanded by Colonel Bricqueville, had made some fine charges, captured two guns which had been abandoned and had been for some time in enemy hands, and also took a howitzer.

Teste's division remained in charge of defending the city, which they did, without cannon, until six in the evening, against the 3rd Prussian Corps, which lost in vain nearly three thousand men. Teste did not leave until everyone in Namur had been evacuated and that the heights of Bouvigne and Dinant had been occupied by our troops.

The local population of Namur was not immune from the fighting that was taking place. One resident writes:[3]

For two days we have been here in a precarious situation, which is hard to describe. After the battle, which had been lost by the French, the army corps which had directed itself towards Wavre saw itself cut off and forced to lay down its arms, or to cut itself a path, which latter it chose to do. On the 19th in the afternoon, the French 12th Dragoons Regiment arrived in front of our gates and asked to pass through to Givet; due to the civilians lacking any troops, they were obliged to receive it; this regiment was followed by a great number of dispersed soldiers and, above all, wounded. On the 20th, the entire army corps successively arrived; among the generals in command one noticed: Marshal Grouchy, Vandamme, Excelmans, Bonnet, Vincent and some others; all these troops were made up of old soldiers. Towards one o'clock they began to defile across the Sambre bridge, during which a very lively cannonade and musketry fire took place at the Brussels gate. The enemy placed several guns on the ramparts and positioned three battalions to cover the retreat; there the enemy defended himself until the evening. Towards eight o'clock the Pomeranians forced a breakthrough and attacked the French within our walls; from the Brussels Gate up to the Sambre bridge one fought ferociously in the streets, which were covered with dead and wounded. One is bound by justice to mention that General Vandamme on this occasion spared our city. But the following event needs to be made public: during the heat of the battle, the Prussians urged General Pirck [sic] to attack the town and take it by force, but the brave general replied he loved the inhabitants too much to befall this terrible disaster upon them. His Pomeranians, who had been in garrison there, cheered for the generous decision of their general. It is thus that one receives the reward if one treats brave soldiers with esteem. The French took all the letters and the newspapers from the post with them, before leaving us.

As General Berton notes, on the march from Wavre to Namur the 22nd Regiment of Line Infantry and other elements of 3rd Corps had not arrived until the very early hours of 20 June. Namur was not gained without a fight, as Colonel Fantin des Odoards writes:[4]

> Already we could see the heights of Namur, which would offer us a good stronghold, when suddenly two cannon shots were heard in our rear. This sound pleases the soldier when he goes to the enemy and it brightens every face, but in retreat, and in the state of mind that we had since the loss of Waterloo, which was no longer a mystery to our subordinates, we would have taken some pains to hide them, it produced an effect exactly opposite: 'there they are!' anxiously said the same men who three days before had faced the Prussians with ardour. The rearguard, after two shots had been fired against them, was charged impetuosity and was at first thrown into disorder and the two cannon they had were captured. Luckily the panic did not spread and was soon repaired. Part of our column arrived, who moved to Namur at the run, and the troops who are at the rear are about-faced; a brilliant charge of our cavalry on the Prussian advance guard tumbled it back and not only captured the canon that we had

lost, but also took one of their howitzers. The beginning was a good omen. Surprised by an unexpected resistance, the Prussians stopped to reinforce those who followed them, and we used their hesitation to take strong positions in Namur and to place the artillery wherever it could be used, we barricaded the bridges, the gates and then did everything to stop the enemy.

Captain Jean Marie Putigny, of 2nd Battalion 33rd Regiment of Line Infantry (part of 3rd Corps), narrates:[5]

Our corps moved to a position in front of Namur to protect the retreat of Comte Gérard, who passed through our lines and entered into the town. We followed progressively after we had sustained an attack from the enemy. My battalion was at the extremity of the rearguard, placed on a road that passed through the orchards and gardens of the suburbs. The English [*sic* Prussians] charged with great obstinacy.

The battalion commander was killed, the captain, an old soldier, also. I took command and I remained so until the end. A spent ball hit me in my right leg. Limping, with my left arm in a sling, I was isolated by the charge, and was stuck in a hollow by the walls. I was fighting against two redcoats who were impossible to break. I defended myself and fought furiously. The larger of the two was a lieutenant of the Guards, he sneered, his boot just missed me and gathering all my remaining strength, thrust at his face, and sent this insolent subject of His Gracious Majesty to God's heaven. He was the last of the enemy that I had killed with my hands on the field of battle. My grenadiers dragged me off, and we closed the heavy gates of Namur in the face of the attackers.

In the early hours of 20 June, the 30th Regiment of Line Infantry arrived at Namur, as Captain François reports:[6]

In the night we crossed Gembloux. At five o'clock in the morning, we stopped on the road from Charleroi to Namur, dying of hunger and fatigue and pursued by the Prussians. The sappers of the 30th found three cattle on a farm, but when they were about to distribute the meat, our generals learned that the Prussians had passed the Sambre. Marshal Grouchy instructed General Bonnemains to stand fast against them with two regiments of dragoons, and we resumed our march on Namur. The 30th formed the rearguard; we had not yet left the scene of the halt when we were attacked: we were forced to abandon our meat, we upturned our cooking pots and we formed into line of battle. The Prussians departed, seeing our defensive movements, but they returned and closely followed us as we marched forward, and they began to bombard us with artillery when we reached the heights, which were about three-quarters of a league from Namur. We answered their artillery with our own. We, as well as the 96th, formed into squares, and we continued our march towards Namur, alone on the road. The 30th is no stronger than three platoons which were formed into two squares. The Prussian cavalry charged us three times, each time it pushed. I command the last four. We marched slowly, often stopping and facing the front until the Prussian cavalry were between ten and fifteen paces away, then stopped and fired in two ranks. In this manner, we gained Namur, where the other regiments of the division were formed. Here, we were identified to support the retirement of the division of General Teste. After various manoeuvres in columns of attack, we entered into the city, while General Teste prepared its defences to stop the enemy at the gates of Namur. We camped on the road to Dinant.

Sub-Lieutenant Gerbet, of the 37th Regiment of Line Infantry, notes that at Namur Marshal Grouchy advantageously placed his artillery and advance guard to defend the town. The 37th Regiment of Line Infantry was formed in square to receive the enemy cavalry charges, which attacked, but without success and left many dead on the field of battle. Vandamme's command, he notes, entered and passed through Namur, and the rearguard was formed from General Teste's command, which fended off the Prussians and forced them to abandon the attack.[7]

Wounded with 4th Corps that day, under General Pecheaux, were officers of the 30th Regiment of Line Infantry. In the attacks, the regiment lost one officer killed (Captain Villeminot) and two wounded (Captain Plancon and Lieutenant-Adjutant-Major Pierre Charles Desfontaines). At Ligny, he took a musket ball to the right leg, as well as a bruise to the kidneys. He had recovered from these wounds sufficiently to remain with the regiment and fought at Namur, where he suffered a contusion from a canister shot to the right leg.[8] The brigaded 96th Regiment of Line Infantry lost two officers killed (Captain Ozenne and Lieutenant Fauville) and two officers wounded (lieutenants Lefort and Ollivero de Rubianca).

Grouchy had conducted a textbook withdrawal from Wavre, and it seems that by the 19th, despite tentative attacks, he had gained the bridge at Limale and cut off some of the Prussians. Given the events taking place on the 19th, this success could not be followed, and Grouchy retired on to Namur. A vigorous defence of the town by General Teste enabled Grouchy to withdraw the vast majority of his command. From Namur, he endeavoured to link up with Marshal Soult and the remnants of the Armée du Nord.

Grouchy still held Namur on the afternoon of 20 June. Sometime that day, he issued the following order to General Vandamme about the evacuation of the place:[9]

> When you evacuate Namur, my dear general, I want you to come take a position on the side of the suburb of Dinant, and that you stay here long enough for the town to be evacuated. I intend to push up tomorrow to Charlemont. And if denied, the outer edges of Namur and Dinant, where you will easily stop the enemy who has only cavalry, and I hope that, without significant loss, we will win Charlemont.
>
> I ordered the cavalry of General Pajol keep our right flank, and to gather news about what is going on in Charleroi, if possible.
>
> If the troops are too tired, they will take a halt before arriving at Charlemont.
>
> Do not forget to give orders to the division of Teste.
>
> Marshal Grouchy.
>
> P. S. There are three gates in Namur, please send infantry sentries and order them that the gates are kept as long as necessary.
>
> I've barricaded the bridges over the Meuse and Sambre, which should also be defended before leaving the city.

Franz Lieber, of the Prussian Kohlberg Regiment, was part of the attacking force:[10]

> Half our army corps, to which I belonged, received orders to pursue Vanamere [sic], who had thrown himself into Namur. We marched the whole of the 19th; the heat was excessive, and our exhaustion and thirst so great that two men of our regiment became deranged in consequence. At four in the afternoon we went into bivouac; we started early again, and now my strength forsook me, I could not keep up with the troops, and began to lag behind. Suddenly, at about noon, I head the first guns. The Battle of Namur had begun. When I arrived where my regiment stood, or, as I should rather say, the little band representing it, I dropped down; but fortunately one of my comrades had some eggs, one of which he gave me great strength. Our colonel came up to us saying 'riflemen, you have twice fought like the oldest of soldiers, I have no more to say. This wood is to be cleared; be steady bugleman, the single!' and off we

went with a great hurrah! Driving off the French before us down a hill toward Namur, which lay on our front. When I saw our men rushing too fast down the hill, I was afraid that the same enemies might be hid under the precipice to receive them. Holding myself a tree with my left hand, I looked over the precipice and saw about seven Frenchmen. They will hit me, I thought, and, turning around to call to our solders, I suddenly experienced a sensation as if my whole body was compressed in my head, and this, like a ball, were quivering in the ear. I could feel the existence of nothing else; it was a most painful sensation. After some time I was able to open my eyes, or to see again with them. I found myself on the ground; over me stood a soldier firing at the enemy. I strained every nerve to ask, though in broken accents, whether, if so, where I was wounded. 'You are shot through the neck.' I begged him to shoot me; the idea of dying miserably of hunger, half of my wound, alone in the wood overpowered me. He of course, refused, spoke a word of comfort that perhaps I might be saved, and soon after he received a shot through both knees, in consequence he died in hospital…my thirst was beyond description; it was a feverish burning. I thought I should die, and prayed for forgiveness of my sins as I forgave all. I recollect I prayed for Napoléon, and begged the dispenser of all blessings to shower his bounty upon all my beloved ones, and if it could be, to grant me a speedy end of my sufferings. I received a second ball, which, entering my chest, gave me more local pain than the first; I thought God had granted my fervent prayer. I perceived, as I supposed, that the ball had pierced my lung and tried to breathe to hasten my death. A week afterward, while I still lay with my two wounds in a house in Liège, one of my brothers was in the hospital in Brussels and another at Aix-le-Chapelle.

About the evacuation of Namur, General Teste reported to Marshal Grouchy on 20 June 1815 as follows:[11]

In accordance with the orders that you gave me on the 19th, before leaving Namur, to hold with my division, this place until six o'clock the next day to allow time for the army and its equipment to operate, without being harassed by the enemy, their retirement through the valley of the Meuse, via Civet, I hastened to be informed of the condition of this important position and that before and during the night, I was told that I was to close and barricade, where possible, the gaps and openings of the square, so as to defend the access with the men under my command.

My arrangements were hardly completed when on the morning of the 20th, a Prussian corps of 12,000 to 15,000 men appeared before Namur to remove it by force. This attack, made with vigour, mainly on the iron gate where I had two companies of grenadiers of the 75th, was repulsed; the enemy left many dead in ditches. It was torn from afar, until noon, when another attempt was made by the Prussians, and had the same result.

At three o'clock the enemy appeared more and more fierce; the men seemed to have drunk a lot of spirits, even the officers, who came to be killed by our bayonets on our barricades, the attackers had retreated at half-past four, leaving the approaches to the place littered with their dead.

Instead of starting my retreat at six o'clock, I delayed until eight, and disputing the ground inch-by-inch, I waited for the enemy on the other side of the Sambre, where I had placed in houses which I had loopholed my two companies of sappers, they had yet to experience a great loss by musketry fire at close-range.

At half-past eight, I occupied the position that I had prepared at the gate of France, under which I had placed a pile of fagots, which was set on fire, to impede the move of artillery to this point, and further delay the enemy.

I write this letter from the bivouacs of Profondeville, having marched very slowly and without being pursued by the enemy.

The Prussians must have had, in the deadliest day of yesterday, 4,000 to 5,000 men out of action: we had only thirteen killed and forty-seven wounded.

General Teste had held back the Prussians to allow 3rd and 4th Corps to evacuate the place. Later the same day, Marshal Grouchy sent his formal report to Napoléon about his operations:[12]

Temploux 19 June 1815
    Marshal Grouchy to the emperor
    Sire,
    It was not until after seven in the evening of 18 June that I received the letter of the Duc de Dalmatie, which directed me to march on to Saint-Lambert, and to attack General Bülow. I fell in with the enemy as I was marching on Wavre. He was immediately driven into Wavre, and General Vandamme's corps attacked that town, and was warmly engaged. The portion of Wavre, on the right of the Dyle, was carried, but much difficulty was experienced in debouching on the other side. General Girard was wounded by a ball in the breast while

endeavouring to carry the mill of Bièrges in order to pass the river, but in which he did not succeed, and Lieutenant-General Aix had been killed in the attack on the town. In this state of things, being impatient to co-operate with Your Majesty's army on that important day, I detached several corps to force the passage of the Dyle and march against Bülow. The corps of Vandamme, in the meantime, maintained the attack on Wavre and on the mill, whence the enemy showed an intention to debouch, but which I did not conceive he was capable of effecting. I arrived at Limale, passed the river, and the division of Vichery and the cavalry carried the heights. Night did not permit us to advance farther, and I no longer heard the cannon on the side where Your Majesty was engaged.

I halted in this situation until daylight. Both Wavre and Bièrges were occupied by the Prussians, who, at three in the morning of the 18th, attacked in their turn, wishing to take advantage of the difficult position in which I was, and expecting to drive me into the defile and take the artillery which had debouched, and make me re-pass the Dyle. Their efforts were fruitless. The Prussians were repulsed, and the village of Bièrges taken. The brave General Penne was killed.

General Vandamme then passed one of his divisions by Bièrges, and carried with ease the heights of Wavre, and along the whole of my line the success was complete. I was in front of Rosierne, preparing to march on Brussels, when I received the sad intelligence of the loss of the Battle of Waterloo. The officer who brought it informed me that Your Majesty was retreating on the Sambre, without being able to indicate any particular point on which I should direct my march. I ceased to pursue, and began my retrograde movement. The retreating enemy did not think of following me. Learning that the enemy had already passed the Sambre, and was on my flank, and not being sufficiently strong to make a diversion in favour of Your Majesty, without compromising that which I commanded, I marched on Namur. At this moment, the rear of the columns was attacked. That of the left made a retrograde movement sooner than was expected, which endangered for a moment the retreat of the left, but good dispositions soon repaired everything, and two pieces which had been taken were recovered by the brave 20th Dragoons, who besides took a howitzer from the enemy. We entered Namur without loss. The long defile which extends from this place to Dinant, in which only a single column can march, and the embarrassment arising from the numerous transports of wounded, rendered it necessary to hold for a considerable time the town in which I had not the means of blowing up the bridge. I entrusted the defence of Namur to General Vandamme, who, with his usual intrepidity, maintained himself there until eight in the evening; so that nothing was left behind, and I occupied Dinant, the enemy has lost some thousands of men in the attack on Namur, where the contest was very obstinate; the troops have performed their duty in a manner worthy of praise.

The retreat of Grouchy from Wavre, via Namur, upon Dinant was executed in a skilful and masterly manner, as was the defence of Namur by General Teste.[13] At 23.00 on the 20th, Grouchy issued the following movement orders for the following day:[14]

> Dinant, 20 June, eleven o'clock in the evening
>
> I am sending herewith, my dear general, the order of march for tomorrow, and ask you to give consideration those that concern you, and give orders as necessary.
>
> I also recommend that you keep, if possible, clear of the village of Rouvines, I expect that there would be a great congestion here, for almost all day tomorrow would be required for its removal.
>
> Marshal Grouchy
>
> Movement Orders:
>
> The 4th Corps will start at five in the morning to make the banks of the stream of Lelle, where it will continue its movement until Givet, and then occupy the camp.
>
> The 3rd Corps, of which Teste's division is part, is to continue to be the rearguard. It will hold as well as possible the village of Rouvines and at the entrance of Dinant, and will defend the approaches as well as they can. It will be important to keep the defensible positions between Dinant and Givet, disputing the ground inch-by-inch, to ensure in this way the return of the wounded of the army into the fortress.
>
> At night, the 3rd Corps will also occupy the camp. M. General-in-Chief Vandamme will appoint one or two regiments of his corps to form the garrison of the city.
>
> All parks and artillery of each corps, other than that belonging to each division, will start at four o'clock, and will not stop at Givet.

Strung out far in front, as Grouchy's avantgarde, were General Bonnemains and his dragoons. He was tasked with securing the line of retreat. From Dinant, he sent the following dispatch:[15]

Dinant 20 June 1815

> General Dumonceau, governor of Givet
>
> I arrived in front of Dinant about midday, where I waited for Marshal Grouchy and his corps to arrive from Namur. It is important that from this position we try and join the army of the emperor.

General Bonnemains, in his report to General Chastel, writes:[16]

> General Bonnemains, being charged by Marshal Grouchy and General Excelmans to use all means to get information on the progress of the emperor and the army, could not get anything positive in the immediate area. He formed small parties to send messengers to Philippeville and Givet. The first was intercepted by the enemy and the second was not and resulted in the response of the general commanding Givet and from the Duc de Dalmatie for rallying the various corps.
>
> Everyone in France believed Grouchy had lost his army. General Dumonceau, commanding Givet, sent the letter from General Bonnemains to the Minister of War at all speed, where the news read to the Chamber and made a great sensation.

General Bonnemains sent the following dispatch to General Chastel from Dinant on 20 June:[17]

> I received your news and will pass around the flank with a troop, to arrive in front of Dinant, where I arrived about midday, where Marshal Comte de Grouchy will also be with the army corps under his command from Namur, and where he will establish his headquarters, and will send to the emperor the dispositions of the army.

Clearly, Bonnemains had headed south from Namur, via Profondeville, and thence to Dinant, and was moving thence onwards to Givet. Bonnemains, writing from Dinant, sent the following dispatch to General Bourke, commanding the garrison at Givet, advising him of the arrival of Grouchy's forces:[18]

> M. general,
>
> I am informing you that my troops arrived at Dinant sometime after midday, and that Marshal Comte de Grouchy is at Namur with the army cops under his orders. [Illegible] I will send you news concerning the arrival of the marshal and the movements he had ordered.

General Vincent, at Givet (no doubt with his brigade), sent the following dispatch to the emperor:[19]

> Sire,
>
> I have the pleasure to inform Your Majesty that General Excelmans had departed Namur at midday and his head of column is heading to Givet. These comprise the dragoons, the corps of General Pajol, as well as the 3rd and 4th Infantry Corps, which have been ordered to debouch from Namur. The enemy pursued General Vandamme to Namur. At the moment of his departure from that town, a part of his artillery and dragoons passed through a defile with the division of Abert [sic], they have not sustained any great loss, but a good number are wounded.
>
> Generals Abert and Gérard are wounded; they were in the rear and are prisoners.
>
> Please accept my most profound respect,
> Your Majesty
> I am your very humble, very obedient servant
> Givet, 20 June at nine o'clock at night
> General Baron Vincent.

21 June

At some time on 21 June, Grouchy wrote to Marshal Soult about his operations:[20]

> At the headquarters of Dinant, 21 June 1815.
>
> M. marshal,
>
> I have the honour to inform you that we have had no news from His Majesty, and have received no orders since the verbal announcement of the loss of the Battle of Waterloo, which was given to me by an officer of staff, while I was struggling with the enemy I fought and pushed back beyond Rosierne, moving from Wavre to Brussels, and I made my retreat on the Sambre, and there onto Charlemont where I will arrive tonight. Every day of my retreat has been marked by bloody battles, but they have been glorious to the French army.
>
> I bring back the corps that were placed under my command, though weakened, forming a total of about twenty-five thousand men, but without losing a single military trophy or cannon, and having beaten off the enemy, we have killed three times more of his men, and the losses I have experienced myself.
>
> I will address His Majesty this evening with the ratio of daily battles that I had to fight and our losses that the army has sustained.

> It is essential after long marches that my corps has done, that these troops take at least one day of rest. The 3rd and 4th Corps and Teste's division are camping in Givet.

Late on 21 June 1815, Grouchy's undefeated troops entered Charlemont. He had managed to escape destruction or capture with 28,000 men, most of his wounded and all his artillery.

22 June

At 06.00 on 22 June, Marshal Soult sent orders (the first since 19 June) ordering Grouchy to move to Mézières, and then to move on to Soissons or Laon and Rheims, depending on the movements of the Prussian troops.[21] Grouchy's movement orders for the day noted Pajol was to move out at 6.00 from cantonments near Givet and move to Rocroy, keeping him informed of the British patrols that had been spotted. Excelmans was to leave at 7.00 to move to Rocroy, one part of the corps moving via the brigade at Houssou, and the other via Roigny. The 4th Corps, under Vichery, was to move out at 8.00 to head to Rocroy and occupy the villages of d'Irauremont, Galichet and Petit-Hougreaux. Vandamme, with 3rd Corps, was to leave at 10.00, and the 5th Hussars were also to operate under his orders.[22]

Marshal Grouchy arrived at Laon at the end of the day. Writing from Laon the same day, he notes to Marshal Soult that:[23]

> The Guard has arrived; there will be about 5,000 infantry under the command of Comte Morand, and 1,600 to 1,800 cavalry under the command of General Lefèbvre-Desnoëttes.
>
> The infantry of the Guard is established in the promenades of Laon, behind the city, and the cavalry to Crépy-Laon and Chavignon-Mons.
>
> I ordered the colonel commanding the artillery of the Guard to move to Lafère, both men and horses, to take two batteries and advance to Soissons.

The same day, General Bonnemains's dispatch had arrived in Paris from Dinant with news that Grouchy's army had not been destroyed or defected to the Allies, as Marshal Ney had claimed the previous day which had directly led to the abdication of the emperor.

In response to Bonnemains's dispatch, Marshal Davout wrote to Grouchy at 20.00 on the 22nd, conveying new orders and informing the marshal of the rapidly changing political situation:[24]

I just learned from a letter from General Bonnemains, passed to me by Dumonceau, which states you were in Dinant and Namur with your cavalry and the 4th and 3rd Corps of generals Vandamme and Gérard. This is an event of very great importance for our country. Because, after the unfortunate events near Genappe concerning 1st, 2nd and 6th Corps and the Guards, there was the greatest concern: the certainty that your corps is not destroyed is an incalculable advantage in the current circumstances. I am ignorant of the orders of the Duc de Dalmatie could have given you, but here are the ones you need to focus upon now.

You must move with the 3rd and 4th Cavalry Corps and artillery to Laon, via Mézières. If you learn in a positive way that the enemy is between you and Laon with a large force, you will direct your march onto Rheims and from there onto Soissons. You are to send to me frequently your news; take all necessary steps to maintain good order in your troops, you inform them about the latest events in Paris. The emperor has abdicated, wanting to remove any pretext for foreign powers to wage war against us, because by all their statements, they announced that it was to him that they were at war and not France.

The Chambers have just appointed a provisional government, commissioners will be sent to all the Allied powers to announce this event which should remove any pretext for war. If the Allied powers, as we hope to have acted in good faith in their statements, in a few days peace shall be restored to the world.

If you feel, M. marshal, in the event that this declaration would be an illusion, it is important for the service of the country to take all measures to prevent malicious rumours, to prevent disorganisation and desertion among the troops. You can even send that you have knowledge of these events to the Allied generals in your neighbourhood, inviting them to suspend all hostilities until they received orders from their sovereigns.

Write to all the prefects and all commanding generals of garrisons to announce these events, invite them to take action to arrest all deserters, to reach those who have abandoned their posts, either soldiers of the line or National Guards. Talk about these events to all generals and implore them in the name of the country to take all measures in order to keep all the troops and remind them of all the duties of the French soldier.

France is counting on you, General Vandamme and General Gérard, and all the generals and officers in this important circumstance. I repeat, the arrival of your body made the biggest impression in Paris. Please accept, M. marshal, the assurance of my highest consideration.

We cannot be sure when Grouchy received the order, but one can see that Marshal Davout was clearly among those wanting an immediate ceasefire when the abdication of Napoléon. How the news was received by Grouchy and the officers and men under his command we can only suppose. He, presumably, gained the news the same day and prepared a proclamation to be read to the army on 23 June.

23 June

On the night of 22 June, Grouchy prepared the following proclamation to be read to the army, based upon the news he had received from Marshal Davout in Paris. It was read out on 23 June:[25]

> Soldiers!
> The movements of the army of the emperor have rendered necessary the painful marches that you make. But make no mistake about their reasons or their results. You're victors of Fleurus, Wavre, in Namur, you beat the enemy wherever you addressed them, your valour has embellished your military trophies and you can boast of not losing a single one. Together with new forces you'll soon take the offensive attitude that suits you. As defenders of our beloved country, you will preserve its sacred ground and the whole of France will proclaim your rights to recognition and public adoration. I am pleased to lead you in these important circumstances where you have increased your fame by earning new laurels. I answer in your name to the country, that faithful to your oath, you will all perish rather than see it humiliated and enslaved.
> *Vive l'Empereur!*

The same day, Marshal Davout sent word about the formation of the new government and the abdication of Napoléon in favour of Napoléon II.

The 3rd and 4th Corps, under the orders of General Vandamme, were at Rheims on 23 June.[26] According to Fantin des Odoards, of the 22nd Regiment of Line Infantry, 3rd Corps was at Givet on 22 June, and thence moved to the town of Maubert-Fontaine on 23 June, in appallingly wet weather.

25 June

On the evening of 25 June 1815, Marshal Soult resigned as commander-in-chief, he told Marshal Davout on health grounds, and was replaced as commander-in-chief of the Armée du Nord by Marshal Grouchy.[27]

Soult said he had no choice but to support Napoléon and abandon the king, and when the time was right he returned as a loyal subject back to the king. Clearly Soult was trying to save his own skin. Other marshals, like Marmont and Victor, who supported the king in 1814 and 1815 did not abandon their new loyalty to the crown when Napoléon returned. For Soult to quickly drop the king and then support Napoléon, and then as quickly drop Napoléon to support king, shows he endeavoured to back what he perceived to be the winning side at all times, and made no display of changes to his allegiances as circumstance dictated.

Once Marmont and MacDonald had changed sides to the king, they remained loyal, unlike Ney or Soult. For this duplicity, Ney was shot and Soult was exiled.

Soult's defection and abandonment of the army had a huge impact on the troops under his command. Grouchy felt that his own two army corps and cavalry were in far better condition to fight than the men Soult had gathered up. He complained to Marshal Davout about Soult's desertion of the army that:[28]

> The departure of the Duc de Dalmatie has totally disrupted and disorganised the officer personnel of the staff of the army. They are all trying to compete against each other in getting to Paris first, using the excuse that he had given them permission to do so. Please send to me General Guilleminot to act as chief-of-staff, and he must bring officers and clerks with him.

Upon Grouchy's orders 1st, 2nd and 6th Corps were placed under the command of General Reille, and the 3rd and 4th Corps under the command of General Vandamme. Marshal Soult, it appears, with the news of the emperor's abdication and the likely restoration of the Bourbons to the throne of France, seemingly wanted to distance himself from the wreck of the army and his defection to Napoléon from the Bourbons.

The cavalry corps of Kellermann, Excelmans and Pajol were still at Rheims on 25 June. Excelmans was inpatient to get to Paris and demanded movement orders.[29] Instead, he was ordered to move at daybreak on 26 June to Corbeny, to keep a line of communications with Laon, and to occupy the place.[30]

26 June

Grouchy arrived at Soissons on the morning of 26 June. He found the men who had gathered here under Soult, disorganised and demoralised. He noted that the Imperial Guard was agitating the troops in the area to desert and to march to Paris to aid Napoléon:[31]

> The disorganisation of the army that we are trying to reform here is still very depressing. No matter what orders I give, no matter the measures I take, I cannot prevent the soldiers leaving the colours and carrying out the most damaging acts. The Imperial Guard is also leaving, inflamed by rabble-rousers who are endeavouring to tell the men that they can best serve the emperor's interest in Paris, they are using this as an excuse to quit their ranks and rush to the capitol.
>
> The troops at Soissons do not appear capable of fighting, though the cavalry is in better mood than the infantry and one can still get some service from them. It is impossible to use such demoralised Infantry in combat.

Grouchy called out the local gendarmerie to stem the tide of deserters flooding to Paris both from the army and mobilised cohorts of the National Guard. Without Soult's guiding hand, nor the emperor to fight for, the troops at Soissons, it seems, had began to drift away from the army, and the work he had done over the previous ten days was undone. Langeron, the garrison commander at Laon, despaired at being able to hold the place without regular soldiers being sent to bolster the garrison, either sent from Paris or detached from the Armée du Nord. However, Grouchy was able to report that Jacquinot's light cavalry was established in the suburbs of Laon, the Imperial Guard infantry and cavalry were between Soissons and Laon, Excelmans was between Craonne and Corbeny, Pajol's light cavalry was behind Coucy while 1st, 2nd and 6th Corps, under Reille, were at Soissons. Parts of 1st Corps were marching to Compiegne under the orders of General Comte d'Erlon. The cavalry of Kellermann and Milhaud were at Senlis.[32]

Furthermore, Grouchy reported to Marshal Davout that the Allies had begun to concentrate at Laon, and in an action, the line of communication with La Fere had been cut, despite the best efforts of General Pajol.[33]

27 June

In the morning of 27 June, the Prussian advanced guard of lancers arrived at Soissons. Grouchy began evacuating the place. Blücher, notes Grouchy, was at Noyon and prevented him from establishing a strong force at Compiegne. As a result, 1st Corps, along with the cavalry of

Kellermann and Milhaud, was ordered to move to Senlis. General Reille with 2nd and 6th Corps, was ordered to move to Nateuil and hold the position, while Grouchy himself and the Imperial Guard was to move to Villiers-Cotterêts, hoping to arrive on the evening of the 27th. General Vandamme, with 3rd and 4th Corps, was ordered to form the rearguard and continue his movement to Paris.[34] Grouchy further notes that the 4,000 men of 1st Corps and the 2,000 sabres of Kellermann and Milhaud were of insufficient strength to fight their way to Compiegne.

Marshal Grouchy, at some point on 27 June, ordered General Morand to unite his command of the infantry of the Guard with the light cavalry of the Guard under Lefèbvre-Desnoëttes at Villiers-Cotterêts, along with the 1st and 2nd Cavalry Brigades commanded by General Jacquinot. They were to take up position by 14.00.[35]

At around 14.00, Marshal Grouchy wrote to Marshal Davout, informing him that the Guard was at that moment arriving and was to be based at his headquarters. General Reille was expected to arrive in the evening.[36]

On the evening of 27 June, around 19.00 the Guard cavalry and elements of the Guard infantry, under the command of General Reille, as well as the troops of Marshal Grouchy occupied the town of Villiers-Cotterêts. General Vandamme noted that at 2.00 on the 28th, he, with 2nd Corps and the Imperial Guard left the place, with the cavalry of General Domon in support, and headed to Dammartin.[37]

29 June

On the 29th, Marshal Grouchy had reached Paris and entered the fortifications to the north of the city. He then resigned command of his troops to General Vandamme. That same day, Blücher ordered General Bülow to attack Saint-Denis, and seized the bridge over the Seine at Saint-Germain.

The Imperial Guard was camped at Charonne on 29 June. Marshal Grouchy's 60,000 men arrived in Paris the same day. The ranks of the chasseurs à cheval were filled out with the men of the 2nd Regiment of Chasseurs à Cheval. Of this number were the 2nd Regiment of Chasseurs à Cheval of the Imperial Guard. The defence of the city of Paris was commanded by Marshal Davout, with his headquarters at d'Aubervillieres. General Vandamme, with 3rd and 4th Corps, was ordered to defend Paris and the cavalry was drawn up on the Boulogne Wood. Paris was to be held at all costs.

The Allies moved on Paris

The Prussian army reached the outskirts of Paris on 29 June 1815. Wellington and his Allied troops, along with the Prussians, may have won the battle, but it was the Prussians who won the war. The outcome of the campaign was due to the tenacity of Blücher in his pursuit of the French.

It had been necessary to place the villages of Vertus and Vilette in a state of siege to guard them from a surprise attack. The defence of the bridges at Pecq and Saint-Germain was entrusted to what remained of the 1st Corps, commanded by General Allix. The bridge at Pecq was defended by the sixty-six year old veteran officer, Jacques-Denis Boivin.

On 30 June 1815, Davout had over 70,000 men available to defend Paris, and this number would continue to swell as mobilised National Guardsmen made their way to Paris, and the command of General Lamarque returned from the Vendée. The army had, in twelve days, found a new sense of confidence and was ready and able to fight. If these men could inflict a major defeat on either Wellington or Blücher, maybe the balance of power could shift back to the French, and the defeat of Waterloo nullified under the walls of Paris. However, the political machinations of Fouché rendered these hopes null and void. On 1 July, the French counter-attacked the Prussians and British at Vertus, but were pushed back by Prussian sharpshooters and artillery fire. The same afternoon at Villacoublay, General Excelmans, at the head of the 5th, 15th and 20th Dragoons and the 6th Hussars, some 3,000 men, moved against the Prussians, while the division of General Piré, comprising the 5th and 6th Lancers and the 1st and 6th Chasseurs à Cheval, supported by the 33rd Regiment of Line Infantry, attacked the Prussian rear situated on the road to Sèvres. Elsewhere around Paris, small actions took place at Versailles and Chenay.[39]

Despite General Piré's victory at Rocquancourt on 1 July, on the morning of 2 July 1815, the Prussians pushed back from Sèvres and elements of General Pully's force moved to Meudon. Here, a rearguard stand was made, before the Prussians drove the French back to Issy.

With the Prussians pursuing the French, at 3.00 on the morning of 3 July, General Vandamme led out two strong columns of infantry; his infantry force comprised fifteen battalions drawn from the 2nd, 3rd and 4th Corps, supported by cavalry and artillery. His goal was to retake the ground which had been lost on the previous day. However, Vandamme failed to take the village of Issy, and fell back in disorder. The French were pursued by the Prussian skirmishers up to the outer defences of Paris. He had nearly succeeded in pushing back Ziethen, who had occupied the place since 22.00 on the previous day.[40] The battle had lasted for some four hours.

At Grenelle, the Prussian troops of General Ziethen faced the rump of the French 3rd and 4th Corps. General Ziethen invited the French government, in a message sent to Marshal Davout, to surrender. The capitulation was signed at 17.00. The armistice began at 8.00 on Tuesday, 4 July 1815; the French army was ordered to move behind the River Loire. Paris had fallen, the army had been vanquished and the emperor was in exile.[41] The city was to be evacuated of troops.

The war was over. The Allies occupied Paris and Louis 'the Inevitable' was restored to his throne. The king entered Paris on 8 July 1815. Paris was not ready to accept the fact that France had lost the war. The peaceful resignation of a year earlier was not repeated. The Parisian National Guard, under the orders of Marshal Masséna, cried 'we have been sold off like beasts'.[42] Could the army, the National Guard and the Federes have fought on? Yes, perhaps. Certainly, Davout had over 100,000 men under his orders, with more men making his force stronger by the day in both morale and manpower. However, peace had been the goal of the Provisional Government since the day it had been formed, and it was peace at any cost. Fouché, the president, refused to continue the fight. As we have seen, peace overtures had been made pretty much from the day the government was formed and had been rejected ostensibly by Blücher, who was out to avenge 1806. Politically, the war could have ended sooner. As it was, the French army, which for fifteen years had come to dominate Napoléon's political actions, found that it had no influence over the course of events and was increasingly marginalised. War for Napoléon had been diplomacy by other means.

With Paris in the hands of the Allies, the army was ordered to retreat behind the Loire river. With the return of the king, keeping men in ranks became an increasing problem, as the lure of home and farm drew men away from the army. With Napoléon gone, the war seemed over, and there was little point in remaining in the ranks.

NOTES:
[1] Lefol, pp. 59-60.
[2] Berton, pp. 68-70.
[3] *Nederlandsche Staatscourant*, 27 June 1815. Transcript by Erwin Muilwijk.
[4] Fantin des Odoards, pp. 437-8.
[5] Miot-Putigny, pp. 245-6.
[6] François.
[7] Gerbet, pp. 21-3.
[8] AN: LH 747/48.
[9] SHDDT: C15 *Registre d'Ordres et de correspondance du major-general a partir du 13 Juin jusqu'au 26 Juin au Maréchal Grouchy*, p. 34.
[10] Thayer, pp. 9-10.
[11] SHDDT: C15 *Registre d'Ordres et de correspondance du major-general a partir du 13 Juin jusqu'au 26 Juin au Maréchal Grouchy*, p. 26.
[12] SHDDT: C15 *Registre d'Ordres et de correspondance du major-general a partir du 13 Juin jusqu'au 26 Juin au Maréchal Grouchy*, p. 28. See also: SHDDT: C15 5. Dossier 19 June 1815. Grouchy

to Napoléon. Copy of the original order made by Comte du Casse in June 1865. See also: *Le Moniteur*, No. 175, 24 June 1815. In the archives of the Service Historique Armée du Térre in Paris, six copies of reports of Grouchy to the emperor dated 19 June 1815 can be found. In themselves they could have their interest, were it not for the fact that they contain a huge amount of overlap and that it is therefore very hard to assess how they relate to each other. However, of these orders, only the order cited here, and a much shorter note written on 19 June at Dinant which did not reach Soult, can be considered authentic, as only these orders appear in Grouchy's own register of correspondence, providing a cross-reference. We note that none of the six orders in the dossier at Vincennes are originals, all are copes by Comte de Casse in 1865 of the now lost originals, except in two cases.

[13] SHDDT: C15 *Registre d'Ordres et de correspondance du major-general a partir du 13 Juin jusqu'au 26 Juin au Maréchal Grouchy*, p. 28.

[14] SHDDT: C15 *Registre d'Ordres et de correspondance du major-general a partir du 13 Juin jusqu'au 26 Juin au Maréchal Grouchy*, p. 34.

[15] *Journal de l'Empire*, 22 June 1815, p. 2.

[16] SHDDT: C15 Bonnemains to Chastel, 23 June 1815.

[17] SHDDT: C15 5. Dossier 20 June. Bonnemains to Chastel. The original handwritten order is difficult to read in many places, the translation is a gist understanding, as Bonnemains's own handwriting is not clear enough to read, not helped by his editing of the letter as he was composing it.

[18] SHDDT: C15 5. Dossier 20 June. Bonnemains to Bourke.

[19] SHDDT: C15 5. Dossier 20 June. Vincent to Napoléon. The original handwritten order is difficult to read in many places.

[20] SHDDT: C15 *Registre d'Ordres et de correspondance du major-general a partir du 13 Juin jusqu'au 26 Juin au Maréchal Grouchy*, p. 44. See also: SHDDT: C15 15. Dossier 21 June. Grouchy to Soult. This is the original handwritten document sent to Soult.

[21] SHDDT: C15 *Registre d'Ordres et de correspondance du major-general a partir du 13 Juin jusqu'au 26 Juin au Maréchal Grouchy*, p. 44.

[22] ibid.

[23] ibid.

[24] ibid, pp. 51-3.

[25] SHDDT: C15 *Registre d'Ordres et de correspondance du major-general a partir du 13 Juin jusqu'au 26 Juin au Maréchal Grouchy*, p. 58.

[26] AN: AFIV 1939, p. 100.

[27] AN: AFIV 1939, p. 123.

[28] SHDDT: C15 6 *Correspondence Armée du Nord 22 Juin au 3 Juillet 1815*. Dossier 26 June. Grouchy to Davout, 26 June 1815 timed at 5.30.

[29] SHDDT: C15 6. Dossier 25 June 1815. Excelmans to Grouchy, Rheims 25 June 1815.

[30] SHDDT: C15 6. Dossier 25 June 1815. Grouchy to Excelmans, Rheims 25 June 1815.

[31] ibid.

[32] ibid.

[33] SHDDT: C15 6. Dossier 26 June 1815. Grouchy to Davout, 26 June 1815 timed at 5.30.

[34] SHDDT: C15 6. Dossier 27 June. Grouchy to Davout, 27 June 1815 timed at 8.30.

[35] SHDDT: C15 5. Grouchy to Morand, Soissons 27 June 1815.

[36] SHDDT: C15 5. Grouchy to Davout, timed at 14.00 27 June 1815.

[37] Ollech, p. 324.

[38] Damitz, Vol. 2, pp. 180.

[39] Damitz, Vol. 2, pp. 285-300.

[40] Damitz, Vol. 2, p. 307.

[41] ibid, pp. 314-6.

[42] *Journal de l'Empire*, 22 June 1815, p. 2.

Chapter 16

The Lie at the Heart of Waterloo

Grouchy was the last of Napoléon's marshals. His reputation since 1815 has been sullied, being blamed for the loss of Waterloo. However, he seems more sinned against than sinner.

The traditional Waterloo myth tells us that Grouchy lost the battle by failing to march to the sound of the guns. This myth is simply that—a story put about by Napoléon and his supporters to blame others for the loss of the battle.

In order to assess the validity of this assertion we have looked critically at the communications between Grouchy and Napoléon made in the lead up to the battle. When Napoléon received the 10.30 dispatch from Grouchy on 18 June, he knew Grouchy could not get to Waterloo. His own order to make the case clearer to the marshal did not arrive with him until 18.00 to 19.00.

Either Napoléon believed that only a small portion of the Prussian army had eluded Grouchy (hardly surprising given the lead they had over the marshal), or he was over-confident in his chances of success against Wellington and the Prussians. Napoléon's judgement on both scenarios was horribly wrong.

For in fact, Napoléon knew from 14.00 that he faced both Wellington and Blücher and that Grouchy was not marching to his aid, regardless of what later French and Anglophone writers have stated. Grouchy's own actions at Wavre were a major concern for the Prussians. Rather than as traditional history tells us, his attacks were not feeble.

Did Napoléon really believe that Grouchy could simply break off the action at Wavre and head to Waterloo? He was experienced enough to realise the difficulty of breaking contact with the enemy once action had begun, as at Eylau in 1807. How could Grouchy break off action until he had reached troop parity with the Prussians? He could not. Only with the arrival of 4th Corps could he make a decisive blow against the Prussians, and even then, he could not have got to Waterloo. Grouchy, unless he left Wavre before 10.00 on 18 June, could not have got to Waterloo to intervene in the action. Robbed of his 'eyes and ears' by Napoléon on 17 June, he had no idea where the Prussians were that day until Pajol and Excelmans found them. Even then, until the infantry caught up there was little Pajol or Excelmans could do to initiate a major cavalry attack. By early evening, Thielemann sent a request to Gneisenau for reinforcements, and had Prussian troops been sent back to Wavre then Waterloo may have had a different outcome. As it was, Grouchy tied down all of Thielemann's command. Grouchy's action at Wavre was vitally important, as it prevented the defeat at Waterloo being far worse than it was.

Despite realising Grouchy could never have got to Waterloo, on the battlefield in the early evening, Napoléon now seems to have set in motion in his own mind, and the minds of his subordinates, that Grouchy would respond to the summons. So confident of this he even announced Grouchy had arrived several hours later to bolster the flagging French army. In doing so, as typified his character, Napoléon was failing to acknowledge his own errors, as it must have been clear to him once the 10.00 dispatch arrived that Grouchy could not get to Waterloo. The blame, however, must fall with Napoléon. General Drouot recalled:[1]

Meantime, the Prussian corps which had joined the left of the English placed itself *en potence* upon our right flank and began to attack about half-past five in the afternoon. The 6th Corps, which had taken no part in the battle of the 16th, was placed to oppose them, and was supported by a division of the Young Guard and some battalions of the Guard. Towards seven o'clock we perceived in the distance, towards our right, a fire of artillery and musketry. It was not doubted that Marshal Grouchy had followed the movement of the Prussians, and was coming to take part in the victory. Cries of joy were heard along our whole line. The troops, fatigued by eight combats ['*huit combats*', perhaps it should be '*huit heures de combats*', or 'eight hours of fighting'] recovered their vigour and made new efforts. The emperor regarded this moment as decisive. He brought forward all his Guard, ordered four battalions to pass near the village of Mont-Saint-Jean, to advance upon the enemy's position, and to carry with the bayonet whatever should resist them. The cavalry of the Guard, and all the other cavalry that remained at hand, supported this movement. The four battalions, upon arriving on the plateau, were received by the most terrible fire of musketry and canister. The great number of wounded who detached themselves from the columns made it believe that the Guard was routed. Panic spread to the neighbouring corps, which precipitately took flight. The enemy's cavalry, which perceives this disorder, is let loose into the plain; it is checked for some time by the twelve battalions of the Old Guard who had not yet charged, but even these troops were carried away by this inexplicable movement, and follow the steps of the fugitives, but with more order.

Drouot writes in the immediate aftermath of defeat, and it seems is the originator of the story of Grouchy losing the battle. Did Drouot know of orders for Grouchy to head to Waterloo which made him think this, and that any trace of such an order being lost? Perhaps, but without any shred of evidence at all to vindicate Drouot, it seems he was making Grouchy a scapegoat. Of interest, Drouot is also the originator of the theory that mud delayed the start of the battle, which can be categorically shown to be wrong. Drouot, therefore, seems to have been clutching at straws to explain the defeat, rather than face facts that Wellington and Blücher made fewer mistakes in the campaign when it mattered, and were able to concentrate their forces at the crucial time, winning Waterloo and the campaign. The emperor sent Grouchy off on a mission that could not succeed, and based on evidence, knew Grouchy was not coming to Waterloo. To bolster the army's morale, he spread the lie that Grouchy had arrived. This would prove fatal to the morale of the army when the lie was exposed for what it was. General Haxo, commanding the Imperial Guard equipment train, engineers, sailors and pontoon train, writes on 25 June that he was sent to look out for Grouchy:[2]

> General Bülow advanced on the right flank of the army, and we began to feel their fire. In the position where the emperor was, already Prussians cannon balls became crossed with those of the English. He [the emperor] persuaded himself that the army corps of General [sic] Grouchy, whom he had ordered to make a great movement, had arrived in the rear of the Prussians. He sent for Haxo to go and recognise the efforts Grouchy made, but he discovered nothing, and remained convinced that it was a fable invented by the emperor to encourage his troops. General Haxo, returning from his reconnaissance, found that the emperor, without waiting for the result of his mission, had committed the Guard. This attack could only have been planned so that Grouchy would have halted the advance of General Bülow, otherwise, even though the French would have broken the British line which was opposed to them, they then would have been taken from behind by Bülow, and

the consequence of their success would have been to make us all prisoners. Instead, the Guard was shaken by a huge loss and it was thrown back, and immediately putting into disorder the army corps that was further back, everything started to flee by pushing into the only road which the French army had.

Captain Jean Baptiste Philibert Vaillant, aide-de-camp to General Haxo, who commanded the Imperial Guard engineers and equipment trains, notes:[3]

> At Waterloo, of terrible memory, I stayed from noon until night with the staff of the emperor, a few feet away, hearing the verbal reports that were made, and the orders he gave. I was one of the officers he sent down the line with the news that the battle was won and that Grouchy arrived behind the English with 40,000 men!

The news of Grouchy's arrival is said to have bolstered the flagging morale of the army. However, any belief they had that Grouchy had arrived was rudely shattered. Battalion Commander Rullieres, of the 85th Regiment of Line Infantry, notes:[4]

> Sometime between three or four o'clock we began to perceive movements of the Prussians on the right of our army. Shortly after, we received musket fire from their scouts. My battalion was ordered to stop them—we succeeded—a vigorous exchange of musketry began and reigned for a half-hour, when the General de La Bédoyère, aide to the emperor, crossing the front of the army, came to announce that Marshal Grouchy was debouching on our right. I remarked that he needed to know it was unlikely as it was the Prussians that we had before us, that had already killed and wounded several men and in the same moment the captain of voltigeurs in my battalion fell wounded, a ball at the thigh.

Captain Robinaux, of the 2nd Regiment of Line Infantry, narrates that:[5]

> The emperor, seeing an army corps that emerged into the plain, immediately announced the arrival of General Grouchy, he ordered the commander of the cavalry to attack immediately the plateau of Mont-Saint-Jean, occupied by the British under the command of General-in-Chief Commander of the Combined Armies Lord Wellington, and there he found a strong resistance and numerous artillery lying in wait, which vomited fire and flames on all sides; the

Imperial Guard advanced at once and quickly took the position; the Guard immediately formed a square and fought hard, and despite being summoned several times to surrender, preferred death to dishonour.

Jacques Martin, an officer with the French 45th Regiment of Line Infantry, narrates the end of the battle as he saw it:[6]

While the Old Guard was preparing its formidable attack, Napoléon had in the army announced the arrival of Grouchy and the certainty of victory. It rekindled a new enthusiasm; his half-destroyed army corps of d'Erlon shook again with the cries of 'long live the emperor', to the right respond where we are, to the left where the Guard started his attack. The divisions of Marcognet and Durutte were already crowning the plateau. Right now (it was half-past seven), a mass of infantry, cavalry and artillery rushed to the battlefield. Who is it that brings us finally to stop destiny? Alas! It is not Grouchy! It was Blücher and his army.

Everything bowed to the flood of enemies. No more hope, No more resistance. Our divisions descend into confusion on the slopes of the valley. The Prussian cavalry was overflowing everywhere. Our soldiers believe themselves betrayed and disperse. Of the army corps of d'Erlon, there remained only one battalion, one company in order; all the artillery is in the hands of the enemy. Everyone fled as fast and as far as they could; I did, like the others.

Other army corps disbanded at the same time. Panic swept through the army. It is only a confused mass of infantry, cavalry, cannons, rushing over each other and roll into the plain like a raging torrent, through which the Prussian squadrons charge and before the battalions descended from the English plateau with shouts of victory. Only a few squares of the Guard, chosen by Napoléon at the foot of La-Belle-Alliance, remain motionless as rocks in a raging sea. Streams of fugitives flow between these heroic squares, and soon the only enemies around them. Then these living redoubts are demolished by shrapnel, and resistance ends.

The indignity of the lie is expressed by Marbot. The following letter, written on 26 June from Laon, gives Marbot's fresh impressions of Waterloo:[7]

I cannot get over our defeat. We were manoeuvred like so many pumpkins. I was with my regiment on the right flank of the army almost throughout the battle. They assured me that Marshal Grouchy would come up at that point; and it was guarded only by my regiment with three guns and a battalion of infantry—not nearly enough. Instead of Grouchy, what arrived was Blücher's corps.

Napoléon had acted cynically to try and wage a propaganda war that totally failed to try and bolster the morale of his soldiers and officers alike. The army was far from a cohesive formation. Rumours of desertion and dubious loyalties were rife. The defection of de Bourmont on the 15th had crippled 4th Corps for some hours; Durutte's staff had defected on 16 June, as had officers in the carabinier brigade. At Waterloo, several officers had defected to the Allies. The men did not know who to trust, the vital bonds of loyalty so crucial to unit morale and cohesion simply did not exist to any great extent. The great lie that Grouchy had arrived, but was in fact the Prussians, resulted in panic and alarm. Were these men really the Prussians, or had Grouchy changed sides too? Several officers thought so. de Brack, an officer serving with the light horse lancers of the Imperial Guard at Waterloo, narrates:[8]

> To make our grief complete, rumours were running through our ranks: our right was routed; Grouchy had sold himself to the enemy; Bourmont, Clouet, du Barail and many officers had deserted; a senior officer of the column that had just attacked the Scots had fallen, hit by a case shot, and 200 white cockades had spilled from his shako.

It is easy to see that the sudden firing in the rear of the French army could easily set off a wave of panic. Coming on top of this sudden realisation that the army was now surrounded, came the shock of the defeat of the Old Guard. Aide-de-camp to Marshal Ney, Octave Lavavasseur, notes the panic that gripped the French army with the arrival of the Prussians:[9]

> ...cannon shots are heard in our rear. There came a great stunned silence, anxiety followed our enthusiasm to succeed. The plain was covered with our horse teams and the multitude of non-combatants who always followed the army; the gunfire continued to approach. Officers and soldiers became muddled up, and mixed with the non-combatants. Appalled, I went to find the marshal, who prescribed me to go find out the cause of this panic. I approached General [name left blank by the author] who said: 'look! These are the Prussians!' I returned to find the marshal, but I could not find him. Our army was

now just a shapeless mass; all the regiments had become intermingled. In that fatal moment there were no orders given, everyone was taken aback in the presence of a danger they could not define.

A study was undertaken into the morale of the French army in the 1860s by General Trochu. In his study, General Trochu describes panics as caused by the instinct of self-preservation and by the spirit of imitation. Their effects may be most disastrous, he notes. He cites the following examples:[10]

- That if one horse of a heard gallops away, the rest follow;
- If the head of a column takes to flight, the rest of the column run also, without knowing why or wherefore;
- Young soldiers, which as we have seen composed the bulk of the French army in 1815, are more liable than old soldiers to panics, which sometimes operate with irresistible force;
- Panics occur at night, when the enemy is supposed to be near; and
- By day, after a defeat, or a hotly-contested action.

General Trochu then dwells on the necessity of the existence of the most absolute confidence between officers and soldiers, and of the award of proper recompenses to those who deserve them. In 1815, the army as a whole lacked this absolute trust and confidence between the officers, sub-officers and men. Trochu notes that the real character of men is revealed in war; in all armies exist braggarts and bullies. Boastful men and loud-talkers, theoretically brave, are apt to become silent and disconcerted at the approach of a combat. Some unable to conquer their feelings practise that part of valour which is considered to be the most discreet, and disappear. Others, a prey to a painful agitation, restrain its appearance by force of character, but are incapable to lead or to be led. A certain number, of a cool, calm, and apparently mild temperament men, he notes, suddenly and unexpectedly become the bravest of the brave and exercise, by the force of their example, an irresistible influence over the masses.

Furthermore, Trochu adds that any unusual sight or sound, or any unexpected appearance, may strike the imagination and cause the greatest havoc, or create the most senseless perturbation. A panic, he notes, may be termed an unreasoning alarm without cause or with insufficient cause, and that it cannot be arrested, but it may be averted by proper instruction and caution. Once the process had started it could not be stopped. Napoléon's lie about Grouchy was a root cause for defeat at Waterloo; he alone was the cause of this, and not Grouchy. As soon as the truth was revealed that the Prussians were behind the

French army, the army panicked and fled—the root cause Napoléon's lie.

When we look at Grouchy's controversial mission in detail, firstly Napoléon was utterly at fault for delaying Grouchy's march on 17 June. He spends most of the day visiting the battlefield and chatting to Prussian prisoners and reviewing his army. The Napoléon of 1806 would have been straight after the Prussians and would not have allowed them to slip away in the darkness of the night of 16 June and the first half of 17 June.

Secondly, Napoléon is at fault for the vagueness of the orders issued to Grouchy. Grouchy however, had had to think beyond the remit of his orders in order to find the Prussians. Napoléon had created a culture of fear around him in his subordinates, which rendered his generals mere marionettes, who were not allowed to think for themselves or to dare to contradict Napoléon's word. Grouchy it seems, was prepared to face some imperial wrath.

Grouchy is usually blamed for squandering his resources, because he outnumbered the Prussians under Thielemann, but this is probably not the case. Thielemann had at his disposal, on 18 June, 19,500 infantry, 3,450 cavalry and forty guns. Grouchy is said to have commanded 35,000 men. This is simply not true. Grouchy commanded 27,000 men, of whom 23,000 were infantry, thus the two forces were approximately equal. However, this belies the fact that until Gérard's 4th Corps arrived about 18.00, followed by Teste's command sometime later, Grouchy was outnumbered at Wavre, Bas-Wavre and Bièrges by almost two-to-one. Only with the full arrival of all his troops in the evening of the 18th did Grouchy obtain troop superiority.

When one takes into consideration the losses sustained by Vandamme's men in the first stage of the action from around 14.00 to 19.00, Gérard's men perhaps did not overtly tip the action in favour of the French numerically, but did provide fresh troops to go into action against weary Prussians who had received no reinforcements, other than the troops of General Borcke's brigade, which was sucked into the action of 19 June near Neuf Cabaret. The two forces that faced each other over the River Dyle were about equal, Grouchy did not have overwhelming troop superiority, neither did he have at Wavre and Bas-Wavre an opportunity to follow up the early success, due to the bottleneck of feeding men over the Dyle onto the northern bank, where Thielemann could operate virtually unmolested and march reinforcements to check Vandamme far quicker than Vandamme could feed men into the action, neither of which are directly attributable to failings of Marshal Grouchy. Not outflanking Thielemann further south by crossing the Dyle at Moustier does not seem to have been a considered option, assuming Grouchy was aware of this bridge. To reach the bridge, his troops would have either had to fight their way past Thielemann at Wavre to head south or retreat south to Mont-Saint-Gilbert and then head to Moustier, which would have taken time—a full-frontal, headlong assault, it seems, was the only initial option Grouchy explored, and only later did he pin down Thielemann at Wavre and send Gérard and Teste south to outflank Wavre and head to Brussels, where Grouchy was convinced the Prussians were heading until he received Napoléon's summons around 19.00. Napoléon seems to have been totally ignorant of the situation Grouchy was in. A quick glance at either the Ferraris map of 1777 or Le Capitaine map of 1789, both of which were used in the campaign, shows the terrain Grouchy had to fight over. Napoléon knew very well the nature of the terrain between Waterloo and Wavre, and yet he still ordered Grouchy to Wavre, knowing that when Grouchy went into action with the Prussians, it was not as simple as he thought to break off the action, pin down and control the Prussians and then send men to Waterloo. Napoléon was asking the impossible.

Grouchy chose to try and fight his way to Saint-Lambert, with Vandamme heading off to Brussels via Louvain on 19 June, and Vichery, with 4th and 6th Corps, heading to Rixensart in the direction of the field of Waterloo. With Napoléon's news received about 19.00, of the three Prussian columns, Grouchy had one in front of him at Wavre, one facing Napoléon, and the third was either heading to Brussels or was linking with Wellington, which history tells us it did. Grouchy's mission-blindness in heading to Brussels, it seems, had clouded his objective judgement, but in heading to Brussels he was executing Napoléon's orders, and when new orders did arrive, it was far too late for Grouchy to change his modus opperandi. Napoléon and Grouchy are equally culpable, Napoléon more so for issuing vague and unrealistic orders.

Finally, the ultimate blame for the mistakes made during the campaign must lie with the commander-in-chief: Napoléon. He foolishly divided his army, so that a river and a dense forest separated the two wings, impeding communication and slowing down any effort to join up. Yet, the failure to 'march to the sound of the guns' is traditionally directly blamed on Grouchy (despite most of the evidence usually used to blame him having little basis in fact), but more importantly, that given the geographical disposition of his men, there is no way he could have arrived in time to alter the course of the Battle of Waterloo. Grouchy was far from an ideal choice as commander of the detached force, but he was severely hampered by errors made by Napoléon. Napoléon alone is to blame for detaching the force under Grouchy and placing them beyond a river and forest, and issuing him vague orders. Napoléon lost the Battle of Waterloo due to mistakes of his own making.

Grouchy, however, bears some responsibility. He repeatedly threw Vandamme's 3rd Corps into Wavre, rather than using his cavalry force to find a ford either up- or downstream, and then be able to cross the Dyle unmolested and out-flank the Prussians, the fact this did not happen is a failure on behalf of Grouchy, and was a direct contributor to his forces getting bogged down in Wavre. Excelmans should have been sent off to reconnoitre both flanks of the Prussians, find a river crossing, and to make contact with Napoléon. Excelmans, on 18 June, appears to have contributed very little to the action at Wavre. He could, and should, have been ordered to move to Waterloo by Grouchy. Instead, an entire cavalry corps was uselessly tied down, just as with d'Erlon's 1st Corps on 16 June. Lack of initiative by Grouchy, and from Excelmans, was a major contributing factor to the outcome of 18 June for the right wing. In defence of Grouchy, he did eventually come to his senses and sent Pajol off to reconnoitre for a river crossing, supported by infantry, out-flanked the Prussians and opened the way to Waterloo. This could, and should, have happened much earlier in the day, as it was it was too little too late, and that falls totally with Grouchy. Excelmans's corps should then have been sent off to Waterloo—we can only speculate about the outcome of the battle if his men came charging into the rear of Bülow!

Grouchy, even if he crossed the Dyle at 15.00, still could not have got to Waterloo with his infantry and artillery until the battle had been lost. He was given an impossible task to perform to get to Waterloo and intervene decisively in the battle. As it was, he did not get the order until 18.00 to 19.00.

What, then, can we say of Grouchy? His track record in the years before 1815, and during the campaign, was faultless. His retreat from 19 June was an almost perfect fighting retreat. Grouchy has often been lambasted for not being fit for independent command, but his actions in the campaign clearly show he was, and far more competent than Ney. Historian George Hooper comments:[11]

> The truth is that on the morning of the 18th, the facts of the situation, if we may be allowed the phrase, rendered it impossible for Grouchy to prevent the junction of Wellington and Blücher. One fact alone ought to settle the question forever. Grouchy, at Gembloux, was separated from Napoléon at La-Belle-Alliance by more than twice the

distance which separated Blücher from Wellington. No manoeuvring could have made the lines of march shorter. Four Prussian army corps were nearer to Wellington than two French army corps were to Napoléon … Turn it which way we may, consider it a question of generalship, or one of time and distance, and we arrive at the same conclusion. It was, on the morning of the 18th, beyond the power of Grouchy to alter materially the Battle of Waterloo.

In Hooper's judgement we concur, and despite Napoléon casting blame on others, if any commander blundered on 15 to 17 June, it was Napoléon himself. Napoléon, on 17 June, was obsessed with Namur, and then a move to Maastricht, and only on 18 June at 10.00 did he ever consider that the Prussians might get to join Wellington. The tipping point in the defeat at Waterloo was Napoléon's failure to pass on the information about the columns headed from Gentinnes and to fully understand what he was told.

The columns had been spotted by Milhaud, and then later on 17 June by Domon. They were seemingly inconsequential to the emperor. He was initially fixated on Namur and then a Prussian line of retreat to Louvain. He could not comprehend of the communication between Wellington and the Prussians, or that the Prussians could carry on the fight. When Excelmans was sent out on the morning of 17 June, he was sent away from where the Prussian 1st and 2nd Corps were moving from. Grouchy never found these troops. When Napoléon reported a troop presence at Wavre, Grouchy assumed these were the same troops that Vandamme had spotted, and were the troops from Gembloux. At no stage did Grouchy ever think otherwise. When General Domon found the Prussians at Moustier on the night of 17 June, and Marbot found the place emptied, Napoléon assumed that the Prussians were not heading to link with Wellington, but were making for the Namur to Louvain road, which was correct. He failed to grasp that the Prussians could pass through Wavre and then turn west to join Wellington, because he felt in his own mind that the Prussians were 100 per cent heading to Louvain. The appearance of the Prussian 4th Corps in no way changed his thinking, as Grouchy had reported the whereabouts of the 1st, 2nd and 3rd Prussian Corps. Where Napoléon thought the 4th Corps had come from we can only guess. Did he assume it was the troops that Milhaud and Domon had spotted? Perhaps. This lulled him into a false sense of security that the only Prussians he would confront were those of the Prussian 4th Corps. It was a logical assumption to make. The truth was Grouchy had pursued only the Prussian 3rd and 4th Corps. He was not aware of the major Prussian troop concentration between him and the emperor. He could not act offensively against troops he did not know existed heading from Gentinnes. He cannot be blamed for the emperor not sending him intelligence reports until far too late to act upon. If Grouchy had known a large body of Prussians was heading to Wavre on 17 June, as a separate body to those moving back from Gembloux, the obvious answer was 'here are the Prussians'. Yet, Napoléon failed to inform him of this fact. When Berton and Excelmans reported to headquarters 'here be 30,000 Prussians' at Gembloux, Napoléon sent no infantry off as soon as the dispatch came in about 9.00. Four hours were wasted, and in those four hours the Prussians got away from Grouchy, and Prussian 1st and 2nd Corps slipped away north. With hindsight, these two command decisions made by Napoléon lost the campaign. These were catastrophic errors. The third mistake was the emperor became mission-blind in that the Prussians were off to Namur, and then Maastricht, and then Louvain, and could not fight and could not get to Wellington. This chain of wrong decisions made by the emperor compounded the other two major mistakes. Napoléon was not betrayed by Soult, nor by Grouchy—he alone bears responsibility for his actions on 17 June.

Yet, since 18 June 1815, the blame for the defeat of the army had been squarely placed with Ney, Soult and Grouchy. Grouchy cannot take blame for what happened. All of Grouchy's reconnaissance reports indicated a Prussian retreat to Louvain, which is of course where Prussian 4th Corps was going before it headed west. As Grouchy was moving north-east, the body of troops Milhaud had found was moving north to join Wellington. In assuming the Prussians could not fight was a blunder of immense proportions made by Napoléon alone. He had preconceived ideas that did not match reality. Napoléon is to blame for the controversial mission of Grouchy, who was denied his light cavalry 'eyes and ears', denied vital information about the Prussians, and sent off far too late to catch the Prussians at Gembloux, which was the only chance Grouchy ever had in catching the Prussians. That failure to send off infantry in response to Excelmans report was a cataclysmic error, and no blame can be ascribed to Grouchy.

NOTES:

[1] *Journal de l'Empire*, 27 June 1815, pp. 1-2.

[2] *Revue Historique dirigée par MM. G. Monod et G. Fagniez*, Part 1, Paris , 1879, p. 376.

[3] *Carnet de la Sabretache*, 1899, p. 243.

[4] SHDDT: GD 2 1135.

[5] Pierre Robinaux, Gustave Léon Schlumberger, *Journal de route du Capitaine Robinaux 1803-1832*, Plon-Nourrit, Paris, 1908.

[6] Jacques François Martin, *Souvenirs d'un ex-officier 1812-1815*, Paris, 1867, pp. 297-8.

[7] Edmond-Charles-Constant Louvat, *Historique du 7e Hussards*, Pairault, Paris, 1889, p. 288.

[8] Digby Smith, personal communication, 2010.

[9] Octave Levavasseur, *Souvenirs militaires 1800-1815*, Librairie des Deux Empirés, 2001, pp. 303-5.

[10] Louis-Jules Trochu, *L'armée française en 1867*, Amyot, Paris, 1867.

[11] George Hooper, *Waterloo, the Downfall of the First Napoleon*, Smith, Elder, London, 1862, pp. 343-4.

Bibliography

Archive Sources
The bulk of this work is based primarily on archive sources held in the Archives Nationales and Service Historique du Armée du Térre, both institutions being in Paris.

Archives Nationales:
AN AFIV 1939 Registre d'Ordres du Major General 13 Juin au 26 Juin 1815

AN LH 62/73	AN LH 910/54	AN LH 2226/19
AN LH 142/69	AN LH 963/46	AN LH 2228/47
AN LH 168/59	AN LH 1026/31	AN LH 2267/29
AN LH 169/57	AN LH 1050/30	AN LH 2276/52
AN LH 256/15	AN LH 1101/66	AN LH 2302/45
AN LH 258/5	AN LH 1121/44	AN LH 2330/17
AN LH 367/78	AN LH 1123/3	AN LH 2337/47
AN LH 377/15	AN LH 1214/28	AN LH 2421/2
AN LH 468/64	AN LH 1225/8	AN LH 2442/29
AN LH 479/47	AN LH 1227/40	AN LH 2459/56
AN LH 494/74	AN LH 1256/7	AN LH 2500/53
AN LH 542/61	AN LH 1311/4	AN LH 2595/11
AN LH 568/79	AN LH 1438/54	AN LH 2603/55
AN LH 616/28	AN LH 1498/10	AN LH 2628/33
AN LH 664/2	AN LH 1620/22	AN LH 2636/49
AN LH 747/48	AN LH 1783/8	AN LH 2725/17
AN LH 771/50	AN LH 1900/46	AN LH 2758/3
AN LH 809/37	AN LH 1959/46	AN LH 2782/98
AN LH 887/64	AN LH 2013/2	
AN LH 897/41	AN LH 2035/60	

Service Historique Armée du Terre:
C15 4 Correspondence Armée du Nord 1 au 10 Juin 1815
C15 5 Correspondence Armée du Nord 11 Juin au 21 Juin 1815
C15 6 Correspondence Armée du Nord 22 Juin au 3 Juillet 1815
C15 22 registre correspondence 2e corps observation Armée du Nord
C15 23 Registre d'Ordres et de correspondance du major-général à 3e Corps d'Armée

C15 35 Situations Armée du Nord 1815
C16 20 Correspondence Militaire General 1 Juin au 7 Juin 1815
C16 21 Correspondence Militaire General 8 Juin au 18 Juin 1815
C16 22 Correspondence Militaire General 19 Juin au 25 Juin 1815
C16 23 Correspondence Militaire General 26 Juin au 6 Juillet 1815
C37 15 Correspondence Ministre de Guerre

Xc 192 4e Chasseurs à Cheval
Xc 238 1e Hussard. Dossier 1814
Xc 249 7e Hussard 1791-1815

GD 2 1135

GR 2 YB 232 Contrôle Nominatif Officiers 32e régiment du Ligne 1 Juillet 1814 a 1 Mai 1815

GR 20 YC 55
GR 20 YC 56
GR 20 YC 137
GR 20 YC 154 registre matricule Dragons Garde Impériale

GR 21 YC 40 4e régiment d'infanterie de ligne dit régiment de Monsieur, 18 Août 1814-13 Avril 1815 (matricules 1 à 1,800)
GR 21 YC 41 4e régiment d'infanterie de ligne dit régiment de Monsieur, 14 Avril 1815-16 Mai 1815 (matricules 1,801 à 2,103)
GR 21 YC 111 12e régiment d'infanterie de ligne, 9 Septembre 1814-11 Décembre 1814 (matricules 1 à 1,824)
GR 21 YC 112 12e régiment d'infanterie de ligne, 11 Décembre 1814-29 Juillet 1815 (matricules 1,825 à 2,453)
GR 21 YC 197 21e régiment d'infanterie de ligne, 18-20 mai 1815 (matricules 1 à 1,800)
GR 21 YC 208 registre matricule du 22e régiment d'infanterie de ligne 29 Janvier 1804 à 3 Juillet 1815
GR 21 YC 215 23e régiment d'infanterie de ligne, 16 Juillet 1814-13 Décembre 1814 (matricules 1 à 1,800)
GR 21 YC 216 23e régiment d'infanterie de ligne, 8 Décembre 1814-11 Août 1815 (matricules 1,801 à 2,358)
GR 21 YC 278 30e régiment d'infanterie de ligne, 20 Février 1813-21 Juillet 1814 (matricules 12,577 à 16,020)
GR 21 YC 279 30e régiment d'infanterie de ligne, 21 Juillet 1814-6 Juillet 1815 (matricules 16,021 à 16,744)
GR 21 YC 280 registre matricule du 30e régiment d'infanterie de ligne 21 Juillet 1814 à 6 Juillet 1815
GR 21 YC 301 32e régiment d'infanterie de ligne (ex 33e régiment d'infanterie de ligne), 13 Août 1814-14 Mars 1815 (matricules 1,801 à 2,253)
GR 21 YC 302 registre matricule du 32e régiment d'infanterie de ligne réorganisation de 1814 29 Mai 1815 à 25 Juin 1815
GR 21 YC 309 33e régiment d'infanterie de ligne (ex 34e régiment d'infanterie de ligne), 19 Juillet 1814-4 Novembre 1814 (matricules 1 à 1,800)

323

GR 21 YC 310 33e régiment d'infanterie de ligne (ex 34e régiment d'infanterie de ligne), 19 Juillet 1814-21 Juillet 1815 (matricules 1,801 à 2,572)

GR 21 YC 336 36e régiment d'infanterie de ligne (ex 37e régiment d'infanterie de ligne), 4 Août 1814-8 Avril 1815 (matricules 1 à 1,800)

GR 21 YC 337 36e régiment d'infanterie de ligne (ex 37e régiment d'infanterie de ligne), 14 Avril 1815-11 Juillet 1815 (matricules 1,801 à 2,233)

GR 21 YC 381 41e régiment d'infanterie de ligne (ex 44e régiment d'infanterie de ligne), 1 Octobre 1814-17 Janvier 1815 (matricules 1 à 1,800)

GR 21 YC 382 41e régiment d'infanterie de ligne (ex 44e régiment d'infanterie de ligne), 17 Janvier 1815-1 Septembre 1815 (matricules 1,801 à 2,358)

GR 21 YC 416 45e régiment d'infanterie de ligne (ex 48e régiment d'infanterie de ligne), 1 Septembre 1814-30 Avril 1815 (matricules 1 à 1,800)

GR 21 YC 424 46e régiment d'infanterie de ligne (ex 50e régiment d'infanterie de ligne), 24 Novembre 1814-3 Mai 1815 (matricules 1 à 1,800)

GR 21 YC 471 52e régiment d'infanterie de ligne (ex 56e régiment d'infanterie de ligne), 5 Août 1814-2 Mai 1815 (matricules 1 à 1,800)

GR 21 YC 472 52e régiment d'infanterie de ligne (ex 56e régiment d'infanterie de ligne), 2 Mai 1815-28 Juillet 1815 (matricules 1,801 à 1,910)

GR 21 YC 500 55e régiment d'infanterie de ligne (ex 59e régiment d'infanterie de ligne), 28 Août 1814-22 Août 1815 (matricules 1 à 1,848)

GR 21 YC 534 59e régiment d'infanterie de ligne (ex 63e régiment d'infanterie de ligne), 25 Août 1814-5 Décembre 1814 (matricules 1 à 1,800)

GR 21 YC 535 59e régiment d'infanterie de ligne (ex 63e régiment d'infanterie de ligne), 5 Décembre 1814-31 Juillet 1815 (matricules 1,801 à 2,197)

GR 21 YC 541 60e régiment d'infanterie de ligne (réorganisation de 1814), 9 Août 1814-21 Janvier 1815 (matricules 1 à 1,800)

GR 21 YC 542 60e régiment d'infanterie de ligne (réorganisation de 1814), 21 Janvier 1815-11 Juillet 1815 (matricules 1,801 à 3,274)

GR 21 YC 550 61e régiment d'infanterie de ligne (ex 65e régiment d'infanterie de ligne), 1 Août 1814-22 Mars 1815 (matricule 1 à 1,800)

GR 21 YC 580 64e régiment d'infanterie de ligne (ex 69e régiment d'infanterie de ligne), 6 Septembre 1814-28 Mai 1815 (matricules 1 à 1,800)

GR 21 YC 590 65e régiment d'infanterie de ligne (ex 70e régiment d'infanterie de ligne), 16 Septembre 1814-15 Mai 1815 (matricules 1 à 1,800).

GR 21 YC 607 67e régiment d'infanterie de ligne (ex 75e régiment d'infanterie de ligne), 1 Septembre 1814-2 Janvier 1815 (matricules 1 à 1,800)

GR 21 YC 608 67e régiment d'infanterie de ligne (ex 75e régiment d'infanterie de ligne), 2 Janvier 1815-5 Août 1815 (matricules 1,801 à 2,187)

GR 21 YC 614 68e régiment d'infanterie de ligne (ex 76e régiment d'infanterie de ligne), 16 Août 1814-20 Juin 1815 (matricules 1 à 1,800)

GR 21 YC 640 71e régiment d'infanterie de ligne (ex 82e régiment d'infanterie de ligne), formation au 11 Août 1814 (matricules 1 à 1,790)

GR 21 YC 641 71e régiment d'infanterie de ligne (ex 82e régiment d'infanterie de ligne), 11-26 Août 1814 (matricules 1,791 à 3,281)

GR 21 YC 673 74e régiment d'infanterie de ligne (ex 86e régiment d'infanterie de ligne), 19 Août 1814-9 Août 1815 (matricules 1 à 1,751)

GR 21 YC 681 75e régiment d'infanterie de ligne (ex 88e régiment d'infanterie de ligne), 7 Juillet 1814-18 Juillet 1815 (matricules 1 à 1,681)

GR 21 YC 725 80e régiment d'infanterie de ligne (ex 96e régiment d'infanterie de ligne), 7 Août 1814-2 Février 1815 (matricules 1 à 1,798)

GR 21 YC 726 80e régiment d'infanterie de ligne (ex 96e régiment d'infanterie de ligne), 2 Février 1815-16 Août 1815 (matricules 1,799 à 2,414)

GR 21 YC 798 90e régiment d'infanterie de ligne (ex 111e régiment d'infanterie de ligne), 1 Août 1814-7 Mai 1815 (matricules 1 à 1,800)

GR 22 YC 81

GR 22 YC 104 12e régiment d'infanterie légère Août 1814-Avril 1815 (matricules 1 à 1,800)

GR 22 YC 105 12e régiment d'infanterie légère Avril 1815-mai 1815 (matricules 1,801 à 2,112)

GR 24 YC 36

GR 24 YC 41

GR 24 YC 55

GR 24 YC 60 Controle Nominiatif Troupe 10e Cuirassiers 15 Avril 1815-27 Juillet 1815 organisation 1814

GR 24 YC 299

GR 25 YC 21 2e Artillerie à Pied

Printed works:

Winand Aerts, *Waterloo, opérations de l'armée prussienne du Bas-Rhin pendant la campagne de Belgique en 1815, depuis, la bataille de Ligny jusqu'a l'entrée en France des troupes prussiennes*, Spineux, Brussels, 1908

Maurice Girod de l'Ain, *Vie militaire du Géneral Foy*, E. Plon, Nourrit et Cie, Paris, 1900

Mameluck Ali, *Souvenirs sur l'empereur Napoléon*, Ed. Christophe Bourachot, Arléa, Paris, 2000

Anon, *Memoires pour servir a l'Histoire de France*, Richard Phillips & Co, London, 1820

Anon, *Tales of War*, William Mark Clarke, London, 1836

Anon, *The Journal of the Three Days of the Battle of Waterloo*, T. Chaplin, London, 1816

Thomas Joseph Aubry, *Mémoires d'un capitaine de chasseurs à cheval*, Jourdan, Paris, 2011

Paul Avers, *Historique du 82e Régiment d'Infanterie de Ligne et du 7e Régiment d'Infanterie Légère, 1684-1876*, Lahure, Paris, 1876

Georges Barral, *L'Épopée de Waterloo, etc*, Paris, 1895

Robert Batty, *An Historical Account of the Campaign of Waterloo*, Rodwell and Martin and Co, London, 1820

Marie Élli Guillaume de Baudus, *Études sur Napoléon* (two volumes), Debecourt, Paris, 1841

Charles Paris Nicholas Beauvais, *Victoires, conquêtes, désastres, revers et guerres civils des Français, de 1792 à 1815*, C. L. F. Panckoucke, Paris, 1821

A. F. Becke, *Napoleon and Waterloo: the Emperor's Campaign with the Armée du Nord, 1815*, Greenhill Books, London, 1995

Stephen M. Beckett, *Waterloo Betrayed: The Secret Treachery that Defeated Napoleon*, Mapleflower House Publishing, 2015

Antoine Nicolas Béraud, *Histoire de Napoléon*, J. B. de Kock, Brussels, 1829

Pierre Berthezène, *Souvenirs militaires de la republique et de l'empire*, J. Dumaine, Paris, 1855

Jean Baptiste Berton, *Précis historique, militaire et critique des batailles de Fleurus et de Waterloo, dans la campagne de Flandres, en juin 1815*, J. S. Wallez, La Haye, 1818

John Booth, *The Battle of Waterloo*, Booth, Egerton, London, 1816

John Booth, *The Battle of Waterloo, also of Ligny, and Quarter-Bras*, London, 1817

Major von Bornstedt, Louise von Bornstedt, *Das Gefecht bei Wavre an der Dyle am 18 und 19 Juni 1815*, Heinicke, Berlin, 1858

Albert Burow, *Geschichte des Könglich Preussischen 18 Infanterie-Regiments von 1813 bis 1847* ed. Rudolph von Wedell, Posen, 1848

Lieutenant Chevalier, *Souvenirs des Guerres Napoleoniennes* ed. Jean Mistler and Helene Michaud, Hachette, Paris, 1970

Silvain Larreguy de Civrieux, *Souvenirs d'un cadet, 1813-1823*, Hachette, Paris, 1912

Tim Clayton, *Waterloo: Four Days that Changed Europe's Destiny*, Little, Brown, London, 2014

John Coates, *The Hour Between Dog and Wolf*, Fourth Estate, London, 2012

Jean-Roch Coignet, *The Narrative of Captain Coignet Soldier of the Empire, 1776-1850*, Chatto & Windus, London, 1897

Combes-Brassard, *Notice sur la bataille de Mont-Saint-Jean* in *Souvenirs et Correspondance sur la bataille de Waterloo*, Librairie historique Teissèdre, Paris, 2000

Emile von Conrady, *Geschichte des Könglich preussischen sechsten Infaterie-regiments*, Glogau, 1857

N. Cornevin, *Les Marchands de Vin de Paris*, Paris, 1869

Edward Cotton, *A Voice from Waterloo*, Mont-St-Jean, Belgium, 1877

Jean Baptiste Pierre Jullien Courcelles, *Dictionnaire historique et biographique des généraux Français*, Paris, 1823

Gregor Dallas, *1815: The Roads to Waterloo*, Pimlico, London, 1996

Karl von Damitz, *Geschichte des Feldzuges von 1815 in den Niederlanden und Frankreich* (two volumes), E. S. Mittler, Berlin, 1838

François-Thomas Delbare, *Relation circonstanciée de la dernière campagne de Buonaparte, terminée par le bataille de Mont-Saint-Jean, dite de Waterloo ou de la Belle-Alliance*, J. G. Dentu, Paris, 1816

François-Thomas Delbare, René Bourgeois, *Relation fidele et détaillée de la dernière campagne de Buonaparte : terminée par la bataille de Mont-Saint-Jean, dite de Waterloo ou de la Belle-Alliance*, Brussels, 1816

Wilhelm Ludwig Victor Henckel von Donnersmarck, *Erinnerungen aus meinem Leben*, Kummer, Zerbst, 1846

Jean-Baptiste Drouët, *Le maréchal Drouet, comte d'Erlon: Vie militaire écrit par lui même*, Guvatve, Paris, 1844

Jacques-Antoine Dulaure, *1814-1830 Historie des Cent-jours*, Paris, 1834

Victor Dupuy, *Mémoires Militaire 1794-1816*, Librairie des deux Empirés, 2001

Pierre Duthlit, *Les Mémoires du Capitaine Duthlit*, Lille, 1909

John Robert Elting, *Swords Around a Throne*, Phoenix Giant, 1996

Charles Sébastien Faivre D'Arcier, Auguste Henri Royé, *Historique du 37e Régiment d'Infanterie, etc*, Paris, 1895

Louis Florimond Fantin des Odoards, *Journal du général Fantin des Odoards*, E. Plon, Nourrit et Cie, Paris, 1895

Théo Fleischmen, *L'Armée impériale racontée par la Grande Armée,* Librairie Académique Perrin, Paris, 1964

Fernand Fleuret, *Description des passages de Dominique Fleuret*, Firmin-Didot et Cie, Paris, 1929

Maurice Fleury, *Souvenirs anecdotiques et militaires du colonel Biot*, Henri Vivien, Paris, 1901

Charles François, *Journal du capitane François (dit le Dromadaire d'Égypte) 1792-1830, publié d'après le manuscrit original par Charles Grolleau*, C. Carrington, Paris, 1904

John Franklin, *Waterloo Hanoverian Correspondence,* 1815 Limited, 2010

Paul Fussell, *The Great War and Modern Memory,* Oxford University Press, Oxford, 1975

John G. Gallaher, *Napoleon's Enfant Terrible: General Dominique Vandamme,* University of Oklahoma Press, Norman, 2008

Jean-Jacques-Basilin de Gassendi, *Aide-mémoire à l'Usage des Officiers d'Artillerie de France Attachés au Service de Terre,* Magimel Anselin et Pochard, Paris, 1819

Frederic Gautier, *Relation de la Bataille de Waterloo,* Berthot, Brussels, 1827

Etienne-Maurice Gérard, *Dernières observations sur les opérations de l'aile droite de l'armée française à la bataille de Waterloo,* Mesner, Paris, 1830

Etienne-Maurice Gérard, *Quelques documents sur la bataille de Waterloo,* Paris, 1829

Philippe Gerbet, *Souvenirs d'un officier sur la campagne de Belgique en 1815*, Émile Javal, Arbois, 1866

Max Gottschalck, *Geschichte des 1. Thüringischen Infanterie-Regiments Nr. 31*, E. S. Mittler und Sohn, 1894

Gaspard Gourgaud, *La campagne de 1815,* P. Mongie, Paris, 1818

Anna Green, Kathleen Troup, *The Houses of History*, Manchester University Press, 1999

Emmanuel Grouchy, George Grouchy, *Mémoires du maréchal de Grouchy*, E. Dentu, 1873

Emmanuel Grouchy, *Mémoires du maréchal de Grouchy*, Paris, 1874

Emmanuel de Grouchy, *Observations sur la relation de la campagne de 1815 publiée par le général Gourgaud et réfutation de quelques-unes des assertions d'autres écrits relatifs à`la bataille de Waterloo, par le maréchal de Grouchy*, Chaumerot Jeune, Paris, 1819

Emmanuel Grouchy, *Relation de la campagne de 1815*, n.d.

Emmanuel Grouchy, *Relation succincte de la campagne de 1815 en Belgique*, Delanchy, Paris, 1843

Guverich, *The French Historical Revolution: The Annales School*, in Hodder et al, *Interpreting Archaeology*, Routledge, London, 1995

J. L. Henckens, *Mémoires se rapportant à son service militaire au 6e régiment de chasseurs à cheval français de février 1803 à Août 1816*, M. Nijhoff, La Haie, 1910

Jean-Baptiste d'Héralde, *Mémoires d'un chirurgien de la grande armée*, Teissèdre, Paris, 2002

Émile Herbillon, *Quelques pages d'un vieux cahier: souvenirs du Général Herbillon (1794-1866)*, Berger-Levrault, Paris, 1928

Colonel Heymès, *Relation de la campagne de 1815, dite de Waterloo*, Gaultier-Laguionie, Paris, 1829

Peter Hofschröer, *1815: The Waterloo Campaign*, Greenhill, London, 1998

Peter Hofschröer, *Waterloo 1815 Quatre Bras and Ligny*, Pen & Sword, Barnsley, 2006

George Hooper, *Waterloo, the Downfall of the First Napoleon*, Smith, Elder, London,

1862

James Hope, *Letters from Portugal, Spain, and France, during the memorable campaigns of 1811, 1812 and 1813 and from Belgium and France in the year 1815*, Michael Anderson, Edinburgh, 1819

E. L. S. Horsburgh, *Waterloo: A Narrative and a Criticism*, Methuen, London, 1895

Henry Houssaye, *1815 Waterloo*, Paris, 1903

François Hue, *Jean-Louis de Crabbé, colonel d'empire*, Canonnier, Nantes, 2006

William Hyde Kelly, *The Battle of Wavre and Grouchy's Retreat*, John Murray, London, 1905

E. F. Janin, *Campagne de Waterloo*, Chaumerot Jeune, Paris, 1820

Christopher Kelly, *A Full and Circumstantial Account Of The Memorable Battle of Waterloo*, London, 1836

Henry Lachouque, *Le General Tommelin*, Tournai, n.d.

Lécrivain, *Histoire des généraux, officiers de tous grades et de toute arme, sous-officiers et soldats qui se sont distingués dans les différentes campagnes des armées française*, 1817

Lefol, *Souvenirs sur le prytanée de Saint-Cyr sur la campagne de 1814, le retour de l'empereur Napoléon de l'île d'Elbe, et la campagne de 1815, pendant les Cent-jours*, Montalant-Bougleux, Versailles, 1854

Jean Baptiste Lemonnier-Delafosse, *Campagnes de 1810 à 1815: souvenirs militaires faisant suite a ceux première et deuxième campagnes se St-Domingue de 1801 a 1809*, Alph. Lemale, Havre, 1850

Hans Oskar von Lettow-Vorbeck, *Napoleons Untergang 1815*, Mittler, Berlin, 1904

Octave Levavasseur, *Souvenirs militaires 1800-1815*, Librairie des Deux Empirés, 2001

Henri Lot, *Les deux généraux Ordener*, R. Roger et F. Chernoviz, Paris, 1910

Edmond-Charles-Constant Louvat, *Historique du 7e Hussards*, Pairault, Paris, 1889

Mackenzie MacBride, *With Napoleon at Waterloo*, J. B. Lippincott & Co, Philadelphia, 1911

Jacques François Martin, *Souvenirs d'un ex-officier 1812-1815*, Paris, 1867

Hippolyte de Mauduit, *Les derniers jours de la Grande Armée* (two volumes), Paris, 1848

William Hamilton Maxwell, *Stories of Waterloo*, Henry Colburn and Richard Bentley, London, 1833

Hubert Miot-Putigny, *Putigny, grognard d'empire*, Gallimard, Paris, 1950

William O'Connor Morris, *The Campaign of 1815: Ligny, Quatre-Bras, Waterloo*, Grant Richards, London, 1900

C. Mullié, *Biographie des célébrités militaires des armées de terre et de mer de 1789 à 1850*, Poignavant et Compie, Paris, 1852

Napoleon I, *Correspondance de Napoleon 1er*, vol.28, H. Plon, J. Dumaine, Paris, 1858

Wilhelm Neff, *Geschichte des Infanterie-Regiments von Goeben (2. Rheinischen) Nr. 28*, Ernst Siegfried Mittler und Sohn, Berlin, 1890

Michel Louis Felix Ney, *Documents inédits sur la campagne de 1815*, Anselin, Paris, 1840

Antoine Noguès, André Maricourt, *Mémoires du général Noguès (1777-1853) sur les guerres de l'Empire*, A. Lemerre, Paris, 1922

Karl Rudolf von Ollech, *Geschichte des feldzuges von 1815 nach archivalischen quellen*, E. S. Mittler und Sohn, Berlin, 1876

Auguste-Louis Pétiet, *Souvenirs militaires de l'histoire contemporaine*, Dumaine, Paris, 1844

328

Julius von Pflugk-Harttung, *Von Wavre bis Belle-Alliance (18 Juni 1815)*, Berlin, 1908

Julius von Pflugk-Harttung, *Vorgeschichte der Schlacht bei Belle-Alliance, Wellington*, R. Schröder, Berlin, 1903

Gustave de Pontécoulant, *Mémoires*, Paris, 1866

Gustave de Pontécoulant, *Souvenirs militaires : Napoléon à Waterloo*, J. Dumaine, Paris, 1866

Colonel du Génie Répécaud, *Napoléon à Ligny et le Maréchal Ney à Quatre-Bras*, Degeorge, Arras, 1847

Pierre Robinaux, Gustave Léon Schlumberger, *Journal de route du Capitaine Robinaux 1803-1832*, Plon-Nourrit, Paris, 1908

John Codman Ropes, *The Campaign of Waterloo*, C. Scribner's Sons, New York, 1892

Marie Théodore de Gueilly Rumigny, *Souvenirs du général comte de Rumigny, aide de camp du roi Louis-Philippe, 1789-1860*, Émile-Paul frères, Paris, 1921

Germain Sarrut, *Biographie des Hommes du Jour, etc*, Paris

Gustave Schlumberger, *Lettres du commandant Coudreux, à son frère, 1804-1815 : soldats de Napoléon*, Plon, Nourrit et Cie, Paris, 1908

Sénécal, *General le Sénécal campagne de Waterloo*, Philadelphia, 1818

C. W. Serjeant, Joseph Butterworth, *Some particulars of the battle at Waterloo*, J & T Clarke, London, 1816

Michael Shanks, Ian Hodder, *Processual, postprocessual and interpretive archaeologies* in Hodder et al, *Interpreting Archaeology*, Routledge, London, 1995

William Siborne, *History of the war in France and Belgium, in 1815, containing minute details of the battles of Quatre-Bras, Ligny, Wavre and Waterloo*, Boone, London, 1848

William Siborne, *The Waterloo Campaign 1815*, A. Constable, 1900

William Siborne, *Waterloo Letters* ed. H. T. Siborne, Greenhill Books, 1993

M. Russell Thayer, *The Life, Character and Writings of Francis Lieber*, Collins, Philadelphia, 1873

Pierre François Tissot, *Histoire de Napoléon, rédigée d'après les papiers d'État, les documents officiels, les mémoires et les notes secrètes de ses contemporains, suivie d'un précis sur la famille Bonaparte* (two volumes), Delange-Taffin, Paris, 1833

William Tomkinson, James Tomkinson, *The Diary of a Cavalry Officer in the Peninsular and Waterloo Campaigns 1809-1815*, S. Sonnenschein, London, 1894

Jean-Phillipe Tondeur, Patrice Courcelle, Jean Jacques Patyn, Paul Megnak, *Carnets de la Campagne No. 1—Hougoumont*, Tondeur Diffusion, Brussels, 1999

Toussaint-Jean Trefcon, *Carnet de la campagne du colonel Trefcon, 1793-1815*, E. Dubois, Paris, 1914

Louis-Jules Trochu, *L'armée française en 1867*, Amyot, Paris, 1867

Andrew Uffindell, *The Eagle's Last Triumph: Napoleon's Victory at Ligny, June 1815*, Greenhill Books, London, 1994

Joseph Émile Vanson, *Carnet de la Sabretache*, Berger-Levrault et Cie, Paris, 1899

Frédéric François Guillaume Vaudoncourt, *Histoire des campagnes de 11814 et 1815, en France*, Chez A. de Gastel, Paris, 1826

Achille de Vaulabelle, *Campagne et bataille de Waterloo*, Perrotin, Paris, 1845

J. B. du Vergier, *Collection complète des lois, décrets, ordonnances, réglements, et avis du Conseil d'Etat*, Guyot et Scribe, Paris, 1827

August Wagner, *Plane der Schlachten und Treffen, welche von der Preussischen Armee in den Feldzügen der Jahre 1813, 14 und 15 geliefert worden*, Reimer, Berlin, 1825

Hans Wellmann, *Geschichte des Infanterie-Regiments von Horn (3-tes Rheinisches) N. 29,*

Lintzcher Verlag, Trier, 1894

Georges de Despots de Zenowicz, *Waterloo: déposition sur les quatre journées de la campagne de 1815*, Ledoyen, Paris, 1848

Online Sources:

Christopher Bassford, Daniel Moran, Gregory W. Pedlow, *The Campaign of 1815 Chapters 30-39*, On Waterloo, available at http://www.clausewitz.com/readings/1815/five30-39.htm [accessed 10 February 2013]

Christopher Bassford, Daniel Moran, Gregory W. Pedlow, *The Campaign of 1815 Chapters 40-49*, On Waterloo, available at http://www.clausewitz.com/readings/1815/five40-49.htm [accessed 10 February 2013]

Christopher Bassford, Daniel Moran, Gregory W. Pedlow, *Clausewitz, Wellington and the Campaign of 1815*, On Waterloo, available at https://www.clausewitz.com/readings/1815/TOC.htm [accessed 12 April 2012]

Paul L. Dawson, *Memoires: Fact or Fiction? The Campaign of 1814*, The Napoleon Series, December 2013, available at http://www.napoleon-series.org/research/eyewitness/c_memoires.html [accessed 28 February 2017]

Lieutenant Pitot, *8e Demi-Brigade Legere 2e Formation 1796-1803 8e Regiment d'Infanterie Legere 1803-1815*, Ancestramil, 2012, available at http://www.ancestramil.fr/uploads/01_doc/terre/infanterie/1789-1815/8_ri_legere_historique_1803-1815.pdf

Index